Reforming the Governance
of the IMF and the World Bank

T0346548

Advance Reviews

'The U.S. cannot afford a diminished IMF and World Bank. Nor can the rest of the world. It should lead not resist the restructuring of voice and votes that would secure their legitimacy and effectiveness for a new century. Here are the reasoned arguments why – and some politically practical ideas how. This book deserves wide attention. I hope it inspires thoughtful debate – not just among international financial insiders in the world's capitals, but on Capitol Hill and Wall Street and their European counterparts, and in the university and business school classrooms of China, India, South Africa, Brazil and beyond.'

Nancy Birdsall
President of the Center for Global Development, Washington D.C.

'Raising the voice and vote of the developing countries in decision making in the IMF and the World Bank will strengthen their governance and legitimacy. The essays by the experts in this volume clarify the positions of developing countries. They constitute an invitation to experts in the industrial countries and the European union to further enrich this debate.'

Leo van Houtven
Former Secretary and Counsellor, IMF

'The construction of more legitimate arrangements in the IMF and the World Bank is one of the principal challenges for effective global economic governance today. This book looks beyond long-standing deadlocks on issues of representation and accountability with innovative and feasible proposals for positive reform.'

Professor Jan Aart Scholte
Professor in Politics and International Studies, and currently Co-Director of the ESRC/ Warwick Centre for the Study of Globalisation and Regionalisation

'You know something is seriously amiss in global economic governance when Belgium, Sweden and Switzerland, with 0.004% of world population and 12% of world GDP, have the same share of IMF and World Bank votes as China and India, with 38% of world population and 19% of world GDP; and when the former do not even borrow from the organizations. This book contributes to the wider process in which the developed countries are slowly being hoist by their own petard: having enjoined the IMF and the Bank to press for governance changes in borrowing countries, borrowing countries are now pressing for the same criteria to be applied to international organizations. The essays provide hard ammunition for the debate about what exactly should be done.'

Robert Hunter Wade
Professor of Political Economy, Development Studies Institute, LSE

This timely volume directs attention to the unreformed governance structures of the twin organizations [the IMF and the World Bank] reflected among other things by the way they still select their leaders, and by their unbalanced voting procedures. If they are to regain credibility and reinforce the right to prescribe governance reforms to member states the IMF and the World Bank need to set an example of transparency and improved functionality by reforming themselves. This volume contains the latest work of the Technical Group of the G24 aimed at assisting that process.'

Laurence Whitehead
Official Fellow in Politics, Nuffield College, Oxford

Reforming the Governance
of the IMF and the World Bank

Edited by
ARIEL BUIRA
for the G-24 Research Program

Anthem Press

Anthem Press
An imprint of Wimbledon Publishing Company
75-76 Blackfriars Road, London SE1 8HA
or
PO Box 9779, London SW19 7ZG
www.anthempress.com

British Library Cataloguing in Publication Data
A catalogue record for this book is available from the British Library.

Library of Congress Cataloging in Publication Data
A catalog record for this book has been requested.

The distribution of this book was supported in part by a grant from the
Foundation Open Society Institute.

1 3 5 7 9 10 8 6 4 2

ISBN 1 84331 211 5 (Pbk)

Typeset by Footprint Labs Ltd, London
www.footprintlabs.com

Printed in the U.S.A.

CONTENTS

The G-24

The Intergovernmental Group of 24 for Intentional Monetary Affairs and Development was constituted in 1972 as a result of a mandate given in Lima by the Group of 77 to their Chairman, to consult member governments on the establishment of an intergovernmental group on monetary issues. Its members, nine African, eight Latin American and seven Asian countries are as follows:

Algeria, Argentina, Brazil, Colombia, Côte d'Ivoire, Democratic Republic of Congo, Egypt, Ethiopia, Gabon, Ghana, Guatemala, India, Iran, Lebanon, Mexico, Nigeria, Pakistan, Peru, Philippines, South Africa, Sri Lanka, Syrian Arab Republic, Trinidad and Tobago, and Venezuela.

The purpose of the G-24 is to further the interests of the developing countries and their effective participation in the discussions of monetary, financial and development issues at the Bretton Woods institutions and other fora. It seeks to provide technical support to its members and to the G77 in their consideration of these issues. To this effect, the G-24 Secretariat, supported by its members and other sources, runs a research programme in which academics and other researchers from countries in the North and South address the main issues of concern to the developing world in their areas of competence. To ensure intellectual freedom in their work, the results of their research and the views expressed in the papers presented to the G-24 are the sole responsibility of the authors.

LIST OF CONTRIBUTORS

V Bhaskar is a member of the Indian Administrative Service (IAS). He currently serves as a Commissioner to the Andhra Pradesh Government, India. He served as a Special Assistant to the Executive Director for India, Sri Lanka, Bangladesh and Bhutan at the IMF.

J Lawrence Broz is an Associate Professor of Political Science at the University of California, San Diego. He earned his PhD at UCLA in 1993 and has held professorships at Harvard University (1993–2000) and New York University (2000–2001). Professor Broz's specialty is the political economy of money and finance.

Ariel Buira is the Director of the G-24 Secretariat; was a staff member and Executive Director at the IMF, Director for International Affairs and member of the Board of Governors of the Bank of Mexico. He has written extensively on macroeconomics and international monetary economics. He has been Ambassador, Senior Member of St. Anthony's College, Oxford and Special Envoy of the President of Mexico for the UN Conference on Financing for Development. For the G-24, he edited *Challenges to the World Bank and IMF* and *The IMF and The World Bank at Sixty*, Anthem Press, London 2003 and 2005.

Praveen Chaudhry teaches in the Political Science department at Ohio University, United States and is also an Associate Scholar at the India Development Foundation, New Delhi. He is currently working on a book titled, *The US and the IMF: Conditionality and Negotiations*.

Laura dos Reis is a Research Associate at the G-24 Secretariat in Washington, DC. She has been a consultant to the World Bank, the Inter-American Development Bank and an analyst at the Ministry of Economics in Argentina. She holds an MA in International Development from the Kennedy School of Government at Harvard University and a MA in Economics from Di Tella University, Argentina.

Cord Jakobeit is a Professor of Political Science and International Relations at Hamburg University, Germany. He heads the Board of Directors at the

Institute of African Affairs in Hamburg and has authored several books and articles on African development, international organizations and matters of regional integration. He is a consultant to the German Ministry of Economic Cooperation and Development (BMZ) and to the German Technical Cooperation (GTZ).

Vijay Kelkar has more than 30 years of experience with economic policy making related to both national and international economic policy issues. Dr. Kelkar was recently Executive Director for India, Sri Lanka, Bangladesh and Bhutan at the IMF. Dr. Kelkar also served as Special Advisor to the Finance Minister, Government of India.

Guillermo Le Fort V holds a PhD in Economics from UCLA, *Magister* and *Licenciado* degrees from *Universidad de Chile* and works as a consultant in Economic and Financial Matters. He was Executive Director at the IMF, Director of International Affairs at the Central Bank of Chile and Senior Economist and Resident Representative for the IMF. He has published several articles in international macroeconomics and finance and taught in universities in Chile and abroad.

Dennis Leech is a Reader in Economics at the University of Warwick, an Associate of the Centre for the Study of Globalization and Regionalization at Warwick University and of the Centre for the Philosophy of Natural and Social Sciences at the London School of Economics. He did his first degree at the University of Manchester and his PhD at Warwick. He has published in a range of leading academic journals including the *Economic Journal, Public Choice, Political Studies, Management Science, Annals of Operations Research, Econometrica* and others.

Robert Leech is currently a Postdoctoral Researcher in Cognitive Science at Birkbeck, University of London. He studied at Cambridge, Birmingham and London. His research focuses on computational modelling in cognitive science and public choice. He has worked with Dennis Leech on a number of theoretical and empirical projects on voting power.

John McLenaghan has held a number of senior positions on the staff of the IMF, where he was Division Chief in the Exchange and Trade Relations Department and Deputy Director of the Statistics Department. He was Director of the Statistics Department, 1988–96 and served as a Special Advisor to the Managing Director in 1999. He has chaired a number of inter-organization statistical committees, including the United Nations ACC Committee on Statistical Activities, 1994–96.

Murilo Portugal is the Deputy Finance Minister of Brazil. Previously, he has been Executive Director at the IMF, Alternate Executive Director at the

IBRD, Advisor to the President of Brazil and Secretary of National Treasury at the Ministry of Finance of Brazil. He holds a degree in Law from *Universidade Federal Fluminense*, Rio de Janeiro, a Diploma on Development Studies from University of Cambridge and MA in Economics from University of Manchester.

David Rapkin is an Associate Professor at the University of Nebraska, where he has served as Graduate Chair and Department Chair. He has also been a visiting professor at the College of International Studies, Tsukuba University in Japan during 1988–90 and 1996–98. His major research and teaching interests are in global political economy, with an emphasis on East Asia. His recent articles have appeared in *Pacific Review*, *International Interactions* and *International Relations of the Asia-Pacific*.

Jonathan Strand is an Assistant Professor in the Department of Political Science at the University of Nevada, Las Vegas. His research interests include international political economy, global governance and the political economy of the Asia Pacific region. He has published several articles on the IMF, the World Bank, the regional development banks and other political economy topics.

Marta Vanduzer-Snow is a Research Scholar in the Department of Politics, New York University and is also an Associate Scholar at the India Development Foundation, New Delhi. She is currently working on a book titled, *The US and the IMF: Conditionality and Negotiations*.

Ngaire Woods is the Director of the Global Economic Governance Programme at University College, Oxford. She is an adviser to the UNDP Human Development Report Office, a member of the Helsinki Process on global governance and a member of the Resource Group of the UN Secretary General's High Level Commission into Threats, Challenges and Change. She sits on numerous boards, including the Advisory Group of the Centre for Global Development. Her most recent book, which is forthcoming, is *Global Mission: the IMF, the World Bank and Their Borrowers*, Cornell University Press.

FOREWORD

In the Monterrey Consensus, agreed at the 2002 International Conference on Financing for Development, held in Monterrey, Mexico, world leaders committed to broaden and strengthen the voice and participation of developing countries in international economic decision-making and norm-setting. This commitment reflected the perceived need to increase the representativeness of the Bretton Woods institutions, which operate within a governance structure largely defined six decades ago. It also reflected the need to adjust other multilateral financial institutions, such as the Bank for International Settlements, to a global environment characterized by the growing importance in the world economy of a dynamic group of developing countries and to give developing countries in general, some representation in policy-making and norm-setting bodies where they have no formal participation, such as the Basle Committee on Banking Supervision and the Financial Stability Forum.

This commitment has translated thus far into some actions and an ongoing discussion on the Bretton Woods institutions. The International Monetary Fund (IMF) and the World Bank have strengthened the offices of African Directors and some European countries have created an Analytical Trust Fund to support the African Chairs. These changes have been motivated by the evident concern to maintain the legitimacy of these institutions as representative global entities. The International Monetary and Financial Committee aptly summarized the major issue at stake in its communiqué of April 2005:

> The IMF's effectiveness and credibility as a cooperative institution must be safeguarded and further enhanced. Adequate voice and participation by all members should be assured, and the distribution of quotas should reflect developments in the world economy. The Group of 24 (G-24), the major group of developing countries in international financial issues, has positioned itself at the forefront of this debate. In its October 2004 communiqué, the G-24 called for the adoption of a new quota formula in the IMF that reflected the relative size of the different economies, by

measuring Gross Domestic Product (GDP) in terms of purchasing power parities (PPP), as well as the vulnerability of different economies to commodity prices, capital account volatility and other exogenous shocks. At the same time, it called for strengthening the voice of smaller sized economies in decision-making, by increasing the weight of the basic votes to its original weight of 11 per cent of the total voting power. Indeed, through time, that weight has declined to only 2 per cent today. Whereas measurement of GDP is particularly important to the dynamic 'emerging' economies of Asia, the issue of basic votes is particularly important to small and poor economies, especially those of sub-Saharan Africa.

This book represents a major contribution by the G-24 to the ongoing debate. Edited by the Director of the Secretariat of the Group, the book offers a rich set of quality papers by current or former Executive Directors of multilateral financial institutions who come from developing countries, as well as by leading academics. The authors analyse the virtues of alternative formulas for the distribution of voting power, which apply measures of GDP based on PPPs; alternative definitions of international trade, which exclude trade among members of the European Monetary Union using a single currency; estimates of the vulnerability of developing countries to commodity shocks and the volatility of capital flows; and restoring the weight of basic votes. They also analyse alternative voting structures, particularly the 'double majority voting procedures' used by some regional development banks, which ensure a greater weight to smaller members, as well as other changes that could increase the accountability and effectiveness of the Executive Boards of the international financial institutions.

This is a timely contribution to an essential debate in international economic governance, a debate that we hope will fulfil the historic promise of voice and representation made at Monterrey.

José Antonio Ocampo
Under-Secretary-General of the United Nations
for Economic and Social Affairs

1

INTRODUCTION

The United Nations Monetary and Financial Conference held at Bretton Woods sixty years ago led to the establishment of the IMF and World Bank. This was a foundational moment. As the most powerful financial institutions of our times were created, hopes ran high of a better world, in which international cooperation through the IMF would sustain economic activity and prevent the adoption of measures destructive of national and international prosperity. The Bank was to assist reconstruction of war ravaged countries and finance the development of the less developed world. For a number of decades, the institutions created in Bretton Woods and the system based on them seemed to work well.

Today, the Bretton Woods Institutions (BWIs) play a diminished role and suffer from a loss of legitimacy and credibility. Several factors account for this diminished role. Among them the expansion of financial markets, the rapid growth of emerging market economies and the rigidity of a governance structure which reflects the political accommodation reached at the end of World War II; an outcome that has become increasingly obsolete and dysfunctional. The current governance structure of the IMF and World Bank fails to take into account the fact that today, the developing countries and economies in transition account for half of the world's output in real terms,[1] for most of the world's population, encompass the most dynamic economies and hold about two-thirds of all international reserves. Yet they are marginalized in the decision-making process. Thus, it is not surprising that the unrepresentative governance of the institutions is leading to a decline in their credibility, influence and effectiveness.

The lack of representation of developing countries and transition economies in the governance of the global economy and the declining commitment of major countries to a multilateral rules-based system of international monetary cooperation has resulted in decisions by major shareholders that are motivated by expediency, which undermine the efficacy of the IMF and World Bank and have adverse consequences for world economic growth and stability. Indeed, the increasingly non-representative character of the governance of these institutions threatens the integrity of the international monetary system, as emerging countries in Asia and elsewhere move away from the IMF and reduce their transactions with the World Bank, diminishing the systemic role of the institutions and leaving them to deal mainly with low income countries.

In keeping with the mandate of the ministerial meeting of October 2004, the Intergovernmental Group of 24 (G-24) for Monetary Affairs and Development held a Technical Group Meeting in Manila on 17 and 18 March 2005 to discuss in depth the reform of the governance of the BWIs. On this occasion, a number of valuable research papers on the subject were discussed. This book presents a selection of papers, that explore various aspects of the issue of governance, consider options for its reform and the obstacles to be overcome.

In the first paper, Buira sets out the challenges to the legitimacy of the existing governance structure. He discusses the proposal for a new quota formula made by the Quota Formula Review Group (QFRG)[2] and points out its major deficiencies, which undermine the validity of the proposal. The paper also lists a number of functional failures of the IMF and World Bank that may be related to their unresponsive governance structure. In addition, the paper presents a calculation of IMF quotas estimated according to a new formula that meets the call of the Ministers of the G-24.[3]

The papers in the first block of analysis present different, although traditional approaches to the reform of the governance of the BWIs. The paper by Kelkar, Chaudhry, Vanduzer-Snow and Bhashar, addresses the democratic deficit and the means to correct it through the revision of quotas, increased basic votes and the reform of the Executive Board. They propose that the link between contributions, access to financing and voting power be broken. They call for an increase in the IMF's resources to keep up with a member's current financing needs and for the creation of an Economic Security Council to socialize risk at the global level.

The comprehensive paper by Portugal presents a proposal for the revision of the quota formula to increase the voting power of developing countries, for strengthening the accountability and effectiveness of the IMF's Executive Board, for making the selection of the Managing Director transparent and inclusive, for strengthening the formation of consensus in decision-making and for turning the Fund into the main forum for economic policy coordination.

In his paper, Le Fort discusses the sources of the growing distortions in IMF representation. By using cross-section regression analysis, he finds that economic growth, population size and credit rating have a high explanatory value. To the extent that high growth economies are not recognized by quota adjustments, the distortions will continue to grow. Simulations are conducted to determine the size of quota increases that are required to bring quotas into line with economic realities, and certain rules are proposed for an all-elected Executive Board intended to improve representation.

The paper by Ngaire Woods, discusses the issues posed by the limited accountability of the IMF and World Bank. It also considers the accountability problems associated with the functioning of the constituency system by which most developing countries are represented. These become greater in the case of constituencies representing a large number of small countries with limited voting power. The limited accountability of international organizations would suggest that in order to avoid power without responsibility, their far reaching conditionality should be limited.

The second part of the book is formed by two papers that develop the analytical case for improving the measurement of the factors included in the quota formulas. The first one by McLenaghan, focuses on the technical merits of the measurement of GDP in terms of Purchasing Power Parity (PPP) to better reflect the size of a country's economy and noting the inconsistency arising from using different measures of GDP for different purposes, challenges the use of GDP measured at market exchange rates in quota calculations. The paper by dos Reis deals with the measurement of vulnerability of developing countries to shocks arising from the volatility of exports and capital flows. This paper considers the methodology applied by the Fund staff to measure volatility and improves on it.

The discussion of quotas and basic votes has been stalled for several years, the next quota review is scheduled to take place in 2008, and an increase of basic votes requires an amendment of the Articles of the Fund and the Bank, which calls for an 85 per cent majority and at best takes several years to complete.[4] Therefore two other alternative options that might help make progress in the reform of the governance of the institutions are explored in the third part. Firstly, Professor Jakobeit analyses the system of double majorities, a procedure for decision-making among countries of unequal size that protects the rights of smaller members. Double majorities are a means of empowering the weaker members and preserving their influence in decision-making. This regime, which is proposed on an experimental basis, also favours consensus building, since under it neither the industrial nor the developing countries alone are able to get their way.

Since successful policies require the cooperation of developed and developing country members, Professors Rapkin and Strand also see double majorities as a means of reconciling the principles of sovereign equality of states and empowering contributors of capital, which contributes to their legitimacy and sense of ownership.[5] They deepen the analysis of alternative measures voting power and discuss different methods to implement double majority voting procedures. Their results indicate that the power of countries and Executive Directors with fewer votes would be enhanced vis-à-vis larger vote holders, requiring them to depend more on consensus and coalition building.

Another innovative analysis is presented by Dennis and Robert Leech, whose starting point is the analytical distinction between the share of votes and voting power, this last defined as the capacity to influence decisions. They explore the implications of two changes. First, the creation of a formal G-7 bloc, which would seem dysfunctional since it would entirely dominate decision making. Second, the consolidation of the European vote in one chair that even with a significant reduction in Europe's total votes, would match the power of the United States. The consolidation of the European chairs into a single chair would considerably increase European influence and power. Moreover, such a consolidation would result in an increase in the voting power of all developing countries and in the number of their representatives in the Boards of the Fund and Bank.

Finally, since the quotas of countries cannot be reduced without their consent, it is difficult to think of a major reapportionment of quota shares without a quota increase. Increases in IMF quotas or World Bank capital require an 85 per cent majority, and since the United States holds 17.1 per cent of the total voting power in the IMF,[6] a quota or a capital increase requires US approval, which under US law, calls for the approval of the US Congress. The paper by Broz analyses the main factors that influence the behavior of the Congress in this regard, i.e. ideology, attitudes toward globalization, the share of highly skilled voters by district and the sources of campaign contributions. These factors help us understand the internal dynamics of the US Congress with regard to the reform of the institutions.

The papers collected in this volume explore different aspects of the governance of the IMF and World Bank. Their purpose is to contribute to a better understanding of the issues involved and to assist the discussions of the necessary reform, a matter crucial to the successful operation and provision of public goods by these major institutions in the future.

The Editor

Notes

1 i.e. measuring GDP in terms of PPP.
2 The Quota Formula Review Group established by the Managing Director of the IMF in 1999 submitted a Report in 2000.
3 In their communique of 1 October 2004, the Ministers of the G-24 stated that 'enhancing the representation of developing countries requires a new quota formula to reflect the relative size of developing country economies. The formula should be simplified to give greater weight to measures of gross domestic product in terms of purchasing power

parity, and take into account the vulnerabilities of developing countries to movements in commodity prices, the volatility of capital movements and other exogenous shocks. In addition, basic votes should be substantially increased to restore their original role in relation to total voting power and to strengthen the voice of small countries.'

4 The Fourth Amendment, which relates to a special SDR allocation, was proposed by the United States in 1994 but has not yet been approved by the US Congress.

5 A number of international financial institutions, including the IADB, African Development Bank, Asian Development Bank operate under a requirement of double majorities—a majority of votes and a majority of members, or of developing country members, for operational and other decisions. The European Union and the Global Environment Fund also operate successfully with a double majority regime.

6 The United States has 16.85 per cent of total voting power in the World Bank.

2

THE BRETTON WOODS INSTITUTIONS: GOVERNANCE WITHOUT LEGITIMACY?

Ariel Buira

Abstract:

Sixty years after their creation, the Bretton Woods institutions face a crisis of legitimacy that impairs their credibility and limits their effectiveness. At the roots of this crisis lies the unrepresentative nature of their structure of governance, which places control of the institutions in the hands of a small group of industrial countries. These countries consider the developing countries and economies in transition as minor partners, despite the fact that they now account for half of the world's output in real terms, most of the world's population, encompassing the most dynamic economies and the largest holders of international reserves. Over time, the effects of the unrepresentative nature of the governance of the BWIs have become aggravated by two trends: First, a growing division among member countries, on the one hand, industrial country creditors who do not borrow from the institutions but largely determine their policies and make the rules and on the other, developing country debtors or potential debtors, subject to policies and rules made by others. Second, the rapid increase in the economic size and importance of developing countries, particularly, emerging market countries in the world economy. This has made the governance structure of the institutions, which reflects the political accommodation reached at the end of World War II increasingly obsolete.

The first part of the paper reviews the existing governance structure of the institutions, the foundations on which it rests, the main formal proposal to reform quotas, its shortcomings and major issues that were not addressed by it.

The second part takes a different approach. Although in their self-interest, the major industrial countries could be expected to favor policies that contribute to the long term success of the institutions, the good performance of the world economy and the stability of the international monetary and financial system, the policies they pursue have often been determined by short term expediency. A brief review of the performance of the institutions in recent times, conducted in the light of their purposes and responsibilities, shows that, despite some conspicuous successes, their limited effectiveness in the pursuit of their objectives has not only not enhanced their legitimacy, but often contributed to their loss of credibility. To conclude, countries' quotas are recalculated according to a revised formula, based on two factors—GDP measured in terms of purchasing power parity (PPP) and the variability of countries' export revenues and capital flows.

The author believes that the reform of the governance of the IMF and World Bank is essential to the preservation of a multilateral system of monetary and financial cooperation.

Introduction

Sixty years after their creation, the Bretton Woods Institutions (BWIs) face a crisis of legitimacy that impairs their credibility and effectiveness. At the root of this crisis lies the unrepresentative nature of their structure of governance, which places the control of the institutions in the hands of a small group of industrial countries. These countries consider the developing countries and economies in transition as minor partners, despite their accounting for half of the world's output in real terms,[1] most of the world's population and encompassing the most dynamic economies and the largest holders of international reserves.[2] Over time, the effects of the unrepresentative nature of the governance of the BWIs have become aggravated by two trends. First, a growing division among member countries, on the one hand industrial country creditors who do not borrow from the institutions but largely determine their policies and make the rules and on the other, developing country debtors or potential debtors, subject to policies and rules made by others. The second trend is the rapid increase in the economic size and importance of developing countries, particularly emerging market countries in the world economy. This trend has made the governance structure of the institutions, which reflects the political accommodation reached at the end of World War II, increasingly obsolete.

The first part of the paper will review the existing governance structure of the institutions, the foundations on which it rests, the main formal proposal to reform quotas and a number of important shortcomings and major issues that were not addressed by their proposal.

The second part takes a different approach. Although in their self-interest, the major industrial countries could be expected to favour policies that contribute to the long-term success of the institutions, the good performance of the world economy and the stability of the international monetary and financial system, the policies they pursued in the institutions, have often been determined by short-term expediency. A brief review of the performance of the institutions in recent times, conducted in the light of their purposes and responsibilities, shows that, despite some conspicuous successes, their limited effectiveness in the pursuit of their objectives has not only hurt their legitimacy, but often contributed to their loss of credibility.

The Unrepresentative Character of the Governance of the BWIs

In 1944 at the Bretton Woods Conference, a compromise solution was adopted between two approaches to the determination of voting power, one which would relate it solely to members' contributions or quotas and another based solely on the legal principle of the equality of states. The compromise based voting rights on a combination of two criteria—it gave each member country 250 basic votes plus one vote for every $100,000 of quota (later for every SDR100,000). Basic votes, and the voice in decision-making they gave smaller countries, were considered to be necessary in view of the regulatory functions of the Fund in certain areas[3] (see Gold, 1972).

Similarly, Article V Section 3(a) of the Bank's Articles of Agreement provides that 'each member shall have 250 votes plus one additional vote for each share of stock held'. All shares of the Bank's capital are valued at US$ 120,635 per share. Note that in 1979, all members of the Bank were offered to subscribe 250 'membership' shares to avoid dilution of the voting power of the smaller members as a result of the 1979 capital increase. New members are also authorized to subscribe 250 shares.

Since the number of basic votes has not been changed with successive quota increases, the participation of basic votes in total votes has declined from 11.3 per cent of the voting power to 2.1 per cent today, despite the entry of 140 new member countries. In fact, as a proportion of the total, the basic votes of the original members declined to 0.5 per cent, as a result of a 37-fold increase in total quotas.[4] This has substantially shifted the balance of power in favour of large quota countries and away from the compromise agreement contained in the Articles in order to protect the participation of small countries in decision-making.

Table 1 below shows the relative share of GNI, quotas and voting power of different country groupings, and underscores the unrepresentative

Table 1. GDP, quotas and votes as shares of the total in 2003

Group of countries	GDP (PPP) 2003 (shares, %)	GDP 2003 (shares, %)	Quotas 2003 (shares, %)	Total votes (shares, %)
G-7 Countries	44.1	64.4	46.1	45.3
Other Industrial Countries	8.3	11.9	15.6	15.5
Total Industrial Countries	**52.4**	**76.3**	**61.7**	**60.8**
Africa	3.4	1.5	5.4	5.7
Asia	26.5	10.0	10.3	10.5
Middle East	3.7	2.6	7.6	7.7
Latin America and the Caribbean	7.6	4.8	7.5	7.7
Transition Economies	6.3	4.8	7.5	7.7
Total Developing and Transition Countries	**47.6**	**23.7**	**38.3**	**39.2**
Total	**100.0**	**100.0**	**100.0**	**100.0**

Source: IMF, *World Economic Outlook*, 2005.

nature of current quotas and voting power in relation to shares of world output.

The large differences between the conversion of measurements of GDP measured at market exchange rates and in terms of PPP are shown in Table 1. The table shows that when properly measured, the output of the developing countries in 2003 approached that of the G-7 countries and the sum of the output of developing countries and economies in transition approached that of all industrial countries. Since the developing countries are growing at a considerably higher rate than industrial countries, the WEO projections indicate that in 2005, the developing country output will equal that of the G-7. The share of global GDP accounted for by developing and transition economies will match that of all industrial countries by 2006.

The Quota Formulas

Given the role of quotas as the determinant of voting power, any review of governance must consider whether they reflect the relative positions of countries in the world economy, the relevance of the variables included and weights assigned to them and the transparency of the quota determination process.

At the time of the Bretton Woods Conference, quotas were assigned several important roles, i.e. the determination of countries contributions to the Fund, that of access to Fund resources and their relative voting power. The logic of having only one formula for determining these different roles has often been questioned. As suggested by Mikesell (1994) and in keeping with the well-known postulate of Prof. Tinbergen (1952), of having one policy instrument for each policy objective, it would make considerable sense to separate the three functions performed by quotas—determination of voting power, determination of contributions to the Fund and access to Fund resources.

However, since at Bretton Woods the membership felt there was merit in having contributions and access to resources based on the same formula, such a far reaching departure from the traditional role of quotas might make an agreement in the discussion of changes in quota formulas considerably more difficult to reach.

The formula developed by Mikesell in 1943 had the political objective of attaining the relative quota shares that the US President and Secretary of State had agreed to give the 'big four' wartime allies, with a ranking which they had decided—the United States was to have the largest quota, approximately \$2.9 billion, the UK including colonies an amount about half the US quota, the Soviet Union a quota just under that of the UK and China somewhat less. To achieve this result, the formula produced by Mikesell[5] after many iterations was based on 2 per cent of national income (NI), 5 per cent of gold and dollar holdings, 10 per cent of average imports, 10 per cent of maximum variation in exports and these last three percentages to be increased by the ratio of average exports/national income.

It is worth noting that with variations in the weight given to these variables and some changes in their definition (i.e. GDP for NI), the IMF continues to use the original formula; this is combined with four other formulas which include the same variables but with different weights. A considerable element of discretion is used in selecting the formula to be applied and in adjusting the results in estimating members' quotas. Consequently, the determination of quotas lacks transparency.

Moreover, while the structure of the world economy has changed rapidly over the last sixty years, as quota increases over the years have been largely (70%) equiproportional, a considerable element of inertia has tended to perpetuate the initial quota structure. Consequently, present day quotas which at best represented the economic structure of the world in 1944, are far from representative of the current sizes of economies, of their ability to contribute resources to the Fund or of their importance in world trade and financial markets.

The Quota Formula Review Group (QFRG)

As dissatisfaction with the structure of quotas increased over the years, pressures to review the system arose. The report of the Executive Board to the Board of

Governors on the increase in quotas under the Eleventh General Quota Review reaffirmed the view of the Interim Committee that the quota formulas should be reviewed, following the completion of that quota review. Accordingly, in 1999, the Managing Director requested a group of external experts to provide the Board with an independent report on the adequacy of quota formulas, including proposals for changes if appropriate. This Quota Formula Review Group (QFRG)[6] was to be headed by Professor Richard Cooper of Harvard University.

The terms of reference for the study given to the group were broad and included the following main areas:

- To review the quota formulas and their working, and to asses their adequacy to help determine member's calculated quotas in the IMF in a manner that reasonably reflects member's relative position in the world economy as well as their relative need for and contributions to the Fund's financial resources, taking into account changes in the functioning of the world economy and the international financial system and in the light of the increasing globalization of markets.
- To propose, as appropriate, changes in the variables and their specification to be used in the formulas.
- To examine other issues directly related to the quota formulas.

After looking at the history of the formulas, how variables affect the calculated quotas under existing formulas and a number of related issues and undertaking a substantial amount of econometric work, the QFRG decided to take a fresh approach and design a new formula. This formula was supposed 'to reflect the underlying changes in the functioning of the world economy and the international financial system, take account of the increasing globalization of markets, and simplify the existing formulas.' (*QFRG Report*, April 2000, p. 55).

The QFRG state their view that:

…any new formula should have a sound economic basis and should reflect changes in the world economy; that the form and content of any new formula should be consistent with the several functions of quotas; that the variables contained should not give members incentives to adjust their policies adversely to IMF principles; that any new quota formula should be more transparent and easier to comprehend than the existing set of formulas and any modification of the quota formulas should be feasible, and where problems of data quality or availability arise, such modification should be contingent on the resolution of these problems. (op. cit., pp. 56–7).

decision-making! This argument is entirely unconvincing.[9] The authors of the report appear to have forgotten the reasons for the compromise that led to basing voting rights on a combination of two criteria and the evolution of basic votes over time.

The importance of basic votes for small countries may be seen from the fact that despite their diminished importance, these still account for 20 per cent of the voting power of one-third of the membership. Nevertheless, quotas (shares in the case of the Bank) account for some 98 per cent of total votes and are virtually the sole determinant of total voting power. Consequently, the voice of small countries in decision-making has been reduced to the point of becoming negligible. A similar process of erosion of the role of basic votes has taken place in the Bank over time as a result of successive capital increases.

Restoring the share of basic votes to, say, the original 11.3 per cent of the total[10] would require a more than five-fold increase in the basic vote of every member country (from 250 to 1324).[11] In addition, to prevent the future erosion of the share of basic votes in the total, a decision could be adopted by which, in every future quota review, total basic votes increase in the same proportion as total quotas.

The preservation of the share of basic votes in the total would not be an exceptional practice among international institutions. Note that being sensitive to the political dimension of its work, the Asian Development Bank's Articles of Agreement provide that the relative importance of basic votes will remain constant over time as a proportion of the total vote (Article 33–1) and that the Articles of Agreement of the Inter-American Development Bank provide that no increase in the subscription of any member will become effective if it would reduce the voting power of certain countries or groups of countries below given percentages of the total.[12]

The Measurement of GDP and the Ability to Contribute

The QRFG agreed unanimously that the most relevant variable for measuring a country's ability to contribute to the Fund is the country's GDP. However, the group differed on how GDP measured in domestic currency was to be converted into a common currency to determine the relative ability of the country to contribute. The majority favoured conversion at market exchange rates, averaged over several years, but a minority preferred to measure GDP for purposes of the quota calculations using PPP-based exchange rates. They considered that market exchange rates do not necessarily equalize prices of tradable goods across countries, even after taking into account transport costs and quality differences and that this creates an index number problem in which the GDP in developing countries is understated in relation to developed countries if market exchange rates are used.

They noted that while real growth rates in these countries have been significantly higher than in industrialized countries, the increase in the relative size of GDP of developing countries is eroded by exchange rate depreciation when converted at market exchange rates.[13]

> The majority view argued that while PPP-based conversion rates were appropriate for measuring relative per capita income for comparing economic well-being across countries, they were not appropriate for indicating a country's ability to contribute to international endeavors. Second, market prices properly reflect the costs of moving goods from one place to another, and equating prices of equivalent goods regardless of location, as is done in PPP calculations, gives a seriously misleading indicator of the ability to contribute to international undertakings... The IMF is a monetary institution, requiring financial resources for use when members are in financial difficulties in their relations with the rest of the world. A country's ability to contribute is therefore determined by its capacity to provide funds at market exchange rates.[14]

In the view of the majority, using PPP-based GDP as a measure of a country's ability to contribute would produce serious anomalies, suggesting for example, that China could contribute one-third more than Japan, or that India could contribute more than France. Are these criticisms valid?

In today's world, where developing country reserves exceed those of industrial countries, in what sense is it meaningful to argue that the ability of Japan to contribute is greater than that of China and that the ability of France to contribute is greater than that of India? Contrary to what is suggested, the relationship between actual contributions as determined by quotas and the ability to contribute as a proportion of GDP is very far from being a binding restriction. Consider first that quotas are a very small proportion of GDP, only 1 per cent at the time of the Eleventh Quota Review in 1998 measured in market exchange rates (Table 1) and today, at nine-tenths of 1 per cent, are an even smaller proportion. Second, note that since conversions of GDP at market rates produce significantly smaller GDPs than PPP-based conversions; the potential contributions by developing countries are such a small proportion of their GDP that the argument loses any significance. Third, note that only 25 per cent of the member's contribution or quota is paid in foreign currencies. Taken together, these facts weaken the 'ability to contribute' argument, the main argument against the use of PPP-based GDP, to the point where it becomes irrelevant. In any case, countries are free to accept or reject quotas proposed and any country that does not feel able or does not wish to accept an increase in its contribution could decline a proposed increase in its quota or accept it at a later date.

Another argument presented against the use of PPP-based GDPs is the lack of data. At the time, PPP-based GDP estimates were available for only 117 countries representing 95 per cent of world GDP. Of course, with effort, data deficiencies can be eliminated over time.[15] You might consider that the availability of data for countries accounting for some 95 per cent of the total world GDP is not a bad starting point if you can work to extend the coverage to other countries, particularly if you have several years in which to prepare the appropriate estimates.

Recall the situation prevalent as regards balance of payments data at the time of the Eleventh Review of Quotas,

> …when data for current receipts and payments through 1994 were used in the quota formulas. At the time, Balance of Payments data supplied for publication in the IMF's Balance of Payments Yearbook were not available for 53 countries (out of the 183 that participated in the quota review). These gaps were filled by information provided by area department desk economists, based on official information, and by staff estimates.[16]

Could not the same be done for PPP-based GDP estimates?

The recent staff calculations[17] that would purport to show developing countries are over-represented and developed countries under-represented in relation to calculated quotas, are contrary to common sense and simply show the biases in existing quota calculations, even when GNP is converted at market exchange rates. Some striking examples of this are shown in Table 2, i.e. the quotas of Denmark, Norway and Austria are larger than that of Korea, which is a larger economy and trading nation than the sum of the three countries cited above. Equally absurd, the Belgian quota is larger than those of India, Brazil and Mexico, which are amongst the world's ten largest economies. Similar bias is obtained when African quotas are compared with those of European countries.

The major bias against developing countries arises from the conversion of measurements of GNP in local currency to US dollars at market exchange rates. By not valuing services and non-tradables at international prices, this conversion substantially underestimates the size of their GNP.[18] As is widely recognized by statisticians, due to the volatility of exchange rates[19] and the fact that the exchange rates do not reflect relative prices across countries or movements in these prices over time, exchange rate conversions of national currency values of GNP yield inconsistent results. 'They fail to reflect the true levels of volumes of goods and services in the aggregates being compared' and 'fail to reflect the movements in relative volumes of these goods and services over time'. Purchasing power parity conversion eliminates both these inconsistencies.[20]

Table 2. Comparison of quotas and GDP for selected countries

	GDP 2003 (SDRs)	GDP (PPP) 2003 (Share in World)	Actual Quota (SDRs)
Small European			
Austria	179,834	0.47	1,872
Belgium	216,136	0.57	4,605
Denmark	151,905	0.33	1,643
Finland	115,535	0.28	1,264
Norway	158,467	0.34	1,672
Sweden	215,119	0.47	2,396
Switzerland	221,320	0.43	3,459
Total	**1,258,316**	**2.88**	**16,910**
Asian			
China	1,008,284	12.69	6,369
India	428,363	5.83	4,158
Indonesia	148,977	1.44	2,079
Korea	432,914	1.86	1,634
Pakistan	49,214	0.64	1,034
Philippines	57,624	0.69	880
Thailand	102,386	0.91	1,082
Total	**2,227,763**	**24.05**	**17,236**
Latin American			
Argentina	92,783	0.85	2,117
Brazil	352,105	2.65	3,036
Chile	51,790	0.31	856
Colombia	55,468	0.57	774
Mexico	447,753	1.82	2,586
Peru	43,633	0.28	638
Venezuela	60,641	0.24	2,659
Total	**1,104,173.40**	**6.73**	**12,667**

Source: The IMF's *World Economic Outlook Database and the IMF's Quotas—A Fact sheet.*

For the above reasons, both the IMF and the World Bank rely on measurements of GNP or GNI in PPP in all estimates which involve international aggregates, i.e. of performance of the world economy in the World Economic Outlook and in economic growth projections. Indeed, measurements of output at market exchange rates are little used in an international context, other than in quota calculations.

The Measurement of Volatility of Receipts

Considering the members' potential need for financial support from the Fund, the QFRG finds that the single most relevant variable for measuring a country's vulnerability to external disturbances is the variability of its international receipts.

It is proposed that the variability of international receipts be measured as the standard deviation from trend of current account receipts over a 13-year period, with the trend measured by the centred 5-year moving average. The report admits the possibility of refining this variable 'by adding to receipts some measure of autonomous net inflows of capital, e.g. net long-term borrowing plus foreign direct investment, assuming that reasonably accurate information was available on a timely basis.' While these are undoubtedly relevant variables and this is the traditional way of looking at balance of payments vulnerability, they are not the whole story.

In looking at external vulnerability, one may consider:

• the degree of openness
• the composition of exports
• the concentration of exports
• the dependence on external financing, particularly on short-term capital flows

The first of these variables, the degree of openness, is estimated in the current quota formula, i.e. openness is measured by the sum of imports and exports as a proportion of GDP. Obviously, a closed economy, say one where the external sector accounts for 6 per cent of GDP will be less affected by external developments than a very open one, where external sector represents say 50 per cent of GDP. In the first case, a collapse of exports will have a limited impact on the level of domestic economic activity while in the second case an export collapse will have major consequences in terms of output and employment. Thus, since an open economy is more vulnerable than a closed one, the degree of openness should be seen as a separate variable, to be distinguished from the variability of current receipts. While this variable is not considered by the QFRG, the appropriate measurement of vulnerability as a proportion of GDP can take care of this factor, thereby making the inclusion of a separate factor for openness unnecessary.[21]

Export composition is an element of vulnerability since exports of commodities are subject to greater price fluctuations than exports of manufactures. Thus, a country with a high concentration of exports in one or two primary products, say cocoa, coffee, copper, etc. is subject to wide fluctuations in export revenues. Similarly, the concentration of exports in one or two markets, whether of manufactures or primary products will result in substantial cyclical variations in export revenues and in a high degree of vulnerability for the exporting country. While these well-known factors are not mentioned explicitly by the QFRG, only the second and third can be subsumed in the proposal for the measurement of variations in current revenues.

However, trade variables and long-term capital flows cannot substitute for the consideration of the volatility of short-term capital flows, which, as is widely recognized, has been the determining factor in the financial crises suffered by emerging market economies that have dominated Fund financial operations in the last decade. Excluded from consideration by the QFRG is the member's dependence on international financial markets, particularly the volatility of short-term capital flows.

The terms of reference for the QFRG refer to 'changes in functioning of the world economy and the international financial system and in the light of the increasing globalization of markets'. Since the increasing role of financial markets and their globalization are probably the single most important change that has taken place in the international economy, it is surprising that the variables proposed exclude the volatility of short-term capital movements, whose reversal played a major role in the financial crises that emerging markets suffered several years before the QFRG was convened.[22]

Adjustment of Quotas for Intra-European Trade

Another important development the QFRG did not consider were the consequences of the emergence of the EU as a major trading block in Europe. This may be surprising since the European Common Market has been in existence for several decades. The IMF recognized the impact of intra-EU trade on quota calculations in its report, *External Review of the Quota Formulas*, EBAP/00/52 Sup. 1, 1 May 2000, which in paragraph 100 states:

> The effect on the calculated quotas of EU countries of excluding all the intra-trade flows within the EU, i.e. not taking into account any domestic valued added of such trade, is illustrated in Table 9.1. The revised calculated quotas would be substantially reduced. In aggregate, the EU-15 countries' share would be reduced by 9.2 percentage points (from about 37.1 per cent to about 28.0 per cent). The largest declines in percentage points are for Germany, the Netherlands, France, and Belgium.

Partly as a result of the distortion generated by intra-trade, the European Union with 15 members in 2003 and a smaller GDP than the United States,[23] had 74 per cent greater voting power than the United States and is currently represented by 8–9 Directors. European countries are over-represented in the IMF and World Bank executive boards, both relative to their share of world GDP (Tables 1 and 2) and compared with the United States. To these voices is added the voice of a European Central Bank representative who participates in the Fund board discussion for a number of issues—the WEO, international financial markets and Financial Stability Reports, the role of the

Euro and consultations with the 25 EU members and with prospective members. In contrast, only two African directors represent the 46 sub-Saharan countries, many of which have Fund programs and Bank loans.

Thus, in addition to the problem arising from exchange rate based conversions of GNI, the substantial over-representation of the EU members arising from the treatment given to intra-EU trade flows, the intra-trade flows considered in IMF calculation are an underestimation as they did not consider trade in services.

Following the IMF methodology of the 12th quota review and using OECD data, we have made a new estimate of the required quota adjustments which includes services.[24]

Moreover, since trade within a single currency area cannot give rise to balance of payments problems, it is more akin to domestic trade than to international trade. When a correction is made for trade in the single currency, the calculated quotas for the 12 euro-zone countries decline sharply, falling from 28.3 per cent to 16.9 per cent, a fall of 11.4 percentage points. See Table 3.

Table 3. Current and adjusted calculated quota for the EU-12 countries

	Current calculated quota (in millions SDR)	Share (in per cent)	Adjusted calculated quota (excluding intra-trade in goods and services) (in millions SDR)	Share (in per cent)
EU-12	**234,860**	**28.3**	**120,926**	**16.9**
Austria	9,572	1.2	4,177	0.5
Belgium	17,709	2.1	6,649	0.8
Finland	4,955	0.6	2,592	0.3
France	38,652	4.7	21,593	2.6
Germany	62,854	7.6	34,872	4.2
Greece	3,087	0.4	2,031	0.2
Ireland	9,323	1.1	6,494	0.8
Italy	30,286	3.6	17,407	2.1
Luxembourg	12,903	1.6	3,580	0.4
Netherlands	24,562	3.0	10,990	1.3
Portugal	4,433	0.5	1,844	0.2
Spain	16,522	2.0	8,697	1.0
United States	**138,060**	**16.6**	**138,060**	**19.3**
Japan	**70,364**	**8.5**	**70,364**	**9.8**
Other countries	**387,271**	**46.6**	**387,271**	**54.0**
Total	**830,556**	**100.0**	**716,622**	**100.0**

If one reduced the actual quotas of the euro-zone member countries by the same proportion as the decline in calculated quotas, the quota share of these 12 countries would fall from 23.2 per cent to 13.84 per cent, a reduction of 9.35 percentage points. (or 40.3 per cent).

Recent Discussions on the Formula[25]

During the discussion of the QFRG report by the Board in August 2000, Directors welcomed the simplification and greater transparency of the proposed formula, but expressed the dissatisfaction and concern that its adoption would lead to greater concentration of quotas and power among the major industrial countries and requested further work should be undertaken on the subject.

In their quota discussion of June 2002, Directors favoured the simpler and more transparent approach to the specification of variables to be included in quota formulas. They agreed that the number of variables should be limited to no more than three or four at most—GDP measuring economic size as the more important variable, a measure of openness, the variability of current receipts and net capital flows to reflect the vulnerability of members and in the opinion of some, international reserves.

In their 2003 discussion, Directors considered that a package approach should be adopted toward the adjustment of quotas, based on a simplified and transparent formula to determine large selective increases and that additional *ad hoc* adjustments would be required for countries whose quotas are more out of line. Basic votes should be increased to correct the erosion of the voting power of the smallest countries. Note however, that any change in basic votes in the Fund or Bank require an amendment of the Articles of Agreement.

Recent discussions on governance have shown increasing pressure on the part of developing countries, particularly emerging market economies, in favour of reforming the governance of the BWIs. For instance, at the April 2005 meetings of the IMFC and Development Committee, most of the developing countries' spokesmen pressed the need for reform.

A recent communiqué of the G-24, stated:[26]

Ministers consider that enhancing the representation of developing countries requires a new quota formula to reflect the relative size of developing country economies. The formula should be simplified to give greater weight to measures of gross domestic product in terms of purchasing power parity, and take into account the vulnerabilities of developing countries to movements in commodity prices, the volatility of capital movements and other exogenous shocks. In addition, basic votes should be substantially increased to restore their original role in relation to total voting power and to strengthen the voice of small countries. Ministers are concerned that the updated quota calculations contained in the report to IMFC and DC continue to understate the role of developing countries in the world economy and run counter to the good governance, legitimacy and best interests of the Bretton Woods institutions.

Table 4 shows the distribution of voting power by country groupings that would result from a new quota formula that followed the G-24 ministers' view; i.e. a formula based on GDP (PPP) and volatility. Since quota formulas may be changed by a simple majority of the Board while the increase in basic votes requires an amendment of the Articles, Table 4 maintains the current level of basic votes. Note that adjustments in the weight given to volatility in the quota formula could achieve a distribution of votes similar to that resulting from a given increase in basic votes simply by revising the quota formula.

As shown by Tables 1 and 4, the measurement of GDP in terms of PPP favours an increase in the quota share of all developing countries by eliminating a measurement bias against them. The introduction of *volatility* as a factor in the quota formula also favours developing countries, particularly exporters of primary products. Despite the volatility of capital movements,

Table 4. Voting power distribution with different weights assigned to GDP (PPP) and volatility with current level of basic votes

Country groupings	GDP (PPP) = 0.60 V = 0.40	GDP (PPP) = 0.70 V = 0.30	GDP (PPP) = 0.80 V = 0.20	GDP (PPP) = 0.90 V = 0.10	GDP (PPP) = 1 V = 0
G-7 Countries	0.26	0.31	0.35	0.39	0.43
Other Industrial Countries	0.08	0.08	0.08	0.08	0.08
Total Industrialized Countries	**0.34**	**0.38**	**0.43**	**0.47**	**0.52**
Africa	0.15	0.12	0.09	0.07	0.04
Asia	0.21	0.22	0.24	0.25	0.26
Middle East	0.08	0.07	0.06	0.05	0.04
Latin America and the Caribbean	0.10	0.09	0.09	0.08	0.08
Transition Economies	0.12	0.10	0.09	0.08	0.06
Total Developing Countries	**0.66**	**0.62**	**0.57**	**0.53**	**0.48**
Total	**1.00**	**1.00**	**1.00**	**1.00**	**1.00**

the inclusion of a volatility factor increases the quotas of primary producers with less diversified exports, more than those of other country groupings, the result being the relative increases of quotas of Africa and the Middle East (Table 4). Consequently, the reduction of the weight assigned to the volatility factor favours emerging market countries, particularly those with a larger GDP and diversified exports. As is apparent from Table 4, the relative weights assigned in the quota formula to these two variables have a major impact on the overall distribution of quotas.[27] Since industrial countries' exports are less dependent on commodities than those of developing countries and industrial countries are less subject to capital account volatility, the greater the weight assigned to volatility, the smaller their quotas.

In the recent April 2005 meeting of the IMFC, statements made on behalf of major industrial countries suggested more openness to the consideration of the subject than in the past. Thus, the United States, which only a year earlier had taken a negative attitude to the discussion of governance, took the view that 'governance should evolve along with the world economy so that countries positions better reflect their global weights and so that all members are more effectively represented…particularly given fast-paced GDP growth in emerging market economies and the advent of currency union in Europe.'[28] However, this is to be achieved without an increase in Fund resources through a 'rebalancing of quotas' from 'over-represented' to 'under-represented' countries. This leaves aside the difficulty posed by the fact that a country's quota can not be reduced without its consent.

Japan pressed for the review of the quotas of emerging markets, stressing that unless the Fund responds to the increasing importance of Asia in the world economy it 'could irrevocably lose relevance in Asia and ultimately in the world'.[29]

European countries that stand to lose quota share were in a difficult position. They had agreed in 2002 in the Monterrey Consensus to strengthen the voice and participation of developing countries and transition economies in decision-making, but with few exceptions, are fighting a rearguard action to avoid structural change and preserve the status quo to the extent possible. Thus, they favour token administrative measures[30] and are generally open to a review of basic votes to favour of African countries, which by itself would have limited systemic impact, and appear prepared to consider selective quota increases to recognize the increasing role of a few emerging markets in the world economy. This changing attitude was reflected in the IMFC Communiqué of 16 April 2005 which states that:

> The IMF's effectiveness and credibility as a cooperative institution must be safeguarded and further enhanced. Adequate voice and participation

by all members should be assured and the distribution of quotas should reflect developments in the world economy. The Committee emphasized that the Thirteenth General Review of Quotas provides an opportunity for the membership to make progress toward a consensus on the issues of quotas, voice and participation.

Nevertheless, the language is vague enough to paper over many deep differences that remain and the way ahead is far from clear.

Among pockets of resistance to the review of governance are smaller European countries which, being over-represented, fear they may lose their chair in the executive board and the committees if a major revision of governance were undertaken. For instance, the Dutch minister[31] expounded the virtues of mixed constituencies as contributing to cooperation between debtor and creditor countries and took the line that the current constituency system, by which countries like Belgium and the Netherlands represent a mixed constituency, is a sound and presumably better solution than having developing countries speak for themselves. He omitted to mention that since the Articles do not allow split voting, the executive directors representing mixed constituencies cast the vote of all the countries in a manner contrary to the interests of the developing/borrowing countries, who are minority members of the constituency, on such policy issues as waivers on conditionality, level of access to Fund resources, the size of the Fund, the allocation of SDRs, the need for a precautionary facility to protect countries against financial crises and others.[32]

Other Aspects of the Legitimacy Problem

In addition to the erosion of basic votes and the unrepresentative character of quotas, the problem of legitimacy of the governance has grown over time for functional reasons, in particular, the diminished effectiveness of the Fund and Bank. It would appear that today, Fund surveillance is only effective over those emerging and developing economies that resort to its financial support, but has little if any impact on industrial countries and on systemic issues. Why did the Fund lose influence over industrial countries and other major economies?

First, the exponential growth of international financial markets has allowed industrial countries easy access to external financing. This access, coupled with the growth of their own domestic financial markets and the development of regional monetary arrangements and reciprocal credit lines among them, make it unnecessary for them to subject themselves to the conditionality associated with IMF support. This trend became apparent by the late seventies—as Europe developed its own monetary arrangements, it walked away from the Fund.

As a result, there has emerged a growing chasm between shareholders and stakeholders, between those who determine IMF policies and decisions and those to whom those decisions and policies are applied. Thus, instead of a cooperative institution to which all members contribute and from which they may borrow from time to time, a distinction has emerged between creditor countries that have the power to make the rules[33] and debtor and prospective debtor countries, which are subject to those rules.

A second factor that has eroded legitimacy is the rapid economic expansion of emerging market countries, their growing importance in the international economy and their accumulation of international reserves. The growth of emerging markets has not been reflected by changes in the governance structure of the Bretton Woods institutions. This lack of representation made possible the contractionary policy prescriptions required by the Fund as a condition for support during the Asian financial crises of 1997–98, perceived by a number of countries as inappropriate and contrary to their interests.

Consequently, in order to avoid having to rely on Fund support in the future, Asian countries decided to build up their reserves and develop regional monetary arrangements as a form of insurance. The Chiang Mai initiative was established to provide liquidity support to its members faced with contagion and speculative attacks against their currencies. Its expansion to allow multilateral currency swaps and the doubling of the size of these, from $39.5 billion to over $70 billion was agreed by the Finance Ministers meeting in Istanbul on 5 May 2005. Reportedly, a four-fold increase in the size of drawings that may be made without IMF conditionality was also agreed. In the words of Masahiro Kawai, a former Japanese finance ministry official who will head the new regional financial integration office at the ADB, 'the Chiang Mai initiative has the potential to become an Asian monetary fund'.[34]

By developing a bond market in domestic currencies, the Asian Bond Fund, also aims at reducing the vulnerability of countries to risks of liquidity and currency mismatches that could lead to financial crises.

Thus, in addition to Europe, a growing number of countries in Asia and Latin America appear to be in the process of moving away from the IMF. To the extent this process advances, the IMF would cease to be a truly multi-lateral institution of monetary cooperation and become an institution dealing mostly with the payment problems of low income countries in Africa and elsewhere.

The Loss of Role and Effectiveness

The IMF

When the Fund was established in 1945, the world lived under an international monetary system centred on fixed parities, which gave the IMF a clear role. The IMF was to enforce a code of conduct designed to prevent the competitive exchange rate devaluations and trade restrictions that had given rise to the 'beggar thy neighbour' policies in the inter-war years. To prevent these, the Fund was to approve exchange rate adjustments only in cases of fundamental disequilibria. Temporary payments imbalances were to be addressed mostly by demand management measures, mainly fiscal and monetary. The support of Fund resources would prevent members from resorting to restrictions on trade and payments or other 'measures destructive of national and international prosperity'.

Following the abandonment of the 'par value' system, which had been at the heart of its role in the international monetary system, the IMF's function was transformed. Since August 1971, when following the inordinate expansion of its liabilities, the United States suspended the convertibility of the dollar into gold to protect its gold holdings; the world has lived in a 'non-system' in which countries choose whether they wish to have floating or fixed exchange rates. Thus, the Fund's central role as arbiter of exchange rates has largely disappeared.

The Articles of Agreement refer to the general obligations of members regarding exchange arrangements and provide the basis for Fund surveillance:

- Article IV Section 1(i) assigns the Fund a role of promoting a stable system of exchange rates. Observing the 65 per cent variations of the exchange rate between two of the world's major currencies, the euro and the US dollar over a small number of years, it can hardly be said to have succeeded.[35]
- Article IV Section 1 (iii) places an injunction on members to avoid exchange rate manipulation in order to prevent effective balance of payments adjustment or to gain unfair competitive advantage over other members. A number of countries, mostly in Asia, have pursued an export driven development strategy based on fixing their exchange rate at very competitive levels in order to promote exports and employment. In this process, these countries run large trade surpluses and have attracted large flows of foreign investment, leading to the accumulation of very high levels of international reserves.

   In the aftermath of the Asian financial crises, reserve accumulation was a deliberate and justifiable policy by these countries to insure themselves against loss of financial market access, the risks posed by volatility of capital flows and the crisis to which they may give rise. Noting that the very high level of international reserves held by some countries goes well beyond the level necessary to ensure stability, the question may arise of whether Fund surveillance has succeeded in promoting international adjustment and preventing exchange rate manipulation.

• Fund surveillance over major economies has proven to be ineffective in dealing with global imbalances. Cumulative US fiscal and current account deficits pose a serious danger to the stability and prosperity of the international economy:

> The dollar depreciation has precipitated rising trade tensions and calls for protection in Europe and other countries whose currencies have appreciated. The rapid growth of Asian exports of textiles and other goods has also given rise to calls for protection in Europe and the United States. Thus, pressures for protectionism are rising in response to political pressures in countries whose industries are unable to compete.

> On current trends, if the US deficits persist, there is the growing risk that at some point the demand for dollars as a reserve asset by foreign central banks, mainly in East Asia, will fall as monetary authorities and private investors choose to hold other reserve assets that maintain their value such as euros, yen or gold. This could take place among the industrial, oil exporting countries and emerging countries that cannot justify either further buildup of reserves or capital losses arising from a declining dollar.

> A loss of confidence leading to a disorderly depreciation of the dollar would lead to a sharp rise in dollar interest rates that would put a sharp brake on the US economy and on the growth of Asian and other countries dependent on the US market.

• The fact that large amounts of capital flow from poor countries to finance the twin deficits of the largest economy, the issuer of the main reserve currency, must be seen as an anomaly and a serious misallocation of resources from a global economic standpoint. This is a resource misallocation from the standpoint of developing countries whose savings should be invested at home to capitalize and develop their economies. But it is a misallocation of resources also from the US medium term perspective. With a rapidly aging population, instead of borrowing to finance consumption, the United States should sustain high rates of investment abroad in order to earn interest, profits and dividends that will increase the income of its population as it ages and the proportion of working population declines.

• While industrial countries are able to, and pursue counter-cyclical policies to combat recession, emerging and developing countries, which account for half of the world output, measured in terms of PPP, are unable to do so. Given the size of their economies, this hinders global economic recovery. Indeed, emerging market countries are forced to pursue pro-cyclical fiscal and monetary policies by the pro-cyclical behavior of international financial markets, as they find it difficult to borrow to sustain their economic activity in times of recession.

- The United States, which was the largest creditor country at the time of the Bretton Woods Conference, always favoured conditionality.[36] As debtors, the European countries had resisted conditionality during the first decade of the Fund and favoured increasing Fund resources, but as their situation changed, they changed their position. This had far-reaching consequences for the character of the institution, since the countries who determine policy and those who are subject to, or governed by, Fund policies are no longer the same. Thus over time, a new situation has emerged, characterized by an increase in conditionality and a relative decline in the resources of the Fund. This has shifted the balance between adjustment and financing in Fund supported programs in favour of more adjustment, increased conditionality and has resulted in a high rate of program failures.[37]

Under Article I Section (v) of the Articles of Agreement, the Fund's purposes include making its resources temporarily available to members under adequate safeguards, providing them with the opportunity to correct balance of payments disequilibria 'without resorting to measures destructive of national and international prosperity'. Thus, the use of Fund resources is intended to mitigate the severity of the adjustment process member countries must undertake. In addressing each case, the Fund should seek to strike a fine balance between adjustment and financing. When a country has unlimited financing, like the United States at present, it is able to resist adjustment, however necessary, for a long period of time. At the other extreme, many developing countries undertake adjustment without adequate financial support. This increases the economic and social costs of adjustment and gives rise to political resistance to the adoption of necessary measures. Consequently, the risk of program failure rises.

To be effective, the Fund must be able to encourage the adoption of adjustment programs in a timely manner by offering a level of financing that limits their contractionary short-term effects. However, with industrial country members no longer resorting to the use of IMF resources, these were allowed to decline as a proportion of world trade. IMF resources thus fell sharply, from 58 per cent in 1944 to under 4 per cent at present and as a result, programs are often under-financed. Moreover, since systemically and strategically important countries have access to Fund resources well beyond the limits established by access policy, there is a lack of transparency and of uniformity of treatment.

A Fund without adequate financial resources can not perform its role. It cannot provide incentives to timely adjustment, nor can it be seen as a friend to whom countries can turn for support and guidance in uncertain times. Indeed, when the Fund puts a premium on the reduction of aggregate demand and acts pro-cyclically, it pursues what Stiglitz called 'beggar thyself policies'.[38]

- Surveillance of countries' economic, fiscal, monetary, exchange rate and debt policies, requiring the timely provision of data to the markets as well as the application of standards and codes, and good regulation and supervision of the financial system may be considered necessary precautionary measures. But however helpful, standards and codes are not sufficient to prevent the emergence of confidence crises that give rise to major reversals of capital flows. Since large outflows inflict damage to an economy very quickly, the currentpolicy of IMF lending to the countries after the crisis has caused a large depreciation of the currency and a deep recession, and must be considered unsatisfactory.

The approach to financial crises that would be consistent with the purposes of the IMF would require it to provide sufficient resources support to sustain or restore market confidence, before the meltdown takes place.[39]

It is clear that the results attained in the management of systemic issues or of the international economy have not gained the Fund greater legitimacy in the eyes of most member countries. Moreover, program results are generally better in terms of improving the external balance than growth and employment. This has been perceived by critics as reflecting the priorities of creditors rather than those of the countries themselves.

The World Bank

The Bank was established with a dual mandate—to help finance the reconstruction of the countries ravaged by World War II and to assist the developing countries in financing their development.[40] Since capital shares of the World Bank are distributed largely in line with IMF quota shares, the under-representation of the developing world undermines its legitimacy and effectiveness.

As emerging market countries gained access to capital markets they diminished their dependence on the Bank as a source of capital. However, most developing countries do not have ready access to international capital markets, except for short term trade finance. The provision of longer term financing for development is an important role of the Bank even for emerging market countries with access to capital markets, since capital market flows are pro-cyclical and market loans are for shorter terms than are required to finance investment projects with long maturities, i.e. in infrastructure, health and education and others. In addition, Bank project financing is usually combined with the transfer of technical knowledge. Drawing on its experience of other countries, the Bank is able to provide its knowledge on the policies and institutions that work better, those most conducive to development and poverty reduction, as well as to provide technical assistance for the solution of the problems of development.

Unfortunately, after a period of rapid expansion followed by years of stagnation, the Bank's lending operations have declined in recent years and as a result, net negative transfers rose sharply (see Table 5). This decline in Bank lending limits the provision of capital and the transmission of knowledge. Moreover, large repayments suggest that the middle income countries are reluctant to resort to the Bank when they have alternative sources of funding. This appears to be due to the high non-financial costs of loans, both in terms of conditionality and the cumbersome administrative procedures leading to delays of disbursements. Additionally, financial costs are not trivial. Since the administrative costs of the Bank exceed $1 billion, the equivalent of over 8 per cent of disbursements, the Bank may be one of the more expensive financial intermediaries in the world.

Table 5. The operations of the World Bank (in millions US$)

	1999	2000	2001	2002	2003	2004
IBRD						
Disbursements	18,205	13,332	11,784	11,252	11,921	10,109
Repayments (−)	10,082	10,398	9,635	12,025	−19,887	−18,479
Net flows	8,123	2,934	2,149	−773	−7,966	−8,370
Interest and charges	−7,649	−8,153	−8,143	−6,861	−5,742	−4,403
Net transfers	474	−5,219	−5,994	7,634	−13,708	−12,773
IDA						
Disbursements	5843	5177	5492	6601	7,019	6936
Repayments	−898	−1285	−1235	−1255	−1,369	−1398
Net flows	4945	3892	4257	5346	5,650	5,538
Interest and charges	−588	−619	−614	−641	−816	−806
Net transfers	4357	3273	3643	4705	5,650	4,732
Total net transfers (IBRD+IDA)	**4,831**	**−1,946**	**−2,351**	**−2,929**	**−8,058**	**−8,041**

The Bank has been slow to adapt to changing circumstances, to streamline its procedures to become more agile, to develop new products more suitable than traditional loans to meet the needs of its members for risk management. For instance, it could be of great assistance by developing risk management instruments to reduce the risks arising from volatility of commodity prices and capital flows. It could also reduce currency mismatches by borrowing and lending in the currencies of emerging market countries without putting its capital at risk.[41]

A fundamental issue arises from the comparison of the poor growth performance and the modest reduction in poverty and inequality in economic reformers pursuing orthodox policies and structural reforms in Latin America compared with the high growth rates, employment creation and poverty reduction achieved by Asian countries pragmatically pursuing heterodox policies. Over the 30-year period ending in 2000, the per capita income of Latin America had risen by 40 per cent while that of Asia had increased by 320 per cent. This differing performance could not fail to undermine the confidence in the pro-market reform policies promoted by international financial institutions.[42] Several of the most successful Asian countries relied on public enterprises and utilized industrial policies, including selective intervention in the allocation of credit, export subsidies, tax incentives and protection.[43]

The issue of ownership arises in the context of both Fund supported programs and of Bank loans. There is ample evidence indicating that country ownership is a requirement for success. However, a combination of excess conditionality and lack of pragmatism, reflecting the unrepresentative character of the governance of both institutions, favours neither adoption of country priorities nor of a plurality of approaches in recognition that developing societies are distinct and often too complex for standard approaches to their problems.

Last, but not least, the exclusion of the great majority of members in the procedure followed for the selection of the new president of the Bank has certainly raised questions regarding the independence and legitimacy of the governance of the institution. Note that in a report of April 2001, the Executive Boards had endorsed a report that called for an advisory group to shortlist potential candidates and carry out an open selection process with the participation of all members, with candidates chosen on merit, irrespective of nationality.[44]

Conclusion

The structure of the world economy has changed considerably since the Bretton Woods Conference of 1944. The developing countries and economies in transition now account for half of the world's output. China,

India, Brazil and Mexico are among the world's ten largest economies measured in real terms, while other emerging countries also became major economic players without attaining adequate representation in the Bank and Fund. Since these political and economic changes have not been reflected in the decision-making structure of the Fund and the Bank, the governance of these institutions and the legitimacy of their decisions are being increasingly questioned.

Quotas should reflect the size of the economies of members, in particular their GDP, their exposure to trade and capital movements, as well as their ability to contribute to the Fund. If quota formulas were determined in accordance with the mandate given to the QFRG[45] and calculated quotas were based on objective measures, i.e. size of GNI, the volatility of receipts, European quotas were adjusted for intra-trade and trade in the single currency in the euro area, the quota share of developing countries and economies in transition as a group, should be about the same as that of industrial countries. Moreover, given the greater number of countries included in the group, with the addition of basic votes, the total voting power of developing countries and transition economies would be greater than that of industrial countries as a group.

However, the determination of quotas is as much a political exercise as a technical one. All participants in the discussion are likely to look at the effect of any proposal on their relative position in the distribution of power before expressing a view on the matter. The major difficulty lies in persuading industrial countries to agree to reducing their share of quotas and voting power.

Consequently, one could suggest that a realistic approach to the problem of distribution of power might start from an acceptable overall outcome, one to which most developed and developing countries will agree and then work backwards to define the precise manner in which this may be reached, i.e. the weights to be given to the components of voting power (basic vote and quotas), that would produce the desired result. While this procedure may seem somewhat lacking in objectivity, it would be far from unprecedented and is probably the only realistic approach to this matter.

A point of departure for the necessary negotiation leading to the reapportionment of quotas and revision of basic votes could be an agreement that the groupings of industrial and developing countries, or of prospective debtor and creditor countries, each have about half of the total vote at the Board. A second stage could be the revision of quota formulas, particularly the weight to be given to GNP (measured by PPP) and other variables. But since it would be difficult to arrive at an agreement on quota formulas without reference to what would happen to the share of basic votes in the total, this would have to be a simultaneous exercise. Consider also that changes in the measurement of GDP and the inclusion of a variability factor in the quota formula will allow any broad overall result to be attained without having to amend the Articles.

Over the past 25 years, the Fund's operations have been conducted exclusively with the developing countries and more recently, also with countries in transition. In recent years, the Fund has extended its conditionality to issues of governance. The explosive growth of international capital markets has given rise to new opportunities and difficult challenges. Thus, while the need for support for emerging market economies rose, the size of the Bank and IMF shrunk relative to world trade and even more in relation to international capital movements. This situation has widened the divide among member countries. On the one hand is a small group of industrial countries with a majority vote, on the other is the large number of primarily debtor developing countries with a minority vote and limited influence on policies. Consequently, major policy decisions on Fund supported programs and Bank policies are often taken outside the institutions on a discretionary basis. This power distribution, which raises questions on the legitimacy, transparency and accountability of Fund and Bank governance, is eroding the relevance of the institutions as Asian and other countries walk away from them.

Short-term self-interest and expediency appear to have blurred the Bretton Woods vision of international cooperation as a means to improve the workings of the world economy. The notion that national goals are best attained through international cooperation tends to be forgotten. If globalization is to work for all countries, the success of the Fund and Bank as multilateral institutions is crucial. For this purpose, the governance of BWIs requires a major reform of the quota and decision making structures to enable them to meet the new challenges of the world economy. Industrial countries should be aware that legitimacy and participation in decision-making are not contrary to the application of sound policies in the exercise of the Bank's and Fund's competences.

Appendix 1

Towards a New Quota Formula

The G-24 Ministerial Communiqué of 1 October 2004 indicates that the quota formula should be simplified to give greater weight to measures of GDP in terms of PPP and take into account the vulnerabilities of developing countries to movements in commodity prices, the volatility of capital movements and other exogenous shocks. In what follows, we have performed some numerical simulations to allow us to visualize the results this approach would lead to.

Since the ministers did not express a view on the proportion in which these factors should be combined, i.e. the relative weight to be assigned to them, Table A1 shows the distribution of quotas by country groupings that would result from assigning GDP (PPP) and Volatility different weights, ranging from GDP at 60 per cent and Volatility at 40 per cent to GDP at 100 per cent and Volatility at 0 per cent.

Table A1. Country distribution of calculated quotas with different weights for GDP (PPP) and volatility, maintaining basic votes at current level

Country	GDP (PPP) = 0.60 V = 0.40	GDP (PPP) = 0.70 V = 0.30	GDP (PPP) = 0.80 V = 0.20	GDP (PPP) = 0.90 V = 0.10	GDP (PPP) = 1 V = 0
G-7 Countries					
Canada	0.0119	0.0137	0.0156	0.0174	0.0192
France	0.0192	0.0223	0.0254	0.0285	0.0315
Germany	0.0270	0.0312	0.0355	0.0397	0.0439
Italy	0.0186	0.0214	0.0243	0.0271	0.0300
Japan	0.0412	0.0480	0.0548	0.0616	0.0684
United Kingdom	0.0195	0.0225	0.0255	0.0285	0.0315
United States	0.1252	0.1459	0.1666	0.1873	0.2080
	0.2626	**0.3051**	**0.3476**	**0.3901**	**0.4326**
Other Industrialized Countries					
Australia	0.0068	0.0079	0.0089	0.0099	0.0110
Austria	0.0032	0.0036	0.0040	0.0044	0.0048
Belgium	0.0044	0.0047	0.0051	0.0054	0.0058
Cyprus	0.0012	0.0010	0.0008	0.0006	0.0004
Denmark	0.0030	0.0031	0.0032	0.0033	0.0034
Finland	0.0026	0.0027	0.0028	0.0028	0.0029
Greece	0.0037	0.0038	0.0039	0.0040	0.0041
Iceland	0.0007	0.0006	0.0005	0.0004	0.0003
Ireland	0.0075	0.0063	0.0052	0.0040	0.0028
Israel	0.0027	0.0027	0.0027	0.0027	0.0027
Luxembourg	0.0098	0.0075	0.0052	0.0029	0.0006
Netherlands	0.0060	0.0068	0.0075	0.0082	0.0089
New Zealand	0.0020	0.0020	0.0020	0.0019	0.0019
Norway	0.0031	0.0032	0.0033	0.0034	0.0035
Portugal	0.0029	0.0031	0.0033	0.0035	0.0037
San Marino	0.0001	0.0001	0.0001	0.0001	0.0001
Spain	0.0113	0.0129	0.0146	0.0162	0.0178
Sweden	0.0037	0.0040	0.0042	0.0045	0.0047
Switzerland	0.0036	0.0038	0.0040	0.0041	0.0043
	0.0786	**0.0799**	**0.0812**	**0.0825**	**0.0838**

continued…

Table A1. (continued)

Country	GDP (PPP) = 0.60 V = 0.40	GDP (PPP) = 0.70 V = 0.30	GDP (PPP) = 0.80 V = 0.20	GDP (PPP) = 0.90 V = 0.10	GDP (PPP) = 1 V = 0
Africa					
Algeria	0.0035	0.0037	0.0038	0.0039	0.0040
Angola	0.0107	0.0082	0.0057	0.0032	0.0007
Benin	0.0021	0.0016	0.0012	0.0007	0.0003
Botswana	0.0019	0.0015	0.0012	0.0008	0.0004
Burkina Faso	0.0012	0.0010	0.0008	0.0006	0.0004
Burundi	0.0015	0.0012	0.0009	0.0005	0.0002
Cameroon	0.0017	0.0014	0.0012	0.0010	0.0008
Cape Verde	0.0015	0.0012	0.0008	0.0005	0.0002
Central African Republic	0.0018	0.0014	0.0010	0.0006	0.0002
Chad	0.0016	0.0012	0.0009	0.0006	0.0003
Comoros	0.0020	0.0015	0.0011	0.0006	0.0001
Congo, Dem. Republic of	0.0025	0.0021	0.0016	0.0012	0.0008
Congo, Republic of	0.0037	0.0028	0.0019	0.0011	0.0002
Cote d'Ivoire	0.0015	0.0013	0.0011	0.0008	0.0006
Djibouti	0.0082	0.0062	0.0042	0.0022	0.0001
Equatorial Guinea	0.0099	0.0075	0.0051	0.0028	0.0004
Eritrea	0.0064	0.0048	0.0033	0.0017	0.0002
Ethiopia	0.0076	0.0060	0.0044	0.0027	0.0011
Gabon	0.0015	0.0012	0.0009	0.0006	0.0003
Gambia, The	0.0023	0.0017	0.0012	0.0007	0.0002
Ghana	0.0021	0.0018	0.0016	0.0013	0.0010
Guinea	0.0010	0.0008	0.0007	0.0006	0.0004
Guinea-Bissau	0.0022	0.0017	0.0012	0.0006	0.0001
Kenya	0.0024	0.0020	0.0016	0.0012	0.0008
Lesotho	0.0020	0.0015	0.0011	0.0007	0.0002
Liberia	0.0026	0.0020	0.0014	0.0007	0.0001
Madagascar	0.0012	0.0010	0.0008	0.0006	0.0004
Malawi	0.0026	0.0020	0.0014	0.0008	0.0002
Mali	0.0012	0.0010	0.0008	0.0006	0.0003
Mauritania	0.0017	0.0014	0.0010	0.0006	0.0002
Mauritius	0.0016	0.0013	0.0010	0.0007	0.0004
Morocco	0.0019	0.0021	0.0022	0.0023	0.0025
Mozambique	0.0116	0.0088	0.0060	0.0033	0.0005
Namibia	0.0012	0.0010	0.0008	0.0006	0.0004
Niger	0.0013	0.0011	0.0008	0.0006	0.0003
Nigeria	0.0055	0.0049	0.0042	0.0036	0.0030
Rwanda	0.0054	0.0041	0.0029	0.0016	0.0003

continued…

Table A1. (continued)

Country	GDP (PPP) = 0.60 V = 0.40	GDP (PPP) = 0.70 V = 0.30	GDP (PPP) = 0.80 V = 0.20	GDP (PPP) = 0.90 V = 0.10	GDP (PPP) = 1 V = 0
Sao Tome and Principe	0.0035	0.0027	0.0018	0.0010	0.0001
Senegal	0.0015	0.0013	0.0010	0.0007	0.0004
Seychelles	0.0021	0.0016	0.0011	0.0006	0.0001
Sierra Leone	0.0019	0.0015	0.0010	0.0006	0.0002
Somalia	0.0001	0.0001	0.0001	0.0001	0.0001
South Africa	0.0059	0.0067	0.0076	0.0084	0.0092
Sudan	0.0019	0.0018	0.0017	0.0016	0.0015
Swaziland	0.0017	0.0013	0.0009	0.0006	0.0002
Tanzania	0.0012	0.0010	0.0009	0.0007	0.0005
Togo	0.0021	0.0017	0.0012	0.0007	0.0003
Tunisia	0.0016	0.0016	0.0015	0.0015	0.0015
Uganda	0.0015	0.0013	0.0012	0.0011	0.0009
Zambia	0.0035	0.0027	0.0019	0.0011	0.0003
Zimbabwe	0.0017	0.0014	0.0012	0.0009	0.0006
	0.1507	**0.1227**	**0.0947**	**0.0667**	**0.0386**
Asia					
Afghanistan, Islamic State of	0.0007	0.0008	0.0009	0.0010	0.0011
Bangladesh	0.0034	0.0038	0.0042	0.0047	0.0051
Bhutan	0.0019	0.0015	0.0010	0.0006	0.0002
Brunei Darussalam	0.0002	0.0002	0.0002	0.0003	0.0003
Cambodia	0.0016	0.0014	0.0011	0.0009	0.0006
China	0.0763	0.0887	0.1011	0.1135	0.1259
Fiji	0.0012	0.0010	0.0007	0.0005	0.0002
India	0.0351	0.0408	0.0465	0.0522	0.0580
Indonesia	0.0104	0.0114	0.0124	0.0134	0.0144
Kiribati	0.0035	0.0026	0.0018	0.0010	0.0001
Korea	0.0121	0.0137	0.0153	0.0169	0.0185
Lao, People's Dem. Republic	0.0015	0.0012	0.0009	0.0006	0.0003
Malaysia	0.0043	0.0044	0.0046	0.0047	0.0048
Maldives	0.0016	0.0012	0.0009	0.0005	0.0002
Marshall Islands	0.0020	0.0015	0.0010	0.0006	0.0001
Micronesia, Fed. States of	0.0030	0.0023	0.0016	0.0008	0.0001
Myanmar	0.0009	0.0011	0.0012	0.0013	0.0015
Nepal	0.0012	0.0011	0.0010	0.0009	0.0008
Pakistan	0.0046	0.0051	0.0055	0.0060	0.0065

continued…

Table A1. (continued)

Country	GDP (PPP) = 0.60 V = 0.40	GDP (PPP) = 0.70 V = 0.30	GDP (PPP) = 0.80 V = 0.20	GDP (PPP) = 0.90 V = 0.10	GDP (PPP) = 1 V = 0
Palau, Republic of	0.0064	0.0048	0.0032	0.0017	0.0001
Papua New Guinea	0.0015	0.0012	0.0010	0.0007	0.0004
Philippines	0.0048	0.0053	0.0059	0.0064	0.0069
Samoa	0.0029	0.0022	0.0015	0.0008	0.0001
Singapore	0.0041	0.0036	0.0031	0.0026	0.0021
Solomon Islands	0.0012	0.0009	0.0007	0.0004	0.0001
Sri Lanka	0.0016	0.0016	0.0015	0.0015	0.0015
Thailand	0.0065	0.0071	0.0078	0.0085	0.0091
Timor-Leste	0.0034	0.0026	0.0017	0.0009	0.0001
Tonga	0.0027	0.0020	0.0014	0.0008	0.0001
Vanuatu	0.0040	0.0030	0.0021	0.0011	0.0001
Vietnam	0.0030	0.0032	0.0034	0.0036	0.0038
	0.2076	**0.2215**	**0.2354**	**0.2493**	**0.2631**
Middle East					
Bahrain	0.0053	0.0041	0.0029	0.0016	0.0004
Egypt	0.0051	0.0052	0.0052	0.0052	0.0052
Iran	0.0065	0.0072	0.0079	0.0085	0.0092
Iraq	0.0001	0.0001	0.0001	0.0001	0.0001
Jordan	0.0046	0.0036	0.0026	0.0016	0.0006
Kuwait	0.0259	0.0196	0.0134	0.0071	0.0009
Lebanon	0.0023	0.0019	0.0014	0.0010	0.0005
Libya	0.0022	0.0019	0.0017	0.0014	0.0012
Malta	0.0023	0.0018	0.0013	0.0008	0.0003
Oman	0.0013	0.0012	0.0011	0.0009	0.0008
Qatar	0.0041	0.0032	0.0023	0.0014	0.0005
Saudi Arabia	0.0049	0.0051	0.0054	0.0056	0.0058
Syrian Arab Republic	0.0026	0.0023	0.0020	0.0017	0.0013
Turkey	0.0063	0.0071	0.0078	0.0086	0.0094
United Arab Emirates	0.0029	0.0027	0.0024	0.0022	0.0020
Yemen, Republic of	0.0063	0.0048	0.0034	0.0019	0.0004
	0.0827	**0.0717**	**0.0606**	**0.0496**	**0.0385**
Latin America and the Caribbean					
Antigua and Barbuda	0.0014	0.0011	0.0008	0.0005	0.0001
Argentina	0.0057	0.0065	0.0072	0.0079	0.0086

continued…

Table A1. (continued)

Country	GDP (PPP) = 0.60 V = 0.40	GDP (PPP) = 0.70 V = 0.30	GDP (PPP) = 0.80 V = 0.20	GDP (PPP) = 0.90 V = 0.10	GDP (PPP) = 1 V = 0
Bahamas, The	0.0013	0.0010	0.0007	0.0005	0.0002
Barbados	0.0009	0.0007	0.0006	0.0004	0.0002
Belize	0.0016	0.0012	0.0009	0.0005	0.0001
Bolivia	0.0008	0.0007	0.0007	0.0006	0.0005
Brazil	0.0162	0.0187	0.0213	0.0238	0.0264
Chile	0.0029	0.0030	0.0030	0.0031	0.0032
Colombia	0.0040	0.0045	0.0049	0.0054	0.0058
Costa Rica	0.0014	0.0013	0.0012	0.0010	0.0009
Dominica	0.0023	0.0017	0.0012	0.0007	0.0001
Dominican Republic	0.0023	0.0021	0.0018	0.0015	0.0012
Ecuador	0.0035	0.0029	0.0023	0.0017	0.0011
El Salvador	0.0014	0.0012	0.0010	0.0008	0.0007
Grenada	0.0014	0.0011	0.0008	0.0005	0.0001
Guatemala	0.0012	0.0012	0.0012	0.0011	0.0011
Guyana	0.0077	0.0058	0.0040	0.0021	0.0002
Haiti	0.0020	0.0016	0.0012	0.0008	0.0004
Honduras	0.0015	0.0013	0.0010	0.0007	0.0005
Jamaica	0.0028	0.0022	0.0015	0.0009	0.0003
Mexico	0.0115	0.0131	0.0148	0.0165	0.0182
Nicaragua	0.0043	0.0033	0.0023	0.0014	0.0004
Panama	0.0026	0.0020	0.0015	0.0010	0.0005
Paraguay	0.0018	0.0015	0.0012	0.0009	0.0006
Peru	0.0023	0.0025	0.0026	0.0027	0.0029
St. Kitts and Nevis	0.0012	0.0009	0.0006	0.0004	0.0001
St. Lucia	0.0008	0.0006	0.0005	0.0003	0.0001
St. Vincent and the Grenadines	0.0014	0.0011	0.0008	0.0004	0.0001
Suriname	0.0058	0.0044	0.0030	0.0016	0.0002
Trinidad and Tobago	0.0017	0.0014	0.0010	0.0007	0.0004
Uruguay	0.0012	0.0010	0.0009	0.0008	0.0006
Venezuela	0.0026	0.0025	0.0025	0.0025	0.0025
	0.0995	**0.0942**	**0.0889**	**0.0836**	**0.0784**
Transition Economies					
Albania	0.0093	0.0071	0.0049	0.0026	0.0004
Armenia	0.0015	0.0012	0.0009	0.0006	0.0003
Azerbaijan	0.0039	0.0031	0.0023	0.0015	0.0007
Belarus	0.0023	0.0020	0.0018	0.0015	0.0013
Bosnia-Herzegovina	0.0023	0.0018	0.0014	0.0009	0.0005

continued…

Table A1. (continued)

Country	GDP (PPP) = 0.60 V = 0.40	GDP (PPP) = 0.70 V = 0.30	GDP (PPP) = 0.80 V = 0.20	GDP (PPP) = 0.90 V = 0.10	GDP (PPP) = 1 V = 0
Bulgaria	0.0024	0.0021	0.0018	0.0016	0.0013
Croatia	0.0040	0.0033	0.0025	0.0018	0.0011
Czech Republic	0.0037	0.0037	0.0036	0.0036	0.0035
Estonia	0.0020	0.0016	0.0012	0.0009	0.0005
Georgia	0.0012	0.0010	0.0008	0.0006	0.0004
Hungary	0.0037	0.0035	0.0033	0.0031	0.0029
Kazakstan	0.0039	0.0035	0.0030	0.0025	0.0020
Kyrgyz Republic	0.0136	0.0103	0.0070	0.0036	0.0003
Latvia	0.0017	0.0015	0.0012	0.0009	0.0006
Lithuania	0.0018	0.0016	0.0013	0.0011	0.0009
Macedonia, FYR	0.0027	0.0021	0.0015	0.0010	0.0004
Moldova	0.0022	0.0017	0.0012	0.0007	0.0003
Mongolia	0.0019	0.0015	0.0011	0.0006	0.0002
Poland	0.0062	0.0068	0.0073	0.0079	0.0085
Romania	0.0027	0.0028	0.0029	0$_3$00.0	0.0031
Russia	0.0159	0.0183	0.0206	0.0230	0.0254
Serbia/ Montenegro	0.0023	0.0021	0.0019	0.0018	0.0016
Slovak Republic	0.0029	0.0024	0.0019	0.0014	0.0008
Slovenia	0.0011	0.0009	0.0007	0.0005	0.0002
Tajikistan	0.0070	0.0054	0.0039	0.0023	0.0007
Turkmenistan	0.0063	.00630	0.0058	0.005	0.0053
Ukraine	0.0026	0.0022	0.0018	0.0014	0.0009
Uzbekistan	0.0070	0.0054	0.0039	0.0024	0.0008
	0.1183	**0.1050**	**0.0916**	**0.0783**	**0.0649**

Notes

1 i.e. measuring GDP in terms of PPP.

2 Developing countries accounted for 63 per cent of total international reserves at the end of 2004.

3 Gold, 1972.

4 Consider the power shift that occurs as quotas increase—a country with a quota of $10 million would be entitled to 350 votes, i.e. 100 votes on account of its quota size and 250 on basic votes for being a member. When the size of quotas is multiplied by 10, the country will have 1000 votes on account of its quota and 250 basic votes, for a total of 1250 votes. Thus the relative share of basic votes declines from over 70 per cent to 20 per cent of the total. In 1945, there were 14 countries, almost a third of the membership whose quota was $10 million or less, and 28 countries, over half of the total, whose quotas were $50 million or less.

5 Mikesell, 1994.

6 The Quota Formula Review Group (QFRG) was formed by eight experts, consisting of Cooper, Richard (Professor at Harvard University) as Chairman; Abbey, Joseph (Executive Director, Center for Economic Analysis, Accra, Ghana), Ahluwalia, Montek (Member, Planning Commission, New Delhi, India); Al-Jasser, Muhammad (Vice-Governor, Saudi Arabian Monetary Agency); Siebert, Horst (President, Kiel Institute of World Economics, Germany); Suranyi, Gyorgy (President, National Bank of Hungary); Utsumi, Makoto (Professor, Keio University, Japan) and Zahler, Roberto (former President of the Central Bank of Chile).

7 This section draws on my earlier work, particularly, Buira, 2001.

8 In light of the broad terms of reference they received, an important issue not considered that has been the object of discussion both inside the Board as well as outside it and would appear to require consideration is the overall adequacy of Fund resources or total quotas. I will not elaborate on this subject here, other than to note that current quotas are equivalent to only nine-tenth of 1 per cent of world GDP and have declined from 58 to under 4 per cent of world trade. Moreover, recall that the desire by some to limit quota increases and avoid adjusting quota shares to changed conditions in the international economy has led the Fund to seek to supplement its available resources by entering into two borrowing arrangements, the General Arrangement to Borrow and the New Arrangement to Borrow, with a number of countries in a strong international reserve position. These arrangements enable the Fund to resort to them to provide additional financing for Fund operations when required.

9 One may ask in what parliamentary body such a small representation would be considered to give a major party an adequate participation in decision-making.

10 op. cit., pp. 32.

11 Restoring the proportion of basic votes per member to what it was in 1945 would raise the total basic votes to nearly half of total voting power ($11.3 \times 4.07 = 46$ per cent). An intermediate solution that would partially restore the role basic votes were meant to have would be to assign to basic votes, say, 25 per cent of the total voting rights. This would mean raising the basic votes of each member country from 250 to 2,927.

12 See *External Review of Quota Formulas,*—Annex, Box 3.1, p. 38.

13 op. cit., pp. 57–58.

14 op. cit., p. 58.

15 *QFRG Report*, p. 58. Under the ICP, a new estimate of GDP converted in terms of PPP is currently under way covering the period 2003–2006; its results could be used in the next quota review to be completed by 2008.

16 *External Review of the Quota Formulas,*—Annex 7, Balance of Payments Data used in the Quota Formulas, p. 77.

17 IMF, 2004.

18 See paper by Ahmed, Sultan, Purchasing Power Parity (PPP) for International Comparisons of Poverty: Sources and Methods, in website http//webworldbank.org/wbsite/external/datastistics/cpext/o,pagePK

19 See paper by McLenaghan, J, former Director of the Statistics Department of the Fund, Purchasing Power Parities and Comparisons of GDP in IMF Quota Calculations, in www.g24.org; also see Chapter 7 in this book by this author.

20 op. cit., 'PPP is defined as the numbers of units of a country's currency needed to buy in the country the same amounts of goods and services as, say, one US dollar would buy in the United States.'

21 See dos Reis in this volume.

22 i.e. the Mexican crisis of 1994, the Asian crises of 1997 and 1998, and several others.

23 The GDP of the EU of 25 members is only marginally larger than that of the United States at 2003 exchange rates.

24 The variables modified in order to exclude intra-trade in goods and services were payments and receipts. The same data as in the 12th review was used in the case of GDP, reserves and variability of current receipts. OECD data on trade in services was converted from US$ to SDR at the average rate for each year taken from IFS.

25 The quota formula may be modified by a simple majority of the Board.

26 See paragraph 10 of their communiqué of 1 October 2004.

27 The detailed calculations underpinning Table 4 may be found in the Appendix. The Appendix also shows the calculated quotas of individual countries under various assumptions.

28 Statement by Secretary of the Treasury, Snow, JW, to the IMFC on 16 April 2005.

29 Statement by the Minister of Finance of Japan, Tanigaki, Sadakazu, to the IMFC on 16 April 2005.

30 i.e. enlarging the staff in the offices of African Executive Directors and others.

31 Statement by Zalm, Gerrit, Minister of Finance of The Netherlands also representing Armenia, Bosnia Herzegovina, Bulgaria, Croatia, Cyprus, Georgia, Israel, Macedonia, Moldova, Romania and Ukraine to the IMFC on 16 April 2005.

32 In fact, the vote of developing countries cast by industrial country directors amounts to some 6.9 per cent of total voting power.

33 Note that an agreement reached among G-7 members on policy issues turns the Board discussion into a mere formality.

34 *Financial Times*, 6 May 2005.

35 Recall that the euro fell from $1.18 dollars per euro at the launching of the new currency on 1 January 1999 to a low of $0.82 dollars per euro on 26 October 2000 and peaked at $1.363 on 28 December 2004.

36 Note that it has become the largest debtor nation and largest importer of capital.

37 See Buira, 2003.

38 Nayyar, 2002, pp. 242.

39 This requires an ongoing dialogue between the Fund and the authorities to enable the country to approach the Fund at short notice, and the Fund to respond promptly. Countries whose policies were considered appropriate by the Article IV consultation and had continued to pursue sound policies would be eligible for immediate Fund support. The above procedure could take the place of a formal precautionary or insurance facility and have the advantage of avoiding the signaling problems of the CCL. Looking ahead, as the cycle matures, countries with substantial external financing requirements and high levels of external debt will be exposed to reversal of current favourable external financing conditions. Rising interest rates and a decline in commodity prices could trigger speculative attacks leading to a new round of financial crises, unless action is taken to prevent it.

40 Development financing was included in the mandate of the Bank in response to a proposal by the Finance Minister of Mexico supported by Keynes.

41 See Dodd, 2005.

42 See Lora, Panizza and Quispe-Agnoli, 2004.

43 See Lall, 2005.

44 The Bank Working Group to Review the Process for the Selection of the President and The Fund Working Group for the Selection of the Managing Director, Draft Joint Report, 25 April 2001.

45 'To review the quota formulas and their working, and to assess their adequacy to help determine member's calculated quotas in the IMF in a manner that reasonably *reflects member's relative position in the world economy as well as their relative need for and contributions to the Fund's financial resources, taking into account changes in the functioning of the world economy and the international financial system* and in the light of the increasing globalization of markets.' (Emphasis added). Terms of reference of the QFRG.

References

Ahmed, Sultan, Purchasing Power Parity (PPP) for International Comparisons of Poverty: Sources and Methods, in website http//webworldbank.org/wbsite/external/datastistics/cpext/o,pagePK

Buira, A, 2001, *A Critique of the Cooper Report on the Adequacy of the IMF Quota Formulas*, Dept. of Economics Discussion Paper Series, No.74, Oxford: Oxford University.

Buira, A, 2003, An Analysis of IMF Conditionality, *Challenges to the World Bank and the IMF*, London: Anthem Press.

Dodd, Randall, 2005, Up from Sin: A Portfolio Approach to Salvation, *The IMF and the World Bank at Sixty*, Buira, A (ed.), London: Anthem Press.

Gold, Joseph, 1972, *Voting and Decisions in the IMF*, Washington, DC: IMF.

IMF, 2000, *External Review of the Quota Formulas*, Washington, DC: IMF.

IMF, 2004, *Quotas-Updated calculations*, Washington, DC: IMF, August.

Lall, Sanjaya, 2005, Reinventing Industrial Strategy: The Role of Government Policy in Building Industrial Competitiveness, *The IMF and the World Bank at Sixty*, Buira, A (ed.), London: Anthem Press, 2005.

Lora, Panizza and Quispe-Agnoli, 2004, Reform Fatigue: Symptoms, Reasons and Implications, *Economic Review*, Federal Reserve Bank of Atlanta, 89:2.

McLenaghan, J, former Director of the Statistics Department of the Fund, Purchasing Power Parities and Comparisons of GDP in IMF Quota Calculations, in www.g24.org

Mikesell, Raymond, 1994, The Bretton Woods Debates: A Memoir, *Essays in International Finance*, No.192, Princeton University, International Finance Section, March.

Nayyar, 2002, Re-examining the Bretton Woods Institutions, *Governing Globalization*, Oxford: OUP, pp. 242.

3

REFORMING THE INTERNATIONAL MONETARY FUND: TOWARDS ENHANCED ACCOUNTABILITY AND LEGITIMACY

Vijay L. Kelkar, Praveen K. Chaudhry,[1]
Marta Vanduzer-Snow and V. Bhaskar

Abstract:

The following article outlines reforms for the IMF so as to enhance financial crisis prevention and management through better surveillance and transparency. With the present quota regime, creditor countries command excessive voting power, resulting in skewed crisis analysis and resource distribution. Consequently, exploring the *democratic deficit* within the governance structure of the Fund reveals much needed changes in the quota regime and voting system of significant import. Expressly, the democratic deficit results from three factors, namely, (1) the decline of basic votes in the Fund's quota regime has reduced the voice of smaller countries in the governance of the Fund; (2) biases in the calculation of economic strength have caused the IMF to neglect the strength of emerging market economies; and (3) the needless complexity and opacity involved in the calculation of quotas. As the governance structure of the Fund is a product of the political and economic agreements embodied in the quota regime, addressing the quota bias, the variable measurement and specification problems will provide the route towards a Fund that is in tune with the growing contiguous democratic consensus. Quota adjustments alone prove insufficient towards this democratic end and therefore we will explore reassessing the Fund size, given the pressing need for a larger Fund as the present size is too small when compared to the global GDP; readjusting access to the resources of the Fund in accordance with the gross financing need of the concerned country; re-examining the voting system and the veto market; restructuring the Executive Board so that every member of the Board is an elected member and; the Fund as an Economic Security Council (ESC), promoting stability in the global economy. Our proposed reforms aim to redress the fundamental flaw of the present quota system, i.e. the mismatch between objectives and instrument.

Introduction

Viable international institutions reflect the historical necessities of a particular period.

The strength of any institution lies in its ability to adapt and serve the changing economic and political forces. The International Monetary Fund (IMF) was the brainchild of John Maynard Keynes and Harry Dexter White, whose world-view was shaped by the Great Wars and the Depression. The IMF served well the dynamic economic forces of the second half of the 20th century. However, a recent report by the United Nations Development Program informs that economically and politically, frustration in the developing countries about the skewed distribution of global power has seldom been greater.[2] Developing and emerging market country members need a unified, coherent and pragmatic platform from which their voices can be heard and incorporated into crisis prevention, crisis management policies and improved governance at the Fund.

The decline of global institutions and the imminent alternative, the resurgence of regional economic blocs, would represent a threat to international peace and security. A crucial lesson of World War II that guided the architects of the Bretton Woods institutions was the precedence of the international monetary order to other spheres of international intercourse. Chronologically, the breakdown of the monetary order preceded the breakdown of international trade and the commencement of war. In actuality, the proper organization of the monetary order is fundamental to the workings of international relations. A stable monetary system is the foundation for international peace and prosperity. International financial institutions that promote stable, cooperative and growth-oriented economic policies provide an essential global public good. While the international community rhetorically recognizes the growing global interde-pendence, global policy has yet to conform to the pressing needs of this reality. Thus, it is important and urgent for politicians and policymakers to undertake reforms of global institutions before another major crisis materializes.

New Global Political Economy

The governance of the global political economy requires global institutions which are flexible enough to reflect the changing distribution of economic power in the international system. There are several economic forces currently shaping the global economy that are profoundly altering the global economic map and power centres. First, the world economy is now riding a new techno-logical wave lifting up economies with faster growth in productivity, which has led to an increase in international economic exchange with an expanding knowledge-based economy and intensified competition as the drivers. Second, the global demographic of the aging populations in the OECD countries, as compared to the working populations in developing countries, are rising to even higher levels. This means that international capital flows are going to increase at an even dizzier pace given the divergence in the productivity of capital and in the growth rates between these two divergent demographic tran-sitions. In other words, the coming years will see further expansion in global capital flows and in economic growth rates, which expands the economic potential of developing countries. Third, the rapid growth of transnationals in production and finance means that private capital flows dominate the global economy. These international capital flows are banks led by short-term capital flows, portfolio flows led by the mutual and pension funds and Foreign Direct Investments (FDI) by transnationals and other actors. This aspect of global-ization is fuelling the engine of global capitalism where an increasing concen-tration of economic decision making, particularly relating to capital flows, challenges the functioning and stability of the money market. The concentra-tion of economic power transforms the business cycles' turning points into tip-ping points, magnifying the scope of economic crises in the global economy. Fourth is the rise of emerging market economies in the global economy. The share of these economies in the global output and trade has grown significantly and is projected to increase further in the first half of the 21st century. Fifth is the rise of Asia in the global economy. Presently, three of the world's four largest national economies in terms of Gross Domestic Product (GDP), valued at Purchasing Power Parity (PPP) terms, are from Asia. They are Japan, China and India and this is going to be the global economic trend for sometime. Of course, if the European Union is seen as a single economy its GDP would exceed that of India, Japan or China. Sixth, the inability of the IMF to restruc-ture itself has initiated a new kind of debate for regional monetary arrange-ments. For example, the 29-year-old Arab Monetary Fund and the ongoing argument made for establishing an Asian Monetary Fund (AMF). Such pro-posals have a potential of being counterproductive to the interests of global as well as regional economies and therefore global security.

Finally, all these economic factors are accompanied by a growing international consensus amongst policymakers, politicians and other elite that emphasizes the critical importance of democracy, human rights, accountability and trans-parency. Unless the Fund sponsored program's political legitimacy is defined by openness and access to information and officials, democracies will fail to successfully carry out decisions executed by the Board. As a result, there is a need for greater parliamentarian oversight of such institutions of global governance. How should the Fund adapt and transform itself to this new global political economy?

The IMF: Present and Future

As the institutional centrepiece of the monetary order, the IMF has a mandate from its member countries

> ...to promote international monetary cooperation through a permanent institution which provides the machinery for *consultation and collaboration* on international monetary problems; [and] ... (v) to give confidence to members by making the general resources of the Fund temporarily available to them under adequate safeguards, thus providing them with opportunity to correct maladjustments in their balance of payments without resorting to measures destructive of national or international prosperity.[3]

The ability of the Fund to carry out its mandate has been recently called into question due to a series of financial crises that threaten to shred the economic, social and political fabric of several emerging markets in Asia, Africa and South America. The Fund will lose relevance if it continues to ineffectively meet the needs of all its constituents.

Not only is the Fund unable to meet the needs of those countries but also those of the G-8. Currently, the Fund is unable to be a credible advisor and guide to the G-3 economies, especially the United States. The decline in the dollar and the continuance of the twin deficits remain unaddressed by the United States, which does not heed Fund counsel. Moreover, the very origin of the G-8 arose from the French and German Finance Ministers', Giscard d'Estaing and Helmut Schmidt, frustration with IMF proceedings.[4] In 1973, accompanied by US, UK and Japanese representatives, they formed a Library Group and met in the Library of the White House. The group discussed issues of common interest and their meeting led to the first G-8 meeting in Rambouillet in November 1975. Despite having the preponderant voting power, the G-8 had already become disenchanted with the workings of the IMF as early as 1973. The alternate body, in their view, could provide collective and effective management of the international system. The general perception that the decisions of the IMF fall in line with the decisions taken at annual G-8 meetings underlines the inability of the IMF as a body to achieve international monetary cooperation. The Funds inability to move forward on its pilot, the Sovereign Debt Restructuring Mechanism (SDRM), underscores a parallel shortcoming. As the time was ripe for such an initiative, the markets were willing to listen, the inability to consummate the issue perhaps points to a weakening of the Fund's authority.[5]

The IMF is attempting to enhance surveillance and harmonize rules related to member countries' banking and financial systems to strengthen the international financial architecture.[6] However, the efficacy of these initiatives is dependent upon the level of participation by the Fund's member countries. Democratizing the Fund will make the organization's initiatives more effective as decisions produced by a democratic process have greater legitimacy and credibility amongst participating members. Concerns for global governance move the IMF reform debate beyond arguments about the proper size and scope of the Fund. Realistic changes in the governance of the Fund will be achieved by rationalizing the Fund's quota regime, or the framework for the organization's decision-making process and the basis for allocating resources. Reforms based on broadly accepted principles will enhance the Fund's legitimacy and accountability as a forum for global economic policy decision-making.

In addition, the IMF needs to undergo institutional reforms so that its structure reflects the aforementioned underlying major economic forces and to ascend the established pre-eminent role of geopolitics. The following agenda proposes an improvement in the functioning as well as the governance of the IMF. A transformed IMF will bolster much needed economic cooperation, enhance economic security and promote globalization that will benefit all, not just any particular region or group of countries. Although the need for reform is urgent, it is important that reforms are transparent and based on principles.

The reform of the Fund should not merely reflect *ad hoc* responses to shifts in economic strength and vulnerability in the international political economy. By grounding reforms on principles, the Fund will enhance its legitimacy and accountability as a rule-making body for international economic policies over the long-term, and among the states that comprise this growing democratic consensus. Of course, realistic proposals for reform must accept that the IMF is an international financial institution in which creditor confidence requires that the majority of the voting power remain with creditor countries. Within this majority, the largest contributor, the United States, will maintain its existing veto power over decisions requiring a supermajority. There remains great latitude for undertaking principled and forward-looking reforms within these constraints.

Reforming the Fund

In an increasingly integrated world economy, the distribution of power within the Fund must adapt to reflect the growing weight of developing and emerging market countries in order to make the Fund more effective as an institution. Giving voice and ownership to member countries will increase the legitimacy and efficacy of global governance.[7] The volume of world trade flows has increased by 6 per cent annually over the past two decades, twice as fast as world real GDP; this is one testimony of the deepening of economic integration.[8] Developing countries as a group have achieved the fastest expansion of trade and now account for one-third of world trade, up from one-quarter in the early 1970s. The developing countries' share of global GDP valued at PPP has increased from 31.86 per cent in 1992 to 37.56 per cent in 2001, while the European countries' share has declined from 34.20 per cent to 29.04 per cent over the same period. The growing contribution of the developing countries to world output and trade is not reflected in the distribution of power in international financial institutions such as the IMF.

At the moment, a great disparity exists between the economic strength and voting power of the emerging market economies and smaller European countries on the IMF's Executive Board (see Table 1).

Evans and Finnemore have recently demonstrated that the quality of information used for surveillance and the design of programs depends critically on the level of member country participation.[9] Therefore, an increase in the effective participation of developing and emerging market countries is desirable in promoting the success of IMF crisis prevention and management policies. What is more, as the IMF increasingly seeks to harmonize and coordinate strategies for crisis prevention and management, the Fund is becoming a rule making institution whose decisions impact international as well as national economic policymaking. The use of a polyarchic framework of governance enhances the legitimacy of a rule making process.[10] A polyarchic

Table 1. The disparity between voting power and economic strength

	Votes on IMF Executive Board in 2001	GDP valued at market exchange rates ($ billion) in 2000	GDP valued at Purchasing Power Parity ($ billion) in 2000	Population (millions) in 2000
Belgium	46,302	$230**	$281**	10**
Italy	70,805	$1,090**	$1,464**	56
Netherlands	51,874	$370	$413	16
Brazil	30,611	$503**	$1,309**	175**
China	63,942	$1,100	$5,900	1,260
India	41,832	$474*	$2,233*	1,003

* Data for 2000–01; **Data for 2001.

Source: Voting data from *IMF Annual Report*, 2001; Economic and population data from *Economist Intelligence Unit Country Reports*, 2002.

process of governance, characterized by the diffusion of power and networks of reciprocal influence, will also better resemble the process of governance among the growing number of democratic states on the Fund's membership roll. These reforms will permit the Fund to act more effectively in times of crisis, as its decisions will hold greater legitimacy amongst the politicians and bureaucrats who will need to monitor and implement Fund programs. Moreover, the diffusion of decision-making power should help to prevent the blind acceptance and application of universal models of macroeconomic management.[11]

The creation of the G-20 in 1999, at the initiative of the Atlantic States, provides a means to deepen the dialogue on global governance with emerging market 'shareholders' such as Argentina, Brazil, China, India, Indonesia, Mexico, Russia, Saudi Arabia, South Africa, South Korea and Turkey.[12] Notably, however, the G-20 continues to exclude a host of other 'stakeholders' in the global policymaking dialogue, especially among developing countries.[13]

Regional Responses

A failure to reform the Fund, coupled with the recurrence of financial crises in the emerging market economies hinders the growth of the global economy. As processes of production are subordinate to the flows of financial capital, financial crises have direct impacts on 'real' economic activity. Even though most financial crises are short lived, they exert detrimental, long-term and asymmetric economic and social consequences on the lives of the most vulnerable members of the global economy. Recent financial crises and global economic trends have already mobilized non-governmental organizations, students and workers around the world to protest the perceived inequities in the operation of the global economic system and the policies of global institutions such as the IMF.

Recurrent crises may also lead to the proliferation of regional international financial institutions and ultimately the marginalization of global economic institutions. This scenario is possible to the extent that emerging market countries, particularly in Asia, believe they are under-represented in the decision-making bodies of international financial institutions relative to their role in the world economy.[14]

The most recent move towards the formal creation of a regional equivalent to the IMF occurred at the 1997 Asia Pacific Economic Cooperation (APEC) meeting of a group of ministers. The Japanese introduced the proposal for a $100 billion 'Asian Monetary Fund' to protect regional currencies from speculative assaults. US and IMF opposition effectively terminated the proposal in 1997.[15] Nevertheless, the 2001 Chang Mai Initiative (CMI), signed by the 10 members of the Association of South East Asian Nations (ASEAN), has created an informal regime that could serve as the basis for an Asian Monetary Fund. The CMI permits bilateral swaps and repurchase arrangements amongst the ASEAN-10, China, Japan and Korea, thereby providing short-term financial assistance to member countries. Currently, any member country can access 10 per cent of the entire credit line in times of emergencies. For the facility to be 100 per cent available, the country has to be under an approved loan program from the IMF.

The Shanghai Cooperation Organization, founded in 2001 by China, Russia, Kazakhstan, Kyrgyzstan, Tajikistan and Uzbekistan, should also be noted here. The pact provides for regional collective security arrangements focused primarily on borders as bilateral trade has eased tensions in the region. The Shanghai group is headed by the Secretary General Zhang Deguang. In November of 2003, at an international conference on Kazakhstan's financial reforms, representatives of the IMF and the World Bank noted that the governor of the People's Bank of China was the most sought-out guest.[16] Analysts find Uzbekistan and Turkmenistan also look to China as opposed to Western dominated international financial institutions. The article's author notes China's central planning, economic and political, resonates with many of the former Soviet Republics in the region. A dangerous conclusion, as perhaps this is true of the elite in these respective countries, but this has yet to be demonstrably proven with respect to its citizenry. The international community should also take note of the rail project that is taking form which will link China with Western Europe. So too should they note that the entry qualifications for Forbes magazine annual list of China's richest was $6m in 1999 and $100m in 2004. Davidoff, the leading Swiss cigar maker, restricts the sale of its Millennium brand, the most expensive cigars in the world, to two markets, the United States and China.[17] These trends will have consequences and if they are not matched by a search for just status, then a regional response will follow.

Size Matters

The central role of the Fund should be to manage the new wave of intensified globalization in such a way that it promotes a stable growth in the global political economy, offering security to all. Towards this, the foremost requirement is to strengthen the resource base of the Fund (see section on Quota). The size of the Fund today is too small when compared to the global GDP, or the levels of global trade, or international capital flows, or to any other comparable indicators for global liquidity. Further, an International Institute of Economics' study of world capital markets suggests that presently, fewer than 200 firms control the international capital market and these firms' share in bond and portfolio markets is even higher.

This indicates that a relatively small number of large players do dominate the global capital market and at time of crises, their herd and pro-cyclical behaviour can severely destabilize a national economy or regional economies. Hence, the global need for a countervailing power; the IMF could serve this role. The IMF needs the ability to act readily so that the concerned economy, or regional economies, can move to a good equilibrium. There is growing theoretical literature to show that in the presence of multiple equilibriums, an appropriate action by a large player has the potential to restore good equilibrium and this is indeed the role IMF will need to play. This means there is a need to dramatically increase the IMF's resource base. The potential losses to the global economy due to a smaller Fund are much higher than the opportunity costs of a larger fund size. This is particularly so as research has shown that the 'moral hazard' argument has little empirical basis.

No precise formula for an optimal Fund size exists, but what needs to be recognized is that the loss function in this regard is asymmetric. The size of the Fund in relation to any of the relevant parameters has shrunk significantly over time. There was no general increase in quotas since the Eleventh review of 1998. Traditionally, the size of aggregate quotas is assessed in relation to key economic indicators that are included in the quota formula. Though the size of the Fund increased from SDR 61.1 billion in 1978 (Seventh review) to SDR 212 billion in 1998 (Eleventh review), between these two reviews, the size of the Fund significantly reduced from 8.5 to 3.7 per cent in relation to current payments, from 1.4 to 0.9 per cent in relation to GDP, from 33 to 18.4 per cent in terms of reserves and in relation to world imports, from 9 to 6 per cent. Due to further expansion in all economic variables since 1998, the present size of the Fund at SDR 212.794 billion (US $312.4 billion) stands very low at 1.8 per cent of current account transactions, 0.8 per cent of GDP, 9 per cent of reserves and 4 per cent of world imports.

The Fund size could be substantially increased. In addition to an increase in quota size, the Fund should, by exploiting the provisions of Article VII, create over time a pool of Tier II capital through market borrowings, of course not to exceed the quota size. This would promote capital markets' monitoring of the Fund and such market discipline may not be a bad thing for an international financial institution. Yet another instrument that the Fund can deploy to fulfil its most critical role as the lender of last resort, is the creation of self-liquidating temporary SDRs to expeditiously meet liquidity needs. This also means the Fund would need to revise the access policy and strengthen bilateral and multilateral surveillance. The access to the Fund facilities, whether by Stand-By Arrangement (SBA), or Supplemental Reserve Facility (SRF), will need to be guided by the financial needs of the member country and not determined by its quota size according to the present policy. The access charges ought to be incentive compatible.

Contribution: Reflections of the Share of Global Output

A member's contribution to the Fund's resources should be based on a member's stake in the global economy as well as the ability to pay, which is a function of its share of global output. The Fund's major potential contribution towards global stability and balanced growth is its crisis prevention and management role. In periods of economic crisis, the Fund acts as a catalyst for private sector involvement and as a *de facto* international lender of last resort. The Fund also carries out extensive economic surveillance and helps to set uniform standards and rules for monitoring the global economy. Members need to support the global public good the Fund provides, consistent with the size of their economies. As a larger economy uses greater resources and has a greater systemic impact in the event of a financial or currency crisis, larger economies ought to contribute more to the resources of the Fund than smaller economies.

With economic integration, a country is now susceptible to contagion even though it may adopt sound economic policies. Developing, emerging and industrialized countries are likely to be affected. These negative spillover effects, which include the 'financial globalization hazard' of rapid capital flow reversal, put a country's stake in the globalized system at risk.[18] A country's stake in the global economic system or its 'value-at-risk' is its GDP, i.e. its national income. Therefore, a member's contribution to the Fund is best determined using that country's value-at-risk as a basis. As the quota regime ought to primarily determine a members' contribution to the Fund resources, one variable could suffice—GDP valued at PPP. The transparency of a single variable would also redress the current mismatch between calculated and actual quotas. For these reasons, our proposal is to determine a country's quota solely using GDP valued at PPP.

Access: Gross Financing Need

Access to the resources of the Fund should be based on gross financing need. Quotas need to be officially decoupled from the determination of access policy. Currently, access to Fund resources is supposed to be limited to 300 per cent of a member's quota. However, as nearly 70 per cent of the Fund's outstanding credit is currently confined to five borrowers, who are borrowing much more than 300 per cent of their quota, it is apparent that the present access policy is not observed.[19] Access to resources is well beyond the present access norms, e.g. Turkey exceeded 2900 per cent of its quota in 2002.[20] It is evident that the rules concerning access to Fund resources were not used as a factor in determining access limits for these large borrowers. By approving large facilities to these countries based on need, the Fund has recognized *de facto* the limitations of the present quota based access limits.

It should be recognized *de jure* and the link between access and quotas should be broken. Moreover, the Fund facilities created to deal with capital account crises, i.e. once the Contingent Credit Lines (CCL) and now the Supplemental Reserve Facility (SRF) implicitly recognize that financing should be based on need rather than quota. The SRF has and CCL had no general access limits linked to a member's quota; however, there was an expectation during the currency of the CCL that it would not exceed 300–500 per cent of a member's quota unless under exceptional circumstances.[21] Uncoupling the quota formula from access considerations would have the added benefit of effectively addressing the pressing need for equality of treatment, an issue raised in recent years by some of the smaller borrowing members.

Access to Fund resources should be on the basis of gross financing need, subject to two prudential norms. First, the Fund should supply only a limited percentage of the gross financing need, thus confirming the role of the Fund as a catalyst for private sector involvement in crisis management.[22] Second, a prudential norm should be in place to limit the individual borrower, such as limiting access beyond 10 per cent of the Fund's total resources. These illustrative numbers are based on a much larger Fund size, a requirement for an access policy based on gross financial need.

The Present Quota Regime

The governance structure of the Fund is a product of the political and economic agreements embodied in the quota regime. While the Fund recognizes a basic number of votes for all members, relative voting power in the Fund is determined by the size of a member's quota.[23] The IMF's quota regime is the basis for

- determining a member's required contribution to the Fund and thus the overall size of the Fund
- the level of access to Fund resources for each member country
- the distribution of voting rights within the organization,[24] including the right to a 'permanent' or elected seat on the 24-member Executive Board.[25]

With the present regime, one policy instrument, a member country's quota, serves three policy objectives and here lays the fundamental flaw of the current system.

The quota regime is not an abstract formula. It is the basis of power relations between member states of the Fund. Moreover, most decisions made by the Fund's Executive Board are the products of a consensus rather than voting process. Member countries will usually not submit issues that are likely to be vetoed by the United States or defeated by the majority of member votes. This shows the effect that distribution of voting power has in implicitly influencing the character and scope of issues on the Fund's agenda.

The formula specifications and the weight of variables involved in calculating members' quotas have become matters of political judgment and compromise that are intended to distribute power in a way that will command wide support from member countries and creditor countries in particular.[26] In addition, the quota regime effectively permits the United States, with 17.38 per cent of the total votes, to retain veto power over decisions that require a super majority of 85 per cent. Hence, any proposed reform of the IMF quota regime must adhere to three basic guidelines. First, reform must be simple and transparent, as an infinite number of permutations are possible through minor manipulation of the quota formulas. Countries whose relative power within the Fund will be diminished can be expected to resist any changes. For this reason, an excessively complex quota reform program will only encounter opposition from members who will have their voting share reduced. A proposal that lacks sound economic criteria for change will inevitably succumb to charges of 'politicization'. Second, as a financial institution, creditors need to have a decisive voice in policy making, as otherwise they may lose confidence in the institution's lending decisions. Third, any proposed reform of the quota system must not seek to remove the veto power of the largest individual creditor, the United States as such a proposal would be politically stillborn.

The IMF conducts reviews of all members' quotas every five years and members may request an *ad hoc* review at anytime, but the basic problem of the quota formula persists—the mismatch between instruments and objectives. This is a classic 'assignment problem'. Presently, there is only one instrument to achieve multiple objectives. In this context, Noble Laureate Tinbergen argued that an optimal arrangement requires one instrument for each policy objective.[27] To achieve an optimal arrangement, three instruments should be used to achieve the three objectives of the quota regime—contribution, access and voting. This is what our proposed quota reform seeks to do, that is, base contribution on GDP at PPP, access based on gross financing need and base voting on a weighted average of the Westphalian principle and a country's contribution.

The Quota Bias Defined: The Variable Measurement and Specification Problems

Variable Measurement Problem

The first bias in the calculation of quotas stems from a problem in how economic output is measured. Currently, the GDP of each individual country is converted from the local currency into a common *numeraire* currency based on prevailing market exchange rates. There are significant problems with the calculation of national income through the GDP at market exchange rates. The underlying theory that has facilitated this technique of comparison is that the exchange rates adjust automatically, through the market, so that the local currency prices of a group of identical goods and services represent an equivalent value in every nation. In practice, however, market exchange rates undervalue the non-tradable sector and they do not necessarily equalize prices of tradable goods across countries even after allowing for quality and transport costs; the latter can be explained in part due to the lagged effect of the exchange rate. As a result, it has long been observed that market exchange rates for a nation's currency often do not reflect that currency's true purchasing power at home and in their region. This can give rise to a significant under or overvaluation of GDP of different countries when making cross-country comparisons of incomes, which, in turn, significantly affects a country's total allocation by the IMF.

Variable Specification Problem

The second bias in the calculation of a member's quota stems from a failure to appropriately reflect *entrepôt*, *maquiladora* and intra-currency union trade. The current calculation of economic 'openness', which sums a country's current receipts and payments, contains a bias in favour of *entrepôt* countries. Current receipts and payments give a rough indication of the resources generated in a country from transactions with the rest of the world and of the amount of resources devoted to consumption of goods and services created elsewhere.[28] *Entrepôt* states engage in the import and export of vast quantities of goods, thereby boosting their receipts and payments, however these transactions have little added domestic value and consequently, they highly overstate the underlying contribution to global output. A similar phenomenon exists in countries where '*maquiladora*' activity is large.[29] Moreover, to the extent that some countries belong to a currency union (e.g. the European Union), intra-currency union trade boosts the 'openness index' even though intra-currency union trade is not subject to balance of payments crises as members share a common currency. Given the growing magnitude of intra-EU trade, this is not a trivial issue. It is estimated that quota figures for members of the EU would fall by as much as 9.2 per cent if intra-currency union trade were subtracted.[30] The IMF should not incorporate intra-currency union trade in the assessment of economic openness.

Critics of this position will argue that sharing a currency with one or more members does not imply that members cannot run into balance of payments difficulties. Nor does a currency union guarantee that a member might not be tempted to raise tariff barriers in a manner that might threaten the prosperity of its trading partners.[31] However, we are not saying it is necessary to terminate Fund interaction with intra-currency members, only that intra-currency union trade should not be used as a factor in the determination of member quotas as this variable is not very relevant in assessing financing needs or balance of payments issues.

Economic openness is not a self-sufficient value. What is important is the value added through trade. However, it is extremely difficult to measure and compare across countries the value added to goods and services. It is for this reason that the IMF commissioned an independent group of academics and policymakers, known as the QFRG (Quota Formula Review Group), or the 'Cooper Group'.

The Board of Governors' International Monetary and Financial Committee (IMFC) has reaffirmed on several occasions that 'quotas should reflect developments in the international economy'.[32] However, recent attempts to reform the quota regime have produced unsatisfactory results. The Cooper Group proposed an alternative quota formula, recommending that the openness index be dropped altogether as a factor in the calculation of quotas. Their approach actually increased the G-7 countries' aggregate calculated quota share to more than 59 per cent, compared to their aggregate calculated quota of 54 per cent at the time (and an actual aggregate quota of 46 per cent). The failures of the Cooper Group may be attributable, in part, to its restrictive mandate not to make any recommendations that would require a change of the IMF's constitution, the Articles of Agreement. In order to discover the best options, it may be necessary to rework the Articles.

A New Quota Regime: Implications

The use of market exchange rates in converting GDP expressed in national currency obscures the relative strength of the economy at the global level for the purpose of international comparison. A country's GDP converted at PPP rates better reflects the real value of total output produced by a country. Global trade distortions have an asymmetric impact on the measurement of output if calculated at market exchange rates, as the consequent undervaluation of the output of developing countries is much greater compared to the overvaluation of the developed countries.[33] PPP raises developing countries' GDP figures because it relies on international market prices to value countries' output and international market prices tend to be higher than domestic market prices in developing countries. Differences between these two methods are sizable for individual countries, in particular for large, relatively closed, developing economies, where PPP GDP can be more than four times higher than GDP at market prices.[34]

Critics of the PPP approach sometimes argue that this method may not always correctly indicate a country's ability to contribute to Fund resources. Also, accurate data for all countries is not readily available.[35] The first objection overlooks the point that a large number of developing countries are now in a position to supply liquidity needs to the Fund as they have reasonably stable currencies, large reserves and comfortable balance of payments positions. Countries that have difficulty in meeting their contribution can be handled on a case by case basis. Thus, a quota increase will not create a significant barrier to contribution by such countries. Issues of data quality and availability can be resolved through a determined effort to replace estimates by actual price surveys. By providing technical assistance, countries can be motivated to support price surveys and suitable transitional arrangements can be worked out in the interregnum. It should be noted that over 95 per cent of world output is currently available through the PPP technique, although there is some variability in the quality of the data.[36] The IMF's own publication, the *World Economic Outlook*, already presents annual calculations of individual country GDP valued at PPP for 176 countries. Similarly, the World Bank publishes PPP-based calculations for a significant number of countries.

Already there is support for the use of PPP within the Executive Board. A recent IMF press release notes:

> A majority of the Board considered that market exchange rates should be used to convert GDP to a common currency, so as to obtain the best measure of the total amount of resources generated by a country. However, many other Directors argued that conversion using Purchasing Power Parities would better reflect the real value of total output produced by developing countries.[37]

The term 'majority' in this press release refers not to the number of Executive Directors who support the market exchange rate calculation but their voting power. There is support amongst the numerical majority of Executive Directors for GDP valued at PPP.

It is important to recall the core principle of calculating quotas using PPP. If voting power were determined through a set of weighted averages for GDP valued at PPP (88.7 per cent) and basic votes at the historic '1945 Ratio' (11.3 per cent), the results would appropriately reflect the economic weight of the developing countries without removing the veto power of the United States. Current voting shares for the advanced economies would drop from 62 to 51 per cent, allowing Asian, Latin American and African countries to have a greater voice. In fact, states in the European Union as well as a coalition of Japan, China and India should hold a veto vote. Similarly, a coalition of the developing countries of Asia, Africa and Latin America could also enjoy veto power. The voting share of Middle Eastern countries, excluding the creditor Saudi Arabia, would remain relatively the same. The voting share of smaller European states would decline significantly, but the European Union would retain a veto power. The proposed reform of the quota regime creates far more 'winners' than 'losers' and thus has a realistic chance of securing approval.

There are ample precedents for quota change. In the past, the distribution of power within the regime has changed to reflect shifting political and economic realities in the post-World War II era. Under the IMF's Articles of Agreement, the quota regime is reviewed every five years through a series of 'General Reviews' and a member may request an *ad hoc* adjustment of its quota at any time. Since 1982, a member's quota is normally increased during the General Review through an 'equiproportional' increase, which is distributed to all members and a selective element, which is intended to reflect a members' relative economic position in the world economy. The selective increase in quota alters the relative share of quotas among members. Significant redistribution of relative gains and losses requires large selective quota adjustments. In practice, however, selective quota adjustments tend to be small. The decision to make equiproportional and selective increases rests with the Board of Governors. The distribution of quotas is generally based on quota formulas, but the Board of Governors ultimately exercises its own judgment. Typically there is a significant disparity between the formally calculated quota and the actual quotas, where the average actual quota is less than half of the average calculated quota.[38]

Changes in the quota distribution often reflect pressing economic developments and political needs of the international community as defined by the dominant voices within the Fund. It is noteworthy that in 1976, the Executive Board decided to increase the liquidity of the Fund by doubling the quota share of the major oil exporting countries. A stipulation was added that the collective share of all the developing countries should not fall, lest their access to resources decline in a period of balance of payments instability. Quota formulas did not play any role in deciding which countries should receive selective increases. In the most recent General Review in 1998, the Executive Board sought to realign calculated and actual quotas. Ten per cent of the total quota increase was distributed selectively to those countries whose ratio of calculated to actual quotas was considered to be most 'out of line'.[39]

The use of *ad hoc* quota adjustments has generally declined in recent decades, but *ad hoc* adjustments were once more frequent. For example, France, Iran, Egypt, Paraguay and the Philippines received *ad hoc* increases in their quota from 1947 to 1959. These members successfully argued that their quotas had been set too low at the time of the Bretton Woods conference.

From 1959 to 1969, the quotas of another nine members were adjusted on an *ad hoc* basis, outside of the scheduled 5-year general review of quotas.[40] From 1970 to 2001, there have only been a handful of *ad hoc* increases in quotas outside the framework of a general review. China received an *ad hoc* increase in 1980 when it 'assumed its seat' at the IMF, while Cambodia received a quota adjustment after the resumption of normal relations in 1994.[41] China received another *ad hoc* increase in 2001 after the resumption of sovereignty over Hong Kong. Saudi Arabia received an *ad hoc* increase in 1981, reflecting that country's role as a major creditor to the IMF after the oil shocks. As a result of an *ad hoc* increase in Japan's quota, new quotas for Germany and Japan were equalized under the Ninth Review in 1990. Quotas for France and the United Kingdom were ranked just below those of Japan and Germany. Adjustments were also made to the quotas of the United States, Canada and Italy so that the total quota for the seven countries as a group was maintained unchanged.[42] Quota increases for the rest of the members were not influenced by the redistribution of voting power amongst the G-7 countries (See Table 2).

Table 2. Present and proposed quota and voting power*

Country category**	GDP (PPP) 1997–99 Average	Present quota share	Proposed quota share on basis of GDP (PPP)	Present voting share	Proposed voting share on basis of GDP (PPP) (87.7%) and BV (11.3%)
	SDR billion	%	%	%	%
Advanced Economies	16,303	62.763	55.492	61.768	50.950
Major Advanced Economies	13,375	46.030	45.523	45.146	40.811
Other Advanced Economies	2,929	16.732	9.969	16.622	10.139
USA	6,315	17.383	21.494	17.030	19.127
Japan	2,282	6.229	7.767	6.110	6.951
EU	5,900	30.106	20.083	29.647	18.740
Developing Countries	11,320	29.697	38.530	30.529	42.019
Africa	1,086	5.493	3.695	5.962	6.427
of which sub-Saharan Africa	873	4.496	2.970	4.952	5.599
Asia	6,181	9.120	21.038	9.250	20.390
Western Hemisphere	2,504	7.456	8.523	7.666	9.536

* BV stands for Basic Votes; PPP refers to GDP valued at Purchasing Power Parity.
** Country categories based upon IMF *World Economic Outlook*.
A country-wise breakdown of data is available on request from Bhaskar, V, vbhaskar@msn.com

Voting: Proportionality and Sovereignty

At the Bretton Woods conference in 1944, two alternate formulas were proposed for determining voting power. In the first formula, voting power would be related solely to members' quota contributions (i.e. one dollar – one vote). The second formula related voting power to the Westphalian principle of the equality of states (i.e. one country – one vote). The Fund settled on a system that combined 'basic votes', which are distributed irrespective of quota size and 'proportional votes' based on a member's quota contribution. The basic votes were designed to increase the voting power of those members whose quotas were below the average quota for Fund membership as a whole. However, a constitutional mechanism was not created to maintain the ratio of basic votes to proportional votes if the size of the IMF's membership fluctuated.

The relative importance of basic votes increased significantly from 1944 when it was 11.26 per cent of the total votes to 15.61 per cent in 1958. Changes made reflected the lower than average quota allocation to countries that joined the Fund during this period which resulted in enhancing the profile of basic votes in the voting structure. However, the relative importance of basic votes has decreased substantially since then. In 1958, basic votes constituted 15.61 per cent of total votes but by 1995, basic votes share reduced to only 3.02 per cent. This decline occurred alongside an expansion in the number of Fund member countries from 68 in 1958 to 181 in 1995.[43] The decline in the relative importance of basic votes reflects, in part, the effects of regular quota increases since 1965 and more recently, the marked slowdown in the new membership of relatively small members. The result of this decline is that smaller countries have very little voice in the governance of the Fund, even if they are able to form a united front.

Voting rights should balance a member's financial contribution with the principle of sovereign equality. Maintaining a strong link between a member's financial contribution to the Fund and its voting power is necessary to inspire confidence among creditor members and financial markets. However, there remains the need to balance the capitalist norm with the principle of sovereignty in order to improve the governance of the Fund. The principle of sovereign equality can be advanced by enhancing the weight of basic votes in the determination of voting power. This is necessary as the share of basic votes has steadily declined over the past and with near universal membership of the Fund, this trend is likely to continue with every further quota increase.

Basic votes continue to be important for countries with small quotas. Table 3 illustrates the current role of basic votes as a per cent of total voting power in the IMF. In 2001, out of 183 members, there were 25 members for whom basic votes comprise more than half of the member's individual voting power,

Table 3. Illustrative voting shares—No change in quotas and increased basic votes (in per cent)

Current members	#	Total voting power with 250 basic votes per member (per cent)	Total voting power with 500 basic votes per member	Total voting power with pasic votes per member (1945 ratio)**
Countries in which Basic Votes are >50% of their Quota	25	0.406	0.678	1.659
Countries in which Basic Votes are >30% of their Quota	34	0.699	1.064	2.379
Countries in which Basic Votes are >20% of their Quota	60	1.919	2.548	4.820

* Table based on actual quotas except for nine countries which have not yet consented to their quota increases, for which the 11th General Review proposed quotas are used.
** In 1945 basic votes constituted 11.3 per cent of total votes. If the basic vote component had not deteriorated, each member would currently have 1488 basic votes.
Source: Data Derived from IMF Staff calculations.

while basic votes make up at least 30 per cent of total voting power for 34 members and 20 per cent of total voting power for 60 members. The aggregate voting power of these 25, 34 and 60 members is 0.406, 0.699, and 1.919 per cent of the total membership's voting power respectively.[44] If basic votes were simply doubled to 500 basic votes per member while maintaining the existing formula for voting rights, the voting power of these countries would increase to 0.678, 1.064, and 2.548 per cent of the total membership's voting power respectively.[45] If the proportion of basic votes to the total number of votes had been kept constant since 1945, these countries would constitute 1.659, 2.379, and 4.820 per cent of the total membership's voting power respectively (See Table 3).

It is apparent that any increase in the size of voting power of these relatively small members, nearly all of which are non-oil producing developing countries, would have an effect upon the highly skewed distribution of voting power within the Fund. Currently the 10 countries with the largest quotas control 54.022 per cent of the total vote, while the next 113 countries control 44.059 per cent and the bottom 60 countries control 1.919 per cent of the total voting share. If each country were given basic votes at the original '1945 ratio' of 11.3 per cent of total votes, it would be possible for the 173 middle and bottom tier countries to hold a simple majority over the top

10 countries. Moreover, the 60 countries in group three of Table 3 would benefit the most by having their total voting power increase from 1.919 per cent to 4.820 per cent. In order to prevent further erosion of voting power amongst the poorest members, it is necessary that basic votes be determined on an *ad valorem* basis. The Fund's Articles of Agreements should be amended to ensure that basic votes would constitute 11.3 per cent of total votes regardless of future quota changes.

The Veto Market and the Democratic Deficit

The redistribution of voting power would not only redress the Fund's current imbalance amongst industrial, emerging and developing countries, it would also create a more contestable 'veto market'. Veto power as determined by different coalitions of states will enable cooperation, which could empower states to prevent policies with which they disagree. A highly contestable veto market would encourage greater dialogue between member countries, as coalitions of member countries would be able to effectively block the approval of programs that influence their interests. This increased pluralism need not lead to deadlock due to the growing global interdependence. As a political institution, the prescribed quota regime reforms would enhance participation and legitimacy, creating dialogue on the governance of the global economy.

These reforms will effectively address the major criticism of the IMF regarding its 'Democratic Deficit'. As the Fund works to set standards and harmonize rules to strengthen national banking and financial sectors of member countries, the ability of different states to participate in the process of global governance will become increasingly important. The legitimacy conferred upon rules agreed through a more democratic framework, particularly amongst the growing number of democratic member countries, represents an important means of reducing transgression or nominal compliance. Moreover, enhancing the diversity of the Fund's governing body will increase inputs from alternative perspectives, thereby contributing to crisis prevention and management while allowing a multiplicity of capitalisms to flourish.[46] A democratic Fund in which different capitalisms exist and compete side by side represents a good start for the next century of capitalism.

The Democratic Deficit, the Westphalian Contradiction

Despite periodic changes to the quota regime, developing and emerging market countries have argued that the distribution of voting power within the Fund does not adequately reflect their importance in the world economy. This 'democratic deficit' results from three factors: (1) the decline of basic votes in the Fund's quota regime, reducing the voice of smaller countries in the governance of the Fund; (2) biases in the calculation of economic strength, causing the IMF to neglect the strength of emerging market economies; and (3) the needless complexity and opacity involved in the calculation of quotas. As the legitimacy and representativity of the organization is in question, the Fund will have to address this growing 'democratic deficit' if it wishes to address global civil demands to improve the governance and provide a greater role for the developing and emerging market economies.

Democratic Deficit and Quota Calculations—Specification Biases

The democratic deficit within the Fund is exacerbated by biases that are built into the calculation of members' quotas. Current quota formulas are composed of five components:

- A country's GDP at current prices for the recent year converted at market exchange rates
- The 12-month average of gold and foreign exchange reserves, including reserve positions in the IMF
- The annual average of current payments (goods, services, income and private transfers) for a recent 5-year period
- The annual average of current receipts (goods, services, income and private transfers) for a recent 5-year period
- The variability of external current receipts for a recent 13-year period[47]

With the exception of the last item, these components are intended to measure a member's economic 'strength' as well as its 'openness' to trade.[48]

An important element of the democratic deficit is the extreme complexity of the quota formulas and the inconsistent process by which these formulas are applied. Currently, there are five different quota formulas. The five formulas use essentially the same set of economic variables, but combine them in different ways with different weights. Members may use whichever formula they prefer to generate higher calculated quotas. Large, closed economies tend to prefer the revised 'Bretton Woods' formula in which GDP is the most heavily weighted variable. Small, open economies tend to prefer one of the four 'derived' formulas in which trade and openness has greater weight and GDP holds relatively less weight.

In practice, the calculation of quotas is inconsistent because the role of quota formulas has declined in the determination of quotas and quota share adjustments have been relatively small.[49] A principled reform of the quota regime would eliminate the unnecessary complexity of the current regime.

A simple and transparent quota formula would have the added benefit of improving relations with civil society groups that have demanded greater transparency in the governance structures of the Fund.

As the IMF is already a political institution, a reformed quota regime would make the politics of the institution legible and create greater space for genuine dialogue on the governance of the global economy. Moreover, through a reform of the quota regime, the IMF staff may acquire greater autonomy to criticize large member countries. In essence, the staff would become accountable to a broader membership base, thus changing the overall tone and tenor of discussions at the Fund. Reforming the quota regime would also change the nationality and regional diversity of the IMF staff. Although the Fund does not pursue a formal policy to recruit and promote nationality diversity amongst the staff, member country quotas are used as a benchmark to assess nationality and regional representation.[50]

As the Fund's quota regime comes to reflect the economic weight of emerging market and developing countries, more staff will be selected from developing countries. A diverse staff may help shape program designs that reflect the concerns of developing countries. At the very least, a diverse staff might help to eliminate 'standardized' solutions that characterized some Fund structural adjustment programs for developing countries in the 1990s. While there is a remarkable homogeneity in the Economics discipline, a diverse staff might introduce heterodox approaches to economic crisis management, enhancing legitimacy for proposed reforms.

Restructuring the Executive Board: Legitimacy and Accountability

The appointment of the Managing Director and the first Deputy Managing Director is the exclusive and unchallenged preserve of the European Union and the United States. In view of this fact, the agreement to objective criterion for filling these posts has yet to be followed. Presently, Europe has ten chairs on the Fund's Board while Asia has six and Africa has even fewer. Today Europe's share in the global GDP valued at PPP basis, an appropriate measure for international comparisons, is 29 per cent while that of Asia is 32 per cent. With the present trends in growth rates, this difference between Asia and Europe will only grow in Asia's favour. Hence, there is little doubt that the Fund's governance structure, in terms of voting and number of chairs in the Board, requires restructuring if the Fund is to reflect a greater balance of the underlying economic forces of the 21st century.

Merely changing the quota shares or reallocating chairs will not be enough to improve governance. The Fund needs to fully empower the Board by making it truly independent, as envisioned by Lord Keynes. The Fund requires a fully independent Board to better manage the global economy just like the parallel demand for independent central banks to better manage national economies. How can this be achieved?

One approach is that every member of the Executive Board should be an elected member, elected by their respective parliaments. In other words, no one should be nominated to the Board even if they represent a single country constituency. The tenure of the Executive Board members should be fixed and it could be for six years with one-third of the Board being elected every two years, providing continuity of the Board. To ensure the independence of the Board members, there should be a single term limit. Enhancing the Board's independence will attract eminent professionals; this would increase objective bilateral and multilateral surveillance and improve crisis management.

Simultaneously, one needs to ensure the Board's accountability, but for now, the Board has little accountability for implemented Fund programs. For instance, there could be a set of benchmarks or a Memorandum of Understanding by which shareholders will measure the Board's performance, providing for a corresponding structure of rewards and disincentives. There have been instances where, because of the failure of a Fund program, the concerned Finance Minister or the central bank governor had to resign. This is a step towards accountability. Similar accountability is needed within the Fund itself. Another way of enhancing the Fund's accountability is by actively engaging parliaments, including those of creditor countries. After all, the Fund's accountability has to be to its shareholders, who in turn represent their parliaments. The added advantage of engaging the parliaments would be improved policies and coherence, particularly amongst the large economies. In other words, surveillance would be more effective.

As the Fund is the custodian of global macroeconomics, improved surveillance is a key consideration. Sensitizing the parliaments to policy externalities and policy coordination will strengthen the Fund's effectiveness in both crisis prevention and crisis management. Towards this, what is required is an active engagement of the IMF with the parliaments of member countries. Just as the Chairman of the Federal Reserve appears regularly before the US Congress, the Managing Director, or the deputy, should annually brief the parliaments of major economies on the IMF assessment of the global economy and the implications of this assessment for the respective country. Equally, the IMF should brief the parliament about the impact of Article IV Consultation on the concerned country and the impact of that countries' policy towards the global economy. The IMF would essentially be the cutting edge of the 'global rationality' for better management of the world economy. Such regular engagements will improve national policies as well as policy coordination among major economies and thus lead to greater stability in the world economy.[51] Such regular engagements will create greater awareness and support for an independent IMF globally.

Economic Security Council

Since the early 1990s, there have been strong recommendations for the creation of an Economic Security Council (ESC). One key recommendation from the Commission on Global Governance was a new institution to address this need as 'the international community has no satisfactory way to consider global economic problems in the round and the linkages between economic, social, environment and security issues in the widest sense'.[52] Later on in 2001, the Zedillo Report made a similar suggestion for the creation of an apex institution in the form of an ESC.[53] Both reports suggest the creation of the ESC within the United Nations (UN). Currently the UN is not only fighting for its political legitimacy, but is also involved in a serious debate on the restructuring of the Security Council. Given this situation, expecting an active and effective role on the part of the UN to create a viable new institution is unreasonable and the reason why we turn to the Fund.

The Fund's institutional reform deficit has created a rather legitimate debate as the IMF has failed to represent all of its 184 constituent members. In the absence of effective surveillance on G-8 Countries, this debate could bring about hazardous consequences. The Asian central banks have accumulated more than $2 trillion foreign exchange reserves. The institution's governance in the hands of the rich nations has led to the belief that it is time to create an Asian Monetary Fund (AMF). Asia contains almost 55 per cent of the world population. According to one author, the region of East and South Asia contains the most dynamic economies, fastest growing trade, highest saving rates, and biggest current account surpluses. As a result, scholars point out that there is no reason for these countries to depend on the Fund and the United States. In order to reduce vulnerability, they suggest the creation of an AMF. Although the case for an AMF seems legitimate, such a Fund would probably lead towards the proliferation of regional financial institutions and eventually may prove to be counterproductive for the global economy. The spread of multiple financial institutions would create greater instability in the international system with respect to effective crisis management. To avoid proliferation of regional financial institutions, the IMF ought to develop an ESC.

The central role of the Fund as an ESC would be to manage the present wave of intensified globalization in such a way that it promotes stable growth in the global economy as the *universal* lender of last resort, providing economic security to all with an enhanced resource base. The ESC is an extension at the global level of the role of the state at the national level, of providing economic security with better risk management through socializing risk, as recently argued in Moss's work, *When All Else Fails*.[54] Through this, the Fund will reduce global political tensions, providing security for smaller countries.

Conclusion

It is perhaps high time to accept the proposal of the distinguished British Chancellor of the Exchequer, Mr. Gordon Brown, calling for a new Bretton Woods Conference to undertake the much needed transformation of the global financial architecture. Foremost, voting power needs to be determined through a set of weighted averages for GDP valued at PPP (88.7 per cent) and basic votes at the historic '1945 Ratio' (11.3 per cent). The results would appropriately reflect the economic weight of the developing countries without eroding the veto power of the United States. Current voting shares for the advanced economies would drop from 62 per cent to 51 per cent. Reforming the governance of the Fund in this manner would help the Fund to embody Keynes' original design for the IMF as an independent international institution.

Keynes' biographer, Robert Skidelsky, has argued recently that one of Keynes' main goals at the Bretton Woods conference was to protect the Fund from preponderant control by a single country. Keynes envisioned the Managing Director position at the Fund as analogous to an independent governor of a central bank. In fact, Keynes, supported by the French and Indian delegates, even fought to locate the headquarters of the Fund outside of Washington, DC in order to promote an international image for the institution and prevent undue influence from the US government.[55]

The proposed reforms are a step towards Keynes' objective of independence. To that end, in summation, the Fund should go through much needed fundamental changes in five areas—the Fund size has to be increased substantially; the Quota Regime requires a new approach so that the redistribution of voting power will redress the current imbalance amongst industrial, emerging and developing countries; the Fund governance structure, in terms of voting and number of chairs in the Board, requires a major rebalancing if the Fund is to reflect current needs; the members of the expanded board should not only be elected, but also held accountable to their Parliaments; and the central role of the Fund should be to manage the new wave of intensified globalization in such a way that it promotes a stable growth in the world economy, offering economic security to all.

Notes

1 The paper, dated 24 April 2005, is a revised version of the paper presented at the March 2005 G-24 annual Technical Group Meeting. We would like to thank James M Boughton, Ariel Buira and John Williamson for their valuable comments. The views

expressed in this paper are personal and not those of the organization with which the authors are associated. The authors wish to thank a number of current and former senior staff at the IMF for their assistance and comments on earlier drafts. Contact Information: Dr. Praveen K. Chaudhry, Department of Political Science, Bentley Annex 257, Ohio University, Athens, Ohio, 45701, Phone: 215-715-9781, Email: chaudhry@ohio.edu

2 *United Nations Development Program*, 2002, pp. 101

3 IMF, 2000a, Article I, i–v, pp. 2.

4 Bayne, Woolcock and Budd, 2003, pp. 123.

5 The G-20, in a recent meeting in Berlin, developed a broad framework for the SDRM.

6 Fischer, 1999,

7 Birdsall, 2003. See also Kapur and Naim, 2005.

8 IMF, 2001, Chapter II.

9 Evans and Finnemore, 2001.

10 Dahl, 1991, pp. 71–80. 'Polyarchy' literally means rule by many. The term is intended to provoke self-reflection among democracies, to right the historical tendency of classifying regime types in terms of extremes. See also McLean and McMillan, 2003.

11 Sakakibara, 1999. The 'constitutionalist' design of the Fund and World Bank, in which duties and actions were carefully prescribed by the Articles of Agreement, were originally intended to keep these institutions from imposing far-reaching structural reforms on sovereign members. However, in the wake of major financial crises, particularly since the 1982 Mexican debt crisis, industrialized members of the IMF and World Bank have cast these institutions into the role of correcting weaknesses in domestic financial systems to ensure growth and poverty alleviation. See Woods 2001, pp. 8. As the IMF agrees, 'Conditionality has evolved substantially over the history of the Fund. Some element of policy conditionality has been attached to Fund financing since the mid 1950s, but the scope for conditionality has expanded particularly since the early 1980s.' See IMF, 2001, paragraph 3.

12 'Atlantic States' are the G-7 countries; just as there was an evolution of the G-3, so too might there be a parallel evolution of the Atlantic States. This term is in response to the untenable IDs many have adopted to refer to a divided globe—Third World *vs* 1st and 2nd or Developed, Developing and Underdeveloped. The reviewers wish to present the dichotomy as Atlantic States and the Developing World.

13 At the 2002 Kananaskis Summit in Canada, the heads of the G-8 did meet with the Presidents of Algeria, Nigeria, Senegal and South Africa, as well as the Secretary General of the United Nations, to discuss the challenges faced by Africa.

14 Six out of 24 Executive Directors (EDs) are from Asian countries (Korea, China, India, Indonesia, Iran, and Japan), whereas there are 10 EDs from European countries (Belgium, Finland, France, Germany, Italy, Netherlands, Russia, Spain, Switzerland, and the United Kingdom). Only three EDs are from African countries (Egypt, Gabon and South Africa), and five from the Western Hemisphere.

15 See *Straits Times*, 24 September 1997; *Business Times (Singapore)*, 22 November 1997; *Los Angeles Times*, 7 November 1997; *Washington Post*, 19 November 1997; *Times*, 20 November 1997; *Financial Times*, 16 December 1998; *Guardian*, 22 April 2000; *Hindu*, 7 May 2000; *New Straits Times (Malaysia)*, 24 April 2002. In the Middle East, the Arab Monetary Fund, which was founded in 1976, is headquartered in Abu Dhabi, United Arab Emirates. There are 21 members devoted to providing short and medium term assistance to members experiencing balance of payments difficulties.

16 French, 2004.

17 Fenby, 2004.

18 Calvo, 2001.

19 The five borrowers are Turkey (SDR 14,510.5 million or 28 per cent of the Fund's General Resources Account or GRA), Argentina (SDR 10,849.8 million or 21 per cent of the GRA), Indonesia (SDR 6,884.9 million or 13 per cent of the GRA), Russia (SDR 5,515.5 million or 11 per cent of the GRA) and Brazil (SDR 3,249 million or 6 per cent of the GRA). IMF, 2002b, pp. 24–25.

20 Although Turkey's quota in the IMF is small, the commitment of IMF loans at almost 10 times the normal limit is unprecedented in the history of the IMF. Mussa, 2002, pp. 12.

21 By enabling countries that are 'basically sound and well managed' to secure precautionary financing in case a crisis should occur, the CCL aimed to prevent the spread of a financial crisis. The SRF was established in December 1997 to provide assistance to members experiencing balance of payments difficulties resulting from 'a sudden and disruptive loss of market confidence' reflected through pressure on the member's capital account and reserve holdings. IMF, 2001c, pp. 184, 196.

22 Sources for bridging the financing gap outside of the private sector could be (a) domestic adjustment effort; (b) multilateral banks; (c) bilateral country assistance; and (d) loan restructuring.

23 The quota regime also determines allocation of SDRs as a reserve asset. A decision to allocate SDRs has only been reached twice. In 2001, SDRs accounted for less than one-half of 1 per cent of members' non-gold reserves. IMF, 2001c, pp. 89.

24 Countries with the five largest quota subscriptions (i.e. US, Japan, Germany, France and the United Kingdom) are allowed to appoint an Executive Director to the Fund's Executive Board. All other members are organized into regional groups and elect an Executive Director to represent their constituency. China, Russia and Saudi Arabia form separate single member country constituencies, thereby effectively retaining a separate and independent seat on the Executive Board.

25 The Board of Governors, whose members are usually ministers of finance or heads of central banks, normally meets once a year. It is the highest policymaking body of the IMF and holds the Executive Board accountable.

26 In fact, there are five quota formulas, including the original Bretton Woods formula that may be used to calculate a member's quota. For each of the formulas, quota calculations are multiplied by an adjustment factor so that the sum of the calculations across members equals that derived from the Bretton Woods formula. The calculated quota of a member is the higher of the Bretton Woods calculation or the average of the lowest two of the remaining four calculations (after adjustment). See IMF, 2001c, pp. 57, Box II.7.

27 Tinbergen, 1952. See also Theil, 1961; Blinder, 1997, pp. 3–19.

28 Quota Formula Review Group, 2001, pp. 15.

29 '*Maquiladora*' economic activity refers to the trade generated by foreign owned assembly plants on international border areas, which import products duty-free for rapid assembly and subsequent export. The term '*maquiladora*' comes from the name for the assembly plants located along the US-Mexican border. IMF 2000b, pp. 108, Table 9.1.

30 Buira 2003, pp. 24 on adjustment of Euro zone countries quotas for trade in a single currency.

31 Quota Formula Review Group, 2000, pp. 63.

32 IMF 2001a, pp. 156, 159.
33 Quota Formula Review Group, 2000, pp. 58; Quota Formula Review Group, 2001, pp. 13; IMF Treasurer's Department and IMF Statistics Department, 2002b, pp. 4.
34 IMF Treasurer's Department and Statistics Department, 2002b, pp. 6. A compromise formula or hybrid exchange rate based on a combination of PPP and market exchange rate is also possible.
35 Quota Formula Review Group, 2000, pp. 57–58; Quota Formula Review Group, 2001, pp. 13–14; IMF Treasurer's Department and Statistics Department, 2002b, pp. 4, 6.
36 op. cit., pp. 58.
37 IMF, 2001f.
38 IMF 2001c, pp. 58.
39 op. cit., pp. 58, 62.
40 IMF, 2001c, pp. 62.
41 Cambodia's quota had not been increased since 1970.
42 IMF, 2001c, pp. 62.
43 The number of countries included in the 1995 tally includes Brunei, Darussalam, Sudan, Zaire (whose voting rights had been suspended), South Africa (which did not participate in the 1994 regular election of Executive Directors), Bosnia and Herzegovina, Iraq, Afghanistan and Liberia—for which data was not available to make quota calculation under the Eleventh General Review.
44 East Timor became the 184th member of the IMF on 23 July 2002.
45 A member's voting power is equal to 250 basic votes plus one additional vote for each SDR 100,000 in quota. IMF, 2001c, pp. 55.
46 Albert, 1993.
47 IMF 2001c, pp. 57.
48 The variability of the current receipts is the only need-based indicator; it takes into account the financial problems that countries are likely to face.
49 The quota formulas play a role in determining the extent of the increase in quota share as well as the proportion of selective increases; see IMF 2001c, pp. 63.
50 IMF, 2002a, chapter 5; IMF, 2001b, chapter 5.
51 Pikoulakis,1995, chapter 9.
52 Commission on Global Governance, 1995, pp. 153.
53 Zedillo, 2001, pp. 67.
54 Studies show that for modern market based economies to perform well, one of the most important roles of the government is the effective management of risks at both the macro and micro level as an integral part of its public policy framework. In this age, international organizations will have to play a role in risk mitigation and risk sharing to provide for global economic security. The Meltzer Commission has already proposed far-reaching reforms; it has suggested that the Fund must focus on short term liquidity crisis assistance and eliminate long term loans for structural reforms.
55 Skidelski, 2001, pp. 466.

References

Albert, Michel, 1993, *Capitalism against Capitalism*, Haviland, Paul (trans.), London: Whurr.
Bayne, Nicholas, Woolcock, Stephen and Budd, Colin, 2004, *The New Economic Diplomacy: Decision-Making and Negotiation in International Economic Relations*, UK: Ashgate Publishing Co.
Birdsall, Nancy, 2003, Why it Matters Who Runs the IMF and the World Bank, *Working Paper 22*, Center for Global Development, January.

Blinder, AS, 1997, What Central Bankers could Learn from Academics, *Journal of Economic Perspectives*, 11, 1: 3–19.

Blustein, Paul, 2001, *The Chastening: Inside the Crisis that Rocked the Global Financial System and Humbled the IMF*, New York: Public Affairs/Perseus Books Group.

Buira, Ariel, 2003, *The Governance of the IMF in a Global Economy*, p. 24, in 'Challenges to the World Bank and the IMF,' Anthem Press, London.

Calvo, Guillermo A, 2001, *Globalization Hazard and Weak Governments in Emerging Markets*, Unpublished manuscript, December.

Commission on Global Governance, 1995, *Our Global Neighborhood*, Oxford: Oxford University Press.

Dahl, Robert A, 1991, *Modern Political Analysis*, 5th Ed., Englewood Cliffs: Prentice Hall.

Evans, Peter and Finnemore, Martha, 2001, Organizational Reform and the Expansion of the South's Voice at the Fund, *G-24 Discussion Paper Series*, No. 15, Geneva: United Nations Publication, December.

Fenby, Jonathan, 2004, Big Money in Modern China, *The Sunday Times*, 17 October.

Fischer, Stanley, 1999, On the Need for an International Lender of Last Resort, paper prepared for delivery at the joint luncheon of the American Economic Association and the American Finance Association, New York, 3 January.

French, Howard, 2004, China Moves Towards Another West: Central Asia, *The New York Times*, 28 March.

Gilpin, Robert, 2000, *The Challenge of Global Capitalism: The World Economy in the 21st Century*, Princeton: Princeton University Press.

Heston, Alan and Summers, Robert, 1988, What We Have Learned about Prices and Quantities from International Comparisons: 1987, *American Economic Review*, May, 78, 2: 467–473.

IMF, 2000a, *Articles of Agreement*, Washington, DC: IMF, March.

IMF, 2000b, Annex. IMF Document – EBAP/00/52, Supplement 1, *External Review of the Quota Formulas*, Washington, DC: IMF, 1 May.

IMF, 2000c, *Selected Decisions and Selected Documents of the International Monetary Fund*, Washington, DC: IMF, Issue 25, 31 December.

IMF, 2001a, Annual Report 2001, Washington, DC: IMF.

IMF, 2001b, Diversity Annual Report 2000, Washington, DC: IMF.

IMF, 2001c, Financial Organization and Operations of the IMF, Washington, DC: IMF Treasurer's Department.

IMF, 2001d, *Conditionality in Fund Supported Programs – Overview*, Washington, DC: IMF, February.

IMF, 2001e, *World Economic Outlook: The Information Technology Revolution*, Washington, DC: IMF, October.

IMF, 2001f, IMF Executive Board Informally Discusses Quota Formulas, *IMF Document—Public Information Notice*: PIN/01/118, Washington, DC: IMF, 7 November.

IMF, 2002a, *Diversity Annual Report 2001*, Washington, DC: IMF.

IMF, 2002b, *International Financial Statistics*, Washington, DC: IMF, July.

International Monetary Fund Treasurer's Department, 2002a, *Twelfth General Review of Quotas—Preliminary Considerations and Next Steps*, Washington, DC: IMF, 22 January.

International Monetary Fund Treasurer's Department and Statistics Department, 2002b, *Alternative Quota Formulas—Further Considerations*, Washington, DC: IMF, 3 May.

Kahler, M, 2000, The New International Financial Architecture and its Limits, in *The Asian Financial Crisis and the Architecture of Global Finance*, Noble, GW and Ravenhill, J (eds), Cambridge: Cambridge University Press.

Kapur, Devesh and Moises, Naim, 2005, The IMF and Democratic Governance, *Journal of Democracy*, January.

Kravis, Irving B, Heston, Alan W and Summers, Robert, 1978, Real GDP per capita for more than One Hundred Countries, *The Economic Journal*, June, 88, 350: 215–242.

McLean, Iain and McMillan, Alistair, 2003, *Oxford Concise Dictionary of Politics*, Oxford: Oxford University Press.

Moss, David, 2002, *When All Else Fails: Government as the Ultimate Risk Manager*, Cambridge: Harvard University Press.

Mussa, Michael, 2002, *Reflections on Moral Hazard and Private Sector Involvement in the Resolution of Emerging Market Financial Crises*, Washington, DC: Institute for International Economics.

Pikoulakis, Emmanuel, 1995, *International Macroeconomics*, St Martin Press: New York.

Quota Formula Review Group, 2000, *Report to the IMF Executive Board of the Quota Formula Review Group*, Washington, DC: IMF, 28 April.

Quota Formula Review Group, 2001, *Alternative Quota Formulations: Considerations*, Washington, DC: IMF, 27 September.

Sakakibara, Eisuke, 1999, The End of Market Fundamentalism, Speech at the Foreign Correspondents Club, Tokyo, 22 January.

Skidelsky, Robert, 2001, *John Maynard Keynes: Fighting for Freedom 1937–1946, Vol. III*, New York: Viking Press.

Summers, Robert and Heston, Alan, 1991, The Penn World Table (Mark 5): An Expanded Set of International Comparisons, 1950–1988, *Quarterly Journal of Economics*, May, 106, 2: 327–368.

Theil, H, 1961, *Economic Forecasts & Policy*, 2nd Ed., Amsterdam: North Holland.

Tinbergen, Jan, 1952, *On The Theory of Economic Policy*, 2nd Ed., Amsterdam: North Holland.

United Nations Development Program, 2002, *Human Development Report 2002: Deepening Democracy in a Fragmented World*, Oxford: Oxford University Press.

Woods, Ngaire, 2001, Accountability, Governance, and Reform in the International Financial Institutions, Working Paper, Oxford: University College.

Zedillo, Ernesto (Chairman), 2001, High-level International Intergovernmental Consideration of Financing for Development, The United Nations, June 26.

4

IMPROVING IMF GOVERNANCE AND INCREASING THE INFLUENCE OF DEVELOPING COUNTRIES IN IMF DECISION-MAKING[1]

Murilo Portugal[2]

Abstract:

The IMF has a generally well-thought out governance structure and has been a relatively effective organization able to adopt and implement complex decisions in a cooperative and timely fashion. The constituency system allows reconciling the legitimacy of an almost universal membership with efficient decision-making and collegiality of a not-too-large Executive Board. Weighted voting based on relative economic strength gives confidence to creditor countries to commit financial resources to the IMF, while consensus decision-making confers some protection to the interests of minority groups, making weighted voting acceptable to debtor countries and may lead to better decisions that are easier to implement.

However, a number of important governance deficiencies need improvements. The influence of developing countries in decision-making is less than desirable, given the major role played by the IMF in these countries and the growing importance of such countries in the world economy. Conversely, there is excessive influence of a small group of large industrial countries and a large part of the membership does not actually participate in a meaningful way in the choice of the main officer of the institution.

The topics discussed in this paper to improve the governance of the IMF centre around increasing the independence and accountability of the Executive Board; moderately improving the aggregate voting share of developing countries; making the selection process of the Managing Director more open and transparent; nurturing the consensus decision-making approach; improving the efficacy and representation of the constituency system; and upgrading the IMF's role as the main forum for international economic policy cooperation.

Introduction

The IMF has a generally well thought out governance structure and is a relatively effective organization that has been able to adopt and implement complex decisions in a cooperative and timely fashion. The constituency system allows reconciling the legitimacy of an almost universal membership with efficient decision-making and collegiality of a not-too-large Executive Board. Weighted voting based on relative economic strength gives confidence to creditor countries to commit financial resources to the IMF, while consensus decision-making confers some protection to the interests of minority groups, making weighted voting acceptable to debtor countries, and may lead to better decisions that are easier to implement. Special voting majorities of 70 per cent for certain key decisions also help to protect sizeable minorities.

There are, however, a number of important governance deficiencies and areas that need improvements. The influence of developing countries in decision-making is less than desirable given the major role played by the IMF in these countries and the growing importance of such countries in the world economy. Conversely, there is excessive influence of a small group of large industrial countries. A large part of the membership does not actually participate in a meaningful way in the choice of the main officer of the institution. The IMF expanded its conditionality to areas beyond its core areas of expertise, while in other key aspects, its mandate remains undeveloped and would benefit from upgrading, such as with respect to international economic cooperation. The cost of the Fund's activities falls disproportionately on borrowing countries, although this topic will not be dealt with in this paper.

It is no secret that the G-7 exercises great influence in the IMF decision-making process that has become excessive, even considering the group's large aggregate voting share. Although, the G-7 countries remain somewhat short of a voting majority, it is highly unlikely that any issue—either policy or country matter—would be approved in the IMF if the group firmly opposed it. The G-7 appears, in some instances, to act as a self-appointed steering committee of the IMF. It drives the policy agenda of the Fund and often acts as a voting bloc. Decision-making in members of this group tends to be kept in their capitals, which raises complex questions regarding governance and accountability.

Given its mandate, financial resources and organizational structure, the IMF is amongst the most powerful official international bodies, perhaps second only to the UN Security Council. Like the Security Council, this power is, in practice, exercised mostly with respect to developing countries. The IMF takes decisions that affect the lives of hundreds of millions of people in developing countries. Developing and emerging market countries are playing an increasingly important role in the world economy and raising their share of global output and trade. They are also home to the majority of the world's population. Yet, their influence in the IMF has not increased correspondingly. The aggregate voting power in the IMF of emerging market countries, developing countries and transition economies has oscillated between 37 and 40 per cent.

As the IMF is a relatively effective international organization, there has been a tendency for important shareholders to use the institution for objectives that go beyond the purposes for which it was originally created. Even when these objectives are laudable international goals, conforming to what could be considered international public goods and not simply national foreign policy interests of powerful shareholders, such practice undermines legitimacy and accountability, while at the same time reducing the Fund's efficiency in its core areas.

The issues of the governance of the IMF discussed in this paper centre around increasing the independence and accountability of the Executive Board; moderately improving the aggregate voting share of developing countries; making the selection process of the Managing Director more open and transparent; nurturing the consensus decision-making approach; improving the efficacy and representation of the constituency system; further focusing Fund conditionality on measures required to ensure repayment capacity; and upgrading the IMF's role as the main forum for international economic policy cooperation.

Reform of international organizations is a difficult and complex undertaking that can only proceed in a balanced and often incremental fashion. There has to be a package of reforms encompassing some benefit for a substantial number of member countries, so as to make the reforms feasible. It requires marshalling the highest qualities of political cooperation amongst member countries. Above all, it depends critically on obtaining support from the large industrial countries, without whose consent little reform is possible. Mobilizing strong support from public opinion internationally and inside countries seems to be the key to help this process. At the same time, while the reform process is by nature incremental, there may be value in discussing bold proposals that initially look ambitious and unfeasible in order to raise public debate and to allow such proposals to be later refined into a feasible and balanced package of reforms. This is the approach taken in this paper where several proposals would require an 85 per cent majority of the IMF voting power and may currently appear far-fetched.

Strengthening the Autonomy, Accountability and Effectiveness of the Executive Board

While the highest decision-making body of the IMF is the Board of Governors, the daily business of the Fund is conducted by a resident Executive Board, which exercises under delegation all the powers not specifically reserved to the Board of Governors in the Fund's Articles of Agreement. The main functions of the Executive Board include approving all policies of the IMF; discussing reports related to bilateral surveillance of member countries' economic and financial policies and multilateral surveillance of the international monetary system; approving all loans extended by the IMF and regular reviews of the implementation of such loan programs, which condition their disbursement; electing the Managing Director; and approving the budget and the administrative and personnel policies of the IMF.

The Executive Board is currently composed of 24 Executive Directors, of which five are appointed without a fixed term by the member countries with the largest quotas and 19 Directors are elected by all other 179 member states for a term of two years. The elected Executive Directors can be re-elected for an indefinite number of periods and there are no limitations with respect to time of service of appointed Executive Directors. About 12 Executive Directors are elected by and represent only emerging market and developing countries.[3] The five appointed Executive Directors represent only large industrial countries. Seven Executive Directors, while being nominated by industrial countries, are elected and simultaneously represent industrial countries, emerging market, transition economies and developing countries. In terms of geographical balance, Europe is represented by nine Executive Directors, Asia by five Directors, the Americas by five Directors, sub-Saharan Africa by two Directors and the Middle East by three Directors.[4]

Some rules and practices related to the appointment, election, term duration of Executive Directors and their relationships with their capitals do not seem to be the most appropriate from the point of view of strengthening the autonomy, accountability and effectiveness of both Executive Directors and the Executive Board. The five Directors appointed by the members with the largest quota have no fixed term and can be removed at will at any time by the authorities that appointed them. As mentioned earlier, some industrial countries retain the decision-making power in their capitals and convey narrow instructions to their representatives that reduce their autonomy and limit their ability to participate in the consensus building process. The 19 elected Directors have no limit for re-elections, which might generate incentives that would also limit their autonomy. Executive Directors who represent multi-country constituencies may enjoy considerably more autonomy in defining their positions, but questions are often raised about the mechanisms by which they are held accountable to their constituent countries.

Executive Directors perform a double role. They are international officials entrusted with the responsibility of ensuring that all operations and activities of the Fund are guided by the purposes of the Articles of Agreement and simultaneously, they act as representatives of the views and interests of the countries that appointed or elected them. While in the long run, these two roles would hopefully converge,[5] there might be divergences in the short run between the interests of a particular government, or even the national interest of a given country and the international objectives of the community of nations. In these instances, the Executive Director has to be able to exercise balanced judgment and to act as an international official while taking into due consideration the long term national interests of the countries they represent.

The issue, in some ways, is analogous to the question of the operational autonomy of central banks to pursue long-term price stability without being affected by time inconsistencies created by the short-term interests of the government of the day. In these instances, the best practice adopted by many countries and often recommended by the IMF has been to ensure the operational autonomy of central banks, a solution that could well be applied to the Executive Board of the IMF, which exercises certain functions of lender of last resort. The Statute of the European Central Bank, for instance, prohibits members of the Board from taking advice from their respective governments.

There is no provision in the Articles of Agreement with respect to the dual role of Executive Directors. While a direct prohibition for Executive Directors receiving advice from the countries that appointed or elected them would clearly be inappropriate, there is merit in including an explicit provision in the Articles of Agreement requiring that, in discharging their functions, Executive Directors appropriately balance the international purposes of the IMF and the national economic, monetary and financial objectives of the countries that they represent. An easier to implement alternative would be to include such a provision in the voluntary Code of Conduct that Executive Directors have drawn for themselves.

While the possibility of re-election may compromise independence, the two-year term for elected Executive Directors is too short for a Director to master all the complexities of IMF operations, to establish productive relations with management, the staff and fellow Directors and to become fully effective. Similarly, the possibility that presently exists that a large part, or even the entire Board, would change in a single election may not be appropriate for the efficient operation of the Board.

It seems that a superior system would be that appointed Directors be appointed for a fixed term during which, like their elected colleagues, they cannot be removed; that the term of both appointed and elected Directors be longer, say six years; that no Director be allowed to serve for more than one term; and that elections be carried out every two years for a staggered renewal of a third of elected Directors each time. All these proposals would require amendments to the Articles of Agreement and therefore, a majority of 85 per cent of the voting power. The introduction of these changes could be simultaneous with the activation of the Council, which would offer member countries political oversight over the Fund's activities, given that according to the Articles of Agreement, the Executive Board should not adopt any decision inconsistent with actions taken by either the Board of Governors or the Council.[6] The Executive Board would be more independent in running the daily business of the Fund, but if there were major issues in which fundamental interests of member countries were inappropriately affected by a too independent Board with insufficient accountability, the Council would be able to redress the situation. A provision could also be established by which an Executive Director could be removed from his office by the Council, with the decision being taken by a majority in terms of number of Councillors rather than voting power. This type of arrangement would seem to appropriately balance independence and accountability for the Executive Board.

Another way of strengthening the autonomy and effectiveness of the Executive Board, which does not depend on changing any rules, would be for the countries to appoint and elect officials that, in addition to being highly competent, have an even higher stature and seniority in their own countries, which would help them to withstand pressure. The proposals presented here for extending the fixed term of Executive Directors could act as a further incentive for countries to appoint their most able representatives as Executive Directors.

Power without accountability often leads to abuse. It is not possible to advocate greater power and autonomy for the Executive Board and Executive Directors dissociated from stronger and more effective accountability. Conversely, it is not logical to demand more accountability if those who are to be held accountable are not given the appropriate means to achieve the goals for which they will be accountable. Strengthening the autonomy of the Executive Board and of Executive Directors should go hand in hand with increasing their accountability and *vice versa*.

Refocusing the IMF on its core areas of expertise and its traditional mandate of ensuring domestic and external macroeconomic stability of member countries and the well-functioning of the international monetary system is another important aspect to strengthen accountability, and will be considered in a section later in this article. If an institution pursues a wide range of objectives that involve significant trade-offs among them, it is more difficult to establish a system of accountability based on ensuring independence of decisionmakers who are to be judged by the quality of the decisions taken and the results achieved. Effective output accountability requires a relatively narrow number of non-conflicting objectives in relation to which the decisionmaker can be held accountable.

In discussing accountability, there are at least three issues that are necessary to specify: accountability to *whom*, in relation to *what* and *how*. Clearly, while each Executive Director should be accountable to the countries that appointed or elected them, the Executive Board as a body should be accountable to the higher organs in the Fund's governance structure and to international public opinion at large. In relation to *what* accountability should be judged, the Fund's Articles of Agreement provide the main yardstick. The Executive Board as a group should be accountable for ensuring that the Fund, in all its activities, is guided by the purposes, rules and limitations enshrined in the Articles of Agreement and that it tries to achieve those purposes in an even-handed manner that is most efficient and cost effective. Individual Executive Directors, in addition to being accountable for the same, should also be accountable for how well they perform their representation role.

Regarding *how* to achieve accountability, the usual instruments are enhanced transparency, public appearance and testimony, regular reporting and evaluation by independent third parties. The Executive Board has already advanced considerably in relation to the transparency of its activities. However, additional steps should be taken in improving regular reporting and providing for independent third party evaluations.

The Executive Board has already created a joint Board staff group to improve the IMF's annual report, which should be the main instrument for the accountability of the Fund and the Executive Board with respect to the Board of Governors and public opinion. The report should give more pre-eminence to how well the Fund is performing with respect to adhering in its activities to the purposes envisaged by the Articles of Agreement and to include a specific section on the Executive Board's work that should be seen and designed as one of the main instruments for accountability of the Board. This could give the Board of Governors and the IMFC a chance to provide an opinion on how well the Executive Board is discharging its responsibilities.

Regarding independent third party evaluations, the Executive Board could ask its Evaluation Committee to arrange an external evaluation of the Board's effectiveness in discharging its obligations according to the Articles of Agreement, to be conducted by a group of eminent persons familiar with the Fund and the Board's work, say, every five years.

Executive Directors have already taken important steps to improve their individual accountability by drafting a voluntary Code of Conduct and establishing an Ethics Committee to oversee compliance. Such a Code, however, deals solely with the personal behaviour of Executive Directors in issues such as financial dealings, avoiding conflicts of interest, maintaining confidentiality of information, treatment of colleagues and subordinates and other standards of personal ethical conduct. It does not include any provisions with respect to the professional conduct of Executive Directors.

One alternative to increase the accountability of individual Executive Directors to their constituents with respect to how well they discharge their representation duties could be to include in such a Code, provisions related to best practices in representation and the obligations to present regular reports to the constituency and to appear and testify in public and private meetings if asked by the constituent countries. Executive Directors may also wish to submit themselves to a process of anonymous and totally confidential evaluations by their fellow Directors and by their constituents on how well they discharge their professional duties to be used as a feedback on their performance.

While the decisions to implement the above proposals related to increasing the accountability of the Executive Board and of Executive Directors do not involve changing the Articles and can be taken by a simple majority, they should be adopted only with a very broad consensus.

Moderately Increasing the Aggregate Voting Power of Developing Countries[7]

The voting power of member countries is based on their quotas and basic votes. Quotas, which are the main component of voting power, are related to a country's relative economic strength in the world economy. Quotas are calculated according to formulas, but for almost all countries, their *actual quotas* differ from their *calculated quotas*. Every five years, the Fund conducts a general review of quotas to determine whether a quota increase is needed. If there is a general quota increase, a part of such an increase is done in an equiproportional fashion, based on the current distribution of *actual* quotas and part in a selective fashion, i.e. based on the *calculated* quotas with an aim of bringing actual quotas more in line with calculated quotas. On average, the equiproportional component of quota increases has been around 70 per cent. Equiproportional quota increases delay the convergence of actual quotas to calculated quotas, introducing an element of inertia favouring the existing quota distribution.

A country's quota determines how much the country should contribute to the IMF's resources, how much the country is able to borrow from the IMF (access to resources is defined as multiples of the quota), what will be the country's share in any allocation of SDRs (Special Drawing Rights) and last but not least, what is its voting power.

Basic votes are the same for all countries. On joining, each member of the IMF receives 250 basic votes. Basic votes are based on the idea of the equality amongst states and resemble the United Nations system of one country – one vote. When the Fund was created, basic votes represented 11.3 per cent of the total voting power. The proportion of basic votes peaked at 15.6 per cent in 1958, but currently is only about 2 per cent. The decline in the importance of basic votes was a result of the repeated increases in the Fund's quotas, which had a much larger effect on the voting structure than the increases in the number of members. An increase in basic votes raises the voting power of small countries. Out of the total membership of 184 countries, for 25 members, basic votes represent more than half of their voting power, but these members account for only 0.4 per cent of the total voting power in the IMF, whereas for 60 countries basic votes account for 20 per cent of their voting power, while these countries represent only 1.9 per cent of the total IMF voting power.[8]

Industrial countries represent about 60 per cent of the voting power, while emerging markets, transition economies and developing countries account for about 40 per cent of the voting power. The United States have the largest voting share with 17.2 per cent, while the Executive Director representing mainly francophone African countries has the smallest voting share of 1.2 per cent. In terms of geographical balance, Europe[9] has 39.1 per cent of the voting power; the Americas have 29.6 per cent; Asia accounts for 18.0 per cent; the Middle East for 8.6 per cent; and sub-Saharan Africa for 4.4 per cent.[10]

Increasing the influence of developing countries in the decision-making process would contribute to good governance. While there is more than one way to achieve this aim, the most important and straightforward one would be a measured increase in the aggregate voting share of developing countries. Narrowing the voting majority of industrial countries, *while preserving their ultimate control of the institution*, would make it somewhat more difficult to impose majority decisions and could create incentives to strengthen the tradition of deciding by consensus rather than by voting. To be politically feasible, an increase in voting power of developing countries needs to respect three constraints—to maintain the majority of voting power in the hands of industrial countries; not to endanger the current veto power held by the United States; and to benefit a large number of developing countries. There could be an objective, for instance, to increase the aggregate voting power of developing countries from the current 40 per cent to say 47–48 per cent.

It would be essential to use the opportunity to correct existing distortions in the individual quota shares of a number of emerging markets, such as Korea, Turkey, China, South Africa, Iran, Mexico and Brazil, whose quota shares are out of line with the increased importance of these countries in the world economy, as well as with their potential need for IMF resources. While the quota shares of some of industrial countries also do not adequately reflect their position in the world economy, the case of emerging markets is more pressing because their actual quotas restrict their normal access to IMF resources, and force some of these countries to pay higher interest rates, face shorter repayment periods and accept more demanding procedural rules to receive IMF loans.

The strategy for achieving a greater voting share for developing countries in the Fund would have to combine three instruments to muster sufficient support within the group—a new, simplified, single quota formula; *ad hoc* selective quota increases for emerging markets whose actual quotas are most out-of-line according to the new formula; and an increase in basic votes. With the exception of a new quota formula, which can be approved by simple majority, the other two decisions mentioned here require an 85 per cent majority to be approved. This indicates that they can only be approved as a *package* and would depend on the highest qualities of cooperation of all members, especially those whose quota shares would be reduced by the proposed changes.

As quota shares and voting power represent a zero sum game, where some countries have to lose what others would gain, there should be a reasonable case not only to identify the countries that would potentially benefit, but also those countries that would have to adjust downward. The most straightforward case would be for a gradual reduction of the aggregate quotas of Western European countries, which currently is over 36 per cent.

As mentioned earlier, Europe—in particular Western Europe—is the continent with the largest aggregate quota. This was justified on historical grounds, since the Fund was created mainly to facilitate and finance the adjustment process and the liberalization of the current accounts of Western European countries after World War II. Since then, however, the situation has changed dramatically for the better. The last time a Western European country borrowed from the Fund was in 1976. Current and capital accounts in Western European countries have been totally and successfully liberalized. More importantly, 12 (to become possibly 25) European countries have adopted a single currency to trade amongst them. The current quota formulas unduly overestimate the quota shares of the European Monetary Union member countries by treating trade conducted amongst them in a single currency as foreign trade. The current 15 members of the European Union have an aggregate quota share close to 30 per cent. This is much higher than the quota share of the United States, with little economic justification, as both have GDP of a similar size.

Any possible adjustment in the quota shares of members of the European Union would have to be phased in gradually over a long period. The first step could be a small, *ad hoc* selective quota increase for a few developing countries, whose actual quotas are most out-of-line according to a new quota formula.

Regardless of what positions are with respect to increasing the voting power of developing countries, there is a strong technical case for *changing the quota formulas*, which are complex and opaque and have several specific problems. There are too many formulas; they contain too many variables; some variables are not directly related to the functions of quotas and produce unwarranted distortions; the specification of some variables seems biased and inappropriate; and the weights used, while being a matter of judgment, have been chosen in a totally *ad hoc* fashion and appear difficult to justify. The quota formulas discriminate against developing countries whose aggregate calculated quotas have tended to fall.

These problems go back to the creation of the IMF. Mikesell, the secretary of the Committee on Quotas in the Bretton Woods conference and the author of the original Bretton Woods formula, confessed in his memoirs that his superior at the US Treasury gave him the quota results for the four largest shareholders, which had been agreed by the highest political level in the United States and that he had to go through several trials using different weights and combinations of trade data until the quota formula produced the predetermined results. He also acknowledged that the lack of candour regarding quotas was unfortunate as it created considerable controversy and mistrust and that assigning quotas had been the most difficult and divisive task of the conference.[11]

Developing countries have long complained about the quota formulas and asked that they be revised. At their insistence, the Interim Committee stated, in its September 1997 press communiqué, 'that the formulas used to calculate quotas be reviewed by the Board promptly after the completion of the eleventh quota review'. In 1999, the Fund commissioned a quota formula review to a group of outside experts chaired by Richard Cooper.

The group produced a valuable report suggesting a reduction in the number of formulas to one, reducing the variables in the formula to three— GDP valued at market exchange rate as a measure of capacity to contribute and variability of external current receipts and long-term capital flows as measures of potential need of Fund resources, attributing to GDP twice the weight of all other variables.[12]

However, the formula proposed in the Cooper report produced an undesirable quota distribution, as it would increase the aggregate calculated quota share of G-7 countries to 59 per cent, compared to an aggregate calculated quota of 54 per cent according to the current formulas and an aggregate actual quota share of 47 per cent. At the same time, the aggregate calculated quota share of developing countries would increase only marginally in relation to the calculated quotas produced by the current formulas, but would still remain below their aggregate actual quota share. Given such an outcome, the Cooper report did not command support. However, this result was mainly due to the fact that the report looked at only one instrument—quotas—as required by its terms of reference, and adopted an inappropriate specification for GDP, valued at market exchange rates. If the proposals in the report are combined, for instance, with a simultaneous increase in basic votes, or with a specification for GDP valued at PPP exchange rates, or a variant of it, the aggregate gain of industrial countries would disappear or be smaller. Therefore, the Cooper report still represents a valuable input on which to build.

The current five formulas are based on six variables—the last observation for GNP at current prices converted at market exchange rate; a 12-month average of official reserves; a 5-year average for current external receipts; a 5-year average for current external payments; variability of external current receipts measured over a 13-year period; the GDP/export ratio. The weights attributed to these variables vary in each of the five formulas.

There are a number of problems with this choice of variables. The inclusion of current external receipts and the GDP/export ratio as measures of capacity to contribute is the main inadequacy. While GDP is a measure of value added, current external receipts is a gross variable, which involves double counting. The problem is greatest with respect to members of a monetary union or *entrepôt* states that engage in vast amounts of imports and exports, with the same goods crossing borders several times in different stages of production. The report estimated that in the case of EMU members, quotas would fall by about 9 percentage points if intra-union trade were excluded. The argument that external current payments indicate the extent to which GDP can be used to meet external obligations is dubious, as what would count here is value added in the tradable sector.

Ideally, the quota formula should contain only a few economic variables that are closely related to the functions that quotas should perform. I would suggest no more than three variables. GDP should be the most important one. It is a comprehensive measure of the capacity to contribute. It is also a measure of potential need for Fund resources and a good criterion to determine voting power in a financial institution. As a measure of vulnerability and, therefore, of potential need for Fund resources, a proxy could be the variability of the current account. This variable would capture different types of shocks that member countries may be exposed to, such as a fall in export values or volumes, or a fall in capital flows leading to compression of imports. International reserves could also be a variable included. Reserves have traditionally played an important role in Fund quotas and are an essential element of the external position of many countries.

An issue that is important for developing countries is how GDP would be valued. Market exchange rates that are currently used underestimate the contribution of non-tradable sectors of developing countries. Even with respect to tradable sectors, market exchange rates may not fully equalize prices across countries even after allowances are made for the costs of transportation and differences in quality. A better alternative would be to use PPP exchange rates, which are already extensively used by the Fund in several reports such as the *World Economic Outlook*. Calculations of GDP at PPP exchange rates are available for 176 countries.

A political problem with the use of PPP exchange rate would be that it would change dramatically the ranking of quota shares of important countries. China, for instance, would become the second largest IMF shareholder, overtaking Japan. One solution to this, proposed by Buira (2002) and by Kelkar, Chaudhry and Vanduzer-Snow (2005), would be to use some agreed combination of PPP and market exchange rate.

With respect to weights, as GDP is the most important variable, it should have a weight that is more than half the total weight. In the 1960s, in order to circumvent the difficulties in reaching consensus on weights, multiple quota formulas were introduced. All formulas are based on the same variables, but in each formula the weights are different. The practice of multiple formulas should be abandoned. This is a non-transparent way of assigning weights. With multiple formulas, the same variable would receive different weights and each member would choose the one that it is more favourable. Normalizing individual quota shares through averaging to sum to100 per cent has the effect of delinking the chosen economic variables from the quota distribution.

The creation of a new, single, simpler and more transparent quota formula, with fewer variables more directly related to the functions of quotas and giving greater weight to GDP, would increase the *calculated* quotas of large member countries, industrial countries and emerging markets alike, at the expense of small countries. However, the introduction of some weighted average of market and PPP exchange rates to value GDP would moderate the increase in calculated quotas of large industrial countries and boost the increase in calculated quotas of large emerging markets. It would also cause most of this adjustment to fall on small European industrial countries rather than small developing countries. This change in the quota formula would require a simple majority and should be the first step in the strategy.

The second step, which would require an 85 per cent majority, could be an *ad hoc* selective quota increase for countries whose quota shares are most out of line with the new formula. This would probably increase the aggregate *actual* quota share of developing countries by some 5 percentage points. It would also increase the actual quota shares of large industrial countries, but probably by a smaller amount.

The third step, which would also require an 85 per cent majority and an amendment of the Articles, should be an increase in basic votes to a higher proportion of the total voting power than the current 2 per cent. This would have the effect of diminishing the voting shares of large member countries, industrial and emerging countries alike, that is, all countries whose individual quota shares are higher than the average. As there are more small developing countries than small industrial countries, the end result would be an increase in the aggregate voting share of developing countries. Increasing the proportion of basic votes to, for instance, 6 per cent of the total voting power would represent an increase in the aggregate voting power of developing countries by some 2 percentage points.

The combination of an *ad hoc* quota increase for emerging markets based on a new formula with an increase in basic votes could generate an increase in the aggregate voting power of developing countries of around 7 percentage points, while correcting distortions in individual quota shares of the countries most out of line.

Making the Selection Process of the Managing Director more Transparent and Inclusive

The Managing Director is the Chairman of the Executive Board and the Chief Operating Officer of the Fund, conducting the ordinary business of the Fund under the direction of the Executive Board. While having a vote only in the unlikely event of a tie, the Managing Director exercises a large influence on the decision-making process, given the nature, considerable authority and prestige of the office. The main source of influence of the Managing Director is a direct command over the staff. Usually, all issues discussed by the Executive Board are based on written proposals presented in papers prepared by the staff which are previously approved by the Managing Director or one of the three Deputy Managing Directors who assist the Managing Director.

The informal agreement between the United States and Western Europe, whereby the latter chooses the Managing Director of the IMF while the former appoints the President of the World Bank, restricts the effective participation of other member countries in these important choices. This arrangement has been increasingly challenged by the excluded member countries and would eventually have to change.

On the occasion of the succession of Michel Camdessus, Executive Director members of the G-11, a country group representing the developing countries, took the unprecedented step of publicly proposing three criteria that should be adopted in the selection process—the process should aim to choose the best person for the job, irrespective of nationality, with a plurality of candidates from all regions being in the best interest of the institution; all Executive Directors should be informed in a timely manner about the candidates and their credentials; all Executive Directors should be consulted in the process of selecting a candidate.

The wide dissatisfaction with the existing closed and non-transparent selection process led to the formation of a Joint Working Group of Fund and Bank Executive Directors to propose better procedures for the selection process. The group presented a report that was endorsed by the Executive Board in 2001, although such endorsement did not constitute a formal decision adopting the specific recommendations. The report proposed that once a vacancy occurs, Executive Directors decide on the required qualifications of the candidates, establish a small advisory group to assist in the selection and decide on the key steps and procedures of the selection process. The advisory group would be formed by eminent persons familiar with the Fund and would have a balanced geographical representation. The Dean—the longest serving Executive Director—would be an observer in the advisory group and act as the liaison with the Executive Board. The advisory group could hire external expertise for the search. The advisory group would review all candidates and provide strictly confidential assessments to the Executive Board without ranking the candidates. The Executive Directors would agree on a shortlist, establish a deadline for candidacies and decide on the modalities to publicize the final shortlist. The final stage would be the formal selection of the Managing Director from the shortlist of candidates.

Due to the sudden departure of Kohler, Executive Directors agreed not to apply the idea of forming an advisory search group for his succession. However, the support for the thrust of the Joint Report was maintained by a large number of Executive Directors. This included the principles that had been suggested earlier by the G-11 Executive Directors, which had been incorporated in the report. A group of Directors including the G-11 Executive Directors plus the Executive Directors representing Australia, Russia and Switzerland expressed public support to those principles. Therefore, the process proposed by the working group, while yet not tested, seems still to offer the best prospects for making the selection of the Managing Director more open to greater participation of all member countries. Thus, the objective should be to implement the process proposed in the Joint Report in the next succession, i.e. when the incumbent Managing Director decides that he will not run for re-election. As the joint nature of the report indicates, any decision in the Fund would have repercussions at the World Bank.

Preserving and Strengthening Consensus Decision-making

The adoption of decisions in the IMF, in addition to formal voting power, is influenced by an informal tradition of *consensus decision-making*. The IMF procedural rules require that the chairman normally ascertains the sense of the meeting rather than placing the issue to the vote. While the sense of the meeting is understood to be the position that, if put to vote, would carry the required majority, an effort is normally made to avoid a narrow simple majority. Thus, while consensus in the sense adopted in the Fund would not require unanimity, it is generally understood that it means a large majority and the absence of explicit, significant and strong dissent. There is an elaborate counting system for gauging support to positions in terms of numbers of Executive Directors rather than voting power, which is normally used to indicate support for specified positions, although on occasion, the summing up of the meeting[13] refers to a majority of Executive Directors. When major disagreements emerge in the discussion of a policy topic, the chairman would try, either in the same or in subsequent meetings, to suggest orally or in additional staff papers, possible avenues for a reconciliation of positions and would encourage further consideration of the topic. Additional papers would be prepared and further meetings would be held until a broad consensus emerges. In addition to the chairman, the Dean usually also plays an important constructive role in consensus building, seeking to suggest alternatives to generate a convergence of views.

The consensus building approach is used mainly for policy decisions. The discussions on bilateral and multilateral surveillance, where no decision is taken, involve no attempts at consensus building. With respect to loan decisions, the proposals presented by the Managing Director are generally accepted.[14] The potential rejection of a proposed loan is internalized by the staff and management so that only loans that have an almost 100 per cent probability of being approved are actually brought to the Executive Board. In practice, the power of the Board of rejecting a loan is exercised *ex ante*. In order to avoid problems and not to pre-empt the Executive Board's powers, informal consultations with the Executive Board are now conducted prior to the negotiations being finalized for loans that involve what is considered an exceptionally large access (more than 100 per cent of quota annually or 300 per cent of quota on a cumulative basis). In addition, in large or contentious cases, management undertakes even earlier informal consultations with the G-7 countries.

The consensus decision-making approach to the adoption of policy decisions has important advantages both for industrial countries and developing countries, as well as for the Fund as an institution. For developing countries, which have a minority voting position, the consensus decision-making approach may yield a voice that is larger than their share of votes and a possibility of having greater influence in policy decisions. This, of course, depends critically on having able Executive Directors who have solid technical expertise, strong ability for oral debate, high powers of persuasion and diplomatic skills.

For industrial countries, consensus decision-making helps to preserve the system of weighted voting that distinguishes the IMF from other international organizations, by making such a system more acceptable to debtor countries. Moreover, as it is applied mainly to policy decisions, it does not disenfranchise the voting majority of industrial countries in the type of decisions that would matter most to them as creditors, namely the decisions on IMF loans.

For the institution as a whole, by increasing the legitimacy and acceptability of policy decisions, consensus decision-making has the advantage of increasing the likelihood that those decisions will be effectively implemented. This is very important since the IMF relies mainly on the cooperation of member countries to implement its decisions, especially those that are not associated with lending. While the consensus decision-making approach is more time consuming and requires more effort up front, it may lead to better decisions. It forces Executive Directors to better argue and justify their positions in terms of the substance of the case rather than voting power. Executive Directors have to articulate the rationale of their positions and to respond to those Directors that counter-argue or present different ideas. This strengthens the power of ideas and contributes to every angle of a problem receiving appropriate scrutiny and attention, ultimately leading to better decisions. It may also act as an incentive for all member countries to appoint or elect able representatives to the position of Executive Directors, thus strengthening the status and the quality of the Executive Board.

A few commentators have proposed abolishing the consensus decision-making approach on the grounds that consensus and compromise are inimical to accountability. The idea is that forcing Directors to take formal votes to make clear their positions would increase accountability.[15] I disagree that consensus and compromise are inimical to accountability. As argued above, consensus decision-making forces participants to make explicit their arguments. As long as all discussions are registered in the Board minutes, there should be no loss of accountability. On the contrary, forcing Directors to justify their positions could help strengthen accountability. Moreover, the approach applies mainly to policy decisions. With respect to lending decisions, Executive Directors occasionally register their dissenting position by abstaining, with the abstentions being registered in the summing up and in the minutes.

The consensus decision-making approach rests solely on tradition and seems to have experienced some erosion in recent times. The reasons for such erosion are unclear. However, several factors may be at work—the disposition to compromise by member governments and Executive Directors may have decreased; the disposition of the chair of the Board to spend the additional time and to undertake the additional work required by consensus decision-making may have diminished; and the tendency of countries to pre-establish inflexible positions within country groupings to exercise a voting majority may have increased. Given that no member country commands a majority alone and considering that the behaviour of the chair, in the end, would conform to the majority, it seems that, out of these factors, the operation of country groupings is the most important one.

Indeed, the functioning of informal country groupings is a major factor in the Fund's decision-making process. There are a number of informal country groupings operating in the IMF, such as the G-7, G-10, G-11, G-20, G-24 and regional caucuses such as the EURIMF and Asian Pacific Group. Country groups are an inevitable reality in the global economy, which goes beyond the IMF. They may be helpful coordinating devices and could contribute to generate consensus around initial positions amongst their members. However, depending on how they function, country groupings may detract from consensus decision-making. If initial positions are non-negotiable and used solely to exercise inflexible majorities, there are the risks that issues would not be analysed on their own merits except inside the groups and that the decision-making becomes more confrontational and polarized. The actions of country groupings should be conducted in a way that does not undermine objective decision-making based on merit of individual cases and preserves the role of the Executive Board.

As mentioned earlier, the way the G-7 operates in some instances creates difficulties to consensus decision-making. The G-7 Finance Ministers regularly adopt and publicize decisions for common positions with respect to initiatives to be introduced in the IMF that are later pushed on the entire IMF membership without enough opportunity for compromise. The G-7 actions set the dynamics for the behaviour of both other country groupings and management. The country groups of developing countries (the G-11 and the G-24) have the incentive to act similarly, but in practice they can do this only in order to take defensive action. Similarly, in order to avoid defeats or embarrassment in Board meetings, management consults informally with G-7 Executive Directors prior to bringing proposals to the Executive Board and prior to undertaking similar informal consultations with the other Executive Directors, who are often not consulted at all prior to the Board meetings, which detracts from good governance.

It is important for all Executive Directors, the Managing Director and the Deputies to be more aware and appreciative of the long-term benefits of consensus decision-making and to make an effort to strengthen consensus decision-making on policy decisions. There is also merit in going somewhat beyond attitudes and trying to achieve greater institutionalization of the tradition of consensus decision-making.

The IMF procedural rules could be amended to instruct the chairman to avoid narrow majorities with respect to policy decisions. In policy decisions, whenever there is a divergence between the majority of voting power and the majority of the number of Executive Directors, and the majority of voting power is a narrow one, the chairman should be required to postpone the decision once in order to try to reach consensus. The chairman and the Dean should be formally given the task of actively seeking to generate consensus during this period. The summing up should avoid using language referring to majority and should generally stick to the methods of indicating support in terms of the number of Executive Directors. These are modest proposals to institutionalize what, in practice, used to happen. If a policy topic is decided by majority voting rather than consensus, then the minutes of the Board meeting and the voting results identifying the positions of each Director could be publicized soon after the decision.

Finally, when there are informal consultations between management and informal groupings of Executive Directors with respect to policy initiatives, there should be a procedural rule instructing the Managing Director to hold similar meetings with all other Board members to ensure that there is no asymmetry of information amongst Executive Directors. *The procedural rules proposed here would apply only to policy initiatives and not to lending decisions*, with respect to which publication of minutes with divergent views could unsettle markets and rigid rules with respect to informal communications could complicate negotiations.

Improving the Constituency System

An important feature of the IMF's organizational structure is the *constituency system*. A constituency is a group of countries that join to elect an Executive Director. The elected Executive Director represents the constituent countries' interests in the Fund and casts these countries' votes as a unit in Executive Board decisions.

Constituencies may be based on informal arrangements or on a written agreement amongst the participating countries. The understandings to form a constituency usually establish the commitment of member countries to vote for a single candidate for Executive Director, the rotation schedule amongst member countries to nominate the candidate for Executive Director and the rotation schedule for the distribution of the positions of Alternate Executive Director, Senior Advisors and Advisors within the office of the Executive Director. The constituencies usually meet regularly, normally twice a year prior to the spring and Annual Meetings, to decide common positions on topics under discussion on the Fund's agenda and other matters of interest to member countries. In addition, there is usually permanent dialogue and consultation between the Executive Director and the members of a constituency, who are regularly canvassed in advance regarding major policy topics to be discussed in the Executive Board.

There are 16 Executive Directors who represent constituencies and eight Executive Directors who represent single countries. The latter are the five Directors appointed by the countries with the largest quotas (United States, Japan, Germany, France and UK) and three Executive Directors elected by single countries, which have sufficiently large quotas and prefer to elect alone an Executive Director (Saudi Arabia, China and Russia). Of the 16 constituencies, there are seven that mix industrial countries, emerging markets, transition economies and developing countries (headed by Belgium, Netherlands, Canada, Italy, a Nordic European country which is currently Sweden, Australia or Korea and Switzerland) and nine that are composed mainly of emerging markets and developing countries (Mexico or Venezuela or Spain, Tanzania, Malaysia or Indonesia, Egypt, Brazil, India, Iran, Argentina or Chile or Peru, Equatorial Guinea).[16]

A number of issues, however, have been raised with respect to the constituency system and surely there is room for improving its efficiency in representing member countries.[17] Do multi-country constituencies that mix industrial countries, transition economies and developing countries manage to adequately reflect the views of all of them, or would more homogeneous constituencies improve representation? Do constituencies where there is a dominant country offer proper representation for the smaller members? Is there an ideal size of a constituency in terms of number of countries in order to maintain efficiency and appropriate representation? Should the number of elected Executive Directors be increased further so as to give more representation to developing countries and transition economies and to reduce the size of constituencies that seem too large? How can Executive Directors elected by multi-country constituencies be made more accountable to their constituents? How to ensure that the voices of all members of a constituency are heard? What can be done further to strengthen the operational capacity and effectiveness of multi-country constituencies?

There are diverging views regarding the role of mixed multi-country constituencies. Some point out to the fact that, by having to represent both types of countries and having first hand experience with problems of debtor countries, some mixed multi-country constituencies function as a middle ground between industrial countries and developing countries and therefore, strengthen consensus building.[18] Developing countries participating in mixed constituencies may succeed in leveraging the voting power of the dominant country to support their positions. Examples are the positions taken by the chair headed by Belgium on the issue of the financial structure of the Fund, by the chair headed by the Netherlands on the topic of streamlining conditionality and by Switzerland and Australia on the question of the election of the Managing Director. Others stress that often, some mixed constituencies tend to adopt positions akin to those of industrial countries and that developing countries and transition economies that are members of those constituencies would be better served if they were part of a more homogeneous constituency.[19] There are elements of truth in both arguments and it is difficult to decide which one should receive the greatest weight. Possibly the only solution would be to let the countries that belong to mixed constituencies decide for themselves. But for that choice to be viable, it would be necessary to create conditions so that those countries can appoint representatives with the same level of seniority and for the same length of time in a more homogeneous constituency as they currently are able to do in mixed constituencies.

Emerging markets, developing countries and transition economies that belong to mixed constituencies account for an aggregate voting share of 6.9 per cent. As the Articles of Agreement require that an Executive Director casts as a unit all votes that elected them, these votes would generally go to the industrial countries camp, if it is true that mixed constituencies tend to align more often than not with those countries' positions. In that case, if developing countries and transition economies that belong to mixed constituencies were to form new constituencies or to move to constituencies whose Executive Directors come from developing countries, this would increase the voting strength of the group of developing countries in the Executive Board by 6.9 percentage points.

A related issue is whether constituencies having a dominant country allow for proper representation of the smaller countries. There are some multi-country constituencies representing developing countries, such as those chaired by Brazil, Egypt, Iran and India, where the Executive Directors always come from these dominant countries.[20] Like in the previous paragraph, again this is a question that is difficult to answer. This, however, is a problem of a different nature from the one raised by mixed constituencies and it would require a different solution. While most mixed constituencies also tend to be dominated by a single country electing the Executive Director, the main difference is that developing countries' constituencies dominated by a single country are homogeneous constituencies where the interests of all members tend to be naturally aligned. All countries share similar socio-economic conditions, normally have closer cultural traditions and belong to the same geographical area, although there might still be differences such as large and small countries, oil producer and oil consumer. However, if the smaller countries in a homogeneous multi-country constituency where there is a dominant country are not adequately represented, it seems more likely that the issue would be more one of an inadequate job performed by the Executive Director than a structural problem of conflicting interests amongst the constituency members. The solution to this problem, to the extent that it exists, would then also have to be different. Rather than redesigning the constituency itself, the case would be to have better mechanisms to hold the Executive Director accountable.

A third topic related to the composition of constituencies is that the two multi-country constituencies representing African countries are too large with 21 and 24 countries each, whereas the average size of multi-country constituencies is 11 members. This increases the burden of the Executive Director, especially because most of the countries are engaged in long term borrowing relationships with the Fund, which are quite demanding in terms of work. The simplest way to begin tackling this issue is to increase the human and material resources available to these constituencies, which has already been done, but this alone may not be sufficient.

The issues posed by constituencies that are too large and by mixed constituencies raise the question of whether the size or composition of the Executive Board or the distribution of countries amongst constituencies should be changed. These are complex and difficult questions to tackle. The organization of constituencies has been appropriately left mostly to the political decisions of member countries and there are only a few rules in the Articles of Agreement that impact the formation or operation of constituencies. The composition of constituencies has varied considerably in the history of IMF with several instances of countries changing constituencies.[21]

There are two rules that affect the formation of constituencies. First, the minimum and maximum shares of votes that each elected Executive Director should receive that are set in the Articles at 4 and 9 per cent of total votes respectively. These proportions may be changed for each election by the Board of Governors. The other rule governs the total number of elected Executive Directors, set in the Articles of Agreement at 15, a number that the Board of Governors may also increase or reduce by an 85 per cent majority and which since 1992, has been set at 19 Directors.

The number and composition of multi-country constituencies is a function of the above rules, as well as of the distribution of voting power amongst the countries that elect Executive Directors, of the number of positions available in the offices of Executive Directors to be shared amongst participating countries and of geographical and cultural factors. Probably the provision of financial development assistance and technical assistance by industrial countries to small developing countries may also exercise an influence in the composition of constituencies. Moreover, there might be rigidities in the form of written long-term constituency agreements, whereby countries agree to participate in a given constituency for a certain period of time.

It seems that the current distribution of countries amongst constituencies represents an equilibrium given the above rules, constraints and preferences of member countries. A change in those variables, for instance an increase in the number of elected Executive Directors, would certainly affect the current distribution. However, given the large number of variables and the complex interplay amongst these variables, a change in one variable alone may affect the distribution in an unpredicted way and not necessarily lead to the result that the proponents of such change might have in mind.

There has been, for instance, a suggestion to create a 25th chair in the Executive Board to allow one additional Executive Director to be elected by African countries with the formation of a new constituency, given the large number of members of the two sub-Saharan African constituencies. Moving of some of these countries to the constituency chaired by Egypt would not solve the problem, as that constituency already encompasses 14 members. Giving Africa a fourth chair in the Executive Board would certainly increase and make the representation of that continent more efficient. Moreover, an additional chair for Africa would lead to a majority in the number of Executive Directors from developing countries, while industrial countries would still retain a majority of the voting power.

However, a mere increase in the number of Executive Directors, without any change in voting power, would not necessarily guarantee the outcome of giving Africa one more chair. The additional chair could, for instance, end up going to the European transition economies that are currently members of mixed constituencies. These transition economies together hold around 4.5 per cent of the voting power, an aggregate voting share similar to that of the two sub-Saharan African constituencies. It seems plausible and justifiable that some of the transition economy countries could try to join to elect an Executive Director of their own if an additional chair is created. Many of these countries are also users or potential users of Fund resources and the case could be made that their representation would improve if, instead of being part of a mixed constituency, they would form a constituency of their own. The influence in the Executive Board of the group of debtor countries and potential users of Fund resources would be equally increased in this way. A similar situation could develop with respect to Asian countries that currently belong to a mixed constituency. This indicates that any increase in the size of the Executive Board has to be part of a larger and carefully negotiated package of reforms that would also alter quotas and increase basic votes.

In addition, consideration should be given to the issue of whether it is desirable, from the point of view of efficiency of decision-making, to further increase the size of the Executive Board. As a result of the increase in the number of members from 45 to 184 countries, the Executive Board has doubled in size since the creation of the IMF. The original number of 12 Executive Directors had increased to 20 by 1964. In 1978, it was increased to 21 Directors to allow Saudi Arabia alone to elect an Executive Director, given that the Saudi riyal was one of the two currencies most used by the Fund in the two preceding years. In 1981, another increase to 22 Directors was done to allow the People's Republic of China to elect an Executive Director. The increase to the current size of 24 Directors was a result of the breakdown of the former Soviet Union and of Russia, other transition economies, as well as Switzerland joining the Fund in the period 1990–92.

If it were feasible, rather than further increasing the size of the Board, a preferable alternative would certainly be an amalgamation of some chairs currently occupied by Executive Directors representing Western Europe, especially members of the European Monetary Union, in order to open space for an additional chair for Africa and another one for the European transition economies.

In addition to the questions of the size and composition of the Executive Board and the distribution of countries amongst constituencies, there are also the issues of how to make all constituencies more efficient in representing the interests of member countries and how to make elected Executive Directors more accountable to their constituencies.

The efficiency of constituencies depends on the amount and quality of the human and material resources that are available to them as well as on the working routines that they follow. The personal qualifications of Executive Directors, Alternates, Senior Advisors and Advisors are one of the most important factors. The Board has already agreed on job descriptions and minimum qualifications for the positions of Senior Advisors and Advisors to be used in a voluntary way as guidance by countries appointing candidates to those positions.

Training is already provided by the Fund to Senior Advisors and Advisors. One area, however, where improvements could be considered is to strengthen the capacity to deal with Fund issues in the capitals of developing countries. Support from capitals is an advantage that is enjoyed by the chairs representing industrial countries. A technical assistance program could be considered to help establish in the Ministries of Finance and Central Banks small units to deal with Fund issues that would offer support to the offices of Executive Directors. Where those units already exist, on the job training could be provided for the staff of those units, who could come to Washington for a short period of time to work temporarily in the offices of Executive Directors, attend a few Board meetings and undertake specially tailored training programs in the IMF Institute.

With respect to best working practices, an effort has already been done to obtain information on how EDs' offices are organized and how they operate in order to identify working procedures that might be of interest to other offices. This effort could be deepened.

Regarding the accountability of Executive Directors, some proposals have already been presented in the first section of this article. In addition, the Secretary could compute and publicize regularly, statistical information relating to the amount of work produced by all EDs' offices. Moreover, the minutes of the Executive Board could be made available immediately to member countries regarding the interventions and statements of their own Executive Director.

Turning the IMF into the Main Forum for International Macroeconomic Policy Coordination

One of the main functions of the IMF is to promote international cooperation on monetary and financial affairs, being the machinery for consultation and collaboration on these issues. However, of all IMF functions, this is the one that is least developed. This function is currently performed by means of exercises of multilateral surveillance of global economic and financial conditions. Two major reports are prepared twice a year for that purpose, the *World Economic Outlook* and the *Global Financial Stability Report*. These reports are discussed by the Executive Board and later taken up by the IMFC, both of which make generic exhortations to certain countries or group of countries to pursue policies that are considered appropriate from their own perspective, but that are also required from a global point of view. There is, however, a clear need to enhance the effectiveness of multilateral surveillance.

In addition to the Executive Board, the main forum where these exercises of multilateral surveillance take place is the IMFC. The IMFC is composed of 24 members, usually Finance Ministers or Central Bank Governors, appointed by the countries or group of countries that appoint or elect an Executive Director. It was created in 1999 as the successor to the Interim Committee. The Interim Committee was established in 1974 with a mandate to oversee the management and adaptation of the international monetary system and was part of the reforms to deal with the breakdown of the Bretton Woods system of fixed but adjustable exchange rates and use of capital controls. The IMFC is an advisory body to the Board of Governors and works in close relation with the Executive Board, discussing and expressing opinions on issues that have already been discussed by the Executive Board and suggesting new topics to be examined by the Executive Board and to be later brought up for discussion in the IMFC.

Like its predecessor, at best the IMFC has a mixed record in promoting international cooperation in economic, monetary and financial issues. In the late 1970s and early 1980s, the Interim Committee was not successful in convincing industrial countries to pursue fiscal discipline, to reduce inflation and to adjust exchange rate to reflect their fundamentals. Similarly, nowadays, the IMFC does not seem effective either in promoting a sufficiently high level of international cooperation that would lead to faster fiscal consolidation in the United States, greater exchange rate flexibility in Asia and the adoption of bolder structural reforms in Europe and Japan in order to increase their potential rate of growth.

The functions of the IMFC are those of cooperation, that is, exchange of information, consultation, mutual encouragement, collective exhortation and generic pledging to certain policies. The IMFC does not play any role in international macroeconomic policy coordination, i.e. in countries collectively agreeing, implementing and monitoring, in an even-handed manner, changes in their domestic policies that due to economic interdependence they believe would be beneficial to all of them. Given the high and rising levels of globalization of production, trade and finances, it seems that international policy coordination could yield a superior outcome than either simple cooperation, or policy independence, where each country pursues totally independent policies and takes the policies of other countries as given. While the IMFC does not have an explicit mandate for policy coordination, like the Interim Committee, it is entrusted with overseeing the management and the adaptation of the international monetary system, which creates the leeway for the exercise of policy coordination.

One question is whether the reason why the Interim Committee and the IMFC were not able to play that role is associated with the fact that neither body had any legal powers or instruments to discharge their functions.

The Second Amendment to the Articles of Agreement approved in 1978 in the wake of the collapse of the Bretton Woods system established a Council with a composition similar to the IMFC. The Council would have three main functions—to supervise the management and adaptation of the international monetary system, including the adjustment process; supervise developments in global liquidity; and review developments in the real transfer of resources to developing countries. It would also consider proposals to amend the Articles of Agreement and to issue Special Drawing Rights. The Council would be an intermediary body between the Board of Governors and the Executive Board. One important difference between the Council and the Executive Board is that Councillors may separately cast the votes of each country that elected them. The Council has never become operational, as this requires the vote of an 85 per cent majority of the Board of Governors, which has never happened.

After the financial crises of the 1990s, there were several proposals to create a body of political oversight of the international monetary system, including the French proposal to activate the Council.[22] However, none of the proposals gained sufficient support.

On the one hand, the largest Fund shareholders did not seem enthusiastic in activating the Council. On the other hand, developing countries were afraid of the effect of the Council in overriding decisions of the Executive Board and were fearful that Ministers from industrial countries would not have either the inclination or the patience to engage in consensus building. But above all, given the poor record with the Interim Committee, developing countries were not convinced of the positive gains that could emerge from the operation of the Council in terms of a firmer management of the international monetary system and the adjustment process of the various countries. Hence, the final outcome was to transform the Interim Committee into the IMFC, keeping its nature of an advisory, not a decision-making, body.

While the Council would have legal power to take decisions on important topics, it is doubtful that simply adding an additional political layer would improve the possibilities for greater international policy coordina-tion if the attitudes and the commitment of the major industrial countries to international economic policy did not improve.

One of the main reasons why neither the Interim Committee nor the IMFC have been very successful is that, to the extent that international economic policy coordination has been occasionally exercised, the major industrial countries have kept this function closely for themselves in the G-7.[23] The Managing Director has been invited to present views on the international economy since the inception of the G-7, but without attending the part of the meeting destined for discussion and deliberation.

A possible approach would be to try to strengthen the type of international cooperation that currently takes place in the IMFC, upgrading it, on an experimental basis, to the higher echelon of policy coordination. For this, the IMF would have to alter somewhat the nature of the WEO, which would have to upgrade its policy implications component. The WEO could include a small but consistent, concrete, even-handed and monitorable set of policy actions to be taken by the major players in the global economy, including both the G-7 and major emerging market countries. In proposing a global action program, it would be critical that the IMF exercise even-handedness amongst countries and good judgment on the feasibility of the proposed actions, given the existing constraints. The overall purpose should be to define and agree on domestic policy actions required to increase global growth in a sustainable fashion while maintaining price stability and to strengthen international financial stability. Hence, only policy actions that have a discernible, medium term international impact for these objectives would be included.

The action program would be discussed in the Executive Board in a cooperative fashion and modified as appropriate, based on the countries' indications on whether or not they would be able to commit. Based on this discussion, the proposal would be revised as appropriate and recommendations on policy actions would then be made to the IMFC. The final decision on the actions to be adopted would be taken by broad consensus in which the consent of each country concerned with respect to actions to be taken by it would be required. While the implementation period could be longer than a year, say three years, monitoring of implementation would take place at each IMFC meeting, based on assessments by the IMF.

Conclusion

This paper has described the main deficiencies and areas for improvements in the governance structure of the IMF. Reform of international organizations is a difficult and complex undertaking that can only proceed in a balanced and often incremental fashion. There has to be a package of reforms encompassing some benefit for a substantial number of member countries, in order to make the reforms feasible. At the same time, while the reform process is by nature incremental, there may be value in discussing bold proposals that initially look ambitious and unfeasible in order to raise public debate and to allow such proposals to be later refined into a feasible and balanced package of reforms. This is the approach taken in this paper where several proposals would require an 85 per cent majority of the IMF voting power and may currently appear farfetched.

The proposed agenda by this paper has emphasized on *strengthening the autonomy, accountability and effectiveness of the Executive Board*, through an explicit provision in the Articles of Agreement requiring that, in discharging their functions, Executive Directors appropriately balance the international purposes of the IMF with the objectives of the countries that they represent. In addition, to increase the two-year term for elected Executive Directors. In the case of *increasing the aggregate voting power of developing countries,* this proposal needs to respect three constraints — to maintain the majority of voting power in the hands of industrial countries; not to endanger the current veto power held by the United States; and to benefit a large number of developing countries. There could be an objective, for instance, to increase the aggregate voting power of developing countries from the current 40 per cent to 45–47 per cent. The strategy for achieving a greater voting share for developing countries in the Fund would have to combine three instruments to muster sufficient support within the group — a new, simplified, single quota formula; *ad hoc* selective quota increases for emerging markets whose actual quotas are most out-of-line according to the new formula; and an increase in basic votes.

Another important issue in the governance of the IMF *is making the selection process of the Managing Director more transparent and inclusive.* In *preserving and strengthening consensus decision-making,* the difficulties in this area centres around the way the G-7 operates in some instances, creating difficulties to consensus decision-making. The G-7 actions set the dynamics for the behaviour of both other country groupings and management. The country groups of developing countries (the G-11 and the G-24) have the incentive to act similarly, but in practice, they can do this only in order to take defensive action. The IMF procedural rules could be amended to instruct the chairman to avoid narrow majorities with respect to policy decisions. In the section on improving the constituency system, the proposal is to create a twenty-fifth chair in the Executive Board to allow one additional Executive Director to be elected by African countries with the formation of a new constituency, given the large number of members of the two sub-Saharan African constituencies. Giving Africa a fourth chair in the Executive Board would certainly increase and make the representation of that continent more efficient. Moreover, an additional chair for Africa would lead to a majority in the number of Executive Directors from developing countries, while industrial countries would still retain a majority of the voting power. However, a mere increase in the number of Executive Directors, without any change in voting power, would not necessarily guarantee the outcome of giving Africa one more chair.

The additional chair could, for instance, end up going to the European transition economies that are currently members of mixed constituencies. In addition, consideration should be given to the issue of whether it is desirable, from the point of view of efficiency of decision-making, to further increase the size of the Executive Board. If it were feasible, rather than further increasing the size of the Board, a preferable alternative would certainly be an amalgamation of some chairs currently occupied by Executive Directors representing Western Europe, especially members of the European Monetary Union, in order to open space for an additional chair for Africa and another one for the European transition economies.

Finally, it is important to *turn the IMF into the main forum for international macroeconomic policy coordination.* One of the main purposes of the IMF is to promote international cooperation on monetary and financial affairs, being the machinery for consultation and collaboration on these issues. However, of all IMF functions, this is the one that is least developed. There is, however, a clear need to enhance the effectiveness of multilateral surveillance.

Notes

1 Presented at the G-24 Technical Group Meeting, 2005, Manila, March 17–18. This paper has been prepared at the request of the Director of the G-24 Secretariat to be used to inform discussions in the group.

2 While I am Executive Director of the IMF, the views expressed here are completely personal and should in no way be attributed to the IMF, its Executive Board or any of the countries that I represent. I wish to thank Jacques Polak, Abbas Mirakhor, Willy Kiekens, Roberto Steiner, Alexandre Tombini and Charles de Silva who were extremely kind to devote their time to read a first draft and who made many valuable comments and suggestions to improve the text. They, however, should not be associated with the views expressed here and are in no way responsible for the mistakes and improprieties that remained in the text, all of which are my exclusive responsibility. I also thank Janice Bramson who helped me with proof reading.

3 There might be a small variation in the number of Directors who are nationals of developing countries due to the rotation schedules of some constituencies.

4 If Egypt is counted as an African rather than an Arabic country, the number of African chairs would be three and the Middle East would have two chairs. It should be mentioned the chair of Iran encompasses African countries as well, namely Algeria, Ghana, Tunisia and Morocco.

5 If this were not the case, the Articles of Agreement would have to be revised and amended.

6 A later section in this article deals in greater detail with the Council.

7 The references in this section to developing countries should be meant to include emerging market countries and transition economies as well.

8 Kelkar, Chaudhry and Vanduzer-Snow 2005, pp. 46–8.

9 This includes Russia and the Eastern European transition economies, but excludes Spain that forms a constituency with Mexico, Venezuela and other Latin American countries and Ireland that forms a constituency with Canada.

10 The sum does not add to 100 as certain countries have been suspended from their voting rights due to arrears and did not vote in the last election of Executive Directors.

11 Mikesell, 1994, pp. 22, 35, 38.

12 QFRG, 2000.

13 The summing up is the summary of the views expressed by Executive Directors and certain portions of it have the legal value of a Board decision.

14 However, there are abstentions sometimes, which on occasion may be large, such as in the loans for Mexico in 1995 and for Argentina in 2002.

15 See, for instance, Woods, 1998, pp. 88–91; de Gregorio, Eichengreen, Ito and Wyplosz, 1999; Bradlow, 2001.

16 The Directorship in the two sub-Saharan African constituencies currently with Tanzania and Equatorial Guinea rotate, with most members of the constituency participating in the rotation schedule.

17 See Woods and Lombardi, 2004.

18 van Houtven, 2002, pp. 21; de Larosière, 2004, pp. 29.

19 See Gerster, 1993, pp. 124; Woods and Lombardi, 2004, pp. 21–2.

20 While the dominance of Brazil and India appears to result from the fact that these countries have a voting majority within the constituency, this is not the case of Egypt and Iran.

21 See Woods and Lombardi, 2004, pp. 3.

22 For a summary of these proposals see de Gregorio, Eichengreen, Ito, and Wyplosz, 1999, pp. 95–104.

23 Since the creation of G-5 in 1985, soon transformed into the G-7, the group engaged in some intermittent experiences at international policy coordination, as in the second half of the 1980s, with the 1985 Plaza Agreement and the 1987 Louvre Accord, being the most well-known outcomes. A description of these efforts and the results may be found in Dodson, 1991.

References

Bradlaw, D, 2001, Stuffing new wine into old bottles: the troubling case of the IMF, *Journal of International Banking Regulations*, August, 3:1 pp. 9–36.

Buira, A, 2002, The Governance of the International Monetary Fund, *Providing Global Public Goods*, Kaul, Inge *et al.* (eds), Oxford: Oxford University Press.

Buira, A, 2003, The Governance of the IMF in a Global Economy, *Challenges to the World Bank and the IMF – Developing Countries Perspectives*, Buira, A (ed.) London: Anthem Press.

Dodson, W, 1991, *Economic Policy Coordination: Requiem or Prologue?*, Washington, DC: IIE.

de Gregorio, J, Eichengreen, B, Ito, T and Wyplosz, C, 1999, *An Independent and Accountable IMF*, Geneva, International Center for Monetary and Banking Studies.

de Larosière, J, 2004, How should the IMF be Reshaped?, *Finance and Development*, September.

Feldstein, M, 1998, Refocusing the IMF, in *Foreign Affairs*, March–April.

Gerster, R, 1993, Proposals for Voting Reform within the International Monetary Fund, *Journal of World Trade*, Vol. 27.

Kafka, A, 1996, Governance of the Fund, *The International Monetary and Financial System: Developing Countries Perspectives*, Helleiner, G (ed.) New York: Saint Martin's Press.

Kelkar VL, Chaudhry PK and Vanduzer-Snow M, 2005, Reforming the Governance of the International Monetary Fund, in, *Finance & Development*, Washington: March, 42:1, pp. 46–8.

Mikesell, R, 1994, The Bretton Woods Debates: a Memoir, *Essays in International Finance*, Department of Economics, Princeton University, March, no. 192.

Quota Formula Review Group, 2000, *Report to the IMF Executive Board of the Quota Formula Review Group*, Washington DC: IMF.

van Houtven, L, 2002, *Governance of the IMF*, Washington DC: IMF.

Woods, N, 1998, Governance in International Organizations: The Case for Reform In the Bretton Woods Institutions, *International Monetary and Financial Issues for the 1990s*, Geneva: UNCTAD, Vol. IX.

Woods, N, 2001, Making the IMF and the World Bank more accountable, *International Affairs* 77.1.

Woods, N and Lombardi, D, 2004, Effective representation and the role of coalitions within the IMF, www.globaleconomicgovernance.org

5

ISSUES ON IMF GOVERNANCE AND REPRESENTATION: AN EVALUATION OF ALTERNATIVE OPTIONS[1]

Guillermo Le Fort V[2]

Abstract:

The current realities of the global economy are far from being reflected in the Fund's quota structure, with EM economies accounting for the bulk of the under- representation. This paper explores the characteristics of the representation distortions using cross-section regression analysis and the results indicate that economic growth, population, credit rating and dummies for the United States and China explain most of them. To the extent that the faster growing countries are not recognized as such in their IMF quotas, the distortions will continue to increase. Eliminating such distortions requires adjusting the quota structure in line with the relative participation in global economic activity, but to the extent that individual quotas cannot be reduced, a large increase in total IMF quotas would be required. Simulations performed under the assumption that all over-represented advanced economies would accept to reduce their quotas indicate that only about one-half of the rate of increase in total quotas would be required. As an initial step towards the elimination of distortions in representation, rules for a professional IMF board are proposed, including that all Executive Directors (EDs) should be elected and be independent from the influence of a permanent employer, that all countries with a common currency be represented by the same ED and that each chair should represent at least three member countries and at most fifteen. In a scenario using these rules and attempting to preserve the existing regional representation, advanced economies would lose three chairs, emerging markets would gain two and developing countries would gain the remaining one.

Introduction

The IMF can be represented as an international organization that provides global public goods in the form of macroeconomic surveillance, support for adjustment programs and technical assistance for the design and implementation of economic and financial policies. Those services are particularly relevant for the EM economies and for developing countries that are particularly exposed to the volatility of global markets, either financial or commodities markets. These countries use the services provided by the IMF to recover from crisis events, or to improve their resiliency against external shocks.[3] The work of the Fund contributes to prevent crisis to the extent that surveillance helps to reduce global volatility and better prepare countries to confront external shocks and contagion. However, experience indicates that it is so in crisis management and recovery, where most of the Fund resources and all its financial facilities have been deployed.

The role of the Fund in the global economy has changed dramatically from its foundation more than 60 years ago, adapting to the changing global environment.[4] From an institution helping advanced economies to correct current account imbalances to an institution devoted to crisis management in EM economies and to support reform programs in low-income countries. The institutional role has changed, but what has not changed is the governance structure, which has yet to respond to the new realities of the global economy that implies different clients and different services. The efficient provision of the Fund services requires an appropriate governance structure, in which the preferences, views and concerns of member countries can be effectively represented. It is a governance problem that the main users of Fund services are under-represented in the decision-making bodies. With the voting power in the Fund decision-making bodies based on the quota structure, the failure to adapt such a structure to the changing world realities generate political problems as a result of distortions in representation.[5]

The distortions of the quota structure have been discussed and well documented.[6] Of the 12 quota revisions that have been completed during the Fund's 60 plus years of history, the Executive Board decided that a quota increase was warranted only in seven. On those seven occasions, the adjustment of individual country quotas was largely determined in proportion to the existing quotas rather than reflecting any formula representing each member country's participation in global economic activity. These quota adjustments have resulted in a steady reduction of the relative importance of the IMF resources relative to global economic activity and the preservation of the quota structure defined when the institution was founded in 1943. Even more, the significant enlargement in the Fund's membership that took place with the collapse of the Berlin Wall and of the socialist regimes was done as a way of preserving the existing quota structure. The incoming members were matched with member countries of comparable economic size and characteristics and given similar quotas sizes. All this has resulted in a quota structure that does not adequately represent the present global economic reality.

Going beyond the existence and quantification of the distortions in the Fund's quota structure, this paper attempts to better describe their characteristics using a simple statistical approach of multiple correlations. The variables that can be associated to the distortions help to understand its nature and the prospects for its evolution over time.

The representation of member countries in the decision-making at the IMF is no doubt a political problem that requires a political solution. However, the discussion could be greatly improved and the probability of success increased to the extent that rules and incentives are considered in shaping such solutions. In this regard, this paper attempts to explore possible solutions to the problems derived from the quota structure and the deficiencies in representation. First, simulations of alternative rules for adjusting individual quotas and eliminating the existing distortions in the structure of representation are attempted. Second, considering the difficulties in garnering the necessary support to modify the quota structure, possible solutions for the under-representation of developing countries and EM countries are analyzed by considering different rules for the conformation of jurisdictions at the Executive Board under the existing quota structure.

Distortions in Representation

In an institution with global membership like the Fund, where the decision-making has been determined not by one country – one vote but on the basis of the financial resources contributed by each country, the relative contributions (quotas) should be defined on the basis of objective rules. The quota formula discussed on numerous occasions by the IMF Executive Board is an effort to define such a standard, taking into consideration both the capacity to contribute resources and the eventual need for Fund credit represented by an ample set of variables and different relationships. Unfortunately, not much progress has been made in defining a consensus around a formula and major differences persist as each country tends to defend the definition of the quota formula more in line with its own interests, namely, the one that maximizes its relative quota position. In addition, the different variables included in the quota formula are very much correlated, so that they all contain similar information which is mainly related to the economic size of each member country.[7]

To simplify matters and to avoid entering into a discussion of quota formulas that would require another paper, the view taken in this article is that a single scale variable can be used to represent the relative importance of each member country in the global economy. This variable is the value of all final goods produced in each country every year, i.e. the Gross Domestic Product (GDP). The GDP in national currencies is readily available and there are no major controversies on its definition, apart from some methodological issues of interest only to specialists in the field. However, a different matter is the exchange rate used to convert the GDP in the national currency into an internationally comparable unit. If we want to measure income and purchasing power of a single country over time, then market exchange rates ought to be used to convert national GDP into a single globally comparable accounting unit like the SDR. Incidentally, to measure purchasing power in each country, instead of GDP the variable of choice would be National Income or GNP at market exchange rates. However, in the case of international comparisons across countries of economic activity or the generation of goods and services, the variable of interest is GDP converted at a globally comparable accounting unit using an exchange rate that maintains purchasing power parity (PPP). With PPP exchange rates, when goods and services are valued at comparable prices across countries, then GDP PPP is a measure of real economic activity that is comparable across member countries.

Moreover, GDP at market rates is quite volatile, as market exchange rates have a wide swing over time, while PPP exchange rates are more stable. The problem with PPP rates is related to their availability and the quality of the statistics. The PPP rates can change significantly when the price surveys in which the estimates are based are revised. A more frequent revision of the surveys would result in more reliable statistics. In any case, the IMF *World Economic Outlook* database present estimates of GDP PPP for almost all member countries and the paper uses the average GDP PPP over the period 2000–04.[8] Using GDP PPP, the current realities of the global economy are far from being reflected in the Fund's quota structure. There are significant deviations in the composition of GDP and quotas implying that the representation of the membership in the Fund's decision-making bodies presents important distortions. The degree of over-representation is defined as the difference between each member country quota share and its share of global GDP PPP. Of course the over-representation adds up to zero, but it varies widely from a maximum of 2.76 to a minimum of –9.55 (see Table 1). Advanced economies account for the bulk of the over-representation (9.32), although large advanced economies like the United States is underrepresented, EM countries account for the bulk of the under-representation (–12.56), while developing countries are in a more neutral position. Advanced economies were defined as those with sovereign debt rated in the first two grades (AAA and AA in Standard and Poor's denomination), EM countries were defined as those with sovereign debt rated in intermediate grades (between A and C in the same denomination), while developing countries were defined as those without access to international markets, they either have a credit rating of selective default (D) or have not been rated at all.[9]

The density of representation in the Executive Board is also an issue. In some cases more than 20 countries are represented by one ED, while in others, the ED represents only one country. In the multi-country constituencies, there could be differences of views, but in the end, it is the ED's opinion that will prevail. Consequently, at the level of the Executive Board, the distortions in representation can then be considered even more marked if the nationality of the Executive Director is used to judge the representation of each country group. Advanced economies control 63 per cent of the Board's voting power, while they represent only 53 per cent of global GDP PPP (see Table 2). EM

Table 1. Over-representation based on GDP PPP (in per cent)

	Developing	Emerging	Advanced	All
Total	3.24	−12.56	9.32	0.00
Average	0.039	−0.206	0.358	0.000
Max	0.577	2.761	1.822	2.761
Min	−0.248	−9.548	−3.946	−9.548
Std Dev	0.096	1.387	1.110	0.951
No. of countries	83	61	26	184

Source: IMF and author's calculations.

Table 2. Representation at the IMF Executive Board (In per cent)

	Share of voting power	Share of GDP PPP
Advanced Economies		
11 Executive Directors*	63.3	53.2
EM Economies		
10 Executive Directors**	30.3	42.0
Developing Countries		
3 Executive Directors***	6.4	4.8

* Including EDs from the US, Germany, France, UK, Italy, Japan, Norway, Belgium, Netherlands, Canada and Switzerland.
** Including EDs from Brazil, India, Indonesia, China, Russia, Iran, Egypt, Mexico, Korea, and Saudi Arabia.
*** Including EDs from Equatorial Guinea, Argentina, and Tanzania.
Source: IMF.

economies control 30 per cent of the Board's voting power while they represent 42 per cent of global GDP PPP. Finally, developing countries account for 6 per cent of the voting power and for 4.5 per cent of global GDP PPP, but developing countries can be considered as being in a rather neutral position.[10]

Explaining the Distortions

After growing faster than other groups, particularly advanced economies, and accumulating more international reserves, EM countries appear as the group more deeply affected by under-representation at the IMF decision-making bodies. However, representation distortions are a political problem and not just an issue of the country type. Some EM countries are over-represented and some advanced economies under-represented; consider Japan that has a quota similar to that of Germany, but has a much larger GDP. Consequently, other variables may play a role in explaining or characterizing this distortion. Therefore, to be able to better represent the general characteristics of the countries that are under- and over-represented, a wide set of potential explanatory variables are used in a cross-section multiple regression against the over-representation variable (OR). Naturally, there could not be any claim of a causal relationship from the explanatory variables to OR, or *vice versa*, or a theoretical model that can be used to define the explanatory variables. The idea is to use a pure statistical method to better characterize the existing over-representation through the variables with which OR is statistically associated in a multiple regression setting.

The explained variable, OR, is defined by the difference between each country share in the IMF quota and its share of GDP PPP. The set of explanatory variables includes regional factors (continent, dummies for specific countries), social factors (per capita income and population), financial factors (credit ratings, international reserves and Fund net asset position) and the country type (advanced, emerging and developing). The results of estimating the multiple regressions, presented in Table 3, basically indicate that altogether, the set of variables considered explain the bulk of the over-representation in the IMF quota structure. The overall goodness of fit measured by a corrected R-squared above 80 per cent is more than adequate for a large cross-section sample like the one used. As expected, other variables in addition to the country group are important to explain over-representation; in particular, average economic growth over the last 20 years appears to be a highly significant explanatory variable. The faster a country grows over the long-term, the lower is the OR variable, or the larger is its degree of under-representation. Thus, growth laggards tend to become over-represented and rapidly growing economies under-represented. In addition, population also appears to be an important factor of under-representation; the more populous countries tend to have a lower OR and this effect remains even when a specific dummy variable is introduced to account for the largest two under-represented countries, China and the United States. This may be just a chance result, but the fact is that the representation distortions of today weight against countries with a large population.

Financial variables like the position at the IMF and credit rating tend to be a factor for over-representation of more advanced economies. Net creditors

Table 3. Multiple regression for over-representation at the IMF

Dependent variable over-representation

Explanatory variables	Equation 1	Equation 2
Constant	0.8366	0.8119
	(0.002)	(0.000)
Growth	−0.031	−0.0318
	(0.057)	(0.023)
Emerging Market Countries	−0.2905	−0.2495
	(0.160)	(0.000)
Developing Countries	−0.120	−
	(0.708)	(−)
Europe	−0.0637	−
	(0.594)	(−)
GDP per capita	0.0000	−
	(0.896)	(−)
Population	−0.0033	−0.0033
	(0.000)	(0.000)
Net International Reserves/GDP	−0.3312	−
	(0.362)	(−)
Net Asset Position at the IMF	0.0002	−
	(0.293)	(−)
Credit rating	−0.0611	−0.0781
	(0.237)	(0.000)
Dummy for China	−5.2387	−5.3055
	(0.000)	(0.000)
Dummy for the US	−3.7086	−3.639
	(0.000)	(0.000)
Adjusted R^2	0.839	0.842
Durbin-Watson statistic	1.786	1.756
N	154	166

Method: Ordinary Least Squares (Cross-section data for 184 countries).
Figures in parentheses correspond to P-values.
Source: Estimations by the author.

to the IMF tend to be over-represented, but the statistical significance of this effect is doubtful.[11] Credit rating has a negative sign, implying that those countries with a lower credit rating score (1 for those rated AAA) tend to be over-represented and those with a high score (8 for those rated D or not rated) tend to be under-represented. Finally, the under-representation of the United States and China is significant and cannot be explained by the other characteristics considered, since the dummy variables included for these countries appear quite significant.

The effect of several variables considered on the OR variable are not statistically significant in the multiple regression setting. This includes net international reserves, that despite the high levels held by EMs in general and Asian countries in particular, do not contribute to explaining over-representation. Moreover, the country net asset position at the Fund; the characteristic of being a developing country; per capita GDP; and the European Dummy (applied to all European countries) are not significant explanatory variables of OR. It is interesting to note that over-representation is not a characteristic of all European countries; some of them are under-represented. Given that the results may be affected by multi-collinearity due to the high correlation between some of the explanatory variables like per capita GDP and developing countries, exclusion restrictions were introduced eliminating the variable that presented 't-test' with absolute value between zero and one. Since those explanatory variables are not significantly related with the degree of over-representation, they were excluded from the second regression performed on a narrow set of variables. The results are reported in Table 3, Equation 2.

After eliminating variables with a low statistical significance in the OR regression, only growth, the condition of being an EM country, population, credit rating (CR) and dummies for the United States and China were left as explanatory variables. All of them have highly significant effects on the OR variable, but perhaps they mask the under-representation affecting some developing countries that could be captured in the effect of the credit rating variable. The credit rating variables were used to precisely define developing countries as those with a higher CR value and its effect on OR has a negative sign.

There are some interesting conclusions that can be obtained from these results. The existing distortions in representation can be associated with incentives that may have important consequences for a global institution like the Fund. To the extent that the faster growing countries are not recognized as such in terms of their IMF quotas and that the faster growing countries continue to be those that are already under-represented, the distortions will continue to increase. Consequently, the IMF runs the risk that those countries that gain importance in the global economy and are not recognized as such by the quotas, may decide to look for substitutes of Fund-like services. Some initiatives associated with the creation of regional monetary funds have already been advanced by Asian countries. The forces behind such initiatives may become stronger, the larger the representation distortions at the IMF, attracting more countries to the idea of joining substitutes. A larger and regionally more diversified base may eventually succeed in creating a multi-regional EM monetary fund, including, for example, countries represented in the Asia Pacific Cooperation (APEC), or some other multi-regional organization. The provision of global public goods by other than a single global institution would clearly be a sub-optimal outcome that should be avoided. First, because pooling resources from a more limited group of countries increases the risk that all of them may require financial support at the same time and second, because there would be repeated efforts in the provision of surveillance and technical assistance. The efficient provision of global public goods requires a single international monetary fund with a solid governance structure and hence no distortions in representation.

Population is growing faster in developing and EM countries than in advanced economies. The political representation of an institution like the Fund is already under question by those that defend the principle of one country – one vote or one man – one vote for the IMF power structure. In principle, the Fund could claim that its voting structure is neutral against the population size of countries, as relative economic importance of countries and not population size determines its quota structure. However, with the existing distortions in representation, the Fund voting structure appears to discriminate against more populous countries. These countries tend to have a lower representation than the one that would be determined by their relative economic importance.

To address the governance issue related to the representation distortions at the Fund, the more radical action would be adjusting the quota structure over time so that it converges towards the relative participation in the global economic activity of different countries. In addition, regular changes in quotas every two to three years would be required for the quota structure to continue responding to the innovations in the composition of global economic activity. However, given the political opposition to changes in quotas in advanced economies, as well as the resistance of countries to accept the reduction in their political influence at the Fund, a substantial reform in the quota structure would take time to become effective. In the mean time, some alternatives could be considered to minimize the effect of the existing distortions. These include modifying the structure of the Executive Board under new rules to elect Executive Directors, while keeping the quota structure unchanged. The next two sections of the paper explore ways of modifying the quota structure and initiatives to modify the structure of the

Executive Board in order to improve governance and address the distortions in representation.

A Representative Quota Structure

It is important to note that given the characteristics of the representation distortions, it would not be possible to eliminate or reduce them significantly without modifying the quota structure. The allocation of additional basic votes to each country, that would benefit small countries at the expense of the larger ones, would not reduce the degree of under-representation of either EM countries, or the faster growing countries, and even less the big member countries. Allocation of additional basic votes equivalent to 9 per cent of the total voting power would minimally reduce the maximum over-representation, but would not reduce the maximum under-representation and the standard deviation of the OR variable.[12] The allocation of basic votes modifies the distribution of power in favour of developing countries and against advancing countries, leaving the participation of EMs barely unchanged. For this reason, the existing distortions in representation as measured by the OR variable remain almost unaltered. In that sense, an increase in basic votes could be part of a reform package that would not exclude a revision in the quota structure (See Table 4).

Only through changes in the quota structure can the existing degree of representation distortions be significantly reduced. An important element to be noted is that, given the size of the initial distortions, more frequent quota reviews would be required, increasing to every other year. By so doing, not only would the quota structure be more in line with the participation in economic activity, but also the quota size could be more representative of the current realities of the global economy.

Table 4. Basic votes adjustment and over-representation* (in per cent unless otherwise indicated)

	Initial conditions	After increase in basic votes
Max over-representation	2.74	2.47
Min over-representation	−9.57	−9.81
Std Dev over-representation	0.92	0.97
Advanced share	61.1	57.5
EMs share	29.3	29.7
Developing countries share	9.6	12.8

* Simulation of allocating 9 per cent of the voting power in additional basic votes.
Source: IMF and author's calculations.

Most likely, simplicity works best to represent the adequate quota structure, with GDP at PPP exchange rates as the preferred indicator of economic activity in member countries. Adding other variables like those used in the quota formulas may contribute some complexity and refinement, but not modify the essence of the problem, particularly considering the high correlation existing between GDP PPP and the other variables considered.[13] Moreover, to avoid falling into the typical quota formula discussion, in which the variables are selected to maximize the participation of the own country in the quota structure, it is better to take a simple and objective rule. This paper uses just GDP at PPP exchange rates as the best representation of economic activity across the Fund membership.

Even GDP PPP may have some cyclical volatility that can be smoothed out by using 5-year averages (the last 5 years for which information is available) to better represent trends in the participation of countries in the global economy. For the purpose of this exercise, averages for 2000–04 *World Economic Outlook* database of September 2004 can be used. An exercise based on official GDP data would require using data with some lags.

Having the 2000–04 shares in global GDP, the problem is how to adjust the quota structure in order to represent actual country shares in global economic activity. Perhaps the most significant political constraint faced in adjusting the quota structure is that countries that are over-represented may dislike the idea of seeing their participation in the decision-making bodies sharply reduced. Since no member country can be forced to reduce its quota, the adjustment in the structure would tend to be expansionary of the total amount of quotas. It can be argued that this is precisely what the Fund needs in order to better perform its role of providing global stability. However, larger shareholders have been resisting any significant adjustment in the total size of the Fund.

The simulations were performed considering two types of quota adjustments. First, the quota adjustment to compensate for under-representation was applied to all the countries with a degree of over-representation of less than –0.1 per cent of total quotas.[14] The quota adjustment applied to them consisted in minus their degree of over-representation times the amount of total Fund quotas. In this way, if nothing else were to change, that particular country would see its under-representation completely corrected. Second, a proportional quota adjustment was applied to those countries with a degree of over-representation between –0.1 per cent and +0.1 per cent to compensate for the increase in total quotas resulting from the global quota adjustment, so that their participation would remain stable. The proportional increase in individual quotas for countries within the range of adequate representation was set equal to the rate of change in total quotas resulting from both types of quota adjustment. Third, the member countries with a degree of over-representation above +0.1 per cent would not have their quotas adjusted, so that their participation would be gradually diluted and their degree of over-representation would converge towards the ±0.1 per cent range.

Simulations performed indicate that to the extent that the quota structure is modified by quota increases only, i.e. all the over-represented countries reject the idea of reducing their nominal quotas, a 210 per cent increase in total IMF quotas would be required to reduce the maximum over-representation from the equivalent of 2.7 per cent of total quotas to 0.5 per cent. At the same time, the minimum over-representation (or maximum under-representation) would shrink from –9.7 to –1.4 per cent, while the standard deviation of the over-representation variable would fall from an initial value of 0.92 to 0.15 (See Table 5).

Repeating the quota adjustment exercise of the type suggested above would result in a gradual convergence of the quota structure to the GDP PPP structure. Under the conditions of the simulation exercise, 10 rounds of quota adjustments were required to yield the commented convergence. So, if the quota adjustment is performed every other year, after twenty years, the quota structure would present distortions of less than one-sixth of their initial value, if the standard deviation of OR is used to represent the degree of distortion. In the real world however, if the 10 rounds of the simulations could be carried out in just one adjustment, the question is whether member countries will agree to increase their individual quota in such a way that total quotas would more than triplicate.

A second quota adjustment exercise is considered on the basis of voluntary quota reductions and presented in Table 6.

Each country that is under-represented in the quota structure, degree of over-representation of less than –0.1 per cent, receives the quota increase that

Table 5. Quota adjustment exercise* (in per cent unless otherwise indicated)

	Initial conditions	Round 1	Round 3	Round 5	Round 7	Round 10
Max over-representation	2.74	2.03	1.39	1.02	0.77	0.52
Min over-representation	–9.57	–4.65	–2.59	–2.06	–1.76	–1.40
Std Dev over-representation	0.92	0.49	0.29	0.22	0.19	0.15
Quotas (SDR Bill)	212.8	271.4	361.7	447.3	534.2	657.7
Change in Quotas	–	27.56	69.99	110.20	151.03	209.08

* Simulation without reductions of individual quotas.
Source: Author's calculations.

Table 6. Quota adjustment exercise* (in per cent unless otherwise indicated)

	Initial conditions	Round 1	Round 3	Round 5	Round 7	Round 10
Max over-representation	2.74	2.33	1.77	1.39	1.11	0.82
Min over-representation	−9.57	−2.69	−2.10	−1.78	−1.54	−1.34
Std Dev over-representation	0.92	0.32	0.26	0.22	0.20	0.17
Quotas (SDR bill)	212.8	243.2	302.3	361.8	422.1	514.0
Change in Quotas	–	14.31	42.05	70.05	98.35	141.55

* Simulation with voluntary reductions of individual quotas.
Source: Author's calculations.

would eliminate its under-representation if no other adjustment were to take place. The member countries, with degrees of over-representation between −0.1 per cent and +0.1 per cent would be subject to the proportional quota increase along with the change in total quotas. Finally, those countries that are over-represented, degree of OR greater than 0.1 per cent, can voluntarily reduce their quotas to the value that would completely eliminate their degree of over-representation if no other quota adjustment were to take place. Those that reduced their quotas would also receive a fraction of the proportional quota increase so as to ensure that their degree of over-representation, after the quota adjustments of all countries, stays within the ±0.1 interval.

An on demand total quota increase would result to the extent that some of the countries that are over-represented may decide not to reduce their quotas. In practice, the total quota will increase until the over-representation of countries that decide not to reduce their quotas is completely diluted through larger quotas of other countries. The simulations were performed under the assumption that all over-represented advanced economies would accept to reduce their quotas, while EMs and developing countries in that condition would elect not to reduce their quotas. Of course, to the extent that fewer countries would volunteer to reduce their quotas, the results would converge towards those of the first simulation. The results in Table 6, in general terms, indicate that the voluntary reduction scenario would allow similar results to those of the first scenario with respect to reducing the distortions in representation, as judged by the maximum, minimum and standard deviation of the degree of over-representation. However in this scenario, a much lower rate of increase in total quotas is required, about 140 per cent, because the voluntary quota reduction implies that a lower dilution effect is required to eliminate over-representation.

Table 7. Quota adjustment exercise* (in per cent unless otherwise indicated)

	Initial conditions	Round 1	Round 3	Round 5	Round 7	Round 10
Max over-representation	2.74	0.09	0.09	0.09	0.09	0.09
Min over-representation	−9.57	−0.57	−0.20	−0.14	−0.15	−0.12
Std Dev over-representation	0.92	0.06	0.04	0.04	0.04	0.04
Quotas (SDR bill)	212.8	218.5	223.6	227.2	228.7	231.3
Change in Quotas	–	2.70	5.08	6.75	7.49	8.71

* Simulation with Mandatory Reductions of Individual Quotas.
Source: Author's calculations.

Finally, the third scenario considered in addition to the quota adjustments to all under-represented countries (OR < −0.1 per cent), is a mandatory reduction of quota to all over-represented countries (OR > +0.1 per cent). This mandatory quota reduction would require a modification in the Articles of Agreement of the Fund. However, this scenario is indicative of what would happen in case of a voluntary reduction, to the extent that an increasing number of the over-represented countries opt for the voluntary reduction. No proportional quota adjustments were considered in this scenario given that no quota dilution effect was required. The results indicate a much sharper reduction in the representation distortions, with the maximum, minimum and standard deviation of OR converging towards zero. At the same time, the total increase in quotas required to produce this result was less than 9 per cent in 10 adjustment rounds. The ±0.1 per cent tolerance for the quota adjustments is the reason why convergence to zero of all the indicators of distortions in representation has not immediately occurred. There seems to be a number of small developing countries with over-representation of less than 0.1 per cent weighted against a few large under-represented countries (see Appendix 2C).

The three quota adjustment scenarios considered yield similar results. In all of them, advanced economies see their share in Fund quota reduced as a result of their initial over-representation. However, in none of the scenarios do the advanced economies lose the absolute majority they presently hold. Also, in the three scenarios, EM economies gain participation at the expense of advanced economies and to some extent, of developing countries also. The latter group see their share in total quotas reduced as the quota structure converges towards that of GDP PPP. Regionally, the quota adjustment scenarios imply gains in participation for Asia and Oceania, to a lesser extent,

Table 8. Quota shares in adjustment scenarios (in per cent)

	Original	No quota reduction	Voluntary quota reduction	Mandatory quota reduction
Advanced economies	62.14	51.46	51.75	52.42
Emerging markets	29.27	41.37	40.94	41.57
Developing countries	8.59	7.17	7.30	6.01
Europe	39.88	27.39	27.93	26.68
Asia and Oceania	19.01	32.35	31.21	33.49
Africa and Middle East	14.58	10.74	10.96	9.12
Western hemisphere	26.54	29.53	29.90	30.70

Source: Quota adjustment simulations.

for the Western Hemisphere and losses for Europe, Africa and the Middle East. Such an outcome is the result of strictly applying the participation in global GDP PPP as the criteria for representation. Accordingly, faster growing economies tend to increase their participation in decision-making bodies at the IMF (see Table 8).

Applying these rules, the representation of several groups is reduced. This is the case with Europe, Africa and the Middle East, as well as the advanced economies and developing countries. These rules would open up the possibility for them to get better represented to the extent that their growth rates pick up. Since it is politically unacceptable that the representation of smaller countries falls further, an increase in basic votes would be the instrument to apply. However, in such a case, the losses of advanced economies and Europe would be even more pronounced.

The reform of the quota structure requires a political consensus that is very difficult to obtain and even if it is obtained, it is most likely that the adjustment would be rather slow. The first barrier to overcome is the resistance of advanced economies that control the absolute majority to changes in the quota structure. The reasons are first, because of the losses in participation implied by the adjustment for many advanced economies, as a group and second, because of the political opposition to an increase in quotas in the advanced economies whose quotas would be increased. A possible way out is that advanced economies agree to voluntarily reduce their quotas to allow the adjustment in the quota structure with a lower increase in total quotas required to eliminate the major distortions. Then the exposition to financial risk of advanced economies in the operations of the IMF would be reduced together with their quotas. One remaining problem could become an important barrier; the larger member country, the United States, would be eligible for a sizeable quota increase under the different scenarios, even in the one of mandatory quota reduction. It remains to be seen whether the political resistance observed in the US Congress against any increase in resources contributed to the IMF can be overcome by a larger participation in the institution's decision-making bodies.

With all the obstacles and the delays that will most likely affect a revision in the quota structure, as an initial step towards the elimination of distortions in representation, a reform at the level of the Executive Board could be considered.

An Independent and Professional Executive Board

The Fund Executive Board is a technical body in which highly competent professionals and well informed people defend the interests of the countries they represent. However, the way that the incentives are set, Executive Directors respond primarily to their own country and to the one that controls the bulk of the voting power of their chair. Otherwise, they would neither be re-elected nor receive the nomination to the next post in their careers as national civil servants. To some extent, the problem of representation of EMs and developing counties in the IMF can be confronted by improving the effectiveness of their representation at the level of the Executive Board. As it was shown, the sum of developing and EM countries are under-represented in the quota structure. Moreover, at the level of the Executive Board and considering the nationality of the ED as the defining variable, their under-representation is more marked. It is possible to argue that a Board composed of 'independent and professional EDs' as opposed to 'political EDs', typically national civil servants representing single member countries, would help in bridging the representation gap affecting EMs and developing countries.[15] At the same time, there are issues of effectiveness of the representation since chairs representing a large number of developing countries contrast against single country chairs of advanced nations.

All the rules for electing the Executive Board that are proposed and considered below cannot become effective unless a political consensus on the need for changes is obtained. In some cases, the new rules may require modification of the Articles of Agreement.

Under the Independent and Professional Board, all EDs should be elected, thus eliminating the ED nominations by the largest five advanced economies (the United States, Germany, France, UK and Japan). If all EDs were to be elected and none was nominated as a representative of a single country and if the rules ensure independence from the influence of a permanent employer as a requisite to become ED, some improvements in representation could materialize under the same voting structure. The Professional ED, as opposed to the ED in mid-career for the Treasury or the Central Bank of any given country, could represent effectively not only their own country, but others as well. As they would not have to follow instructions from a single source, the professional ED is in a better position to balance the interest of the whole constituency and seek consensus among members of the Board. Consensus building at the level of the Executive Board is an important tool to improve the decision-making process in the institution. It must be noted however, that the Professional Board would be fully accountable, first because all important decisions have to be confirmed by the Board of Governors, which should be the instance of political representation. And second, because the ED would have to seek re-election after a few years. In this respect, more independence could be granted at the expense of some accountability through longer terms in office for EDs and the prohibition of re-election. However, well-founded proposals along these lines have not received significant support.[16]

Some additional conditions for forming the Executive Board chairs could be considered on the basis of the Fund being a Monetary Institution. All countries that have a common currency and thus a common monetary policy should be represented by the same ED at the Board of the Global Monetary Institution. Whether the use of a common currency is the result of a bilateral or multilateral treaty, or just the unilateral decision of one country to adopt the currency of the other, the fact is that they all have a common monetary policy and can benefit from information exchange and coordination. Belonging to the same chair at the Fund Executive Board would facilitate such exchanges and create instances for coordination, either improving existing channels or creating new ones for information sharing among members of the currency union. Moreover, at the Executive Board, such policies can be represented by a single chair, favouring the discussions. In this regard, all countries that have adopted the euro should be represented by the same chair. Similarly, all the countries that use the US dollar as their official currency should also be represented by the same ED.

In addition, requirements of minimum and maximum density of country representation in each ED chair are required for better representation. Single country chairs play a very limited role in coordinating decisions or contributing to consensus building, often acting under the well-defined instructions of their Governor. Extremely large chairs of more than 20 member countries result in a heavy burden for the ED, who has to stretch resources in an attempt to represent such large constituencies. For a more effective representation and hence better governance conditions, an ED should represent at least three countries and at most fifteen countries.[17] These limits in the number of countries per constituency would improve the effectiveness of chairs by avoiding the concentration of a large number of countries under a single representation and forcing the coordination of members by each and every chair.

Table 9. Independent Professional Board scenario

	Number of Chairs			
	Current Board	Professional Board	Current Board	Professional Board
Advanced economies	63.3	61.7	11	8
EM economies	30.3	31.9	10	12
Developing countries	6.4	6.4	3	4
Total	**100.0**	**100.0**	**24**	**24**

Source: IMF and author's estimations.

Applying the rules set to the selection mechanism, a market for EDs and representation would be created. Each ED would need to keep the confidence of the represented, otherwise risk not obtaining the required votes to be elected, or attract the support of the minimum of three countries considered. For those representing constituencies arranged within a single currency area, the persons that better represent the group would be in competition and various forms of rotating representation agreement between the members are also possible (see Table 9).

There are many possible solutions under these rules, as only two chairs are clearly defined, namely those of the euro and the dollar. A simulated Board was generated using the proposed rules and attempting to preserve as much as possible the existing structure in terms of the regional representation at the Board. Details are presented in Appendix 3 only as a reference of the type of results that could be expected. Some competition may be generated between the different regions to increase their representation and perhaps, some transversal representation of countries may arise. In any case, the scenario presented seems to be stable, that is, under the assumed rules the large chairs cannot be divided into two or more chairs with voting power greater than those of the African chairs (the smallest ones). This is because of the minimum number of member countries by constituency, the concentration of countries with a common currency in a single chair and the indivisibility of the voting power of larger constituents.

The Board would retain the 24 chairs. In the simulation, the chair with the largest voting power would be the euro chair and the one with the lowest, the smallest of the three African chairs. Under the new Board composition, the participation of EMs would increase slightly to 31.9 per cent of the voting power at the Board level, basically as the result of reducing the representation of advanced economies to 61.7 per cent (see Table 8). Under the new rules, the number of chairs controlled by advanced economies would fall from 11 to 8, thus allowing EMs (most from Eastern Europe) to take control of two chairs in which they were previously represented by one advanced economy. A third chair, previously controlled by one advanced economy (Italy), is assumed to be taken by a group of EMs including Korea, but that implies that the chair previously under the control of Korea, is taken by Australia, an advanced economy, hence neutralizing the additional gain by EMs.

The number of chairs controlled by developing countries would increase from 3 to 4, but their representation would stay stable. The number of chairs controlled by developing countries would increase as a reflection of the limits between 3 and 15 of the number of countries in each chair, allowing a third African chair to reduce the concentration in representation that affect developing countries.

Some minimum advances in representation and in the working of the Executive Board can be obtained by imposing a number of rules to ensure a professional Board that improves incentives to represent EM and developing countries. A key role is played by the imposition of limits on the number of countries in each constituency and conditions to ensure the independence of the Executive Director.

Conclusion

Using GDP PPP to represent the participation of each member country in global economic activity, the current realities of the global economy are far from being reflected in the Fund's quota structure. Advanced economies account for the bulk of the over-representation, EM countries for the bulk of the under-representation, while developing countries are in a more neutral position. At the level of the Executive Board, the distortions in representation can be even more marked as chairs controlled by advanced economies represent a large number of EMs and developing economies.

To explore the general characteristics of the countries that are under- and over-represented, a cross-section regression is attempted. The results basically indicate that economic growth, population, credit rating and dummies for the United States and China, all with negative signs and thus associated to under-representation, are highly significant in explaining representation distortions. The distortions in representation can be associated with perverse incentives. To the extent that the faster growing countries are not recognized as such in terms of their IMF quotas, the distortions will continue to increase. Consequently the IMF runs the risk that those countries that gain importance in the global economy and are not recognized may decide to look for Fund substitutes in which they could be better represented. In addition, while population is growing faster in developing and EM countries than in advanced economies, already the existing distortions in representation indicate that the Fund voting structure appears to discriminate against more populous countries.

To address the representation distortions, the more radical action would be adjusting the quota structure in line with the relative participation in global economic activity of different countries. The allocation of additional basic votes to each country would not reduce the degree of under-representation of EM countries, or the one affecting the faster growing countries, and even less that of the big member countries. The allocation of basic votes modifies the distribution of power in favour of developing countries and against advancing countries, leaving the participation of EMs unchanged.

Perhaps the most significant problem in adjusting the quota structure is that those that are over-represented may reject the idea of seeing their participation sharply reduced. To the extent that the quota structure is modified by quota increases only, a large increase in total IMF quotas would be required to significantly reduce over-representation. Repeated quota adjustment exercises would result in a gradual convergence of the quota structure into the GDP PPP structure. Under the conditions of the simulation exercise, 10 rounds of quota adjustments and more than tripling existing quotas were required to reduce distortions in representation to one-sixth of its original value. A second quota adjustment exercise is considered on the basis of voluntary quota adjustments. The total quotas will increase until the over-representation of countries that decide not to reduce their quotas is completely diluted through the increase in quotas of other countries. The simulations were performed under the assumption that all over-represented advanced economies would accept to reduce their quotas and the results indicate that the voluntary reduction would allow a similar cut in the degree of over-representation, but requiring about one-half of the rate of increase in total quotas. Finally, the third scenario considered a mandatory reduction of quota to all over-represented countries, where a much sharper reduction in the representation distortions is obtained with a very small increase in total quotas.

The reform of the quota structure requires a political consensus that will be difficult to obtain. As an initial step towards the elimination of distortions in representation, a reform at the level of the Executive Board could be considered. In that sense, a less political and more professional and independent Board would contribute to reduce distortions in representation by better defending the views of smaller economies. At the same time, effectiveness can also be improved by reducing the size dispersion among the chairs. The rules considered that all EDs should be elected and none nominated as a representative of a single country, that independence from the influence of the permanent employer is a requisite to effective representation of more than one country, that all countries that have a common currency and thus a common monetary policy should be represented by the same Executive Director and finally, that each ED chair should represent at least three member countries and at most 15.

There are many possible solutions under these rules, as only two chairs are clearly defined, those of the euro and the dollar. The new Board was generated attempting to preserve as much as possible the existing structure in terms of the regional representation. The Board would retain the 24 Chairs; the Chair with the largest voting power would be the Euro Chair, and the one with the lowest, the smallest of the three African Chairs. Under the new Board composition, the participation of EMs would slightly increase, basically as the result of reducing the representation of advanced economies. Under the new rules, the number of chairs controlled by advanced economies would fall from 11 to 8, thus allowing EM to take control of two additional chairs and the developing countries would obtain the other.

Some advances in representation and in the working of the Executive Board can be obtained by imposing a number of rules to ensure a professional Board that better represents all member countries, even under the existing quota structure. A key role is played by the imposition of limits to the number of countries in each constituency and conditions to favour the independence of the Executive Director.

Appendix 1A

Country Data Set A

Country name	Credit rating	Developing and EMs	LDCs	EMCs	Advanced economies	Europe	Net IMF position
Albania	8	1	1	0	0	1	−118.02
Algeria	8	1	1	0	0	0	−46.20
Angola	8	1	1	0	0	0	0.00
Antigua and Barbuda	8	1	1	0	0	0	0.05
Argentina	7	1	0	1	0	0	−493.42
Armenia	8	1	1	0	0	0	−157.00
Australia	2	0	0	0	1	0	42.68
Austria	1	0	0	0	1	1	41.16
Azerbaijan	5	1	0	1	0	0	−108.42
Bahamas, The	8	1	1	0	0	0	4.79
Bahrain, Kingdom of	3	1	0	1	0	0	51.63
Bangladesh	8	1	1	0	0	0	−9.25
Barbados	8	1	1	0	0	0	7.44
Belarus	8	1	1	0	0	0	−4.53
Belgium	2	0	0	0	1	1	39.35
Belize	8	1	1	0	0	0	22.55
Benin	6	1	0	1	0	0	−75.96

continued...

Appendix 1A. (continued)

Country name	Credit rating	Developing and EMs	LDCs	EMCs	Advanced econonomies	Europe	Net IMF position
Bhutan	8	1	1	0	0	0	16.19
Bolivia	6	1	0	1	0	0	−104.17
Bosnia & Herzegovina	8	1	1	0	0	0	−53.29
Botswana	8	1	1	0	0	0	48.12
Brazil	5	1	0	1	0	0	627.66
Bulgaria	4	1	0	1	0	1	−119.71
Burkina Faso	8	1	1	0	0	0	−127.25
Burundi	8	1	1	0	0	0	−24.53
Cambodia	8	1	1	0	0	0	−79.66
Cameroon	6	1	0	1	0	0	−125.45
Canada	1	0	0	0	1	0	40.65
Cape Verde	6	1	0	1	0	0	−51.20
Central African Rep.	8	1	1	0	0	0	−43.66
Chad	8	1	1	0	0	0	−126.78
Chile	3	1	0	1	0	0	45.82
China, P.R.: Mainland	3	1	0	1	0	0	40.13
Colombia	5	1	0	1	0	0	36.93
Comoros	8	1	1	0	0	0	4.59
Congo, Dem. Rep. of	8	1	1	0	0	0	−88.81
Congo, Republic of	8	1	1	0	0	0	−21.72
Costa Rica	5	1	0	1	0	0	12.19
Cote d'Ivoire	8	1	1	0	0	0	−87.78
Croatia	4	1	0	1	0	1	0.04
Cyprus	3	1	0	1	0	1	47.86
Czech Republic	3	1	0	1	0	1	38.40
Denmark	1	0	0	0	1	1	41.78
Djibouti	8	1	1	0	0	0	−79.57
Dominica	8	1	1	0	0	0	−64.90
Dominican Republic	7	1	0	1	0	0	−40.00
Ecuador	6	1	0	1	0	0	−81.11
Egypt	5	1	0	1	0	0	0.00
El Salvador	5	1	0	1	0	0	0.00
Equatorial Guinea	8	1	1	0	0	0	−0.56
Eritrea	8	1	1	0	0	0	0.03
Estonia	3	1	0	1	0	1	0.01
Ethiopia	8	1	1	0	0	0	−73.78
Fiji	8	1	1	0	0	0	21.61
Finland	1	0	0	0	1	1	41.31
France	1	0	0	0	1	1	39.50
Gabon	8	1	1	0	0	0	−25.43
Gambia, The	6	1	0	1	0	0	−70.79
Georgia	8	1	1	0	0	0	−129.24
Germany	1	0	0	0	1	1	39.61
Ghana	6	1	0	1	0	0	−82.63
Greece	3	1	0	1	0	1	40.61
Grenada	8	1	1	0	0	0	−25.04
Guatemala	8	1	1	0	0	0	0.00
Guinea	8	1	1	0	0	0	−85.55
Guinea-Bissau	8	1	1	0	0	0	−97.00
Guyana	8	1	1	0	0	0	−70.60
Haiti	8	1	1	0	0	0	−11.03
Honduras	8	1	1	0	0	0	−82.47
Hungary	3	1	0	1	0	1	43.81

continued...

Appendix 1A. (continued)

Country name	Credit rating	Developing and EMs	LDCs	EMCs	Advanced econonomies	Europe	Net IMF position
Iceland	2	0	0	0	1	1	15.80
India	5	1	0	1	0	0	21.33
Indonesia	6	1	0	1	0	0	−325.57
Iran, I.R. Of	6	1	0	1	0	0	0.00
Ireland	1	0	0	0	1	1	46.12
Israel	3	1	0	1	0	0	38.22
Italy	2	0	0	0	1	1	39.63
Jamaica	8	1	1	0	0	0	−2.19
Japan	2	0	0	0	1	0	39.09
Jordan	8	1	1	0	0	0	−166.28
Kazakhstan	4	1	0	1	0	0	0.00
Kenya	8	1	1	0	0	0	−23.18
Kiribati	8	1	1	0	0	0	0.17
Korea	3	1	0	1	0	0	31.08
Kuwait	2	0	0	0	1	0	37.85
Kyrgyz Republic	8	1	1	0	0	0	−153.00
Lao People's Dem.Rep	8	1	1	0	0	0	−56.43
Latvia	3	1	0	1	0	1	−2.96
Lebanon	6	1	0	1	0	0	9.28
Lesotho	6	1	0	1	0	0	−41.07
Libya	8	1	1	0	0	0	35.20
Lithuania	3	1	0	1	0	1	−20.92
Luxembourg	1	0	0	0	1	1	43.09
Macedonia, FYR	8	1	1	0	0	1	−66.76
Madagascar	8	1	1	0	0	0	−94.85
Malawi	7	1	0	1	0	0	−95.79
Malaysia	3	1	0	1	0	0	39.43
Maldives		0	0	0	1	0	18.95
Mali	6	1	0	1	0	0	−112.23
Malta	3	1	0	1	0	1	39.47
Mauritania	8	1	1	0	0	0	−108.97
Mauritius	8	1	1	0	0	0	21.53
Mexico	4	1	0	1	0	0	20.36
Moldova	6	1	0	1	0	0	−77.88
Mongolia	8	1	1	0	0	0	−65.09
Morocco	8	1	1	0	0	0	11.98
Mozambique	6	1	0	1	0	0	−123.89
Myanmar	8	1	1	0	0	0	0.00
Namibia	8	1	1	0	0	0	0.04
Nepal	8	1	1	0	0	0	−2.69
Netherlands	1	0	0	0	1	1	39.81
New Zealand	2	0	0	0	1	0	48.41
Nicaragua	8	1	1	0	0	0	−110.39
Niger	8	1	1	0	0	0	−121.38
Nigeria	8	1	1	0	0	0	0.01
Norway	1	0	0	0	1	1	40.05
Oman	8	1	1	0	0	0	39.98
Pakistan	8	1	1	0	0	0	−137.82
Panama	5	1	0	1	0	0	-8.78
Papua New Guinea	6	1	0	1	0	0	−61.85
Paraguay	8	1	1	0	0	0	21.50
Peru	5	1	0	1	0	0	−14.67
Philippines	5	1	0	1	0	0	−81.65

continued...

Appendix 1A. (continued)

Country name	Credit rating	Developing and EMs	LDCs	EMCs	Advanced econonomies	Europe	Net IMF position
Poland	4	1	0	1	0	1	39.30
Portugal	2	0	0	0	1	1	41.60
Qatar	8	1	1	0	0	0	39.22
Romania	4	1	0	1	0	1	−38.89
Russia	4	1	0	1	0	0	−57.35
Rwanda	8	1	1	0	0	0	−77.20
Samoa	8	1	1	0	0	0	5.99
Sao tome & Principe	8	1	1	0	0	0	−25.70
Saudi Arabia	3	1	0	1	0	0	43.62
Senegal	8	1	1	0	0	0	−98.77
Serbia & Montenegro	8	1	1	0	0	1	−131.91
Seychelles	8	1	1	0	0	0	0.02
Sierra Leone	8	1	1	0	0	0	−109.69
Singapore	1	0	0	0	1	0	43.97
Slovak Republic	3	1	0	1	0	1	0.00
Slovenia	2	0	0	0	1	1	42.01
Solomon islands	8	1	1	0	0	0	5.29
South Africa	4	1	0	1	0	0	0.03
Spain	1	0	0	0	1	1	41.11
Sri Lanka	8	1	1	0	0	0	−52.44
St. Kitts and Nevis	8	1	1	0	0	0	0.92
St. Lucia	8	1	1	0	0	0	0.04
St. Vincent & Grens.	8	1	1	0	0	0	6.02
Sudan	8	1	1	0	0	0	−237.39
Suriname	6	1	0	1	0	0	6.65
Swaziland	8	1	1	0	0	0	12.92
Sweden	1	0	0	0	1	1	41.25
Switzerland	1	0	0	0	1	1	40.00
Syrian Arab Republic	8	1	1	0	0	0	0.00
Tajikistan	8	1	1	0	0	0	−77.19
Tanzania	8	1	1	0	0	0	−142.91
Thailand	4	1	0	1	0	0	6.93
Timor-Leste	8	1	1	0	0	0	0.01
Togo	8	1	1	0	0	0	−38.02
Tonga	8	1	1	0	0	0	24.81
Trinidad and Tobago	8	1	1	0	0	0	38.53
Tunisia	4	1	0	1	0	0	7.05
Turkey	6	1	0	1	0	0	−1,670.12
Turkmenistan	7	1	0	1	0	0	0.01
Uganda	8	1	1	0	0	0	−87.98
Ukraine	6	1	0	1	0	0	−90.05
United Arab Emirates	8	1	1	0	0	0	39.12
United Kingdom	1	0	0	0	1	1	39.64
United States	1	0	0	0	1	0	40.82
Uruguay	6	1	0	1	0	0	−530.47
Uzbekistan	8	1	1	0	0	0	−10.55
Vanuatu	8	1	1	0	0	0	14.68
Venezuela, Rep. Bol.	6	1	0	1	0	0	12.11
Vietnam	5	1	0	1	0	0	−69.24
Yemen, Republic of	8	1	1	0	0	0	−110.93
Zambia	8	1	1	0	0	0	−118.15
Zimbabwe	8	1	1	0	0	0	−57.33
Total		**149**	**88**	**61**	**26**	**34**	

Appendix 1B

Country Data Set B

Country name	Net Intern. reserves (US$)	GDP PPP share	Over-representation	Population	GDP Per cap	LT growth
Albania	681,723,000	0.0275	−0.0046	3,166,160	2,230	2.49
Algeria	22,487,400,000	0.3873	0.2052	31,799,700	2,448	2.31
Angola	426,792,000	0.0618	0.0734	13,624,800	1,348	2.85
Antigua and Barbuda	76,561,000	0.0020	0.0043	73,010	11,482	4.49
Argentina	9,525,040,000	0.8987	0.1010	38,427,800	3,740	1.35
Armenia	343,337,000	0.0188	0.0246	3,060,930	795	1.14
Australia	21,751,400,000	1.1114	0.4169	19,730,700	29,712	3.30
Austria	6,057,270,000	0.5007	0.3834	8,116,190	34,627	2.10
Azerbaijan	552,399,000	0.0543	0.0217	8,370,060	1,047	−0.07
Bahamas, The	330,497,000	0.0113	0.0502	313,837	17,432	2.28
Bahrain, Kingdom of	1,202,030,000	0.0249	0.0388	724,323	13,423	4.46
Bangladesh	1,738,740,000	0.4997	−0.2479	146,736,000	394	4.34
Barbados	496,607,000	0.0085	0.0234	270,369	10,381	1.20
Belarus		0.1124	0.0700	9,895,120	2,458	1.12
Belgium	7,685,630,000	0.5856	1.5891	10,318,400	32,979	2.05
Belize	56,989,000	0.0030	0.0058	255,916	3,977	5.44
Benin	343,058,000	0.0146	0.0146	6,736,290	560	3.47
Bhutan	246,705,000	0.0047	−0.0017	2,257,390	804	6.68
Bolivia	514,263,000	0.0446	0.0364	8,808,430	1,118	2.03
Bosnia & Herzegovina	1,208,360,000	0.0179	0.0620	4,161,490	2,071	12.24
Botswana	3,593,460,000	0.0298	0.0000	1,785,010	5,503	7.65
Brazil	33,065,200,000	2.8311	−1.3974	178,470,000	3,182	2.38
Bulgaria	4,278,460,000	0.1185	0.1838	7,896,520	3,059	0.32
Burkina Faso	292,584,000	0.0282	0.0003	13,002,500	405	4.95
Burundi	45,098,700	0.0097	0.0266	6,825,060	96	1.35
Cambodia	562,816,000	0.0435	−0.0022	14,143,500	321	5.72
Cameroon	431,499,000	0.0585	0.0292	16,017,900	832	3.25
Canada	24,379,900,000	1.9684	1.0392	31,510,300	30,439	2.80
Cape Verde		0.0049	−0.0003	463,212	2,033	5.82
Central African rep.	89,497,100	0.0095	0.0168	3,864,920	339	0.99
Chad	126,302,000	0.0184	0.0080	8,597,640	506	5.50
Chile	10,659,700,000	0.3172	0.0871	15,805,500	5,571	4.78
China, P.R.: Mainland	357,922,020,000	12.5560	−9.5484	1,311,713,351	1,227	9.46
Colombia	7,268,560,000	0.5728	−0.2073	44,222,300	2,033	3.08
Comoros	63,479,500	0.0020	0.0022	768,221	530	2.12
Congo, Dem. Rep. of	n.a.	0.0660	0.1857	52,771,200	116	−1.29
Congo, Republic of	23,807,700	0.0071	0.0329	3,723,600	1,331	4.10
Costa Rica	1,235,810,000	0.0760	0.0015	4,172,860	4,308	3.71
Cote d' Ivoire	1,501,020,000	0.0543	0.0993	16,630,800	836	1.55
Croatia	5,511,900,000	0.0928	0.0796	4,427,900	7,336	2.12
Cyprus		0.0296	0.0363	801,884	18,098	4.81
Czech republic	18,031,100,000	0.3235	0.0634	10,235,500	10,058	1.88
Denmark	25,045,100,000	0.3415	0.4342	5,363,820	43,896	1.91
Djibouti	67,383,300	0.0030	0.0045	702,504	794	0.33
Dominica	32,124,000	0.0010	0.0029	78,620	3,643	3.22
Dominican Republic	170,998,000	0.1108	−0.0074	8,744,910	1,822	3.96
Ecuador	576,424,000	0.0988	0.0439	13,002,500	2,082	2.61
Egypt	9,229,820,000	0.5151	−0.0695	71,931,000	1,083	4.21
El Salvador	1,323,930,000	0.0563	0.0246	6,515,400	2,009	1.31
Equatorial Guinea	159,957,000	0.0257	−0.0103	494,168	4,032	13.14

continued...

Appendix 1B. (continued)

Country name	Net Intern. reserves (US$)	GDP PPP share	Over-representation	Population	GDP Per cap	LT growth
Eritrea	16,627,400	0.0018	0.0057		138	4.84
Estonia	924,498,000	0.0332	−0.0024	1,323,130	8,058	1.96
Ethiopia	643,087,000	0.0980	−0.0349	70,678,000	114	2.99
Fiji	285,108,000	0.0091	0.0241	838,777	2,143	2.66
Finland	7,131,340,000	0.2868	0.3100	5,206,730	34,318	2.54
France	23,717,900,000	3.3105	1.7604	60,144,100	32,153	2.03
Gabon	132,734,000	0.0168	0.0561	1,328,630	5,140	1.73
Gambia, The	78,614,100	0.0051	0.0096	1,425,590	268	3.89
Georgia	128,348,000	0.0243	0.0467	5,125,610	866	−1.79
Germany	37,985,600,000	4.6536	1.4890	82,475,600	32,404	1.82
Ghana	920,226,000	0.0881	0.0861	20,922,300	424	3.52
Greece	3,055,870,000	0.4069	−0.0183	10,976,300	18,036	1.93
Grenada	56,007,800	0.0018	0.0037	80,312	4,386	3.23
Guatemala	1,914,340,000	0.1009	−0.0016	12,346,900	1,953	2.53
Guinea		0.0334	0.0172	8,480,320	381	3.46
Guinea-Bissau	110,623,000	0.0020	0.0047	1,492,700	199	1.99
Guyana	185,998,000	0.0069	0.0360	765,480	1,034	1.21
Haiti	41,793,700	0.0284	0.0103	8,326,310	557	−0.17
Honduras	963,104,000	0.0363	0.0249	6,940,590	1,026	2.83
Hungary	8,575,310,000	0.2866	0.2037	9,876,920	10,015	1.38
Iceland	535,372,000	0.0176	0.0379	289,574	41,875	2.84
India	66,983,900,000	5.6763	−3.7128	1,065,460,000	603	5.61
Indonesia	23,636,800,000	1.4537	−0.4718	219,883,000	1,003	4.91
Iran, I.R. of		0.8977	−0.1907	68,919,600	2,429	3.50
Ireland	2,750,850,000	0.2730	0.1229	3,955,550	43,862	4.96
Israel	17,709,000,000	0.2775	0.1608	6,433,360	17,165	3.89
Italy	23,194,100,000	3.1564	0.1753	57,423,000	28,649	1.84
Jamaica	804,094,000	0.0211	0.1081	2,650,920	2,986	1.52
Japan	447,229,000,000	7.1746	−0.8881	127,654,000	36,184	2.56
Jordan	3,509,940,000	0.0450	0.0355	5,472,830	1,903	4.32
Kazakhstan	2,911,690,000	0.1833	−0.0106	15,433,000	2,580	1.45
Kenya	997,284,000	0.0668	0.0613	31,987,100	466	2.94
Kiribati		0.0000			760	0.58
Korea	104,516,000,000	1.6621	−0.8907	47,700,000	13,806	6.53
Kuwait	5,187,900,000	0.0707	0.5815	2,521,360	19,534	1.49
Kyrgyz republic	248,269,000	0.0176	0.0243	5,137,780	381	−0.52
Lao People's Dem Rep		0.0201	0.0049	5,657,340	401	6.08
Latvia	972,679,000	0.0442	0.0157	2,307,470	5,633	1.02
Lebanon	8,747,870,000	0.0407	0.0551	3,652,510	5,225	2.82
Lesotho	309,787,000	0.0095	0.0070	1,801,690	536	3.98
Libya	13,341,100,000	0.1045	0.4261	5,550,930	5,209	0.05
Lithuania	2,275,730,000	0.0741	−0.0060	3,443,630	6,212	0.49
Luxembourg	190,991,000	0.0549	0.0769	453,147	66,279	4.80
Macedonia, FYR	607,468,000	0.0282	0.0044	2,055,910	2,399	0.11
Madagascar	278,789,000	0.0277	0.0300	17,403,600	242	1.32
Malawi	85,551,800	0.0136	0.0192	12,105,300	165	2.59
Malaysia	29,997,900,000	0.4726	0.2294	24,424,600	4,418	6.26
Maldives	107,395,000	0.0041	−0.0002	318,251	2,256	8.36
Mali	611,494,000	0.0203	0.0238	13,006,700	412	3.98
Malta	1,625,200,000	0.0154	0.0328	394,258	12,029	3.87
Mauritania	279,903,000	0.0103	0.0201	2,892,900	432	3.45
Mauritius	1,063,610,000	0.0273	0.0206	1,221,320	4,841	5.46
Mexico	39,680,800,000	1.9060	−0.6850	103,457,000	6,377	2.78

continued...

Appendix 1B. (continued)

Country name	Net Intern. reserves (US$)	GDP PPP share	Over-representation	Population	GDP Per cap	LT growth
Moldova	203,416,000	0.0134	0.0448	4,266,560	630	−5.30
Mongolia	159,435,000	0.0087	0.0154	2,593,920	512	3.12
Morocco	9,346,060,000	0.2366	0.0412	30,565,900	1,541	3.42
Mozambique		0.0423	0.0113	18,863,300	278	4.09
Myanmar	378,378,000	0.1414	−0.0194	49,485,500	142	4.74
Namibia	218,859,000	0.0253	0.0391	1,987,490	2,241	1.95
Nepal	828,032,000	0.0679	−0.0342	25,164,200	239	4.31
Netherlands	8,550,966,000	0.9473	1.4904	16,370,010	34,836	2.18
New Zealand	3,304,220,000	0.1665	0.2559	3,875,380	23,120	2.76
Nicaragua		0.0269	0.0344	5,465,890	777	1.53
Niger	76,756,800	0.0190	0.0120	11,971,700	265	1.80
Nigeria	4,821,210,000	0.2516	0.5763	124,009,000	496	2.80
Norway	25,088,900,000	0.3589	0.4305	4,533,060	52,861	2.98
Oman	2,418,300,000	0.0719	0.0197	2,850,980	10,235	6.12
Pakistan	7,436,210,000	0.6384	−0.1503	153,578,000	538	4.99
Panama	680,343,000	0.0389	0.0587	3,120,400	4,615	3.52
Papua New Guinea	334,766,000	0.0253	0.0368	5,711,340	686	2.63
Paraguay	653,227,000	0.0519	−0.0047	5,878,080	1,155	2.71
Peru	6,618,430,000	0.2815	0.0199	27,167,200	2,290	2.20
Philippines	9,343,930,000	0.6958	−0.2803	79,999,000	1,019	2.73
Poland	22,040,200,000	0.8534	−0.2069	38,587,300	5,912	1.72
Portugal	4,536,160,000	0.3782	0.0314	10,061,500	16,021	2.98
Qatar	1,986,640,000	0.0375	0.0871	610,102	33,570	3.40
Romania	6,176,140,000	0.3054	0.1810	22,333,900	3,012	0.74
Russia	49,683,000,000	2.5238	0.2837	143,246,000	4,016	−0.52
Rwanda	144,484,000	0.0207	0.0172	8,387,230	184	2.85
Samoa	56,467,900	0.0020	0.0035	178,013	1,750	2.02
Sao Tome & Principe		0.0000		160,599	398	0.88
Saudi Arabia	15,383,200,000	0.5410	2.7576	24,217,000	10,663	2.00
Senegal	534,688,000	0.0336	0.0428	10,094,500	715	2.86
Serbia & Montenegro		0.0753	0.1455		2,796	2.42
Seychelles	45,349,400	0.0020	0.0021	81,007	8,567	2.89
Sierra Leone	44,830,800	0.0057	0.0433	4,970,860	193	−0.08
Singapore	64,433,300,000	0.2062	0.2011	4,252,840	23,999	6.76
Slovak Republic	7,898,410,000	0.1430	0.0258	5,402,430	7,329	2.86
Slovenia	5,726,590,000	0.0784	0.0310	1,984,130	16,439	3.12
Solomon Islands	25,036,800	0.0018	0.0031	477,018	518	1.47
South Africa	4,510,360,000	0.9372	−0.0549	45,026,500	3,687	2.02
Spain	13,905,800,000	1.8211	−0.3814	41,060,400	23,447	2.69
Sri Lanka		0.1442	0.0510	19,065,400	982	4.56
St. Kitts and Nevis	43,609,300	0.0010	0.0032	41,756	8,195	4.42
St. Lucia	71,941,000	0.0020	0.0052	149,187	4,021	3.79
St. Vincent & Grens.	34,450,000	0.0010	0.0029	119,846	3,512	4.22
Sudan	570,352,000	0.1333	−0.0531	33,609,900	586	4.09
Suriname	71,896,600	0.0051	0.0384	435,529	2,760	0.54
Swaziland	186,755,000	0.0101	0.0138	1,077,280	1,906	4.58
Sweden	13,453,300,000	0.5029	0.6283	8,876,250	37,363	2.10
Switzerland	33,906,200,000	0.4373	1.1958	7,168,660	47,493	1.56
Syrian Arab Republic		0.1270	0.0116	17,799,500	1,328	4.20
Tajikistan	75,751,300	0.0126	0.0285	6,244,940	261	−1.52
Tanzania	1,371,770,000	0.0421	0.0518	36,976,600	290	3.72
Thailand	27,734,200,000	0.8951	−0.3842	62,833,300	2,556	6.06
Timor-Leste		0.0010	0.0028		402	6.26

continued...

Appendix 1B. (continued)

Country name	Net Intern. reserves (US$)	GDP PPP share	Over-representation	Population	GDP Per cap	LT growth
Togo	122,795,000	0.0142	0.0205		354	1.52
Tonga	28,685,000	0.0010	0.0022	103,622	2,059	5.51
Trinidad and Tobago	1,651,610,000	0.0271	0.1313	1,302,710	9,545	1.48
Tunisia	1,989,740,000	0.1392	−0.0039	9,832,300	2,881	4.36
Turkey	23,005,300,000	0.9182	−0.4630	71,325,200	4,428	4.06
Turkmenistan		0.0547	−0.0192		2,518	3.73
Uganda	726,973,000	0.0677	0.0176	25,827,000	287	4.73
Ukraine	4,546,920,000	0.4963	0.1516	48,523,100	1,293	−2.45
United Arab Emirates	10,153,500,000	0.1614	0.1274	2,994,780	21,410	3.33
United Kingdom	28,516,000,000	3.2530	1.8179	59,250,600	35,505	2.35
United States	59,554,900,000	21.5011	−3.9587	294,043,000	39,991	3.02
Uruguay	1,402,190,000	0.0861	0.0586	3,415,300	3,489	1.68
Uzbekistan		0.0851	0.0451		357	0.42
Vanuatu	29,486,800	0.0010	0.0070	211,960	1,394	2.61
Venezuela, Rep. Bol.	11,192,200,000	0.2694	0.9863	25,698,800	4,019	1.16
Vietnam		0.3688	−0.2134	81,376,700	494	6.03
Yemen, Republic of	3,357,770,000	0.0324	0.0826	20,010,300	526	5.29
Zambia	166,712,000	0.0180	0.2129	10,812,100	454	1.21
Zimbabwe	66,249,200	0.0573	0.1096	12,891,200	498	1.36
Total		**100.0000**				

Appendix 2A

Final Quota Adjustment in the No Reduction Scenario

Country name	Adjusted quota	Quota share	Over-rep	Change in quota		
				Correcting over-rep	Proportional	Total
Afghanistan, I.S. of	488,894,117	0.074	0.074	0	326,994,117	326,994,117
Albania	147,060,800	0.022	−0.005	0	98,360,800	98,360,800
Algeria	2,970,252,362	0.452	0.064	0	1,715,552,362	1,715,552,362
Angola	864,548,398	0.131	0.070	0	578,248,398	578,248,398
Antigua and Barbuda	40,766,341	0.006	0.004	0	27,266,341	27,266,341
Argentina	6,393,068,160	0.972	0.073	0	4,275,968,160	4,275,968,160
Armenia	277,815,063	0.042	0.023	0	185,815,063	185,815,063
Australia	7,661,532,435	1.165	0.053	0	4,425,132,435	4,425,132,435
Austria	3,780,533,402	0.575	0.074	0	1,908,233,402	1,908,233,402
Azerbaijan	485,874,388	0.074	0.020	0	324,974,388	324,974,388
Bahamas, The	393,470,682	0.060	0.048	0	263,170,682	263,170,682
Bahrain, Kingdom of	407,663,408	0.062	0.037	0	272,663,408	272,663,408
Bangladesh	2,739,245,154	0.416	−0.083	823,304,520	1,382,640,634	2,205,945,154
Barbados	203,831,704	0.031	0.022	0	136,331,704	136,331,704
Belarus	1,166,823,266	0.177	0.065	0	780,423,266	780,423,266
Belgium	4,605,200,000	0.700	0.115	0	0	0
Belize	56,770,904	0.009	0.006	0	37,970,904	37,970,904
Benin	186,921,222	0.028	0.014	0	125,021,222	125,021,222
Bhutan	19,024,292	0.003	−0.002	0	12,724,292	12,724,292
Bolivia	517,883,515	0.079	0.034	0	346,383,515	346,383,515
Bosnia & Herzegovina	510,636,165	0.078	0.078	0	341,536,165	341,536,165
Botswana	190,242,924	0.029	−0.001	0	127,242,924	127,242,924

continued...

Appendix 2A. (continued)

Country name	Adjusted quota	Quota share	Over-rep	Change in quota		
				Correcting over-rep	Proportional	Total
Brazil	17,409,014,506	2.647	−0.185	14,372,914,506	0	14,372,914,506
Brunei Darussalam	509,443,140	0.077	0.077	0	294,243,140	294,243,140
Bulgaria	1,292,686,794	0.197	0.078	0	652,486,794	652,486,794
Burkina Faso	181,787,683	0.028	−0.001	0	121,587,683	121,587,683
Burundi	232,519,129	0.035	0.026	0	155,519,129	155,519,129
Cambodia	264,226,283	0.040	−0.003	0	176,726,283	176,726,283
Cameroon	560,763,666	0.085	0.027	0	375,063,666	375,063,666
Canada	12,860,638,436	1.955	−0.013	0	6,491,438,436	6,491,438,436
Cape Verde	28,989,398	0.004	0.000	0	19,389,398	19,389,398
Central African Rep.	168,198,903	0.026	0.016	0	112,498,903	112,498,903
Chad	169,104,821	0.026	0.007	0	113,104,821	113,104,821
Chile	2,585,189,954	0.393	0.076	0	1,729,089,954	1,729,089,954
China, P.R.:						
Mainland	77,210,231,109	11.739	−0.819	70,841,031,109	0	70,841,031,109
Colombia	3,140,083,217	0.477	−0.096	781,118,599	1,584,964,618	2,366,083,217
Comoros	26,875,588	0.004	0.002	0	17,975,588	17,975,588
Congo, Dem. Rep. Of	946,801,618	0.144	0.078	0	413,801,618	413,801,618
Congo, Republic of	255,469,069	0.039	0.032	0	170,869,069	170,869,069
Costa Rica	495,537,521	0.075	−0.001	0	331,437,521	331,437,521
Cote d'Ivoire	982,015,855	0.149	0.095	0	656,815,855	656,815,855
Croatia	1,102,503,040	0.168	0.075	0	737,403,040	737,403,040
Cyprus	421,554,161	0.064	0.035	0	281,954,161	281,954,161
Czech Republic	2,474,063,929	0.376	0.053	0	1,654,763,929	1,654,763,929
Denmark	2,610,438,826	0.397	0.055	0	967,638,826	967,638,826
Djibouti	48,013,690	0.007	0.004	0	32,113,690	32,113,690
Dominica	24,761,777	0.004	0.003	0	16,561,777	16,561,777
Dominican Republic	661,018,667	0.101	−0.010	0	442,118,667	442,118,667
Ecuador	912,864,062	0.139	0.040	0	610,564,062	610,564,062
Egypt	2,849,718,210	0.433	−0.082	0	1,906,018,210	1,906,018,210
El Salvador	517,279,569	0.079	0.022	0	345,979,569	345,979,569
Equatorial Guinea	98,443,164	0.015	−0.011	0	65,843,164	65,843,164
Eritrea	48,013,690	0.007	0.007	0	32,113,690	32,113,690
Estonia	196,886,328	0.030	−0.003	0	131,686,328	131,686,328
Ethiopia	403,737,761	0.061	−0.037	0	270,037,761	270,037,761
Fiji	212,286,945	0.032	0.023	0	141,986,945	141,986,945
Finland	2,244,967,888	0.341	0.054	0	981,167,888	981,167,888
France	21,683,094,555	3.297	−0.014	0	10,944,594,555	10,944,594,555
Gabon	465,944,177	0.071	0.054	0	311,644,177	311,644,177
Gambia, The	93,913,570	0.014	0.009	0	62,813,570	62,813,570
Georgia	453,865,261	0.069	0.045	0	303,565,261	303,565,261
Germany	28,616,449,043	4.351	−0.304	15,608,249,043	0	15,608,249,043
Ghana	1,114,279,983	0.169	0.081	0	745,279,983	745,279,983
Greece	2,485,236,926	0.378	−0.029	0	1,662,236,926	1,662,236,926
Grenada	35,330,829	0.005	0.004	0	23,630,829	23,630,829
Guatemala	634,747,025	0.097	−0.004	0	424,547,025	424,547,025
Guinea	323,412,971	0.049	0.016	0	216,312,971	216,312,971
Guinea–Bissau	42,880,151	0.007	0.004	0	28,680,151	28,680,151
Guyana	274,493,362	0.042	0.035	0	183,593,362	183,593,362
Haiti	247,315,801	0.038	0.009	0	165,415,801	165,415,801
Honduras	391,054,899	0.059	0.023	0	261,554,899	261,554,899
Hungary	2,458,205,191	0.374	0.087	0	1,419,805,191	1,419,805,191
Iceland	355,120,125	0.054	0.036	0	237,520,125	237,520,125
India	34,905,217,322	5.307	−0.370	30,747,017,322	0	30,747,017,322
Indonesia	8,916,717,441	1.356	−0.098	5,687,859,369	1,149,558,072	6,837,417,441

continued...

Appendix 2A. (continued)

Country name	Adjusted quota	Quota share	Over-rep	Change in quota		
				Correcting over-rep	Proportional	Total
Iran, I.R. of	5,503,049,277	0.837	−0.061	2,399,099,382	1,606,749,895	4,005,849,277
Iraq	606,192,095	0.092	0.092	0	102,192,095	102,192,095
Ireland	1,984,745,023	0.302	0.029	0	1,146,345,023	1,146,345,023
Israel	2,197,328,639	0.334	0.057	0	1,269,128,639	1,269,128,639
Italy	19,409,363,458	2.951	−0.206	12,353,863,458	0	12,353,863,458
Jamaica	647,456,779	0.098	0.077	0	373,956,779	373,956,779
Japan	44,118,530,644	6.708	−0.468	30,805,730,644	0	30,805,730,644
Jordan	514,863,786	0.078	0.033	0	344,363,786	344,363,786
Kazakhstan	1,104,314,877	0.168	−0.015	0	738,614,877	738,614,877
Kenya	819,554,437	0.125	0.058	0	548,154,437	548,154,437
Kiribati	16,910,482	0.003	0.003	0	11,310,482	11,310,482
Korea	10,220,961,081	1.554	−0.108	8,587,361,081	0	8,587,361,081
Kuwait	1,381,100,000	0.210	0.139	0	0	0
Kyrgyz Republic	268,151,931	0.041	0.023	0	179,351,931	179,351,931
Lao People's Dem.Rep	159,743,661	0.024	0.004	0	106,843,661	106,843,661
Latvia	382,901,631	0.058	0.014	0	256,101,631	256,101,631
Lebanon	613,004,977	0.093	0.052	0	410,004,977	410,004,977
Lesotho	105,388,540	0.016	0.007	0	70,488,540	70,488,540
Liberia	215,306,674	0.033	0.033	0	144,006,674	144,006,674
Libya	1,290,010,274	0.196	0.092	0	166,310,274	166,310,274
Lithuania	435,444,915	0.066	−0.008	0	291,244,915	291,244,915
Luxembourg	842,806,350	0.128	0.073	0	563,706,350	563,706,350
Macedonia, FYR	208,059,325	0.032	0.003	0	139,159,325	139,159,325
Madagascar	369,010,878	0.056	0.028	0	246,810,878	246,810,878
Malawi	209,569,189	0.032	0.018	0	140,169,189	140,169,189
Malaysia	3,519,229,427	0.535	0.062	0	2,032,629,427	2,032,629,427
Maldives	24,761,777	0.004	0.000	0	16,561,777	16,561,777
Mali	281,740,711	0.043	0.023	0	188,440,711	188,440,711
Malta	308,012,353	0.047	0.031	0	206,012,353	206,012,353
Marshall Islands,Rep	10,569,051	0.002	0.002	0	7,069,051	7,069,051
Mauritania	194,470,544	0.030	0.019	0	130,070,544	130,070,544
Mauritius	306,804,461	0.047	0.019	0	205,204,461	205,204,461
Mexico	11,720,600,022	1.782	−0.124	9,134,800,022	0	9,134,800,022
Micronesia, Fed.Sts.	15,400,618	0.002	0.002	0	10,300,618	10,300,618
Moldova	372,030,607	0.057	0.043	0	248,830,607	248,830,607
Mongolia	154,308,149	0.023	0.015	0	103,208,149	103,208,149
Morocco	1,776,204,568	0.270	0.033	0	1,188,004,568	1,188,004,568
Mozambique	343,041,209	0.052	0.010	0	229,441,209	229,441,209
Myanmar	780,297,961	0.119	−0.023	0	521,897,961	521,897,961
Namibia	412,193,002	0.063	0.037	0	275,693,002	275,693,002
Nepal	215,306,674	0.033	−0.035	0	144,006,674	144,006,674
Netherlands	6,209,139,032	0.944	−0.003	0	1,046,739,032	1,046,739,032
New Zealand	1,589,134,572	0.242	0.075	0	694,534,572	694,534,572
Nicaragua	392,564,763	0.060	0.033	0	262,564,763	262,564,763
Niger	198,698,165	0.030	0.011	0	132,898,165	132,898,165
Nigeria	2,108,682,502	0.321	0.069	0	355,482,502	355,482,502
Norway	2,656,361,447	0.404	0.045	0	984,661,447	984,661,447
Oman	585,827,416	0.089	0.017	0	391,827,416	391,827,416
Pakistan	3,913,720,966	0.595	−0.044	1,309,320,125	1,570,700,841	2,880,020,966
Palau	9,361,160	0.001	0.001	0	6,261,160	6,261,160
Panama	623,876,001	0.095	0.056	0	417,276,001	417,276,001
Papua New Guinea	397,396,330	0.060	0.035	0	265,796,330	265,796,330
Paraguay	301,670,922	0.046	−0.006	0	201,770,922	201,770,922
Peru	1,927,794,962	0.293	0.012	0	1,289,394,962	1,289,394,962

continued...

Appendix 2A. (continued)

Country name	Adjusted quota	Quota share	Over-rep	Change in quota		
				Correcting over-rep	Proportional	Total
Philippines	3,933,734,425	0.598	−0.098	1,334,587,607	1,719,246,818	3,053,834,425
Poland	5,231,125,136	0.795	−0.058	2,334,770,148	1,527,354,988	3,862,125,136
Portugal	2,619,312,891	0.398	0.020	0	1,751,912,891	1,751,912,891
Qatar	796,604,497	0.121	0.084	0	532,804,497	532,804,497
Romania	2,438,793,324	0.371	0.065	0	1,408,593,324	1,408,593,324
Russia	15,519,519,263	2.360	−0.165	9,574,119,263	0	9,574,119,263
Rwanda	241,880,289	0.037	0.016	0	161,780,289	161,780,289
Samoa	35,028,856	0.005	0.003	0	23,428,856	23,428,856
San Marino	51,335,392	0.008	0.008	0	34,335,392	34,335,392
Sao Tome & Principe	22,345,994	0.003	0.003	0	14,945,994	14,945,994
Saudi Arabia	6,985,500,000	1.062	0.521	0	0	0
Senegal	488,592,144	0.074	0.041	0	326,792,144	326,792,144
Serbia & Montenegro	1,107,186,602	0.168	0.093	0	639,486,602	639,486,602
Seychelles	26,573,615	0.004	0.002	0	17,773,615	17,773,615
Sierra Leone	313,145,892	0.048	0.042	0	209,445,892	209,445,892
Singapore	1,741,553,201	0.265	0.059	0	879,053,201	879,053,201
Slovak Republic	1,079,553,100	0.164	0.021	0	722,053,100	722,053,100
Slovenia	699,671,198	0.106	0.028	0	467,971,198	467,971,198
Solomon Islands	31,405,181	0.005	0.003	0	21,005,181	21,005,181
Somalia	133,472,020	0.020	0.020	0	89,272,020	89,272,020
South Africa	5,642,363,543	0.858	−0.080	0	3,773,863,543	3,773,863,543
Spain	11,198,715,706	1.703	−0.119	8,149,815,706	0	8,149,815,706
Sri Lanka	1,248,355,948	0.190	0.046	0	834,955,948	834,955,948
St. Kitts and Nevis	26,875,588	0.004	0.003	0	17,975,588	17,975,588
St. Lucia	46,201,853	0.007	0.005	0	30,901,853	30,901,853
St. Vincent & Grens.	25,063,750	0.004	0.003	0	16,763,750	16,763,750
Sudan	512,448,003	0.078	−0.055	0	342,748,003	342,748,003
Suriname	278,117,036	0.042	0.037	0	186,017,036	186,017,036
Swaziland	153,100,258	0.023	0.013	0	102,400,258	102,400,258
Sweden	3,806,492,700	0.579	0.076	0	1,410,992,700	1,410,992,700
Switzerland	3,458,500,000	0.526	0.088	0	0	0
Syrian Arab Republic	886,592,420	0.135	0.008	0	592,992,420	592,992,420
Tajikistan	262,716,419	0.040	0.027	0	175,716,419	175,716,419
Tanzania	600,624,088	0.091	0.049	0	401,724,088	401,724,088
Thailand	5,486,907,661	0.834	−0.061	2,802,970,706	1,602,036,955	4,405,007,661
Timor-Leste	24,761,777	0.004	0.004	0	16,561,777	16,561,777
Togo	221,648,105	0.034	0.020	0	148,248,105	148,248,105
Tonga	20,836,130	0.003	0.002	0	13,936,130	13,936,130
Trinidad and Tobago	794,466,161	0.121	0.094	0	458,866,161	458,866,161
Tunisia	865,152,344	0.132	−0.008	0	578,652,344	578,652,344
Turkey	5,628,457,214	0.856	−0.063	3,021,091,403	1,643,365,811	4,664,457,214
Turkmenistan	227,083,617	0.035	−0.020	0	151,883,617	151,883,617
Uganda	545,061,075	0.083	0.015	0	364,561,075	364,561,075
Ukraine	3,247,936,751	0.494	−0.003	0	1,875,936,751	1,875,936,751
United Arab Emirates	1,448,077,923	0.220	0.059	0	836,377,923	836,377,923
United Kingdom	20,003,489,516	3.041	−0.212	9,264,989,516	0	9,264,989,516
United States	132,216,090,636	20.103	−1.403	95,066,790,636	0	95,066,790,636
Uruguay	925,546,923	0.141	0.055	0	619,046,923	619,046,923
Uzbekistan	832,237,299	0.127	0.041	0	556,637,299	556,637,299
Vanuatu	51,335,392	0.008	0.007	0	34,335,392	34,335,392
Venezuela, Rep. Bol.	2,659,100,000	0.404	0.135	0	0	0
Vietnam	1,858,443,596	0.283	−0.086	455,947,496	1,073,396,100	1,529,343,596
Yemen, Republic of	735,303,999	0.112	0.079	0	491,803,999	491,803,999
Zambia	702,575,231	0.107	0.089	0	213,475,231	213,475,231
Zimbabwe	836,604,116	0.127	0.070	0	483,204,116	483,204,116

Appendix 2B

Final Quota Adjustment in the Voluntary Quota Reduction Scenario

Country name	Adjusted quota	Adjusted quota share	Adjusted over-rep	Change in quota		
				Correcting over-rep	Proportional	Total
Afghanistan, I.S. of	488,894,117	0.074	0.074	0	326,994,117	326,994,117
Albania	147,060,800	0.022	−0.005	0	98,360,800	98,360,800
Algeria	2,970,252,362	0.452	0.064	0	1,715,552,362	1,715,552,362
Angola	864,548,398	0.131	0.070	0	578,248,398	578,248,398
Antigua and Barbuda	40,766,341	0.006	0.004	0	27,266,341	27,266,341
Argentina	6,393,068,160	0.972	0.073	0	4,275,968,160	4,275,968,160
Armenia	277,815,063	0.042	0.023	0	185,815,063	185,815,063
Australia	7,661,532,435	1.165	0.053	0	4,425,132,435	4,425,132,435
Austria	3,780,533,402	0.575	0.074	0	1,908,233,402	1,908,233,402
Azerbaijan	485,874,388	0.074	0.020	0	324,974,388	324,974,388
Bahamas, The	393,470,682	0.060	0.048	0	263,170,682	263,170,682
Bahrain, Kingdom of	407,663,408	0.062	0.037	0	272,663,408	272,663,408
Bangladesh	2,739,245,154	0.416	−0.083	823,304,520	1,382,640,634	2,205,945,154
Barbados	203,831,704	0.031	0.022	0	136,331,704	136,331,704
Belarus	1,166,823,266	0.177	0.065	0	780,423,266	780,423,266
Belgium	4,605,200,000	0.700	0.115	0	0	0
Belize	56,770,904	0.009	0.006	0	37,970,904	37,970,904
Benin	186,921,222	0.028	0.014	0	125,021,222	125,021,222
Bhutan	19,024,292	0.003	−0.002	0	12,724,292	12,724,292
Bolivia	517,883,515	0.079	0.034	0	346,383,515	346,383,515
Bosnia & Herzegovina	510,636,165	0.078	0.078	0	341,536,165	341,536,165
Botswana	190,242,924	0.029	−0.001	0	127,242,924	127,242,924
Brazil	17,409,014,506	2.647	−0.185	14,372,914,506	0	14,372,914,506
Brunei Darussalam	509,443,140	0.077	0.077	0	294,243,140	294,243,140
Bulgaria	1,292,686,794	0.197	0.078	0	652,486,794	652,486,794
Burkina Faso	181,787,683	0.028	−0.001	0	121,587,683	121,587,683
Burundi	232,519,129	0.035	0.026	0	155,519,129	155,519,129
Cambodia	264,226,283	0.040	−0.003	0	176,726,283	176,726,283
Cameroon	560,763,666	0.085	0.027	0	375,063,666	375,063,666
Canada	12,860,638,436	1.955	−0.013	0	6,491,438,436	6,491,438,436
Cape Verde	28,989,398	0.004	0.000	0	19,389,398	19,389,398
Central African Rep.	168,198,903	0.026	0.016	0	112,498,903	112,498,903
Chad	169,104,821	0.026	0.007	0	113,104,821	113,104,821
Chile	2,585,189,954	0.393	0.076	0	1,729,089,954	1,729,089,954
China, P.R.: Mainland	77,210,231,109	11.739	−0.819	70,841,031,109	0	70,841,031,109
Colombia	3,140,083,217	0.477	−0.096	781,118,599	1,584,964,618	2,366,083,217
Comoros	26,875,588	0.004	0.002	0	17,975,588	17,975,588
Congo, Dem. Rep. of	946,801,618	0.144	0.078	0	413,801,618	413,801,618
Congo, Republic of	255,469,069	0.039	0.032	0	170,869,069	170,869,069
Costa Rica	495,537,521	0.075	−0.001	0	331,437,521	331,437,521
Cote d'Ivoire	982,015,855	0.149	0.095	0	656,815,855	656,815,855
Croatia	1,102,503,040	0.168	0.075	0	737,403,040	737,403,040
Cyprus	421,554,161	0.064	0.035	0	281,954,161	281,954,161
Czech Republic	2,474,063,929	0.376	0.053	0	1,654,763,929	1,654,763,929
Denmark	2,610,438,826	0.397	0.055	0	967,638,826	967,638,826
Djibouti	48,013,690	0.007	0.004	0	32,113,690	32,113,690
Dominica	24,761,777	0.004	0.003	0	16,561,777	16,561,777
Dominican Republic	661,018,667	0.101	−0.010	0	442,118,667	442,118,667
Ecuador	912,864,062	0.139	0.040	0	610,564,062	610,564,062
Egypt	2,849,718,210	0.433	−0.082	0	1,906,018,210	1,906,018,210
El Salvador	517,279,569	0.079	0.022	0	345,979,569	345,979,569

continued...

Appendix 2B. (continued)

Country name	Adjusted quota	Adjusted quota share	Adjusted over-rep	Change in quota		
				Correcting over-rep	Proportional	Total
Equatorial Guinea	98,443,164	0.015	−0.011	0	65,843,164	65,843,164
Eritrea	48,013,690	0.007	0.007	0	32,113,690	32,113,690
Estonia	196,886,328	0.030	−0.003	0	131,686,328	131,686,328
Ethiopia	403,737,761	0.061	−0.037	0	270,037,761	270,037,761
Fiji	212,286,945	0.032	0.023	0	141,986,945	141,986,945
Finland	2,244,967,888	0.341	0.054	0	981,167,888	981,167,888
France	21,683,094,555	3.297	−0.014	0	10,944,594,555	10,944,594,555
Gabon	465,944,177	0.071	0.054	0	311,644,177	311,644,177
Gambia, The	93,913,570	0.014	0.009	0	62,813,570	62,813,570
Georgia	453,865,261	0.069	0.045	0	303,565,261	303,565,261
Germany	28,616,449,043	4.351	−0.304	15,608,249,043	0	15,608,249,043
Ghana	1,114,279,983	0.169	0.081	0	745,279,983	745,279,983
Greece	2,485,236,926	0.378	−0.029	0	1,662,236,926	1,662,236,926
Grenada	35,330,829	0.005	0.004	0	23,630,829	23,630,829
Guatemala	634,747,025	0.097	−0.004	0	424,547,025	424,547,025
Guinea	323,412,971	0.049	0.016	0	216,312,971	216,312,971
Guinea-Bissau	42,880,151	0.007	0.004	0	28,680,151	28,680,151
Guyana	274,493,362	0.042	0.035	0	183,593,362	183,593,362
Haiti	247,315,801	0.038	0.009	0	165,415,801	165,415,801
Honduras	391,054,899	0.059	0.023	0	261,554,899	261,554,899
Hungary	2,458,205,191	0.374	0.087	0	1,419,805,191	1,419,805,191
Iceland	355,120,125	0.054	0.036	0	237,520,125	237,520,125
India	34,905,217,322	5.307	−0.370	30,747,017,322	0	30,747,017,322
Indonesia	8,916,717,441	1.356	−0.098	5,687,859,369	1,149,558,072	6,837,417,441
Iran, I.R. of	5,503,049,277	0.837	−0.061	2,399,099,382	1,606,749,895	4,005,849,277
Iraq	606,192,095	0.092	0.092	0	102,192,095	102,192,095
Ireland	1,984,745,023	0.302	0.029	0	1,146,345,023	1,146,345,023
Israel	2,197,328,639	0.334	0.057	0	1,269,128,639	1,269,128,639
Italy	19,409,363,458	2.951	−0.206	12,353,863,458	0	12,353,863,458
Jamaica	647,456,779	0.098	0.077	0	373,956,779	373,956,779
Japan	44,118,530,644	6.708	−0.468	30,805,730,644	0	30,805,730,644
Jordan	514,863,786	0.078	0.033	0	344,363,786	344,363,786
Kazakhstan	1,104,314,877	0.168	−0.015	0	738,614,877	738,614,877
Kenya	819,554,437	0.125	0.058	0	548,154,437	548,154,437
Kiribati	16,910,482	0.003	0.003	0	11,310,482	11,310,482
Korea	10,220,961,081	1.554	−0.108	8,587,361,081	0	8,587,361,081
Kuwait	1,381,100,000	0.210	0.139	0	0	0
Kyrgyz Republic	268,151,931	0.041	0.023	0	179,351,931	179,351,931
Lao People S Dem. Rep	159,743,661	0.024	0.004	0	106,843,661	106,843,661
Latvia	382,901,631	0.058	0.014	0	256,101,631	256,101,631
Lebanon	613,004,977	0.093	0.052	0	410,004,977	410,004,977
Lesotho	105,388,540	0.016	0.007	0	70,488,540	70,488,540
Liberia	215,306,674	0.033	0.033	0	144,006,674	144,006,674
Libya	1,290,010,274	0.196	0.092	0	166,310,274	166,310,274
Lithuania	435,444,915	0.066	−0.008	0	291,244,915	291,244,915
Luxembourg	842,806,350	0.128	0.073	0	563,706,350	563,706,350
Macedonia, FYR	208,059,325	0.032	0.003	0	139,159,325	139,159,325
Madagascar	369,010,878	0.056	0.028	0	246,810,878	246,810,878
Malawi	209,569,189	0.032	0.018	0	140,169,189	140,169,189
Malaysia	3,519,229,427	0.535	0.062	0	2,032,629,427	2,032,629,427
Maldives	24,761,777	0.004	0.000	0	16,561,777	16,561,777
Mali	281,740,711	0.043	0.023	0	188,440,711	188,440,711
Malta	308,012,353	0.047	0.031	0	206,012,353	206,012,353
Marshall Islands, Rep	10,569,051	0.002	0.002	0	7,069,051	7,069,051
Mauritania	194,470,544	0.030	0.019	0	130,070,544	130,070,544

continued...

Appendix 2B. (continued)

Country name	Adjusted quota	Adjusted quota share	Adjusted over-rep	Change in quota		
				Correcting over-rep	Proportional	Total
Mauritius	306,804,461	0.047	0.019	0	205,204,461	205,204,461
Mexico	11,720,600,022	1.782	−0.124	9,134,800,022	0	9,134,800,022
Micronesia, Fed.Sts.	15,400,618	0.002	0.002	0	10,300,618	10,300,618
Moldova	372,030,607	0.057	0.043	0	248,830,607	248,830,607
Mongolia	154,308,149	0.023	0.015	0	103,208,149	103,208,149
Morocco	1,776,204,568	0.270	0.033	0	1,188,004,568	1,188,004,568
Mozambique	343,041,209	0.052	0.010	0	229,441,209	229,441,209
Myanmar	780,297,961	0.119	−0.023	0	521,897,961	521,897,961
Namibia	412,193,002	0.063	0.037	0	275,693,002	275,693,002
Nepal	215,306,674	0.033	−0.035	0	144,006,674	144,006,674
Netherlands	6,209,139,032	0.944	−0.003	0	1,046,739,032	1,046,739,032
New Zealand	1,589,134,572	0.242	0.075	0	694,534,572	694,534,572
Nicaragua	392,564,763	0.060	0.033	0	262,564,763	262,564,763
Niger	198,698,165	0.030	0.011	0	132,898,165	132,898,165
Nigeria	2,108,682,502	0.321	0.069	0	355,482,502	355,482,502
Norway	2,656,361,447	0.404	0.045	0	984,661,447	984,661,447
Oman	585,827,416	0.089	0.017	0	391,827,416	391,827,416
Pakistan	3,913,720,966	0.595	−0.044	1,309,320,125	1,570,700,841	2,880,020,966
Palau	9,361,160	0.001	0.001	0	6,261,160	6,261,160
Panama	623,876,001	0.095	0.056	0	417,276,001	417,276,001
Papua New Guinea	397,396,330	0.060	0.035	0	265,796,330	265,796,330
Paraguay	301,670,922	0.046	−0.006	0	201,770,922	201,770,922
Peru	1,927,794,962	0.293	0.012	0	1,289,394,962	1,289,394,962
Philippines	3,933,734,425	0.598	−0.098	1,334,587,607	1,719,246,818	3,053,834,425
Poland	5,231,125,136	0.795	−0.058	2,334,770,148	1,527,354,988	3,862,125,136
Portugal	2,619,312,891	0.398	0.020	0	1,751,912,891	1,751,912,891
Qatar	796,604,497	0.121	0.084	0	532,804,497	532,804,497
Romania	2,438,793,324	0.371	0.065	0	1,408,593,324	1,408,593,324
Russia	15,519,519,263	2.360	−0.165	9,574,119,263	0	9,574,119,263
Rwanda	241,880,289	0.037	0.016	0	161,780,289	161,780,289
Samoa	35,028,856	0.005	0.003	0	23,428,856	23,428,856
San Marino	51,335,392	0.008	0.008	0	34,335,392	34,335,392
Sao Tome & Principe	22,345,994	0.003	0.003	0	14,945,994	14,945,994
Saudi Arabia	6,985,500,000	1.062	0.521	0	0	0
Senegal	488,592,144	0.074	0.041	0	326,792,144	326,792,144
Serbia & Montenegro	1,107,186,602	0.168	0.093	0	639,486,602	639,486,602
Seychelles	26,573,615	0.004	0.002	0	17,773,615	17,773,615
Sierra Leone	313,145,892	0.048	0.042	0	209,445,892	209,445,892
Singapore	1,741,553,201	0.265	0.059	0	879,053,201	879,053,201
Slovak Republic	1,079,553,100	0.164	0.021	0	722,053,100	722,053,100
Slovenia	699,671,198	0.106	0.028	0	467,971,198	467,971,198
Solomon Islands	31,405,181	0.005	0.003	0	21,005,181	21,005,181
Somalia	133,472,020	0.020	0.020	0	89,272,020	89,272,020
South Africa	5,642,363,543	0.858	−0.080	0	3,773,863,543	3,773,863,543
Spain	11,198,715,706	1.703	−0.119	8,149,815,706	0	8,149,815,706
Sri Lanka	1,248,355,948	0.190	0.046	0	834,955,948	834,955,948
St. Kitts And Nevis	26,875,588	0.004	0.003	0	17,975,588	17,975,588
St. Lucia	46,201,853	0.007	0.005	0	30,901,853	30,901,853
St. Vincent & Grens.	25,063,750	0.004	0.003	0	16,763,750	16,763,750
Sudan	512,448,003	0.078	−0.055	0	342,748,003	342,748,003
Suriname	278,117,036	0.042	0.037	0	186,017,036	186,017,036
Swaziland	153,100,258	0.023	0.013	0	102,400,258	102,400,258
Sweden	3,806,492,700	0.579	0.076	0	1,410,992,700	1,410,992,700
Switzerland	3,458,500,000	0.526	0.088	0	0	0
Syrian Arab Republic	886,592,420	0.135	0.008	0	592,992,420	592,992,420

continued...

Appendix 2B. (continued)

Country name	Adjusted quota	Adjusted quota share	Adjusted over-rep	Change in quota		
				Correcting over-rep	Proportional	Total
Tajikistan	262,716,419	0.040	0.027	0	175,716,419	175,716,419
Tanzania	600,624,088	0.091	0.049	0	401,724,088	401,724,088
Thailand	5,486,907,661	0.834	−0.061	2,802,970,706	1,602,036,955	4,405,007,661
Timor-Leste	24,761,777	0.004	0.004	0	16,561,777	16,561,777
Togo	221,648,105	0.034	0.020	0	148,248,105	148,248,105
Tonga	20,836,130	0.003	0.002	0	13,936,130	13,936,130
Trinidad And Tobago	794,466,161	0.121	0.094	0	458,866,161	458,866,161
Tunisia	865,152,344	0.132	−0.008	0	578,652,344	578,652,344
Turkey	5,628,457,214	0.856	−0.063	3,021,091,403	1,643,365,811	4,664,457,214
Turkmenistan	227,083,617	0.035	−0.020	0	151,883,617	151,883,617
Uganda	545,061,075	0.083	0.015	0	364,561,075	364,561,075
Ukraine	3,247,936,751	0.494	−0.003	0	1,875,936,751	1,875,936,751
United Arab Emirates	1,448,077,923	0.220	0.059	0	836,377,923	836,377,923
United Kingdom	20,003,489,516	3.041	−0.212	9,264,989,516	0	9,264,989,516
United States	132,216,090,636	20.103	−1.403	95,066,790,636	0	95,066,790,636
Uruguay	925,546,923	0.141	0.055	0	619,046,923	619,046,923
Uzbekistan	832,237,299	0.127	0.041	0	556,637,299	556,637,299
Vanuatu	51,335,392	0.008	0.007	0	34,335,392	34,335,392
Venezuela, Rep. Bol.	2,659,100,000	0.404	0.135	0	0	0
Vietnam	1,858,443,596	0.283	−0.086	455,947,496	1,073,396,100	1,529,343,596
YEMEN, Republic of	735,303,999	0.112	0.079	0	491,803,999	491,803,999
Zambia	702,575,231	0.107	0.089	0	213,475,231	213,475,231
Zimbabwe	836,604,116	0.127	0.070	0	483,204,116	483,204,116

Appendix 2C

Final Quota Adjustment in the Mandatory Quota Reduction Scenario

Country name	Adjusted quota	Adjusted quota share	Adjusted over-rep
Afghanistan, I.S. of	161,900,000	0.070	0.070
Albania	48,700,000	0.021	−0.007
Algeria	824,278,316	0.356	−0.031
Angola	286,300,000	0.124	0.062
Antigua and Barbuda	13,500,000	0.006	0.004
Argentina	2,117,100,000	0.915	0.016
Armenia	92,000,000	0.040	0.021
Australia	2,365,489,078	1.023	−0.089
Austria	1,065,698,743	0.461	−0.040
Azerbaijan	160,900,000	0.070	0.015
Bahamas, The	130,300,000	0.056	0.045
Bahrain, Kingdom of	135,000,000	0.058	0.033
Bangladesh	1,063,543,203	0.460	−0.040
Barbados	67,500,000	0.029	0.021
Belarus	386,400,000	0.167	0.055

continued...

Appendix 2C. (continued)

Country name	Adjusted quota	Adjusted quota share	Adjusted over-rep
Belgium	1,246,332,955	0.539	−0.047
Belize	18,800,000	0.008	0.005
Benin	61,900,000	0.027	0.012
Bhutan	6,300,000	0.003	−0.002
Bolivia	171,500,000	0.074	0.030
Bosnia & Herzegovina	169,100,000	0.073	0.073
Botswana	63,000,000	0.027	−0.003
Brazil	6,513,099,121	2.815	−0.016
Bulgaria	252,198,125	0.109	−0.009
Burkina Faso	60,200,000	0.026	−0.002
Burundi	77,000,000	0.033	0.024
Cambodia	87,500,000	0.038	−0.006
Cameroon	185,700,000	0.080	0.022
Canada	4,443,754,392	1.921	−0.048
Cape Verde	9,600,000	0.004	−0.001
Central African Rep.	55,700,000	0.024	0.015
Chad	56,000,000	0.024	0.006
Chile	856,100,000	0.370	0.053
China,P.R.: Mainland	28,886,062,919	12.487	−0.072
Colombia	1,219,173,157	0.527	−0.046
Comoros	8,900,000	0.004	0.002
Congo, Dem. Rep. Of	140,541,177	0.061	−0.005
Congo, Republic Of	84,600,000	0.037	0.029
Costa Rica	164,100,000	0.071	−0.005
Cote d'Ivoire	325,200,000	0.141	0.086
Croatia	365,100,000	0.158	0.065
Cyprus	139,600,000	0.060	0.031
Czech Republic	819,300,000	0.354	0.031
Denmark	726,847,929	0.314	−0.027
Djibouti	15,900,000	0.007	0.004
Dominica	8,200,000	0.004	0.003
Dominican Republic	218,900,000	0.095	−0.016
Ecuador	302,300,000	0.131	0.032
Egypt	1,174,474,438	0.508	−0.007
El Salvador	171,300,000	0.074	0.018
Equatorial Guinea	32,600,000	0.014	−0.012
Eritrea	15,900,000	0.007	0.007
Estonia	65,200,000	0.028	−0.005
Ethiopia	133,700,000	0.058	−0.040
Fiji	70,300,000	0.030	0.021
Finland	610,448,794	0.264	−0.023
France	7,573,644,664	3.274	−0.037

continued...

Appendix 2C. (continued)

Country name	Adjusted quota	Adjusted quota share	Adjusted over-rep
Gabon	154,300,000	0.067	0.050
Gambia, The	31,100,000	0.013	0.008
Georgia	150,300,000	0.065	0.041
Germany	10,646,383,147	4.602	−0.052
Ghana	369,000,000	0.160	0.071
Greece	823,000,000	0.356	−0.051
Grenada	11,700,000	0.005	0.003
Guatemala	210,200,000	0.091	−0.010
Guinea	107,100,000	0.046	0.013
Guinea-Bissau	14,200,000	0.006	0.004
Guyana	90,900,000	0.039	0.032
Haiti	81,900,000	0.035	0.007
Honduras	129,500,000	0.056	0.020
Hungary	610,017,686	0.264	−0.023
Iceland	117,600,000	0.051	0.033
India	12,942,772,970	5.595	−0.083
Indonesia	3,325,749,373	1.438	−0.016
Iran, I.R. of	1,910,670,238	0.826	−0.072
Iraq	0	0.000	0.000
Ireland	581,133,457	0.251	−0.022
Israel	590,617,831	0.255	−0.022
Italy	7,261,474,108	3.139	−0.018
Jamaica	44,835,222	0.019	−0.002
Japan	16,580,490,154	7.167	−0.009
Jordan	170,500,000	0.074	0.029
Kazakhstan	365,700,000	0.158	−0.025
Kenya	271,400,000	0.117	0.050
Kiribati	5,600,000	0.002	0.002
Korea	3,776,503,973	1.633	−0.030
Kuwait	150,456,659	0.065	−0.006
Kyrgyz Republic	88,800,000	0.038	0.021
Lao People S Dem.Rep	52,900,000	0.023	0.003
Latvia	126,800,000	0.055	0.011
Lebanon	203,000,000	0.088	0.047
Lesotho	34,900,000	0.015	0.006
Liberia	71,300,000	0.031	0.031
Libya	222,451,679	0.096	−0.008
Lithuania	144,200,000	0.062	−0.012
Luxembourg	279,100,000	0.121	0.066
Macedonia, FYR	68,900,000	0.030	0.002
Madagascar	122,200,000	0.053	0.025
Malawi	69,400,000	0.030	0.016

continued...

Appendix 2C. (continued)

Country name	Adjusted quota	Adjusted quota share	Adjusted over-rep
Malaysia	1,005,774,744	0.435	−0.038
Maldives	8,200,000	0.004	−0.001
Mali	93,300,000	0.040	0.020
Malta	102,000,000	0.044	0.029
Marshall Islands,Rep	3,500,000	0.002	0.002
Mauritania	64,400,000	0.028	0.018
Mauritius	101,600,000	0.044	0.017
Mexico	4,302,915,088	1.860	−0.046
Micronesia, Fed.Sts.	5,100,000	0.002	0.002
Moldova	123,200,000	0.053	0.040
Mongolia	51,100,000	0.022	0.013
Morocco	588,200,000	0.254	0.018
Mozambique	113,600,000	0.049	0.007
Myanmar	258,400,000	0.112	−0.030
Namibia	136,500,000	0.059	0.034
Nepal	71,300,000	0.031	−0.037
Netherlands	2,016,291,675	0.872	−0.076
New Zealand	354,370,698	0.153	−0.013
Nicaragua	130,000,000	0.056	0.029
Niger	65,800,000	0.028	0.009
Nigeria	535,436,019	0.231	−0.020
Norway	763,923,209	0.330	−0.029
Oman	194,000,000	0.084	0.012
Pakistan	1,358,852,119	0.587	−0.051
Palau	3,100,000	0.001	0.001
Panama	206,600,000	0.089	0.050
Papua New Guinea	131,600,000	0.057	0.032
Paraguay	99,900,000	0.043	−0.009
Peru	638,400,000	0.276	−0.006
Philippines	1,480,855,656	0.640	−0.056
Poland	1,816,257,606	0.785	−0.068
Portugal	867,400,000	0.375	−0.003
Qatar	263,800,000	0.114	0.077
Romania	650,110,722	0.281	−0.024
Russia	5,644,491,705	2.440	−0.084
Rwanda	80,100,000	0.035	0.014
Samoa	11,600,000	0.005	0.003
San Marino	17,000,000	0.007	0.007
Sao Tome & Principe	7,400,000	0.003	0.003
Saudi Arabia	1,151,489,216	0.498	−0.043
Senegal	161,800,000	0.070	0.036
Serbia & Montenegro	160,372,141	0.069	−0.006

continued...

Appendix 2C. (continued)

Country name	Adjusted quota	Adjusted quota share	Adjusted over-rep
Seychelles	8,800,000	0.004	0.002
Sierra Leone	103,700,000	0.045	0.039
Singapore	438,867,848	0.190	−0.017
Slovak Republic	357,500,000	0.155	0.012
Slovenia	231,700,000	0.100	0.022
Solomon Islands	10,400,000	0.004	0.003
Somalia	44,200,000	0.019	0.019
South Africa	2,096,072,481	0.906	−0.031
Spain	4,111,318,763	1.777	−0.044
Sri Lanka	413,400,000	0.179	0.034
St. Kitts And Nevis	8,900,000	0.004	0.003
St. Lucia	15,300,000	0.007	0.005
St. Vincent & Grens.	8,300,000	0.004	0.003
Sudan	169,700,000	0.073	−0.060
Suriname	92,100,000	0.040	0.035
Swaziland	50,700,000	0.022	0.012
Sweden	1,070,440,930	0.463	−0.040
Switzerland	930,761,968	0.402	−0.035
Syrian Arab Republic	293,600,000	0.127	0.000
Tajikistan	87,000,000	0.038	0.025
Tanzania	198,900,000	0.086	0.044
Thailand	1,905,065,835	0.824	−0.072
Timor–Leste	8,200,000	0.004	0.004
Togo	73,400,000	0.032	0.018
Tonga	6,900,000	0.003	0.002
Trinidad And Tobago	57,768,459	0.025	−0.002
Tunisia	286,500,000	0.124	−0.015
Turkey	1,954,212,136	0.845	−0.074
Turkmenistan	75,200,000	0.033	−0.022
Uganda	180,500,000	0.078	0.010
Ukraine	1,056,214,369	0.457	−0.040
United Arab Emirates	343,593,001	0.149	−0.013
United Kingdom	7,442,041,930	3.217	−0.037
United States	49,464,977,092	21.383	−0.123
Uruguay	306,500,000	0.132	0.046
Uzbekistan	275,600,000	0.119	0.034
Vanuatu	17,000,000	0.007	0.006
Venezuela, Rep. Bol.	573,373,514	0.248	−0.022
Vietnam	785,047,496	0.339	−0.030
Yemen, Republic Of	243,500,000	0.105	0.073
Zambia	38,368,604	0.017	−0.001
Zimbabwe	122,003,537	0.053	−0.005

Appendix 3

Independent Professional Board Scenario

Chair	Voting power in per cent	Number of countries
1. Euro (Germany, France, Belgium, Netherlands, Finland Italy, Spain, Portugal, Greece, Austria, Luxembourg, Iceland, Ireland, Malta, San Marino)	23.065	15
2. U.S. Dollar (U.S., Panama, El Salvador, Ecuador)	17.436	4
3. East Asia (Japan, Fiji, Myanmar)	6.305	3
4. Anglo (UK, St. Kitts, St Lucia, St. Vincent)	4.997	4
5. Arabian (Saudi Arabia, United Arab Emirates, Bahrain)	**3.589**	3
6. West/Central Asia (Russia, Tajikistan, Azerbaijan, Kyrgyzstan, Turkmenistan, Uzbekistan)	3.118	6
7. North/Central Asia (China, Mongolia, Lao)	3.010	3
8. Anglo American (Canada, Antigua and Barbuda, Belie, Dominica, Grenada)	3.009	5
9. Middle East (Egypt, Jordan, Lebanon, Kuwait, Iraq Libya, Maldives, Oman, Qatar, Syria, Yemen)	2.891	11
10. Latin North (Mexico, Venezuela, Costa Rica, Guatemala Honduras, Nicaragua)	2.771	6
11. North Europe (Sweden, Norway, Denmark)	**2.659**	3
12. North Africa and Mid East (Iran, Morocco, Afghanistan, Tunisia Algeria, Ghana, Pakistan	2.467	7
13. South East Asia (Indonesia, Cambodia, Brunei, Malaysia, Philippines, Nepal, Tonga, Vietnam)	2.462	8
14. Trinidad, Jamaica, Bahamas, Barbados	2.460	10
15. Indo (India, Bangladesh, Sri Lanka, Bhutan, Timor, Leste)	2.411	5
16. Mixed I (Turkey, Kazakhstan, Singapore, Thailand, Korea)	2.314	5
17. East Europe (Belarus, Ukraine, Romania, Moldova, Macedonia, Georgia, Bosnia and Herzegovina, Armenia Albania, Bulgaria, Serbia and Montenegro)	2.217	11
18. Slovak Republic, Estonia, Latvia, Lithuania,	2.180	9
19. Slovak Republic, Estonia, Latvia, Lithuania,	2.116	11
20. Mixed II (Switzerland, Israel, Cyprus) Slovak Republic, Estonia, Latvia, Lithuania,	2.115	3
21. Latin South (Argentina, Bolivia, Chile, Paraguay, Peru, Uruguay)	1.995	6
22. Africa I (Mozambique, Cameroon, Sudan, Sao Tome, Djibouti, Guinea-Bissau, Madagascar, Guinea, Mauritius, Congo Republic Botswana, South Africa, Namibia	1.524	13
23. Africa II (Nigeria, Benin, Burundi, Ethiopia, Eritrea, Sierra Leone, Gambia, Lesotho, Malawi, Cape Verde, Burkina Faso, Comoros Swaziland, Tanzania, Uganda	1.455	15
24. Mauritania, Niger, Rwanda, Senegal, Togo	1.433	15

Notes

1 Draft, February 10 2005. Paper prepared for the Technical Group Meeting of the Group of XXIV, Manila Philippines, March 2005. Preliminary and for discussions only, please do not quote or cite without the author's permission and direct comments to glefortv@glefort.cl

2 The views expressed in this paper, as well as all errors remaining are the author's.

3 Bordo and James, 2000, describe the market failures and the public goods provided by the IMF.

4 Krueger, 1997, describes how the roles and responsibilities of the Fund have evolved over time as the institution adapted in the service of the membership.

5 Buira, 2004, discusses the relationship between governance and Fund effectiveness.

6 Buira, 2001a and 2001b, refer to the need for a more representative quota structure; Alberich and Martinez, 2000, ask for the effective quota structure to better reflect that of the quota formula.

7 See IMF 2000b; 2001a; 2004, for information on the status of the discussion on quota formulas. Variables like exposure to the volatility of terms of trade or capital flows are not represented as volatility ratios but as standard deviation and consequently, highly correlated to the scale variables.

8 IMF, 2004.

9 Standard and Poor's sovereign credit rating as of December 2004 was used. See Appendix IA and IB for the list of countries and data set on the variables used.

10 The over-representation of developing countries could be an issue of classification. To the extent that Argentina is successful in its debt exchange and is reinstated among the borrowing nations, it would be classified among EMs rather than as a developing country, thus reducing the over-representation of the latter group at the Executive Board.

11 The value of the 't-test' for the IMF Position coefficient is just over 1, indicating that this coefficient is different from 0 with 30 per cent of significance.

12 Such an increase in basic votes would restore their original level of 11 per cent of the voting power.

13 A different matter would be to consider the additional variables like reserves or volatility of external payments as ratios to a scale variable like GDP, imports or some other. In such a case, the information content of the additional variables could be significant. However, developing and testing quota formulas would be quite an exercise in itself, especially if the purpose is to convince regarding its special practicality and usefulness.

14 The tolerance used of ±0.1 per cent of total quotas greatly simplifies the adjustment procedure, concentrating the effort in the large distortions. However, this procedure implies disregarding distortions that are small in absolute terms but not relative to small countries quotas. The tolerance could be reduced over time as the major distortions are corrected and more precision could be demanded.

15 The term independent professional Executive Director is used in contrast to the political representative ED, who defends the interest of the single country that nominates them. To the extent that the Executive Board functions as a parliament in which the larger groups are more than proportionally represented, the under-representation of EMs and developing countries is amplified.

16 Eichengreen and De Gregorio, 1999.

17 It is possible to consider other limits. However more than 15 countries in a single chair would almost repeat the current condition of the African chairs and less than 15 as a maximum would require a second Euro chair. Increasing to four the minimum number of countries would not have a major impact on the structure of the Board. Four small countries would move to the two advanced country chairs (Nordic and Swiss) and two EM chairs (China and Saudi Arabia) with only three constituents.

References

Alberich, I and Martínez, M, 2000, *Quotas and Representation in the International Monetary Fund*, International Department, Bank of Spain.

Bordo, Michael and James, Harold, 2000. The International Monetary Fund: It's Present Role in Historical Perspective, *NBER Working Paper 7724*, Cambridge: National Bureau of Economic Research.

Buira, Ariel, 2001, *A new voting structure for the IMF*, Washington G24, http://www.g24.org/newvotig.pdf

Buira, Ariel, 2001b, *The Governance of The International Monetary Fund*, Kaul, Inge *et al* (eds), Oxford: Oxford University Press.

Buira, Ariel, 2004, *Can More Representative Governance Improve Global Economic Performance?*, Washington:G24, http://www.g24.org/001gva04.pdf

De Gregorio J, Eichengreen, B, Ito, T, Wyplosz, C, 1999, *An Independent and Accountable IMF by CEPR*, The Brookings Institution, pp. 134, http://www.cepr.org/pubs/books/p130.asp

Feldstein, Martin, 1998, Refocusing the IMF, *Foreign Affairs*, 77, 2: pp. 20–33.

IMF (International Monetary Fund), 1993. *Articles of Agreement*, Washington, DC: IMF, http://www.imf.org/external/pubs/ft/aa/

IMF, 2000b, *Report to the IMF Executive Board of the Quota Formula Review Group*, Washington, DC: IMF.

IMF, 2001a, *Alternative Quota Formulas: Considerations*, Washington, DC: IMF.

IMF, 2001b, *Review of the Fund's Experience in Governance Issues*, Washington, DC: IMF, http://www.imf.org/external/np/gov/2001/eng/report.htm

IMF, 2004, *Quotas—Updated Calculations*, Washington, DC: IMF.

IMF, 2004a, *World Economic Outlook*, Database for the September 2004 round, Washington, DC: IMF.

IMF, Various issues, International Financial Statistics, Washington, D.C. Data series in: http://ifs.apdi.net/imf/logon.aspx

Krueger, Anne O, 1997, Whither the World Bank and the IMF?, *NBER Working Paper 6327*, Cambridge: National Bureau of Economic Research.

Mikesell, Raymond F, 1994, The Bretton Woods Debates: A Memoir, *Essays in International Finance 192*, Princeton: Princeton University, International Finance Section.

Standard and Poor's Sovereign Credit Ratings, December 2004.

World Bank, 2001, *World Development Indicators*, Washington, DC.

World Bank, Various years, *World Development Report*, New York: Oxford University.

6

MAKING THE IMF AND THE WORLD BANK MORE ACCOUNTABLE

Ngaire Woods[1]

Abstract:

Accused of being secretive, unaccountable and ineffective, both the IMF and the World Bank are seeking to become more transparent, participatory and accountable. Yet, few attempts have been made to dissect the existing structure of accountability within the International Financial Institutions (IFIs). This paper critically examines the existing accountability of the institutions and offers some recommendations for making them more accountable. It also warns that the limits of their accountability should limit the legitimacy of their activities.

Introduction

During the 1990s, the International Monetary Fund (IMF) and the World Bank (the Bank)[2] found themselves accused of being secretive, unaccountable and ineffective. Not only radical non-governmental organizations (NGOs) but equally, their major shareholders are demanding that the institutions become more transparent, accountable and participatory. Accountability became the catch cry of officials, scholars and activists in discussing the reform of the institutions. However, few attempts have been made to dissect the existing structure of accountability within the International Financial Institutions (IFIs), to explain its flaws and to propose solutions and is the aim of this paper.

The first section examines the structure of accountability planned by the founders of the IMF and the Bank. The second section discusses the defects in this structure. Section three analyses the recent attempts to make the institutions more accountable. The conclusion offers some recommendations for improving the institutions and a warning about the limits of accountability at the international level.

How are the IMF and the World Bank Accountable to their Government Members?

Like many international organizations, the IMF and the Bank face complex problems of accountability which begin when one tries to answer the simple question: to whom should they be accountable and how? Within democratic political systems, several mechanisms exist to prevent the abuse or misuse of political power.[3] These measures range from elections, through to the appointment of ombudsmen and judicial review. The aim is to ensure that political actions are predictable, non-arbitrary and procedurally fair, that decisionmakers are answerable and that rules and parameters on the exercise of power are enforced. For all these reasons, accountability within public institutions, whether national or international, is a desirable thing.[4]

Unlike a democratically elected government, international institutions cannot claim that voters elect them and can vote them out of office. Nor, in the past, have the institutions been subjected to the normal restraints politicians face from the checks and balances of government, including the role played by judges, ombudsmen and the like. Rather, international organizations grapple with an unwieldy structure of government representation which makes ensuring their own accountability extremely difficult. In the past, when such institutions were required to perform a narrow range of technical functions, the problem was less acute. Today, however, the international financial institutions are being required to perform a much wider range of tasks directly affecting a wider range of people. This makes their accountability all the more important.

The basic structure of accountability in the international financial institutions works through representatives of governments. At the top of the system are the Boards of Governors—the Ministers of Finance or Development, Central Bank Governors and equivalents—who meet just once per year and are supposed to maintain overall oversight and control of the institutions. However, the day to day operations and main work of the institutions is overseen by representatives of member states who sit on the Executive Boards of each institution. The Executive Directors (as they are called) have a dual role—to represent a country or a group of countries (this is further described below); and to collectively manage the organization. Executive Directors appoint and can dismiss the head of each organization, who in turn controls the management and staff.

The chain of representative accountability described is in practice a long and imperfect one. Flaws in each link highlight how weak the relationship between most member governments and the IMF and the Bank are. Simply put, member governments (with the obvious exception of the United States) are too far removed from the workings of the representative body (the Executive Board) which in turn, exercises too little control over the staff and management of the institutions for its role to be described as an exercise of vertical accountability.

Why do the IMF and World Bank not Seem Accountable?

The core of the problem of accountability lies in the flawed representativeness of the Executive Board in both the Fund and Bank. The Board should reflect governments who are members of each organization. Yet, representation is inadequate in two respects. In the first place, the Board does not adequately represent all members, and it particularly fails adequately to represent countries with the most intensive relationships with the institutions, for example, the African members. Secondly, the representatives on the Boards of the institutions are too distant from the governments they represent and stakeholders most affected by the work of the institutions. Let us examine each of these arguments in turn.

Representation on the Executive Boards is too Unequal

The Board of Executive Directors (the Board) is the vital link from countries (and voters) to both the IMF and the Bank. Yet, only the largest member countries (United States, Germany, France, Japan, UK, Saudi Arabia, Russia and China) are directly represented by their own Executive Directors. All other economies are grouped within constituencies represented by just one Executive Director. This means that most national governments have only the weakest link to the formal deliberations and decision-making processes of the institutions.

For example, in the IMF, there are 24 African countries, 21 of whom are very low income (IDA eligible) and most of whom have an 'intensive care' relationship with the institution. They are all deeply affected by the work of the institution. However, they are represented by just one Executive Director, with a voting share of 1.41 per cent. Likewise, in the Bank, their voting share is tiny. Further exacerbating this lack of representation is the fact that these countries also lack influence in the informal processes of consultation and decision-making with both the IMF and the Bank.

When the Board makes decisions, each country has voting power which is exercised by the Executive Director representing it. This voting power depends upon a country's quota, which is determined by a formula which attempts to translate relative weight in the world economy into a share of contributions and votes (and in the IMF, access to resources) in respect of each institution. The formula has been criticized for some time and its technical elements were reviewed for the Managing Director of the IMF in 2000.[5] The real problem with quotas and voting power, however, is that they were created to govern institutions with very different world roles to those played by the IMF and the Bank today.

Voting shares in the Bank and IMF are allocated according to rules formulated in 1944. At that time, members of both institutions were expected to be contributors as well as borrowers (with the exception of the United States). European countries expected to draw both upon the IMF for assistance in crises and on the International Bank for Reconstruction and Development (later part of the Bank group) for post-war reconstruction and development. Hence, 'shareholding members' were also 'stakeholders' in the work of the institution. Their accountability was largely 'constitutionalist', with duties and actions carefully proscribed by the *Articles of Agreement*. Neither the Bank nor the Fund were given an explicit mandate to enter into policy conditionality and to attempt to alter in any far reaching way, the economic structure of a member's economy.

These founding presumptions of the IMF and Bank were rapidly superseded by events. The role of the Bank (then actually the IBRD) was transformed in 1947 when the Marshall Plan was announced to deal with reconstruction in Europe. This left the Bank lending exclusively to developing countries. In the 1970s, the IMF's role changed dramatically when the Bretton Woods system of exchange rates collapsed. By the 1980s, both institutions had become heavily involved in conditionality and policy based lending. Throughout this time, the membership of both institutions more than trebled, as decolonization brought a host of new, independent states into their midst.

The result of these changes has been to dramatically expand the 'stakeholders' in the institutions. The original stakeholders made large contributions to the basic capital of the institutions. A subsequent group of stakeholders have become those who pay most of the running costs of the institutions through loan charges (non-concessional borrowing countries). A further (overlapping) group of stakeholders are those whose cooperation is vital if the IMF and Bank are to fulfil their respective purposes. This now embraces a much wider, indeed universal, category of countries.

By 2000, in the wake of the financial crises of the 1990s, the powerful industrialized members of the IMF and the Bank had cast the institutions into the role of ensuring 'forceful, far reaching structural reforms' in the economies of all members in order to, among other things, correct weaknesses in domestic financial systems and ensure growth and poverty alleviation.[6] The result is not only that all members have a high stake in the institutions but that equally, the institutions have a high stake in gaining a deep political commitment to change in all member countries. Yet, the stake of countries whose commitment is now being sought is not reflected on the Executive Boards of either the Fund or the Bank—indeed it has even been diminished.

When the IMF and Bank were created, there was a clear and explicit concern to ensure some equality among members to reinforce the 'universal' and 'public' character of the institutions as opposed to giving them a structure which simply reflected economic and financial strength in the world economy.[7] This was achieved by giving every member of the institution 250 'basic votes'[8], to which were added weighted votes apportioned on the basis of the quota mentioned above. In this way, two kinds of stake were recognized—to a degree, every member had an equal stake in the institution and to a degree, the different contributions and influences of states was also recognized. As I have argued elsewhere, this balance which was explicit in the foundation of the institutions, has subsequently been dramatically eroded. The proportion of basic votes to total votes has diminished from its high point of 14 per cent of all votes in 1955, to around 3 per cent in both the Fund and the Bank.[9] Yet if anything, the role of basic votes should have increased as the stakes in the institution changed in the ways described above.

The Executive Boards do not Adequately Hold the Staff and Management to Account

The Executive Boards are the lynchpin of accountability of the Fund and Bank. For this reason, the quality and depth of their oversight and control of each institution's work is vital. In each organization, the Board is expected to appoint and oversee the senior management and work of the institutions. However, in practice, the whole Board rarely holds the management and staff of the institutions tightly to account. Most Executive Directors have little incentive to do so.

In the first place, it is difficult for the members of the Executive Boards to prepare positions on all countries, papers and issues brought to the Board meetings. Many Executive Directors are in the job only for a short time. Indeed, in some multi-country constituencies, there is regular and short-lived rotation of the Executive Directorship.

In the second place, the Executive Board is not assisted in playing an active role by the staff and management of each institution, who seldom divulge internal disagreements to the Board, tending instead to attach considerable importance to presenting a unified view in Board discussions.[10]

A third feature of the Executive Boards is that many decisions are taken, or agreement reached on them, prior to Board meetings. As reports on both the

Fund and the Bank aver, real debates over policy and issues are conducted outside of the Board.[11] Controversial cases and stand-off debates are rare. A loan, for example, that does not meet with US approval would seldom be presented to a Board for discussion. Before getting that far, in most (but not all) cases, staff and management would have been in dialogue with those whose agreement was necessary for the loan to go through.

Finally, the Executive Board's limited oversight has also been attributed to Directors being protective about the countries they represent and expecting (and reciprocating) similar deference from their colleagues on the Board. Hence, in the words of the External Evaluation into Surveillance, what is supposed to be 'peer pressure' in fact becomes 'peer protection'.[12]

Underscoring the particular inability of Directors representing developing countries to exercise oversight are political and institutional features of the Fund and Bank. Mustering a coalition of countries within the IMF or Bank requires extensive preparation and lobbying. Each Director on the Board is supported by an Alternative Director and a set number of advisers is allocated and paid for by the institution. Clearly, this greatly benefits countries which have their own chair or are in a small constituency. Conversely, it means that the resources spent on supporting any chair representing a large number of countries are tiny if measured on a per country basis.

The workload imposed on many developing country representatives is simply unwieldy. As mentioned above, in the 24-country African constituency within the IMF, some 21 countries are IDA eligible (very low income). If we assume that all are within PRGF supported programs, the Executive Director's office should be involved in some 42 onsite missions which present PRGF semi-annual reviews to the Executive Board. On top of this, there is the work required to prepare 24 countries' Article IV Consultations (typically on an annual basis), PRSP Joint Staff Assessments or informal Board meetings on country matters designed to provide Board members with timely updates on country developments. Further to this work, since most countries (21 out of 24) are eligible for debt relief under the HIPC Initiative, the Executive Director and other officials will also have to prepare for considerations by the Board of decision and completion points, preparing documents of the respective countries as they progress under the Initiative. On top of all of this, there are field missions for those members undertaking a voluntary assessment of inter-national standards,[13] other missions related to Financial Sector Assessment Programs,[14] as well as possible technical assistance missions. Importantly, this exercise only takes into account the duties related to the Executive Director holding the chair of the constituency that elected them and does not consider the heavier workload resulting from their being members of the Executive Board, which is '...responsible for conducting the business of the Fund...'

(Article XII, Section 12a) and oversees the whole range of activities and policies carried out by the institution.

In numerous constituency consultations, report and accountability to each member country is more difficult. A modest recognition of this has been made in the recent decision to introduce a communication system which will enable video conferencing and access to Bank and Fund documents from the capitals. However, the fact that there is already very little support from member country bureaucracies suggests that this will not resolve the problem. Unlike the British, American or Dutch chairs, to name but three who benefit from substantial back-up technical support from their home bureaucracies, many developing country Chairs do not.

The Heads of both Organizations are Selected by A Non-Transparent, Process which Excludes most Member Countries

A further, very obvious way in which the IMF and the Bank seem inadequately accountable to their membership lies in the appointment of the heads of each organization. Appointed by the Executive Boards, it is to these heads of the organizations that all staff must eventually account. Yet, in neither the Bank nor the Fund is there an open and transparent process of appointment: whether aimed at achieving political representation or technical excellence. Rather a 60-year-old political compromise means that in each organization, the head is appointed by convention according to the wishes of the United States (in respect of the Bank) and Western Europe (in respect of the IMF). This process has come under scrutiny during the last two appointments of the Managing Director of the IMF and the latest appointment of the President of the Bank—leading to press and policy attention not so much to the personalities involved but to the lack of transparency and accountability in the process of selection. Although both institutions have established committees to propose improvements in the appointment procedure, until the United States and European countries are prepared to give up their privilege, change in this procedure will not occur.

The Role of the IMF and World Bank has Expanded, their Accountability has not

The problems of accountability highlighted above have all been magnified by the increase and transformation of the activities of the IMF and Bank. Previously, the need to respect the sovereignty of member governments limited their range of activities. However, both now reach deep into policy making within member governments, going well beyond the delicately respectful parameters set out in the original Articles of Agreement.

Specifically, both the IMF and the Bank have embraced areas of policy it was inconceivable for them to touch prior to the 1980s. The expansion was tracked in the early 1990s by measuring numbers of performance criteria on which loans are conditional that have increased. In a sample of 25 countries, there were between 6 and 10 measures in the 1980s as contrasted with around 26 measures in the 1990s.[15] More recent work by the IMF details the growth in that institution's conditionality, expressed in performance criteria, prior actions and program reviews. In this work, we find instances of borrowers facing dozens of 'prior actions': Ukraine's programme in 1997, for example, had 45 specified prior actions and its 1998 programme had 38 prior actions.[16]

Deeper and wider conditionality has extended the purview of the international financial institutions within member countries to a degree that has led both institutions to review their conditionality (the IMF in 2002, the Bank in 2005). By the early 1990s, they were no longer engaged in monitoring specific macroeconomic policy targets in the context of a crisis, or specific project loans and conditions. Both institutions had become engaged in negotiations with borrowers which cover virtually all issues of economic policy making—and beyond (with good governance extending into the rule of law, judicial reform, corporate governance and so forth). This new wide ranging domain of advice and conditionality directly affects a wider range of policies, people, groups and organizations within countries.

Yet the IMF and the Bank were neither created nor structured, to undertake, or to be accountable for, such wide ranging activities. They were created to deal with a narrow, clearly stipulated range of technical issues. For this reason, at their birth, it was decided that they should only deal with member countries through the Treasury, Finance Ministry, Central Bank or similar institution of a country and that only a representative of these agencies could sit on the Boards of the institutions.[17] This is still true today.

Meanwhile, the work of both the IMF and the Bank has broadened and deepened far beyond the purviews of the Finance Ministries or Central Banks with whom they are negotiating. This means that, through conditionality and loan agreements, the Fund and Bank are making Finance Ministries or Central Banks formally accountable for policies which should properly lie within the scope of other agencies and for which those other agencies are domestically accountable. A policy affecting the distribution of healthcare, for example, we would expect to be the responsibility of the Minister of Health whom we could expect to be answerable to voters and the society at large. Yet, as the Fund and Bank intrude further into these kinds of decisions, the risk is that the line of accountability they establish with the Finance Ministry or Central Bank will override other agencies and local or democratic accountability.[18]

A further implication is that while in theory, different agencies within the government compete for and debate competing priorities and goals, negotiations with the Fund and Bank heavily sway these debates, subjecting broad areas of policy to the narrower focus, priorities and analysis of the Central Bank and Finance Ministry—even though neither necessarily have the desire, mandate, accountability, or expertise to evaluate and formulate policy in respect of these broader issues. In a subtle way, this point is underscored by a remark in the External Evaluation into IMF Surveillance, where the evaluators found that 'the most favourable appraisals came from those whose lines of work bore close similarities to the Fund's—central banks, and, to a lesser extent, finance ministries'.[19] Turned on its head, this statement emphasizes the degree to which the Fund's core mandate remains as that shared with central bankers. Yet at the same time, the institution is now formulating directions for policy in areas outside this formal mandate and expertise.

In the extreme, the problem becomes that succinctly expressed by Martin Feldstein in response to the IMF's intervention in East Asia:

> The legitimate political institutions of the country should determine the nation's economic structure and the nature of its institutions. A nation's desperate need for short term financial help does not give the IMF the moral right to substitute its technical judgements for the outcomes of the nation's political process.[20]

The accountability problem underscored here is: who makes particular policy decisions, by whose rules and under whose scrutiny?

Making the IMF and World Bank more Accountable

Aware of the criticisms they face and also frustrated by their limited effectiveness in implementing wider policy reform, both the IMF and the Bank have begun more explicitly to recognize a wider range of stakeholders in their work. Both institutions have undertaken a number of steps to make themselves more accountable to such stakeholders, including more transparency, new mechanisms of horizontal accountability and working more closely with non-governmental organizations. The implications for accountability are worth examining.

Transparency

First and foremost among the steps taken by the institutions in improving their own accountability is an increase in transparency and evaluation. Both the IMF and the Bank now publish a large amount of their own research and explanation of what they are doing (and to what effect) on their websites. They are also pressing governments to permit greater disclosure and publication of policies and agreements made with governments (which are confidential if the government so wishes). Both the IMF and the Bank each evaluate what they do, including their overall effectiveness and impact on the world. The Bank has an Operations Evaluation Department which reports to the President. The IMF has an Independent Evaluation Office which reports to its Board.

Transparency and internal evaluation are crucial pre-conditions for improving the accountability of both institutions. However, for information to feed into accountability requires outside institutions and actors to interpret and debate what they are doing, as well as monitoring and publicizing their activities, thereby helping to hold the institutions to account.

Ensuring Member Governments are Accountable to their Own People for Policies Agreed with the IFIs

A second part of the new transparency policies of both the Fund and the Bank has been to promote transparency within the countries with whom they work. The rationale here is that the IFIs advise and assist member countries, but it is governments in those countries who are accountable for all policies both to global markets and to their own people. Of course, this formulation glosses over the fact that some governments perceive little choice but to accept Fund or Bank advice and assistance, having resorted to the IFIs for assistance precisely because they have no alternatives.

The transparency being pursued by the IMF involves releasing their documentation and agreements with countries, with the agreement of the member governments concerned. The result has been the publication of information such as Public Information Notices (PINs) following about 80 per cent of its Article IV consultations and publishing Letters of Intent (LOIs) and related country documents that underpin Fund supported programs with respect to about 80 per cent of requests for, or reviews of, Fund resources.

Going further, in some cases, the IMF and the Bank now require governments to consult more and to be more actively accountable to their own people. At the behest of their largest contributors, both IFIs are requiring governments wanting enhanced debt relief under the Heavily Indebted Poor Countries (HIPC) initiative to produce a plan on how they intend to reduce poverty. The plan (labelled the Poverty Reduction Strategy Paper or PRSP) must be 'nationally owned' and produced in consultation with 'civil society'. Uganda and Mauritania were the first to qualify for enhanced debt relief under this programme, having each had a pre-existing well-developed plan for poverty reduction. Bolivia also qualified early by producing an interim PRSP on the basis of a 'national dialogue' already undertaken which sets out future plans for reducing poverty and for engaging civil society in the formulation of its full PRSP.[21]

The new disclosure and consultation measures highlight the sensitivity of the IFIs to concerns about accountability not just within the institutions, but within countries with whom they are working. Significantly, neither the Fund nor the Bank any longer describes their interlocutors in member countries exclusively as 'national authorities'. Rather, the Bank writes of 'development partners'[22] and the IMF of 'authorities and civil society', and of the need for its programmes to enjoy 'ownership by the societies affected'.[23] Along with this recognition has come the opening up of new mechanisms through which these groups can question or probe the legitimacy of the international financial institutions' assumptions and recommendations.

Agencies of Horizontal Accountability

The terms 'constitutionalism' and 'democracy' have been used to contrast different kinds of accountability.[24] For example, in the US political system, while democracy is served by the US Congress, constitutionalism is served by the Supreme Court. This simple contrast usefully highlights the way 'horizontal' or 'sideways' accountability can add to vertical accountability by contributing agencies and processes which exist to monitor and to enforce the mandate, obligations, rules and promises of institutions.

Within the international financial institutions, several agencies and processes have recently emerged with the aim of enhancing horizontal accountability. For example, the IMF created the Independent Evaluation Office mentioned above, after commissioning independent external evaluations of its work.[25] The Bank has long had an Operations Evaluation Department (OED) which reports to the Executive Board, rating the development impact and performance of all the Bank's completed lending operations, as well as the Bank's policies and processes and reports its findings to the Board. In 1993, in the context of a broad review of the Bank's Disclosure Policy, access was opened up to the OED's *Annual Review of Evaluation Results* and summaries of evaluation reports ('Précis') for selected projects. Since that time, much more of the OED's work has become publicly available.

A more powerful and unprecedented step towards greater horizontal accountability was taken in the Bank in 1993 when an Inspection Panel was created by the Executive Board. The Panel opens up the possibility for complaints to be made by any group that is able to show that:

- they live in the project area (or represent people who do) and are likely to be affected adversely by project activities

- they believe that the actual or likely harm they have suffered results from failure by the Bank to follow its policies and procedures
- their concerns have been discussed with Bank management and they are not satisfied with the outcome

The three-person Inspection Panel has powers to make a preliminary assessment of the merits of a complaint brought by a group, taking into account Bank management responses to the allegations. Subsequently, it can recommend to the Board that a full investigation be undertaken, and make recommendations on the basis of such a full investigation.

The Executive Board retains the power to permit investigations to proceed and to make final decisions based on the Panel's findings and Bank Management's recommendations. The Inspection Panel thus enhances the power of the Executive Board, as well as of a wide group of affected 'stakeholders' in the Bank's work.

One highly publicized case in the 1990s was that of the Western Poverty Reduction Project in Qinghai, China. The case resulted from a complaint filed by the International Campaign for Tibet (ICT), a US based NGO, acting on behalf of local people affected by the project, claiming in particular that it would harm Tibetan and Mongolian people. The final report of the inspection panel found that the Bank had failed to comply with some of its own policies, including those on environment, indigenous peoples and disclosure of information.[26] The case became notorious in the media, mobilizing US and international Tibet campaign groups as well as environment lobbies and supporters of indigenous groups.

Behind the media glare of such cases, a couple of serious questions of governance emerge regarding the role and implications of such inspections, as highlighted in retrospect by one of the expert consultants who advised the Inspection Panel in the China case. Wade points out that an initial problem with the Panel is that its 'image of success is to find projects out of compliance', he then writes that

> …since almost any project can be found to be out of compliance if one pushes hard enough, and since there is no limit to the cases that affected groups can bring—assisted by Washington based NGOs—the Bank is likely to be deluged with Inspection Panel investigations.[27]

The problems hinted at here are worth examining further for they touch on the core question of how widely or narrowly accountability should be defined and what kind of breach should trigger an enforcement action.

If the triggering mechanism for inspection is unlawfulness, this not only presumes that actions that are legal must also be legitimate in the eyes of the citizenry, but opens up the risk that minor legal infractions can be used as weapons for much larger political purposes. This point has been made in a study of accountability in which one scholar, alluding to the Clinton/ Lewinsky scandal, reminds us that 'minor legal infractions can be used by partisan opponents to thwart the clearly expressed preference of the public at large'.[28] In other words, beware of the fact that agencies of horizontal accountability can be abused.

That said, in many parts of the world, there is no recourse for people affected by Bank projects (or indeed other projects). Sometimes this may be due to failure of representation at the national level—a government fails to offer adequate representation or consideration of minority interests or significantly disenfranchises particular peoples. At other times, it may be due to a failure of representation at the international level—a particular group or interest falls outside the special relationship between a particular government agency and the Bank. The Inspection Panel offers a possible 'second best' recourse, whereby people affected by Bank projects have some way to try to hold the institution (and indirectly their own government) to account.

An alternative model of accountability is that provided by the new Office of the Compliance Adviser/Ombudsman (CAO) of the IFC and the Multilateral Investment Guarantee Agency (MIGA). This new ombudsman's office was created in June 1999, after consultations with shareholders, NGOs and members of the business community. The aim was to find a workable and constructive approach to dealing with environmental and social concerns and complaints of people directly impacted by the IFC and MIGA financed projects. The CAO or ombudsman and the staff are independent of the Bank and IFC and report directly to the President of the Bank. The emphasis of the office's work, however, is very much dialogue, mediation and conciliation. Other than the power to make recommendations, the CAO has no formal powers. Indeed, the draft operational guidelines of the office state, 'The ombudsman is not a judge, court or policeman'.

In the absence of enforcement powers, one must ask whether an ombudsman can really be considered a mechanism of accountability. Clearly the CAO office provides for transparency and monitoring, which are vital to accountability. It also provides for a very light form of indirect enforcement. For this reason, it avoids the costs highlighted with the Inspection Panel above and possibly, also the incentive for users to abuse the process of accountability in the pursuit of other goals. However, it remains to be seen whether this mechanism has enough power to hold decisionmakers to account. More generally, such mechanisms cannot be seen as sufficient in and of themselves to patch up the accountability of international institutions. They operate alongside the vertical accountability already outlined above, affording another check on IFI officials.

The experiments in compliance enforcement being undertaken in the Bank and IFC highlight how little horizontal accountability exists for the international financial institutions. Obviously, the primary agencies which should hold the institutions to account are their member governments, through bolstered and improved forms of vertical accountability. However, both IFIs are now working in a world political system in which groups both within and across countries are becoming increasingly effective at demanding more account of the work of international organizations, both through governments and directly from the organizations concerned. It is for this reason that horizontal accountability has become a large plank in both IFIs responses to those who criticize their unaccountability. A further part of this response has been to engage more directly with their critics, and in particular with non-governmental organizations.

Engagement with Non-governmental Organizations

In the late 1990s both the IMF and the Bank began to recognize non-state actors and non-governmental organizations (NGOs). The trend was welcomed by the US Secretary of the Treasury in discussing the Fund's modus operandi:

> ...it should become more attuned, not just to markets, but the broad range of interests and institutions with a stake in the IMF's work. Just as the institution needs to be more permeable for information to flow out, so too must it be permeable enough to let in new thoughts—by maintaining a vigorous ongoing dialogue with civil society groups and others.[29]

The Fund and Bank have both begun to make much more information and analysis available to NGOs. The Bank's NGO-World Bank Committee (established in 1982) has become more active. Both the Bank and Fund now consult with lobbying organisations in Washington DC, with grassroots organisations in member countries, trade unions, church groups and such like. These contacts are taking place at regional, country and local levels. Bank regional directors and IMF resident representatives are being told to seek out and maintain such contacts. At the annual and spring meetings, both institutions have been actively involved in more dialogue and meetings with a select group of transnational NGOs. In addition to these measures which increase transparency and consultation, the institutions have also moved more recently to permitting some level of local participation by non-state actors, such as in the poverty reduction strategy papers being required of countries seeking enhanced debt relief.

It is worth clarifying that NGOs have not taken a place as major stakeholders in the institutions. They have not acquired control, or a formal participatory role in decision-making except at the behest of their own governments. However, where 'Northern' NGOs have allied with or used political leverage in major shareholding countries—at any rate in the United States—they have exercised considerable informal power and influence. Indeed, in such cases, the position of some NGOs starts looking much stronger than that of many smaller developing countries—whose formal right to participate in decision-making is diluted by the problems of representation described earlier. For this reason, the recognition of NGOs as stakeholders has led to a vociferous debate about the accountability and legitimacy of the NGOs themselves.

In further analysing this debate, it is useful to distinguish local or 'Southern' NGOs within borrowing countries and transnational or 'Northern' lobbying organizations, usually based in Washington DC or one of the G-7 capitals. The implications of developing relations with each are somewhat different for the accountability of the IFIs.

Engagement with Southern NGOs

Local or Southern NGOs are stakeholders in a direct sense of the term. They represent groups directly affected by the programs and policies of the IFIs. Their inclusion in discussions and strategy formulation is required because of the way in which the activities of the IFIs have broadened. Both IFIs recognize that, to quote the Bank, 'policy reform and institutional development cannot be imported or imposed'.[30] In countless publications, both IFIs recognize that wider participation and ownership is required for policies to be successfully implemented. For these reasons, the IMF and the Bank are encouraging both their own local representatives and government officials (such as in the PRSP process outlined above) to develop consultative links with local NGOs. At the same time, NGOs now have access to the complaints procedures described above (Bank Inspection Panel and IFC Ombudsman).

However, new relations with Southern NGOs do not resolve the problems of accountability faced by the IFIs, even if they add some positive additional elements. Neither the Fund nor the Bank has been structured as agencies of forceful, far reaching domestic reforms. Their governance structure gives them neither the necessary elements of legitimacy nor accountability for such tasks. They are being forced, for practical and political reasons, to look beyond their traditional and narrow points of contact with 'national authorities' (Finance Ministries, Central Banks and the like) to the wider 'civil society'. However, such relations should not divert attention from the core lack of accountability to developing country governments. Are the IFIs beginning to step around governments and themselves attempting to persuade societies to support certain kinds of reform? The problem here is that the government itself should be the agent of persuasion. Also, borrowing governments will not be able to persuade their own societies to accept changes required by international institutions in which they (developing country governments) cannot claim to have an effective voice.

Relations with NGOs also bring their own problems of accountability and legitimacy. Foremost is the question of which civil society groups ought to be consulted or recognized. As Scholte has documented in the case of the IMF, some non-governmental groups (such as business groups) are being consulted much more than others.[31] This poses the question: to who are local NGOs accountable and for what? Until now, both the IMF and the Bank have been pursuing relations with NGOs in an *ad hoc* and reactive way. However, as Abugre and Alexander have noted, one needs to consider more systematically criteria such as the effectiveness, representativeness, internal decision-making structure, membership and accountability of groups being so consulted.[32]

The problem of accountability of local NGOs is further heightened where they are given a more active role in implementation or formulation of policy. In such cases, the accountability of local NGOs ought to be compared with that of local government agencies. In the 1980s and early 1990s, it was sometimes too readily assumed that the former was preferable. In the Bank's work in Africa, it was criticized for undermining the capacity of the governments in the region.[33] A decade later, it has become more obvious that using NGOs to bypass government institutions risks thwarting the 'institution building' and 'state modernization'.

A final problem concerning relations with Southern NGOs is about who shapes and influences the modalities and processes of consultation with such groups. In the PRSP process described above, no framework was spelled out. There is nevertheless a risk that certain kinds of consultations become recognized in a *de facto* way as preferable to others, not on the grounds that they enhance existing mechanisms of local accountability, but rather on the grounds that they please the political sensitivities and preferences of major shareholders in the IFIs. In other words, there is a risk that a new 'Washington consensus' on the politics of participation and consultation will be forged and that this will pay insufficient attention to the complex social and political arrangements which give life to accountability at the local level.[34]

Nonetheless, the vociferous debate about NGOs and their lack of accountability risks being overplayed in the context of Southern NGOs. Certainly, they now have access to more information. Also, transparency is a powerful step towards holding governments and institutions accountable. NGOs are, with government approval, being consulted more regularly. In the Bank and

IFC, they have the right (although not necessarily the resources) to access the new complaints procedures. These steps, however, do not amount to a transfer of decision-making power or substantial influence. Indeed, the argument has been made that Southern NGOs should be strengthened and more robustly used by developing country governments in order:

- to enhance their own information and analysis about the IFIs
- as a bargaining counter (in alliance with Northern NGOs) to pressure by major shareholders, who face demands from their own public to pay attention to NGOs
- to counter the power of Northern NGOs[35]

New consultation mechanisms with NGOs in borrowing countries do not, however, resolve the deeper problems of accountability, both within the IFIs and in relation to their government interlocutors. Indeed, these problems may well be exacerbated by new developments in the IFIs' relations with the other category of new lobbyists and stakeholders, namely, Northern NGOs.

Engagement with Transnational and Northern NGOs

Transnational NGOs do not have the same stake in the IFIs as directly affected local groups. In defining their stake in international organizations, one needs to consider their broader place in global governance. Even there, they are not part of the state based system of representation in world politics. But politics is not just about representation, it is equally about debate. In international politics, NGOs open up and contribute to an active debate about the IFIs and their policies. Their role is to speak for different views and interests which are not necessarily expressed through the formal channels of representation, i.e. to act as lobbyists for particular interests relevant to notions of justice, development, the environment and so forth.

In more academic terms, the argument for the place of NGOs in an international 'deliberative democracy' is voiced by theorist James Bohman:

> In the case of a political setting where there is no public to whom appeal can be made or institutions in which voice is important, international institutions and the NGOs that attempt to influence their procedures and standards themselves can function as a public to whom equal access of political influence is guaranteed and open'.[36]

The accountability problem posed by transnational NGOs lies first and foremost in the question, to whom are they themselves accountable. Most TNGOs are accountable in various ways to at least three constituencies—their membership (actual and potential and predominantly Northern); their major funders or clients (which include governments and corporations); and in many cases, NGO partners (some in the South). Overall, there is a tendency for such groups primarily to be accountable to Northern groups, funders and partners. For this reason, a longstanding concern about TNGOs has been that they magnify Northern views—both outside of governments and through governments—in the international organizations, adding yet another channel of influence to those people and governments who are already powerfully represented.

The risk here is that TNGOs further distort the inequalities of power and influence already emphasized in this paper. As Abugre and Alexander found, 'Activism by US NGOs has probably expanded the already disproportionate role of the United States in the international financial institutions, especially the Bank'.[37] Similarly, where TNGOs deploy their considerable resources and expertise in representing and assisting local groups bringing cases to the Inspection Panel, it is not always the case that the interests of those being represented are the same as the interests of those to whom the TNGO is primarily accountable (members and funders). The TNGO has an incentive to favour an outcome which maximizes publicity and support for itself. Yet in some cases, the quieter compromise decision may well do more for the group they claim to represent.

The difficulty for critics is that while the work of many TNGOs has undoubtedly magnified Northern influence in the IFIs, other TNGOs have used their influence with the US government (both Congress and the Executive) and other G-7 governments effectively, to campaign for greater transparency, disclosure and new forms of horizontal accountability, which are of interest to all stakeholders. Hence, some TNGOs have assisted in enhancing the accountability of the IFIs, even while, at the same time, further undermining the relative power and participation of both developing countries and Southern NGOs.

The devil with TNGOs lies not so much in the detail, but in the objectives, priorities and constitutions of the organizations. Some TNGOs working on and with the IFIs are fully aware of the risks mentioned and steer clear of them by prioritizing multilateralism, local accountability and capacity building in developing countries. In so doing, such groups are implicitly respecting the claims of more directly affected stakeholders to have priority in holding the institutions to account. TNGOs that do not delimit their priorities this way, it is argued here, are wrong to claim that their stake in the institutions gives them a right of account.

Bolster and Build on Networks

Underpinning the influence of powerful countries and groupings within the IMF and Bank who do hold the institutions to account is a degree of networking.

As detailed elsewhere, in the G7, the EURIMF and the Asia Pacific groupings, countries bolster pre-existing links to one another to coordinate their policies, to share information and to leverage their access to senior management and staff within each organization.[38] One has to ask whether developing countries could build on existing partnerships to attempt to build similar, albeit not as powerful, networks.

One first step towards better networking in the IMF and the Bank could be for countries to shift constituencies within the Boards of the Fund and the Bank in order to group themselves into more cohesive units, making the most of the fact that there are no set rules governing how countries group together either within the Bank or the IMF.[39] As detailed in another paper, the 'constituency system' has permitted significant change in groups within the institutions. Indonesia has shifted constituency in the IMF three times. The Australian led constituency began as a partnership, with South Africa and other southern African countries, but then as members shifted, became an Asia Pacific grouping.[40]

Conclusion

In the late 1990s, the G-7 pressed the IMF and the Bank to become more accountable. In so doing, they emphasized making the institutions more transparent and opening up dialogues with new groups of stakeholders. This paper has shown that these measures may improve governance, but they do not solve the core accountability deficit in the IFIs. The institutions are supposed to be directly accountable to their member governments through their Executive Boards. Yet there are deep flaws in this structure. Furthermore, as the activities of both IFIs expand to embrace wider and deeper conditionalities, the accountability deficit is further widened. This is because, just as the activities of the Fund and Bank are widening, so too are the categories of affected groups who might legitimately claim to be stakeholders in the institutions and therefore to have some right to hold them to account.

The implications for the institutions are several. First, the flaws in the vertical structure of accountability needs redress. This means working to put into place:

- an open and legitimate process of appointment for the heads of the institutions
- a stronger role for the Executive Board in overseeing the work of the institutions
- a structure of representation which better reflects the stakes of all state members
- measures which assist in enhancing the accountability of Executive Directors representatives to their governments and voters

These measures, along with positive steps towards independent evaluation, inspection and transparency would doubtless improve the accountability of the IMF and Bank. However, ultimately, there are limits to how accountable the IMF and Bank can be to the governments and people most affected by their lending and policies. This raises a more profound issue about how far reaching the activities of relatively unaccountable agencies should be.[41] In Kapur's essay on whether international institutions can be democratic, political theorist Dahl warns that we should be 'wary of ceding the legitimacy of democracy to non-democratic systems'.[42] His point is that domestic political systems have a potential to be democratically accountable in a way that international organizations cannot. The implication is that the IMF and the Bank should be reined in from far reaching policy conditionality. Their activities should be limited to those for which they can claim to be effectively accountable.

Notes

1 University College, Oxford, email: ngaire.woods@univ.ox.ac.uk
2 The terms 'World Bank' and 'the Bank' are widely used (and also in this paper) to refer to the World Bank Group of institutions which comprises the International Bank for Reconstruction and Development (IBRD), the International Development Association (IDA), and the International Finance Corporation (IFC).
3 Schedler, Diamond and Plattner, 1999.
4 An earlier version of this article appeared in *International Affairs*, January 2001. A more thorough and radical argument for reforming the IMF and World Bank is made in my forthcoming book, Woods, 2006.
5 See the Report to the IMF Executive Board of the Quota Formula Review Group, 2000c. For earlier critiques see Wagner, 1995; Buira, 1996.
6 IMF, 1998b.
7 Gold, 1972, pp. 18 and 173–4.
8 Horsefield, 1996, Vol 1.
9 Woods, 2000, 28:5.
10 IMF, 1999; World Bank, 1992.
11 IMF, 1998a; World Bank, 1992.
12 IMF, 1998a, pp. 34.
13 Currently, such assessments are available in 12 areas. More information is available at http://www.imf.org/external/standards/index.htm
14 More details are available at http://www.imf.org/external/np/fsap/fsap.asp
15 Kapur, 2001, 4:3; Kapur and Webb, 2000.
16 IMF, 2002, pp. 33.
17 See in the Articles of Agreement of the IMF, Article V, Section 1 and the World Bank, Article III, Section 2.
18 Of course, the external line of accountability does not always produce the outcomes desired by the IFIs, as argued by Collier in Schedler *et al.*, 1999, pp. 313–332.
19 IMF, 1998a, pp. 35.
20 Feldstein 1998, pp. 24, 22–33.
21 For an updated list of countries preparing PRSPs see www.imf.org/external/np/prsp/

22 World Bank, 1998.
23 IMF, 2000a.
24 Schedler *et al.*, 1999, see comments by Richard Sklar on Guillermo O'Donnell, pp. 29–51.
25 IMF, 2000b, in www.imf.org/ieo
26 World Bank, 2000; see www.worldbank.org/eap/eap.nsf/
27 Wade, 2000.
28 Schedler *et al.*, 1999, see comments by Philippe Schmitter on Guillermo O'Donnell, pp. 29–51.
29 Summers, 1999.
30 World Bank, 1999.
31 Scholte, 1998, pp. 42–5.
32 Abugre and Alexander, 1998, pp. 107–25.
33 op. cit., 1998, pp. 114.
34 For the original statement of the Washington consensus, see Williamson, 1990. For subsequent analysis, see Naim, 2000, 118, pp. 86 ff; Stiglitz, 1998; Broad and Cavanagh, 1999, 16:3, pp. 79–88.
35 Abugre and Alexander, 1998.
36 Bohman, 1999. pp. 511.
37 Abugre and Alexander, 1998, pp. 116.
38 Woods and Lombardi, 2005, at www.globaleconomicgovernance.org
39 Constituencies are not written into the IMF's Articles which provide for the membership-wide elections of 15 Directors (Schedule E), increased to 19 by a Resolution of the Board of Governors in 1992.
40 Woods and Lombardi, 2005.
41 I am grateful to Devesh Kapur for spurring me to think about this issue.
42 Dahl, 1999, 19–36 at pp. 33.

References

Abugre, Charles and Alexander, Nancy, 1998, Non-governmental organizations and the international, monetary and financial system, *International Monetary and Financial Issues for the 1990s Volume IX*, Geneva:UNCTAD.

Bohman, James, 1999, International regimes and democratic governance: political equality and influence in global institutions, *International Affairs*, 75:3, pp. 499–513 at pp. 511.

Broad, Robin and Cavanagh, J, 1999, The death of the Washington consensus?, *World Policy Journal*, 16:3, pp. 79–88.

Buira, Ariel, 1996, The Governance of the International Monetary Fund, *Development and Global Governance*, Culpeper, Roy and Pestieau, Caroline (eds), Ottawa: International Development Research Centre, the North-South Institute.

Dahl, Robert A, 1999, Can international organizations be democratic?, *Democracy's Edges*, Shapiro, Ian and Hacker-Cordon, Casiano (eds), Cambridge: Cambridge University Press, 19–36 at pp. 33.

Feldstein, Martin, 1998, Refocusing the IMF, *Foreign Affairs*, March/April, 77:2, pp. 20–33.

Gold, Joseph, 1972, *Voting and Decisions in the International Monetary Fund*, Washington DC: IMF, pp. 18 and pp. 173–4.

Horsefield, Keith J, 1996, *The International Monetary Fund, 1945–1965: Twenty Years of International Monetary Cooperation*, Washington DC: IMF, Vol. 1.

IMF, *Articles of Agreement*, Article V, Section 1.

IMF, 1998a, *External Evaluation of the ESAF*, Report by a Group of Independent Experts, Washington DC; IMF.

IMF, 1998b, *The IMF's Response to the Asian Crisis*, Washington DC; IMF.

IMF, 1999, *External Evaluation of IMF Surveillance*, Report by a Group of Independent Experts, Washington DC: IMF, p. 34.

IMF, 2000a, The IMF in a Changing World, Remarks by Horst Köhler, Managing Director, Given at the National Press Club, Washington, DC, 7 August.

IMF, 2000b, *Report to the IMFC on the Establishment of the Independent Evaluation Office and its Terms of Reference*, Washington DC: IMF, 12 September, www.imf.org/ieo

IMF, 2000c, *Quota Formula Review Group Report*, Washington DC: IMF, 28 April.

IMF, 2002, The Modalities of Conditionality – Further Considerations, 8 January, accessed 30 May 2005, pp. 33.

Kapur, Devesh, 2001, 'Expansive Agendas and Weak Instruments: Governance Related Conditionalities of the International Financial Institutions', *Journal of Policy Reform*, 4:3.

Kapur, Devesh and Webb, Richard, 2000, *Governance-related Conditionalities of the International Financial Institutions*, Geneva: UNCTAD.

Naim, Moises, 2000, Washington consensus or Washington confusion?, *Foreign Policy*, 118, pp. 86 ff.

Schedler, Andreas, Diamond, Larry and Plattner, Marc, 1999, *The Self-restraining State: Power and Accountability in New Democracies*, Boulder: Lynne Rienner.

Scholte, Jan Aart, 1998, The IMF meets Civil Society, *Finance and Development*, September, 35:3, pp. 42–5.

Stiglitz, Joseph, 1998, *More instruments and broader goals: moving towards the post-Washington consensus*, Helsinki: WIDER/United Nations University.

Summers, Lawrence, 1999, The right kind of IMF for a stable global financial system, Remarks to the London Business School, US Treasury: LS-294, 14 December.

Wagner, Nancy, 1995, A Review of PPP-Adjusted GDP Estimation and its Potential Use for the Fund's Operational Purposes, *IMF Working Paper*, Washington DC: IMF.

Williamson, John, 1990, *Latin American adjustment: how much has happened?*, Washington DC: Institute for International Economics.

Woods, Ngaire, 2000, The Challenge of Good Governance for the IMF and the World Bank Themselves, *World Development*, May, 28:5.

Woods, Ngaire and Lombardi, Domenico, 2005, Effective Representation and the role of coalitions in the IMF, *Global Economic Governance Programme Working Paper*, 28 February, at www.globaleconomicgovernance.org

World Bank, 1944, *Articles of Agreement*, Article III, Section 2.

World Bank, 1992, *Report of the Ad Hoc Committee on Board Procedures*, Washington DC: World Bank, 26 May.

World Bank, 1998, *Partnership for Development: From Vision to Action*, Washington DC: World Bank.

World Bank, 1999, *Annual Review of Development Effectiveness*, Washington DC: World Bank.

World Bank, 2000, *China Western Poverty Reduction Project Inspection Panel Report*, Washington DC: World Bank, www.worldbank.org/eap/eap.nsf/

7

PURCHASING POWER PARITIES AND COMPARISONS OF GDP IN IMF QUOTA CALCULATIONS

John B. McLenaghan[1]

Abstract:

The governance of the IMF and the distribution of IMF quotas have come under much scrutiny in recent years, with a focus on the voting rights of member countries consistent with their relative size in, or contribution to, the world economy. Quota increases resulting from general quota reviews since the IMF came into being in 1945 have fallen far short of the amounts needed to maintain the relationship of total quotas to world GDP. At the same time, the distribution of quotas between the industrial and developing countries has been broadly maintained despite the enormous and disparate growth of the world economy over this period. On the basis of the formula that guides the IMF in deciding members' quotas in these reviews, giving prominence to GDP as the primary variable, the share of developing countries would be appreciably greater if GDP were to be converted by Purchasing Power Parities (PPPs), rather than at market exchange rates. For many purposes, inter-country comparisons of GDP converted by PPP are seen as the preferred approach, a view which has received increased support in light of the expected strengthening of the quality of PPP data compiled under the International Comparison Program. Market exchange rates, which continue to serve as the conversion factor for GDP in IMF quota calculations, are regarded by statisticians and analysts alike as unsuitable for many applications because of their short-term volatility. While a significant change in quota distribution involving a shift to the developing countries would require much more than a change in formula, the adoption of PPPs for the conversion of GDP would set that process in motion.

Introduction

Issues of governance have assumed great importance for the IMF in recent years in terms of its financial programs with member countries and with respect to its internal operations. With the vastly extended ambit of IMF support programs for a number of Asian countries in 1997 and 1998, and subsequently for emerging and developing countries in other regions, the need to address shortcomings of governance in member countries has assumed a prominent place in many of its programs. Concomitantly, a sharp light has been thrown on to the Fund itself in terms of aspects of its internal governance. Prominent among them has been the size and distribution of quotas allocated to member countries and the related question of members' voting rights. In particular, much attention has been given to the limited voice assigned in the IMF's decision-making processes to developing countries, both individually and as a group and to redressing perceived imbalances in voting entitlements.[2]

The formula adopted at the Bretton Woods Conference in 1944 for the establishment of countries' quotas and voting rights, itself a compromise of the at times conflicting views and priorities of the participants, remains an ingredient in the IMF's quota determination. There have been adjustments to the original formula in subsequent quota reviews and a more comprehensive set of formulas has been adopted, although increases in quotas since the IMF was established have not relied on calculations derived from the formula. Importantly, the inherent rigidities of the quota determination procedure have ensured that the distribution of quotas across member countries, geographically and by country grouping (e.g. developed and developing) has remained largely unchanged despite some selective quota increases and the large increase in the number of members. It can be shown that the vast and uneven growth of the world economy over the last 60 years has generated a greatly altered pattern of global resources, real and financial, as well as their distribution, than is portrayed by the Fund's present formulaic approach to quotas. Putting it another way, there can be little doubt that if the IMF were to be created today with the present membership of 184 countries on the basis of the each country's 'share' of the global economy, the distribution of quotas across countries would certainly give rise to a very different outcome.

Within the present quota formula, there are, in fact, five component formulas used in the quota calculations. The weightage given to a country's GDP and its relationship to global GDP constitutes the most important measure. GDP converted at market exchange rates has been the preferred approach for quota calculations, notwithstanding the volatility of exchange rates. At the same time, it has been shown that adjusting GDP for PPP to take account of changes in relative prices in many cases yields significantly different results in quotas for individual countries. The use of PPP adjusted GDP data rather than GDP data adjusted at market exchange rates is seen by many observers as a preferred approach. Moreover, the IMF itself has made use of PPP adjusted GDP data in the regular reviews presented in its *World Economic Outlook*. Other international organizations, including the United Nations and the OECD, as well as the European Union, have incorporated GDP data calculated by the use of PPPs as a regular feature of their analyses. Nevertheless, the IMF has consistently viewed the existing arrangements based on the use of market exchange rate adjusted GDP as appropriate for quota calculations.

Against the background of IMF quotas and their determination, the primary objective of this paper is to assess the relative merits of market exchange rates and PPPs as a basis for conversion of GDP. Section 2 looks at the framework of calculating PPP and the issues that arise in making inter-country comparisons of GDP and discusses the criticisms that have been directed at both conversion techniques from a conceptual and practical stand-point. It then reviews the PPP program for the advanced countries of the OECD. Section 3 deals with the compilation of PPPs under the International Comparison Program and the program's place as an important tool in the international statistical system. Section 4 considers the use of PPP data for analytical and operational purposes by the international organizations and Section 5 summarizes the IMF's data dissemination standards as a relatively new instrument for improving countries' statistics. Section 6 compares GDP data adjusted for market exchange rates and PPPs for selected countries and country groupings. Sections 7 and 8 then turn to IMF quotas and the measurement of GDP as a key ingredient in the formula for quota calculations. Conclusions are given in Section 9.

Approaches to PPPs

The PPP between two countries (A and B) is defined as the rate at which the currency of A needs to be converted into the currency of B in order to enable a given amount of A's currency to purchase the same volume of goods and services in both countries. The methodology of PPPs can be likened to country price indexes in an interspatial context, with rather similar requirements for data inputs. Country specific price indexes measure price changes over time, based on a representative basket of goods and services and using the expenditure pattern within the country concerned. For the calculation of PPPs, there is likewise a need for a representative basket of goods and services, but for this purpose the basket applies to each of the countries incorporated in the calculation. Difficulties in PPP computations may arise because expenditure patterns across countries can vary markedly. Moreover, the larger the number of countries involved, the more complex are the issues of determining similar expenditure patterns and in specifying selected products to be included.

Proceeding from the establishment of a list of goods and services with the necessary specifications for pricing in each of the participating countries, the estimation of PPPs is linked to the expenditure patterns in the countries covered, using GDP as measured by final expenditure—household and government consumption, gross capital formation and net exports. These data are taken from the national accounts using the classifications of the UN System of National Accounts (SNA) in order to ensure conceptually consistent GDP data of different countries valued in their own currencies. For this purpose, the so-called basic headings are chosen as a beginning point for determining expenditures on groups of commodities deemed representative of purchases made in countries for which a detailed specification of items can be identified. To the extent possible, participating countries provide average prices for the individual items specified. These prices are expressed in national currency and, ideally, are transaction prices. On the basis of the price data submitted by individual countries, unweighted bilateral price ratios, or parities, are combined using the expenditure data provided to determine PPPs. Purchasing power parities thus derived are used to construct price indexes and as the basis for converting GDP volumes.

Due to its onerous data requirements, the calculation of PPPs from the production side of the national accounts has had only limited application, while because of statistical problems, the derivation of PPPs from the income side of the national accounts has had little support.

Perhaps the first major work on international price comparisons and the relative value of money in different countries was undertaken by Clark, who compared the purchasing power of selected countries for a number of consumption goods. The results were published in 1940 in the first edition of his *Conditions of Economic Progress*. A first comprehensive effort to compile inter-country comparisons of national incomes took place in the 1950s in the Organization of the European Economic Community (OEEC, later, the OECD) under the direction of Kravis and Gilbert, who compared physical quantities and average values of more than 250 goods and services in four European countries and the United States. Expenditure on each item was then extrapolated with that of related goods and services to obtain total expenditure. Purchasing power parities were derived from the valuation of different currencies. Their methodology was applied in a refined form in a number of benchmark studies in the early to mid 1970s.[3]

In 1982, the OECD reinstituted a program for the calculation of PPPs, jointly with the Statistical Office of the European Community (Eurostat). Employing an updated methodology, it compared national incomes and price levels for the European and other OECD member countries. Benchmark results under this program have been released at three yearly intervals since 1990 and, for the countries covered by the joint survey, PPPs for GDP are extrapolated both monthly and annually from the most recent benchmark year.

A report issued in 1997 reviewing the OECD/Eurostat PPP program (the *Castles Report*) noted that the use of market exchange rates as proxies for PPPs had become unacceptable as a result of major fluctuations in exchange rates, which had made them erratic currency converters for statistical purposes.[4] The report, in providing a strong endorsement of the usefulness of PPPs, pointed to empirical work which supported this conclusion and noted that it was impossible to make price or volume comparisons between countries without them. Furthermore, the report concluded that a fully functioning world statistical system would include, as a central element, the capacity to make such comparisons. At the same time, the report pointed to shortcomings in a number of areas of the program that impacted on the quality of its results which could be eliminated by assigning an appropriate level of resources for this important exercise. The conclusions of the report were accepted by the OECD and Eurostat.

The eighth joint comparison under the OECD/Eurostat program is to take place in 2005 and will cover 45 countries. It will include those countries that have applied to join the European Union as well as certain countries of the former Soviet Union and the former Yugoslavia with which Eurostat and the OECD have a program of technical cooperation in statistics.

The International Comparison Program

The most comprehensive approach to the compilation of PPPs, in terms of country coverage, is that of the International Comparison Program (ICP). The ICP began as the International Comparison Project in the late 1960s under arrangements for joint work by the United Nations Statistical Office and the International Comparison Unit of the University of Pennsylvania, with initial support from the Ford Foundation and the World Bank. The project began on a pilot basis with just 10 countries and the first results for the years 1967 and 1970 were published in 1975. Subsequent phases of the program resulted in an increase in country participation and its frequency was adapted to a 5-year cycle. In its early stages, the ICP was coordinated under the central direction of the University of Pennsylvania but a number of changes in organizational responsibility occurred as the program evolved. Mainly in order to reflect the increased country participation, the program and its overall management and structure moved to a regional basis. Drawing on the advanced work on PPPs undertaken by OECD/Eurostat for their respective member countries and with oversight and funding support from the World Bank and other international agencies, the ICP established country groupings by region, following which world comparisons were obtained by linking results across these groups.

By the late 1980s, however, there was a loss of momentum in the ICP, reflecting a questioning by some observers of the value of the program in terms of its conceptual soundness, the quality of data inputs and the credibility of results. Perhaps more importantly, its heavy resource costs led to doubts about the program's viability. Many of the smaller developing countries remained outside of the program which, even for some of those participating, was seen more as a statistical activity meeting the needs of the international agencies than as one of immediate or even potential benefit to them. These concerns and problems in the collection of relevant price data, have been factors in the criticism of the program. From the initial phase based on limited participation in 1970, the first of the global comparisons took place in 1975. While there was a steady progression in the number of industrial countries participating, only slow progress was made in encouraging developing country participation. Moreover, as noted above, it was not possible to complete effectively the ICP rounds of 1990 and 2000 (Table 1).

Some of the problems of PPP calculations identified in countries participating in the ICP have stemmed from the fact that data on private expenditure in the national accounts of many countries are derived as a residual, making them difficult to validate. Another limitation of ICP data is that price surveys are designed to permit comparisons of goods of the same quantity and quality across countries, but differences in these dimensions may be seen, incorrectly,

Table 1. ICP surveys (Number of Countries)

Year	Developing	Industrialized	Total
1970	4	6	10
1973	8	8	16
1975	21	13	34
1980	42	18	60
1985	42	22	64
1993/1996	93	24	117
2003/2006	126	24	150

Source: ICP and OECD.

as differences in price. There have also been problems in determining prices of services such as medical, education, housing and transportation. In addition to these concerns at the technical level, a major criticism of ICP has centred on the difficulty in generating commitments by countries to ensure good quality data inputs in the price surveys, with the attendant problem of inadequate resources.

The conclusions of the *Castles Report*, with its strong endorsement of PPPs and their widespread application as a tool for international comparisons, were echoed in a second report issued in 1998 under the sponsorship of the World Bank, the IMF and the United Nations, which evaluated the ICP.[5] Although taking somewhat different approaches, both studies concluded that the availability of sound PPP data was essential for the purpose of international comparisons in a number of important policy making areas and for research. Indeed, they asserted that a fully functioning world statistical system should include, as a key component, the capacity to make such comparisons.

In a frank and hard hitting report, Ryten noted that in a long and costly process that began in the 1980s, the international statistical community undertook an exhaustive revision of the United Nations System of National Accounts which, when it was adopted in 1993, provided a universal basis for statisticians to compile macroeconomic statistics. Ryten concluded that the enormous investment in the revision would only yield full returns when the (resulting) data permit comparisons of the rates of growth and levels of the broad aggregates of GDP. For this reason, he observed that

> ...we must not find ourselves deterred by the existence of different currencies or become exclusively dependent on market exchange rates among them. Conceptually, theoretically and practically, the United Nations national accounts program will only be complete when it encompasses ICP.

The report sounded a warning, however, that in view of questions about the quality of the program's output its future was questionable. It concluded that the most serious problem facing the ICP was a lack of credibility of its results, especially at the detailed level. This was linked to poor management and supervision of data collection, editing and processing at the country level and a lack of coordination between national statistical offices and coordinating agencies at the regional level. On a broader plane, the program had languished because of insufficient funding and the lack of coordination at the global level.

To address these problems as a matter of urgency, Ryten recommended sweeping changes in organization at all levels of the program, the establishment of a research program to deal with quality issues, the institution of a major funding initiative and firm commitments by national statistical offices to participate in the program.

The *Ryten Report* has proved to be a catalyst for change for the ICP. The positive acceptance of its conclusions and recommendations by the United Nations Statistical Commission at its 2000 session was followed by the implementation of far reaching improvements and structural change in the program. A governance structure for the ICP was established with a consortium of national, regional and international institutions coordinating the global program with the assistance of the Global Executive Board. (Appendix 1). An international secretariat serving as a Global Office, with a Global Manager operating within the World Bank, was established to manage the program on a day to day basis. Substantial funding commitments by a wide range of contributors, international organizations and national agencies, have been directed to meeting the ambitious operational targets of the next ICP round.

All five ICP regions—Africa, Asia Pacific, the Commonwealth of Independent States (CIS), Latin America and West Asia—have mobilized staffing, funding and other resources to implement and monitor the current round of the ICP in 2003–06. The overhauled operational structure of the ICP has been accompanied by a number of new support initiatives. They include the establishment of an ICP Technical Advisory Group to deal with technical and methodological issues, a revised *ICP Handbook* and the preparation of the *ICP Operational Manual* and *Price Collectors Guide*. The ICP Global Office is coordinating the global Ring Comparison, which is using the multilateral approach to link regional PPPs in order to generate global PPPs expressed in a common currency. For this sub-program, a number of selected countries or areas from each region participate in a separate comparison program in order to provide links across regions. In late 2004, the Technical Advisory Group reached an agreement, on the basis of its research program, to obtain PPPs for the government, construction and housing sectors.

Data collection for most household consumption items for the 2003–06 round of the ICP began in the first quarter of 2005. For other items, as well as non-household items, including government compensation, equipment and construction, data collection will take place in the second half of 2005. Final PPPs for the 2005 reference period will be prepared in the first half of 2007 and will encompass the results of the global linking from the Ring Program. It is expected that 150 countries will participate in the current round of the ICP, including 45 countries that now form part of the OECD/Eurostat program.

The International Organizations as Users of PPPs

In recent years, the international organizations have extended their use of PPPs in a number of applications. The OECD incorporates data on GDP converted by PPPs in much of its statistical and analytical work. For example, cross-country comparisons of GDP per capita converted by PPPs are seen as a primary instrument for the purpose of measuring economic welfare. Measurement of the relative size of countries is likewise based on GDP valued at PPPs. The productivity of labour is another useful indicator that uses PPP-based volume comparisons of output, while PPPs are also applied to spatial comparisons of prices across countries.

Eurostat applies PPPs in the context of its budget allocations for its Structural Funds used to reduce economic disparities between EU member states. The list of regions for fund allocations is established on the basis of GDP per capita converted by PPP. Purchasing power parities also provide the basis for monitoring price convergence in the EU in the context of competition policy and consumer protection. They are used in the programs of a number of UN agencies and by the World Bank in comparing per capita GDP and in measuring poverty reduction in the context of the UN's Millennium Development Goals.

The IMF has at times acknowledged the limitations of market exchange rates for converting GDP in the context of quotas for newly joining member countries. This was the case for the centrally planned economies that joined the IMF in the 1980s and 1990s, when official exchange rates were considered not to reflect market conditions and a PPP conversion factor was adopted. In the case of Russia, GDP was converted partly at official exchange rates and partly on the basis of PPPs.[6]

In the Eleventh General Review of Quotas in 1996, the Executive Board of the IMF was asked to consider the circumstances of a number of countries whose GDP data adjusted by market exchange rates appeared to understate the substantial real economic growth achieved over several years. China and India were singled out in this context. As a result, the IMF staff at that time proposed the use of a version of a PPP exchange rate for the purposes of quota calculations However, the Executive Board decided in favour of the continuation of using market exchange rates, largely on the grounds of maintaining a uniform approach to conversion factors. In contrast to the approach taken for quota calculations, the IMF, in its *World Economic Outlook*, has made use of annual GDP calculations for countries as well as regional and industrial/developing and other country groupings, valued on the basis of PPPs. The IMF is not a primary source of these data and it applies certain conventions depending on the data series, as follows:

- Country group composites for exchange rates, interest rates and the growth rates of monetary aggregates are weighted by GDP converted to US dollars at market exchange rates (averaged over the preceding three years) as a share of group GDP.
- Composites for other data relating to the domestic economy, whether growth rates or ratios, are weighted by GDP valued at PPPs as a share of total world or group GDP.

For those series using PPP weights, the IMF's data calculations have been based on the surveys undertaken by the OECD and the International Comparison Program (see below). Where price survey data are not available, PPPs for the most recent years are based on estimates using the OECD/Eurostat data for the countries coming within the coverage of that program and, for the remaining countries included, on the World Development Indicators prepared by the World Bank. For a small group of countries, mostly small economies, for which these sources are not available, an estimation procedure is utilized for aggregative analysis and research.

The IMF's Data Dissemination Standards

In 1996, in the wake of the first of the global financial crises of that decade and recognizing the negative influences on the capital markets flowing from non-current, incomplete and poor quality statistics, the IMF established new standards for country data dissemination designed to improve information available to government policy makers and the financial markets. The first of two standards, the Special Data Dissemination Standard (SDDS), was directed at countries already having a high degree of access to the international markets and which were likely in large degree to be undertaking, or prepared to undertake, commitments to these demanding standards, which were voluntary. In subscribing to the SDDS, IMF member countries undertook to compile and disseminate data for the main areas of economic statistics in accordance with identified best practice. A key element in the implementation of the SDDS was the commitment of a subscribing country to register its implementation of the various elements of the standards with the IMF, which publishes the results on its Dissemination Standards Bulletin Board and which is available to data users via Internet access.

The General Data Dissemination Standard (GDDS), structured in the same fashion as the SDDS but with less demanding requirements, became operational in 2000. In directing the GDDS at countries whose statistical systems were less developed than those acceding to the SDDS, the IMF recognized that these countries would need assistance and time in order to reach a higher level of statistical capacity. Nevertheless, the IMF's Executive Board encouraged all members to subscribe to the standards, which like the SDDS were voluntary.

By early 2005, 53 countries, comprising all the industrial countries and the major emerging market countries, had subscribed to the SDDS. Fifty eight countries were subscribers to the GDDS. Commitments to such rigorous statistical standards by a large and still growing, proportion of the IMF's membership are a manifestation of the increased awareness of the importance of high quality statistics in policy formulation and analysis. At a specific level, these standards bring into prominence the increasing importance given by countries to implementing the United Nations SNA and to the global statistical commitment of the ICP.

Comparisons of GDP – Adjusting for Market Exchange Rates or PPPs

There is a considerable body of opinion which supports the view that inter-country comparisons of national expenditures or GDP, when converted at market exchange rates, are far from meaningful because they do not take into account price differences across countries. The volatility of market exchange rates, the propensity for them to have long periods of misalignment and the very large declines that occur in foreign currency denominated GDP immediately after a large devaluation, have all been cited as negative factors in the use of market exchange rates for adjusting GDP data.

Calculations of GDP converted at market exchange rates, in many instances, exhibit marked differences from those based on PPP conversions. While these differences vary in their extent from country to country, they may be pronounced when comparisons are made by region or by selected groups of countries.

Table 2, compares GDP converted at market exchange rates for high income countries and middle to low income countries for the years 1999 to 2003 and shows GDP converted by PPPs for these countries over the same period.

For the latter group of countries, the disparity between the two conversion series is considerable, with GDP converted by PPPs more than three times greater than when converted by exchange rates. Note that for the high income countries, however, differences arising from the two methods of conversion are less than 5 per cent in any one year.

Table 2. GDP at market exchange rates and GDP based on PPP valuations

	1999	2000	2001	2002	2003
1. High income countries in billions of current US dollars	25,096	25,456	25,060	26,118	29,270
2. Low and middle income countries In billions of current US dollars	5,656	6,121	6,196	6,297	7,087
3. All countries	30,752	31,577	31,256	32,415	36,357
1 as per cent of 3	81.6	80.6	80.2	80.6	80.5
4. High income countries PPP in billions of current international dollars	24,385	25,719	26,623	27,456	28,591
5. Low and middle income countries PPP in billions of current international dollars	17,793	19,170	20,402	21,566	23,247
6. All countries	42,178	44,889	47,025	49,022	51,838
4 as per cent of 6	57.1	57.3	56.5	56.1	55.2

Source: World Bank, 2003, *World Development Indicators*.

Table 3. Comparisons of GDP weights–

	PPP weights	Market exchange Rate weights
Advanced economies	57.0	79.9
Major industrial countries	45.4	66.4
-United States	21.9	30.2
-Japan	7.4	15.1
Other advanced economies	11.6	13.5
Developing countries	37.2	17.9
Africa	3.3	1.4
Asia	21.6	7.7
-China	11.6	3.3
-India	4.6	1.5
Middle East & Europe	3.9	2.6
Western Hemisphere	8.4	6.2
Transition countries	5.7	2.2

Source: IMF, 2000, Annex and Statistical Appendix, *World Economic Outlook*, May.

Differences in GDP weights when converted at market exchange rates and at PPPs are also significant for individual countries and for certain regions. Table 3 shows the PPP weights applied in the IMF *World Economic Outlook* in 2000 in comparison with the market exchange rate weights for the same year. For the major industrial economies, especially the United States and Japan, the PPP weights for that year are substantially below those derived from market exchange rates. For the regional groupings of the developing and transition countries, on the other hand, PPP weights were appreciably above those derived from market rates. For China and India, there was a more than two-fold increase in weights, from 3.3 per cent and 1.5 per cent, to 11.6 per cent and 4.6 per cent, respectively. Comparable data for 2003 show that the weights for China and India had risen to 12.6 per cent and 5.7 per cent of world GDP.

IMF Quotas and their Determination

The quota of each member of the IMF is, in essence, its capital contribution to the Fund, with one-quarter of its allocated subscription to be paid in reserve assets, expressed in Special Drawing Rights (SDRs) and the remaining portion to be paid in its own currency. The size of quotas is determined by the IMF's Board of Governors taking into account the relative economic weight of the country.

Quotas serve a number of purposes. First, they provide the major part of the IMF's reserve assets (although the IMF has found it necessary at times to access borrowed and administered resources to meet exceptional borrowing requirements of members). Second, quotas play a role in determining members' access to the IMF's resources, subject to limits set by the Executive Board and the *Articles of Agreement*. It should be noted, however, that waivers to these limits have increasingly been invoked in light of the exceptional demands on the IMF's resources to support its role in crisis management. To a large extent, such waivers have also recognized the lessened significance of quotas and of the IMF's available resources more generally in the face of the growth of capital flows and members' financing needs. Third, quotas play a crucial role in the determination of voting power in the IMF. As such, the size of a member's quota (and, for groupings of members, the aggregate of their quotas) is important in the IMF's decision-making processes and representation in the Executive Board. While many decisions of the Board require a simple majority, there are some that require a majority of 70 and 85 per cent of votes. Voting entitlements are therefore critical to the determination of IMF policies and operations. A fourth function of quotas, now of limited operational significance, is in determining a member's share in a general allocation of SDR.

The Bretton Woods Conference agreed on a two-pronged approach to quotas. In the interest of recognizing the individual member states, each country was allocated 250 basic votes. Also, to reflect differences in countries' economic significance and in their contributions to the IMF's financing needs, each member's quota was represented by a voting entitlement in the ratio of one vote per US$100,000 of quota (subsequently, one vote per SDR100,000). Since the Fund's inception, there has been no change in the number of basic votes allocated to each member, including newly accredited members. Thus, with increases in the size of quotas agreed at general reviews, the number of basic votes as a proportion of countries' voting entitlement has diminished appreciably.[7]

General reviews of quotas take place to consider the need for an overall increase in quotas and their distribution among members. Of the 12 reviews completed thus far, all but four have provided for an increase in total quotas. However, when increases in overall quotas have been approved and accompanied by a selective increase for certain members, the latter increase has been limited, both with regard to the size of the selective increase and to the number of countries affected. Over the life of the IMF, the review process has not yielded much change in the distribution of quotas among members. Changes in the distribution of quotas, when they have occurred, have been implemented largely in response to developments of major significance, such as the accession to membership of the countries of the former Soviet Union.

The formula for quotas agreed at the Bretton Woods Conference incorporated a number of variables such as national income, official reserves, current payments, export variability and the ratio of exports to national income. However, the formula itself played only a qualified role in the determination of quotas agreed upon by the 45 countries represented at the conference. In fact, the initial quotas and their distribution among the 45 participating countries, while taking the formula calculations into account, reflected a compromise reached by the major participating countries—the United States, United Kingdom, France, China and Russia.[8] The Bretton Woods formula gave the highest weighting among the component variables to national income but, starting in the 1960s, the IMF adopted a multi-formula approach using the same basic variables but with larger weights for other components, particularly external trade and the variability of exports. There are now five formulas that are applied in the review process and, among them, the modified Bretton Woods formula continues to give the largest weight to GDP (replacing GNI). The current quota formulas are detailed in Appendix 2.

While the formulas have provided a guide to calculating quotas, in practice they have not been the definitive factor in determining the outcome of reviews, either in terms of a general increase in quotas or in adjusting quota shares. The Executive Board of the IMF has viewed quota calculations as one step, although an important one, in its reviews, but it has, in general, taken the opportunity to approve more or less equiproportional increases in quotas and has not used them to achieve any meaningful rebalancing of quotas for individual countries or groups of countries. Only in exceptional circumstances, such as the increase awarded to the quota for China in 2000 following the addition of Hong Kong SAR, have selective quota increases taken place.[9]

Measurement of GDP in the Quota Formula

In 1999, the IMF Executive Board appointed an independent body of experts, the Quota Formula Review Group (QFRG), to review quota formulas. The QFRG was asked to assess quota formulas with respect to their adequacy to help determine members' calculated quotas that reasonably reflect members' relative position in the world economy, as well as their need for and contribution to the IMF's financial resources, against the background of changes in the functioning of the world economy and the international financial system and the increasing globalization of markets. The expert body was not asked to consider the question of the absolute level of quotas or their distribution among members.

In its report to the IMF Executive Board in 2000, the QFRG noted the great changes that had occurred in the world economy since the Bretton Woods conference. They included the extended openness of countries in terms of trade and capital flows; the expansion of capital markets and the rise of private capital flows, contrasting with a reduced reliance on official financing; greater exchange rate flexibility; a vast expansion of the world's population; and the extension of IMF membership to cover almost all countries.

The expert group considered a list of variables that could be included in a new formula or set of formulas for IMF quotas. In addition to those already incorporated, the QFRG identified a country's capital flows, external debt and population—all of which were seen as having some correlation with historical quotas. Other variables that entered into this review included GDP converted at PPP exchange rates, measures of the openness of an economy, per capita income, access to capital markets and the variability of exchange rates.

While this paper does not discuss the methods of assessing the quota formulas considered by the QFRG, it can be noted that its report emphasized that the IMF's resources reflect creditor positions in the IMF, which are based on quotas and represent a component of each member's official reserves. The QFRG concluded that a quota formula that is applicable to potential creditor countries should rely on variables that represent those members' ability to contribute to the IMF. The report noted that for debtor countries the use of IMF resources is correlated with variables that measure their economic vulnerability, such as weakness in the balance of payments. It was the ability of a country to contribute to the IMF that provided an underpinning to the choice of variables included in the formula calculations and the QFRG concluded that the single most important variable for measuring ability to contribute is GDP.

A minority of the QFRG favoured a measure of GDP for quota calculations using PPP-based exchange rates. They considered that market exchange rates did not necessarily equalize prices of tradable goods across countries, even after allowing for transport costs and quality differences. They pointed to an index number problem which resulted in an understatement of GDP in developing countries when market exchange rates are used for conversion. Although for a prolonged period, real growth rates in these countries had been significantly higher than those in the industrialized countries, the developing countries had been shown to have a much lower GDP when market exchange rates are applied for conversion. This, to a large extent, reflected the high incidence of non-tradables in the developing economies.

While acknowledging the merits of PPP-based GDP for welfare measurement across countries in terms of per capita income, the majority view of the QFRG was that this measure was not appropriate for indicating a country's ability to contribute to 'international endeavours'. The IMF's role as a financial institution and its need for financial resources for the support of members requiring financial assistance were seen to be of overriding importance in this context. The ability of a member to contribute to the IMF was therefore considered to be determined by its capacity to provide funds at market exchange rates.

There was also a view presented by the majority of the QFRG that as a measure of a member's ability to contribute to the IMF, the use of PPP adjusted GDP would produce some anomalous results. The QFRG instanced China and India as countries which, on a PPP based GDP calculation, would be required to contribute significantly more than Japan and France, respectively, an outcome that was seen as improbable. However, one only needs to recall the substantial growth of China and India in the five years since the release of the report and to note the shift in their relative positions in world GDP, even when measured by market exchange rates, to view these examples as adding support to the minority position. Moreover, it can be noted that consideration of the ability of members to contribute to the Fund did not encompass official reserves which were excluded because they 'may fluctuate and may reflect international short-term borrowing'. However, the large and sustained increases in official reserve holdings of these two countries in recent years and of other emerging and developing countries more generally, are clearly not of a transitory nature (Table 4). As such, the assessment of just what should constitute a member's ability to contribute to the IMF warrants review.

Table 4. Official reserves (in billions of SDRs*)

	2000	2001	2002	2003	2004
All countries	1,589	1,742	1,889	2,156	2,514
Industrial countries	684	717	757	847	929
Developing countries	905	1,025	1,132	1,309	1,585
Africa	42	52	54	62	83
Asia	550	633	721	843	1036
Europe	99	114	140	170	214
Middle East	93	99	98	102	109
Western Hemisphere	121	127	119	132	143
Addendum: Developing countries as per cent of all countries	57.2	59.1	60.1	60.71	63.0

* Includes gold valued at SDR 35 per ounce.
Source: IMF, International Financial Statistics, various issues.

Other concerns were cited by the QFRG in its consideration of the compilation and use of PPPs. First, for the non-ICP countries included in the IMF's *World Economic Outlook*, the ICP estimates were extended through the use of regression techniques based on ICP benchmark countries, but because of differences in the composition of these two groups of countries, the regression results were considered likely to have large residual errors. There was also the familiar problem that the price surveys undertaken should relate to goods of the same quantity and quality across all countries. This was seen to be difficult to validate in practice. These concerns, it should be noted, did not impede the use of PPPs in the IMF's *World Economic Outlook*.

The report also considered the problems of data quality in PPP calculations to be a major impediment to their use in GDP conversions, but noted that data deficiencies could be eliminated over time. While conceding that short run variations in market exchange rates were at times a major problem in GDP conversion, the QFRG nevertheless recommended the retention of the conversion of GDP by market exchange rates, with an amended approach that called for averaging GDP data over a three-year period.

In an added comment on the report of the QFRG, the staff of the IMF noted that GDP data converted at market exchange rates included in quota calculations were drawn from the IMF's statistical publication *International Financial Statistics (IFS)*, which reported data submitted to the IMF by national statistical agencies on an official basis and which were, in principle, compiled in accordance with the United Nations System of National Accounts. In accepting these data for quota calculations, the IMF staff observed that GDP data in the IMF's *World Economic Outlook* based on PPPs were not necessarily calculated on a consistent basis and included, where necessary, staff estimates.

However, it can be noted that in 2000, less than 60 countries submitted GDP data for the *IFS* in accordance with the revised methodology of the 1993 SNA. Data submitted by the remaining countries continued to adhere to the earlier (1968) edition of the SNA in which the methodology on the compilation of expenditure was markedly different. In the years since the issuance of that report, of course, an appreciably larger number of countries have doubtless adopted the newer methodology.

In accepting the report of the QFRG, the IMF Executive Board endorsed the position that a member's ability to contribute remained of paramount importance and that exchange rate conversions should continue to apply to GDP in the calculations. However, the extraordinary volatility of the major currencies over the period since the issuance of this report, as evidenced by the sharp adjustments that have occurred in the euro/US dollar rate since the euro's introduction in 1999, highlights the difficulty of continuing with this approach. Furthermore, the application of a three-year average of market rates as an alternative conversion factor, as suggested by the QFRG, is not fully consistent with the report's position on determining a country's ability to contribute. It should also be noted that when a member is allocated an increase in quotas which it deems unacceptable, it has the option to reject the increase and to retain its previously determined quota.[10] Let us consider further the meaning of 'ability to contribute'. At any time when quotas are increased and members are required to subscribe to the new, higher level of quotas, they do so by providing to the IMF 25 per cent of the increase in the form of foreign exchange, gold or SDRs. As total IMF quotas have been reduced over time to under 1 per cent of global GDP, the requirement to fund a quota increase is now of diminished significance for many members, particularly the emerging market countries, as was seen in the data on official reserves presented in Table 4.

In assessing the results of general quota reviews and the sporadic selective increases that have been approved, the reality has been that significant changes in quota shares have been viewed by the Executive Board and eventually, by the IMF's Board of Governors, as too politically sensitive to warrant substantive action. Although the IMF Executive Board has recognized that quota shares have become misaligned, indicating a need for the developing countries to assume a more appropriate role in the IMF's governance, steps in that direction will require a preparedness on the part of the industrial countries to accede to in a reduction in their collective voting power.

Conclusions

Inter-country price comparisons and the methodology of PPPs are well documented and well tested. Early empirical work of note, stemming from the studies of Kravis and Gilbert at the OEEC, was directed at a limited range of products and a limited number of countries. From this modest beginning, there emerged the full scale price comparison exercises for the advanced economies and the development of PPPs by the OECD/Eurostat and the comprehensive multilateral initiative of the ICP encompassing a growing number of developing countries operating on a regional basis under the direction of the United Nations.

Problems in the operation of the ICP that surfaced in the early 1990s cast doubt on the credibility of the program's results at the time and led to calls for change by statisticians and data users. Responding to these concerns, the UN Statistical Commission, at its 2000 session, approved a reorganization of the program on a global basis, placed its management under the responsibility of the World Bank and established substantially enhanced funding arrangements for data collection, research and software development. With these reforms in place, the 2003/2006 ICP round can be expected to provide the most comprehensive and robust results to date. At the same time, the ICP research program will need to address outstanding issues, including elements of the measurement of expenditure and price collection, as well as extending coverage of the program to the remaining countries. Nevertheless, the ICP can be expected to take its place as a major component of the international statistical system.

Purchasing power parities are recognized by analysts and other data users as an important instrument of analysis and policy development involving calculations of GDP for inter-country comparisons of volume and growth, poverty assessment and comparisons of productivity across countries. Due to their short-term volatility, propensity to long periods of misalignment and, in the case of countries experiencing large currency depreciation, the likelihood of an early and large decline in foreign currency denominated GDP, market exchange rates are seen as inappropriate for GDP comparisons in many areas. The OECD, as a compiler of PPPs for the industrialized and advanced emerging market economies, as well as a primary user in its research and published work, supports the use of PPPs for GDP comparisons across countries. So too does the IMF in its *World Economic Outlook*, for which it relies on the OECD and World Bank/ICP data on PPPs for benchmark years, with estimates compiled by the IMF staff for intervening years obtained by regression. Increasingly, PPPs have found a place in academic research and in the private sector.

The IMF continues to assign a major role to GDP as the primary variable in quota calculations and has remained committed to the use of market exchange rates for GDP conversion. In doing so, the IMF's Executive Board has taken the position that this approach is consistent with the role of quotas in meeting the financing requirements of the IMF which need to be aligned with a member's ability to contribute. However, with quotas now representing less than 1 per cent of world GDP and in light of the large and sustained increases in official reserves for many countries, an increase in quotas, with a corresponding subscription requirement of 25 per cent of that increase should not prove burdensome for most developing countries choosing to accept them.

Recall that at the commencement of the IMF, the quota formula served only as a guide to the determination of the level of quotas and their distribution. The outcome was essentially one of political compromise, especially among the major countries. Subsequent general quota reviews and the large increases in quotas that followed have, for the most part, served to maintain the broad pattern of quota distribution and voting entitlements between the industrial countries and developing countries, with only limited recognition given to the emerging economies and their substantially enhanced share of the global economy. Despite calls for an improved share of quotas and voting rights for developing countries, including from within the IMF itself, they have remained largely unchanged.

The IMF has recognized the shortcomings of using market exchange rates for the conversion of GDP for country comparisons and has applied PPP converted data in its *World Economic Outlook*, a position that stands in contrast with its approach to quota calculations. The results of the 2003/2006 ICP round should provide an opportunity to the IMF to revisit its approach to quota calculations.

Appendix 1

International Comparison Program: Participating Organizations

- African Development Bank (AfDB)
- Arab Fund for Economic and Social Development (AFESD)
- Asian Development Bank (ADB)
- Australian Agency for International Development (Aus/AID)
- Australian Bureau of Statistics (ABS)
- Bureau of Economic Analysis Foundation, Moscow
- Canadian International Development Agency (CIDA)
- Economic Commission for Africa (ECA)
- Eurostat
- Federal State of Statistical Service of the Russian Federation (Rosstat)

- Interstate Statistical Committee, Commonwealth of Independent States
- International Labor Organization (ILO)
- International Monetary Fund (IMF)
- Norwegian Agency for Development Cooperation (NORAD)
- Office for National Statistics, UK (ONS)
- Organization for Economic Cooperation and Development (OECD)
- Statistics Canada (Stat Canada)
- Statistical Institute for Asia and Pacific
- United Nations Economic and Social Commission for Asia and Pacific (UN ESCAP)
- United Nations Economic Commission for Europe (UN ECE)
- United Nations Economic and Social Commission for Western Asia (UN ESCWA)
- United Nations Economic Commission for Latin America and the Caribbean (UN ECLAC)
- United Nations Development Program (UNDP)
- United Nations Educational, Scientific and Cultural Organization (UNESCO)
- World Bank
- World Health Organization (WHO)

Appendix 2

IMF Quota Formulas

The present five quota formulas, with the Bretton Woods formula listed first, are:

$$CQ = (0.01Y + 0.025R + 0.05P + 0.2276VC)(1 + C/Y)$$
$$CQ = (0.0065Y + 0.0205125R + 0.078P + 0.4052VC)(1 + C/Y)$$
$$CQ = (0.0045Y + 0.03896768R + 0.07P + 0.76976VC)(1 + C/Y)$$
$$CQ = 0.005Y + 0.042280464R + 0.044\,(P + C) + 0.8352VC$$
$$CQ = 0.0045Y + 0.05281008R + 0.039\,(P + C) + 1.0432VC$$

where CQ = calculated quota

Y = GDP at current market prices for a recent year

R = 12-month average of gold and foreign exchange reserves, including SDR holdings and reserve positions in the IMF, for a recent year

P = annual average of current payments (goods, services, income, and private transfers) for a recent 5-year period

C = annual average of current receipts (goods, services, income, and private transfers) for a recent 5-year period

VC = variability of current receipts

For each of the four non-Bretton Woods formulas, quota calculations are multiplied by an adjustment factor so that the sum of the calculations across members equals that derived from the Bretton Woods formula. The calculated quota of a member is the higher of the Bretton Woods calculation or the average of the lowest two of the remaining four calculations (after adjustment).

Notes

1 Presented at G-24 Technical Group Meeting, 2005, Manila, 17–18 March.
2 See, for example, Buira, 2002.
3 Vachris and Thomas, 1999.
4 Castles, 1997.
5 United Nations Economic and Social Council, Report of the Consultant on the Evaluation of the International Comparison Programme, E/cn.3/1998/8. The report was prepared by a consultant expert, Jacob Ryten, and is referred to hereinafter as the *Ryten Report.*
6 IMF, 2000a.
7 The *Articles of Agreement* provide that a general review of quotas shall be undertaken at 5-year intervals. The 12th review took place in 2003.
8 Several countries which were represented at the Bretton Woods Conference and received proposed quotas, did not subscribe to the *Articles of Agreement* when the Fund commenced business in December 1945, while a similar number that did not participate were part of the group of the 45 founding members.
9 Following the transfer of responsibility for Hong Kong to China from the United Kingdom, there was no change in the latter country's quota.
10 These issues were discussed in detail by Buira, 2001.

References

Ahmad, Sultan, 2004, *Purchasing Power Parity (PPP) for International Comparison of Poverty: Sources and Methods*, Washington, DC: World Bank.

Belkindas, Misha, 2005, Thoughts about the Future of the International Comparison Program, International Statistical Institute, 55th Session, Sydney.

Buira, Ariel, 2002, *A New Voting Structure for the IMF*, Washington DC: IMF.

Buira, Ariel, 2001, *A Critique of the Cooper Report on the Adequacy of IMF Quota Formulas*, Dept. of Economics Discussion Paper Series, Oxford: Oxford University, No. 74.

Castles, Ian, 1997, *Review of the OECD-Eurostat PPP Program*, Paris: OECD, STD/PPP (97)5.

Clark, Colin, 1940, *Conditions of Economic Progress*, 1st Ed., London: MacMillan and Co.

Gulde, Anne Marie and Shulze-Ghattas, Marianne, 1993, *Purchasing Power Parity Weights for the World Economic Outlook*, IMF Staff Studies for the World Economic Outlook, Washington, DC: IMF, December.

Heston, Alan and Summers, Robert, 1997, *PPPs and Price Parities in Benchmark Studies and the Penn World Tables*, Eurostat Conference on the Value of Real Exchange Rates, Belgium.

IMF, 1996, Data Dissemination Standards, *Annual Report*, Washington, DC: IMF.

IMF, 2000a, *Report to the Executive Board of the Quota Formula Review Group*, Washington, DC: IMF, April.

IMF, 2000b, *Staff Commentary on the External Review of the Quota Formulas*, Washington, DC: IMF, June.

IMF, 2001a, *External Review of Quota Formulas*, Washington, DC: IMF, April.

IMF, 2001b, *Financial Organization and Operations of the IMF*, Pamphlet Series No. 45, 6th Ed., Washington, DC: IMF.

IMF, 2002, *Alternative Quota Formulas –Further Considerations*, Washington, DC: IMF, May.

McCarthy, Paul, 2005, International Comparison Program: Extrapolating PPPs from the 2005 ICP Benchmark, International Statistical institute, 55th Session, Sydney.

OECD, 2005, *The Eurostat – OECD PPP Program and the ICP – A Shared Commitment*, OECD, Paris.

Ryten, Jacob, 1998, *Report on the Evaluation of the International Comparison Programme*, Report of the Consultant on the Evaluation of the International Comparison Programme, United Nations Economic and Social Council, E/CN.3/1999/8, New York: UN Statistical Commission, November.

Ryten, Jacob, 2005, Purchasing Power Parities: Combining Countries and Multinational Institutions in a Complex Statistical Project, International Statistical Institute, 55th Session, Sydney.

Taylor, Alan and Taylor, Mark, 2004, *The Purchasing Power Parity Debate*, NBER Working Paper No. 10607, Cambridge: National Bureau of Economic Research, June.

United Nations Statistical Division, 1992, *Handbook of the International Comparison Programme*.

United Nations Statistical Commission, 1999, *Report of the World Bank on measures to improve the effectiveness of the International Comparison Programme*, December.

United Nations Statistical Commission, 2004, *Report of the World Bank on the International Comparison Programme*, December.

Vachris, Michelle and Thomas, James, 1999, International Price Comparisons Based on Purchasing Power Parity, *Monthly Labor Review*, US Bureau of Labor Statistics, October.

van Houtven, Leo, 2002, *IMF Decision Making, Institutional Oversight, Transparency and Accountability*, IMF Pamphlet Series No.53, Washington, DC: IMF, August.

Wagner, Nancy, 1995, *A Review of PPP-Adjusted GDP Estimation and its Potential Use for the Fund's Operational Purposes*, IMF Working Paper WP/95/18, Washington, DC: IMF.

World Bank, 2003, *World Development Report*.

8

MEASURING VULNERABILITY: CAPITAL FLOWS VOLATILITY IN THE QUOTA FORMULA

Laura dos Reis[1]

Abstract:

This paper discusses a proposal to include capital flows volatility as an additional variable in the quota formula. The motivation is to capture macroeconomic volatility associated with capital accounts shocks as well as countries' vulnerabilities to balance of payment crisis. A proposal to this effect was requested by the G-24 Ministers in the communiqué of October 2004 and also introduced in recent quota reviews at the IMF.

However, the methodology put forward by IMF staff papers measures capital flows volatility in dollar terms. This measure does not fully capture the vulnerabilities of balance of payment crises because it does not take into account the differential macroeconomic impact of volatility among developing and industrial countries. In particular, fluctuation in capital flows implies a bigger adjustment for developing countries since capital flows to these countries represent a larger share of their economies and tend to be more volatile.

We propose an alternative measurement of capital flow volatility based on the volatility of net capital flows as a proportion of GDP and argue that it is a more appropriate measure to capture the economic effects of capital flow volatility. We also measure volatility in exports and capital flows altogether as a share of GDP to capture countries' total vulnerabilities to balance of payment crisis arising not only from capital account shocks but also from current account shocks, i.e. commodity shocks.

Introduction

This paper discusses a proposal by the G-24 Ministers and also by the IMF to include capital flow volatility as an additional variable in the quota formula. The objective is to capture countries' vulnerabilities to both capital account shocks and balance of payment crisis.

In the communiqué of October 2004, Ministers of the G-24 stated that enhancing the representation of developing countries requires a new quota formula that:

> ...takes into account the vulnerabilities of developing countries to movements in commodity prices, the volatility of capital movements, and other exogenous shocks.

A proposal to this effect was introduced in recent quota discussions at the IMF.[2] This issue is important given the increasing number of financial crises that many Fund members have faced since the late 1980s and during the 1990s.

The current quota formula estimates a country's vulnerability to current account shocks as it includes variables such as trade openness and export volatility.[3] However, during the 1980s and 1990s, crises episodes have been related to capital account reversals, often linked to exogenous factors, i.e. contagion and 'sudden stops'.

The current account indicators that are presently included in the quota formula are only partially and imperfectly related to the potential effects of changes in capital flows on an economy. In particular, the current quota formula takes into account variables that are important in what are called 'first generation' models of financial crises, which link countries' vulnerabilities to domestic fundamentals and economic fragility.[4]

The inclusion of capital flow volatility in the quota formula constitutes an effort to incorporate variables that better reflect the growing integration of financial markets. Since the early 1990s, balance of payments and currency crises episodes have been related to developments in financial markets, often exogenous to the economies affected. For example, self-fulfilling crises (second generation models) and crises related to moral hazard and imperfect information (third generation models) may take place irrespective of countries' good fundamentals. In addition, models of sudden stops and contagion, which reflects a sudden reversal of capital flows, have also been identified as a potential cause of balance of payment crises as a result of investors behaviour in the financial centres.[5]

The first section of this paper presents the stylized facts on capital flows as reported by data and empirical studies. The next section describes the methodology proposed in recent IMF staff papers to measure capital flow volatility and their inclusion in the quota formula. Next, we analyse shortcomings of the proposed methodology and develop an alternative method for the measurement of volatility of capital flows. We also measure volatility in exports and capital flows altogether to capture countries' overall vulnerabilities to balance of payment crises. Finally, we analyse the impact of our proposed new methodology across countries and within country groups.

Stylized Facts on Capital Flows

The literature identifies a series of stylized facts on capital flows. They can be summarized in the following list:

- As a result of international financial integration, capital flows increased sharply in volume during the 1990s for both industrial and developing countries.
- Capital pulled out from developing countries during the Russian crises.
- On average capital flows represent a higher proportion of GDP in developing countries than in industrial countries.
- Volatility of capital flows has increased during the 1990s for both groups.
- Volatility of capital flows, measured as a proportion of GDP, is higher for developing countries than for industrial countries. However, it appears to be smaller for developing countries if it is measured in absolute (dollar) terms, given the smaller size of these flows.
- Capital flows behave procyclically.
- Volatility in capital flows contributes to a more volatile macroeconomic environment in the case of developing countries due to the procyclicality of capital flows and their limited market access.

Capital Flows in the 1990s

Financial flows have increased sharply among industrial countries, in particular, after members of the European Community eliminated capital controls during the 1980s, and also after the Russian crisis in 1998. Following the closing of the markets after the debt crises during the 1980s, the volume of capital flows to developing countries also increased during the 1990s, a period of increasing financial integration which led to a number of currency crises in Asia, Russia and Latin America.

As can be seen in Figure 1, following the resolution of the Latin American debt crisis of the 1980s, capital flows to emerging markets (EM) rose sharply during the 1990s, reaching a maximum of US$200 billion in 1996, then fell by about half after the Asian crisis and continued to decline after 1998 following the Russian crisis, with only a small recovery during 2001–2002.

In contrast, after receiving net private capital inflows to the amount of US$100 and US$200 billion during the 1980s, industrial countries experienced

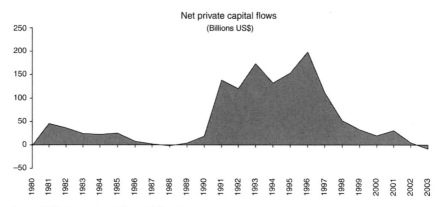

Source: IMF, *International Financial Statistics*.

Figure 1. (1980–2003).

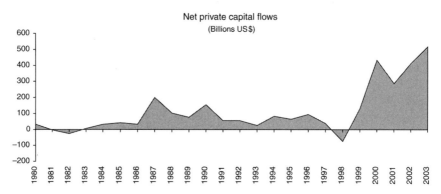

Source: IMF, *International Financial Statistics*.

Figure 2. (1980–2003).

a surge in flows more recently, starting in 1999. Possibly, this is related to a revaluation of EM risk following the Russian crisis. Since then, capital flows reached a maximum of US$500 billions dollars between 2000 and 2003 (Figure 2).

Capital Flows as a Proportion of GDP

Figure 3 compares the share of net private capital flows as a per cent of GDP for industrial and developing countries. In contrast to Figures 1 and 2, notice that when measured as a share of GDP, capital flows have been larger in the case of developing than for industrial countries.

As shown in Figure 3, while inflows as a percentage of the GDP started to increase at the beginning of the 1990s for both groups of countries, for

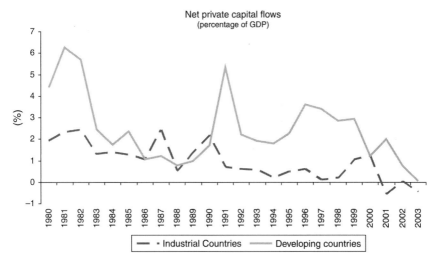

Source: IMF, *International Financial Statistics.*

Figure 3. Net private capital flows (per cent of GDP): Advanced economies and developing countries (1980–2003).

developing countries, these flows declined steadily after 1997. In the case of developing countries, private flows reached a maximum of 5 per cent of GDP during the 1990s and more recently declined to 2 and 1 per cent. For industrial countries, capital flows reached a maximum of 2 per cent and have remained at between 0 and 1 per cent of GDP in recent years.

Volatility and Procyclicality of Capital Flows

Volatility of net capital flows has increased for both industrial and developing country groups during the 1990s as compared to 1980s (Table 1). In addition, notice that capital flow volatility, measured in dollar terms, appears to have been higher for industrial countries because their flows are larger. However, when measured as a share of GDP, seem to be considerably higher for developing countries.

Capital flows have behaved procyclically[6] for both industrial as well as for developing countries. That is, when the economy is growing, capital is flowing in. During recessions, capital inflows slow down, or in many cases, capital outflows occur. Table 2 presents the correlation between the cyclical component of net capital flows and real GDP for different levels of income.[7]

As the table and figures above show, capital flows have behaved procyclically for both groups of countries. Also, procyclicality has been higher for middle–high income countries and represent a bigger share of developing

Table 1. Volatility of net capital flows (1980–2003)

Volatility	1980–89	1990–99
Standard Deviation of net capital flows	(*billions dollars*)	
Industrial countries	38.6	44.4
Developing countries	7.1	27.6
Standard Deviation of net capital flows/GDP	(%)	
Industrial countries	0.54	0.33
Developing countries	0.58	0.87

Source: IMF, *International Financial Statistics.*

Table 2. Correlation between the cyclical components of net capital flows and real GDP

Countries	Correlations	
	HP filter	Band-Pass filter
OECD	0.30(*)	0.25(*)
Middle–High income	0.52(*)	0.26(*)
Middle–Low income	0.24(*)	0.20(*)
Low Income	0.16(*)	0.10(*)

* Statistical significance as the 10 per cent level.
Source: IMF, *International Finanacial Statistics*. This table is from Kaminsky (2004).

countries' economies. These factors make developing countries more vulnerable to changes in the amount of capital flows, resulting in a more volatile macroeconomic environment. Furthermore, in extreme cases, they can explain why developing countries have been more prone to balance of payments crises, including cases of sudden changes in capital flows. Gavin and Hausmann (1996), in a study of developing countries, find that there is a significant and positive association between the volatility of capital flows and output volatility. In contrast, O'Donnell (2001) finds that higher financial integration in OECD countries is associated with lower output volatility.

As a result, lower correlation between capital flows and GDP among industrial countries imply lower volatility and lower financing needs when the economy is in a recession, therefore requiring lower real adjustments. In contrast, the fact that procyclicality of capital flows is higher among developing countries requires larger macroeconomic adjustment. In extreme cases, developing economies can even lose access to financial markets.

Table 3 presents the magnitude of the sudden reversals in capital flows as a proportion of GDP for several developing countries. Reversal in capital

Table 3. Selected large net capital flows reversals

Country/Episode	Reversal	% of GDP
Argentina	1982–83	20
Ecuador	1995–96	19
Malaysia	1993–94	15
Mexico	1981–83	12
Philippines	1996–97	7
Venezuela	1992–94	9
South, Korea	1996–97	11
Thailand	1996–97	26
Turkey	1993–94	10

Source: Calvo and Reinhart (2000).

flows represented between 7 and 26 per cent of the countries' economies. As stated above, this illustrates how emerging markets tend to have sharper real adjustments, usually associated with large real currency depreciations, banking crises and output collapses.

Furthermore, the possibility of sudden stops amplifies the impact of volatile capital inflows among developing countries.[8] For example, for the period 1990–2001, 63 per cent of all devaluations in developing countries have been associated with a sudden reversal in capital flows, compared with only 37 per cent for developed countries.[9]

Capital Flows Volatility in the Quota Formula

Recent IMF quota reviews emphasized the need for a more transparent and simpler quota formula and the need to include a measure of capital flows volatility.[10] The inclusion of additional variables such as capital inflows and terms of trade volatility have also been discussed at the G-24 ministerial meetings, as mentioned in the October 2004 communiqué.

Currently, the quota formula computes a country's vulnerability through current account variables,[11] for example, trade openness and export volatility. As a result of Board discussions, there is a broad support 'to include capital flows into the traditional variability measure to capture more fully countries' vulnerability to balance of payments shocks'.[12] In recent publications,[13] the IMF Finance Department describes a broad agreement among Board members to incorporate two new variables in the quota formula: capital flow volatility and financial integration.

The proposed measure—as described in the publications[14]—incorporates volatility in capital flows, computing the standard deviation from a centred

3-year moving average trend in dollar value capital flows. The data used for these estimates is as follows:

- Current receipts (export in goods, services, income and current transfers) for 13 years (1990–2002), defined as the credit component of all economic transactions between resident and non-resident entities other than those relating to financial transactions and reserves.
- Net capital flows for 13 years (1990–2002). Capital flows relate to cross-border transactions in all foreign financial assets and liabilities except reserve assets, Fund credit and loans and exceptional financing. Errors and omissions have not been included in the measure of variability of current receipts and net capital inflows.

Table 4 compares volatility of current receipts (exports in goods, service, income and current transfers) as they are currently considered in the quota formula (column 1) with the IMF staff proposed methodology described above (column 2).

As shown in column 2, about 61 per cent of the volatility in exports and capital flows is explained by industrial countries, 32 per cent by developing countries and about 8 per cent by transition economies.

Table 4. Volatility in exports and net capital flows* (1990–2002) (in per cent)

	(1) Variability of current receipts	(2) Variability of current receipts plus net capital flows	(2)–(1)
Advanced economies	58.1	60.8	2.7
Major industrial	40.5	43.2	2.7
Of which US	13.4	20.8	7.4
Other industrial	17.6	17.6	0.0
Developing	32.6	31.5	−1.1
Africa	4.3	3.7	−0.7
Asia	14.9	12.8	−2.1
Middle East	8.0	7.6	−0.4
West Hemisphere	5.4	7.4	2.0
Transition economies	9.3	7.7	−1.6
	100.0	100.0	

* Standard Deviation from centred 3-year trend. Shares represent the regional distribution of the volatility in dollar terms.
Source: IMF (2004).

Column 3 compares the difference in percentage points between the methodology currently in place and IMF staff calculations including capital flow volatility. Notice that by including volatility in capital flows, industrial countries would gain about 3 percentage points in the total volatility shares. Developing and transition economies would loose about 1 and 2 percentage points respectively.

An Alternative Measurement of Capital Flows Volatility

The problem with the IMF staff calculations is that it does not capture the countries' macroeconomic vulnerability to capital account shocks. As a result, it is not a good measurement for the amount of resources potentially required to stabilize a given country. For example, if two countries experience the same volatility in absolute (dollar) terms, its impact will impose a greater burden on the smaller economy. The natural alternative is to compare net capital flows as a proportion of the size of the economy, which is the alternative evaluated in this paper, by measuring volatility of capital flows as a proportion of GDP.[15]

An additional factor to consider is the cyclical nature of capital flows, as it is key in assessing their macroeconomic impact. For example, two countries having the same volatility in capital flows would have very different macroeconomic effects depending on their behaviour along the business cycle. Countercyclical flows would have a stabilizing effect and the opposite would hold true in the case of procyclical flows. The fact that procyclicality is much higher among developing countries implies that for a given identical volatility of capital flows in dollar terms, developing countries will have greater financial needs, as compared to industrial countries.

In addition, more intense procyclicality among developing countries may result in the underestimation of the real volatility of capital flows as a share of GDP, since capital flows behave procyclically with output. The reason for this is that the macroeconomic effect of capital flows would be included in the denominator. With our proposed measure, countries in which capital flows are more procyclical would tend to exhibit both a lower numerator and a lower denominator in periods of low inflows in the net flows/GDP ratio, and *vice versa*. As a result, the inclusion of capital flows volatility measured as a share of GDP in the IMF quota formula would be an improvement over the IMF staff methodology, but may still underestimate its macroeconomic impact.

The Data

Volatility is estimated with data on net capital flows and exports (current receipts or export in goods, services and income) from IMF, International

Financial Statistics (IFS) as in the database used in IMF quota reviews,[16] and GDP at market prices in dollars from World Bank, World Development Indicators (WDI) for the period 1990–2003. We consider all the 184 country members of the IMF, with only a few exclusions for extreme cases where data appears to be questionable.[17]

Replicating the methodology used in Table 4 of the previous section, we calculate volatility in dollar terms and compare the results with the volatility as a proportion of GDP. In Table 5, we compare the volatility of capital flows in dollar terms and as a proportion of GDP to reflect countries' vulnerabilities to capital account shocks. In Table 6, we compare the volatility of current receipts (exports in goods, services and income) and net capital flows altogether in dollar terms and as a percentage of GDP, to reflect countries' vulnerabilities to capital account and current account shocks.

As shown in Table 5, when capital flow volatility is measured in absolute dollar terms, as presented in recent IMF staff papers (first column),[18] industrial countries' share of total volatility represents 60 per cent and that of developing countries, 30 per cent. This result only shows that industrial countries attracted larger amounts of capital flows during the period 1990–2002 and that relative to the trend, changes in flows have been larger in absolute

Table 5. Variability of net capital flows* (1990–2002) (Shares)

	Variability	
	Net capital flows (US$ billions, share of total)	Net capital flows/GDP (per cent, share of total)
Advanced economies	60.9	8.2
Major industrial	43.2	1.0
Of which US	19.4	0.1
Other industrial	17.7	7.2
Developing	31.3	73.2
Africa	2.6	26.0
Asia	12.2	13.7
Middle East	8.3	13.9
Western Hemisphere	8.3	19.7
Transition economies	7.8	18.6
	100.0 .	100.0

* Standard Deviation from centred 3-year trend. Shares represent the regional distribution of the volatility in dollar terms and as percentage of GDP.
Note: Country outliers excluded are Angola, Congo, Dem. Rep. of Congo, Equatorial Guinea, Mozambique and Kuwait. Appendix II includes all the countries where data is available.
Source: IMF, *International Financial Statistics*.

values than flows to developing countries. However, this does not measure the vulnerability of industrial countries to financial crises. In fact, over the period 1990–2002, industrial countries have been subject to fewer balance of payment crisis than developing countries. Indeed, industrial countries only had a major currency crisis at the beginning of the 1990s during the EMS devaluations.

In contrast, when capital flow volatility is measured as a proportion of GDP (second column), industrial countries' share of total volatility represents only 8 per cent, while developing countries account for 73 per cent and transition economies about 19 per cent of total volatility.

Table 6 computes the combined volatility of exports and capital flows and compares these results with that obtained as percentage of GDP. In the first column, industrial countries represent 62 per cent of the total volatility measured in absolute terms for the period 1990–2002, developing countries account for 30 per cent, and transition economies for 8 per cent of total volatility.

In contrast, when capital flows and export volatility are measured as shares of GDP, volatility in industrial countries falls to 9 per cent, while developing

Table 6. Variability of net capital flows and current receipts* (1990–2002) (Shares)

	Variability	
	Current receipts + Net capital flows (US$ billions, share of total)	(Current receipts + Net capital flows)/GDP (in per cent, share of total)
Advanced economies	62.5	9.1
Major industrial	44.5	0.8
Of which US	21.4	0.1
Other industrial	18.0	8.3
Developing	29.6	67.2
Africa	2.9	26.9
Asia	12.9	14.7
Middle East	6.0	10.2
Western Hemisphere	7.7	15.5
Transition economies	7.9	23.7
	100.0	100.0

* Standard Deviation from centred 3-year trend. Shares represent the regional distribution of the volatility in dollar terms and as percentage of GDP.
Note: Country outliers excluded are Angola, Congo, Dem. Rep of., Congo, Equatorial Guinea, Mozambique and Kuwait. Appendix II includes all the countries where data is available.
Source: IMF, *International Financial Statistics*.

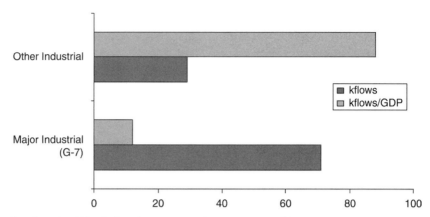

Note: Standard Deviation from centered 3-year trend. Shares represent the regional distribution of the volatility in dollar terms and as percentage of GDP.
Source: IMF, *International Financial Statistics*.

Figure 4. Volatility of net capital flows (1990–2003).
(Industrial countries, in shares)

countries' share rises to 67 per cent and that of transitions economies to 24 per cent of total volatility.

If we analyse the same figures within country groups, the ranking changes radically when comparing volatility in absolute terms with volatility as percentage of GDP. Among industrial countries, volatility in the G-7 countries measured in absolute (dollar) terms accounts for a higher share of the total. This would imply that these countries are the most vulnerable to balance of payment crisis, more than other industrial economies. In contrast, the opposite result is obtained when volatility is measured in relation to GDP. That is, smaller industrial countries would appear to be significantly more vulnerable to crises. This result also holds when we measure volatility for both exports and capital flows (Figure 4).

Measuring volatility in absolute terms and comparing the ranking within developing economies shows Asian countries as the most vulnerable, followed by the Middle East, the Western Hemisphere and Africa. In contrast, when volatility is measured as a share of GDP, Africa appears as the most vulnerable region, followed by the Western Hemisphere, Middle East and Asia (Figure 5).

The same result holds when computing volatility of both exports and capital flows altogether, as a proportion of GDP. In particular, when exports are included in the measurement of volatility, total volatility for Africa and the Western Hemisphere increases considerably, reflecting the fact that these economies are the most affected by volatility of commodity exports (Figure 6).

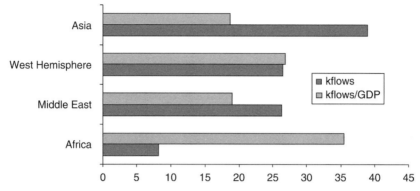

Note: Standard Deviation from centered 3-year trend. Shares represent the regional distribution of the volatility in dollar terms and as percentage of GDP.
Source: IMF, *International Financial Statistics*.

Figure 5. Volatility of net Capital flows (1990–2003).
(Developing countries, in shares)

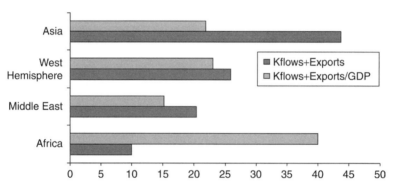

Note: Standard Deviation from centered 3-year trend. Shares represent the regional distribution of the volatility in dollar terms and as percentage of GDP.
Source: IMF, International Financial Statistics.

Figure 6. Volatility of net capital flows and exports (1990–2003).
(Developing countries, in shares)

Conclusions

The introduction of volatility of capital flows as a new variable in the quota formula, in addition to export volatility, is necessary in order to take into account countries' vulnerabilities to financial crises and capital account shocks. The proposal to include this variable has gained wide support among IMF Board members in recent quota reviews as well as among G-24 Ministers.

In response, recent IMF staff publications have included capital flows volatility as a new variable by computing volatility in dollar denominated flows as a deviation from countries' 3-year moving average trend. This measure does not fully capture the vulnerabilities explained above, as it does not take into account the differential macroeconomic impact of volatility among developing and industrial countries. In particular, fluctuations in capital flows of a given dollar amount implies a greater real adjustment for developing countries since capital flows to these countries represent a larger share of their economies. In addition, capital flows to these countries tend to be more volatile. For example, sudden stops and financial crises are more frequent among developing countries and also have a more severe negative macroeconomic impact.

The differential macroeconomic effects of volatility in capital flows among developed and developing countries can be better addressed through a variable that relates volatility to the relative size of the economy. This would better capture the potential changes in the countries' financing needs resulting from variations in capital flows.

This paper attempted to measure total volatility in exports and capital flows as a proportion of GDP. Such measures would capture better the economic burden arising from fluctuation in capital flows and commodity prices. For example, when the impact of capital flow volatility is computed as a percentage of GDP, the volatility experienced by developing countries is much higher. Within country groups, volatility measured as a proportion of GDP, is higher for small industrial countries than for G-7 countries. Among developing countries, African countries appear as the most vulnerable group, followed by the Western Hemisphere, Middle East and Asian countries. In addition, if we measure total volatility in exports and capital flows, the same result holds for industrial and developing countries. Among developing countries, African countries and Latin America are the most vulnerable, with total volatility being higher than that of the rest of the countries.

Appendix 1

The Five Existing Quota Formulas[19]

Computation of calculated quota shares under the status quo is a complex process that reflects the evolution of quota formulas. The current five formulas, used from the Eighth to the Eleventh Reviews, are:

Bretton Woods: $Q_1 = (0.01Y + 0.025R + 0.05P + 0.2276VC)(1 + C/Y)$
Scheme III: $Q_2 = (0.0065Y + 0.0205125R + 0.078P + 0.4052VC)$
                $(1 + C/Y)$
Scheme IV: $Q_3 = (0.0045Y + 0.03896768R + 0.07P + 0.76976VC)$
                $(1 + C/Y)$

Scheme M4: $Q_4 = 0.005\Upsilon + 0.042280464R + 0.044\,(P + C) + 0.8352\,VC$
Scheme M7: $Q_5 = 0.0045\Upsilon + 0.05281008R + 0.039\,(P + C) + 1.0432\,VC$

where:

Q_1, Q_2, Q_3, Q_4 and Q_5 = calculated quotas for each formula
Υ = GDP at current market prices for a recent year
R = 12-month average of gold, foreign exchange reserves, SDR holdings and reserve positions in the IMF, for a recent year
P = annual average of current payments (goods, services, income and private transfers) for a recent 5-year period
C = annual average of current receipts (goods, services, income and private transfers) for a recent five-year period
VC = variability of current receipts, defined as one standard deviation from the centred 5-year moving average, for a recent 13-year period

For each of the four non-Bretton Woods formulas, quota calculations are multiplied by an adjustment factor so that the sum of the calculations across members equals that derived from the Bretton Woods formula. The calculated quota of a member is the higher of the Bretton Woods calculation and the average of the lowest two of the remaining four calculations (after adjustment).

Appendix 2

Table A1. Variability of net capital flows* (1990–2002) (Shares)

	Variability	
	Net capital flows (US$ billions, share of total)	Net capital flows/GDP (in per cent, share of total)
Advanced economies	59.1	6.5
Major industrial	41.8	0.8
Of which US	18.8	0.1
Other industrial	17.2	5.7
Developing	33.4	78.8
Africa	3.1	30.3
Asia	11.8	10.8
Middle East	10.5	22.2
Western Hemisphere	8.0	15.5
Transition economies	7.6	14.7
	100.0	100.0

* Standard Deviation from centred 3-year trend. Shares represent the regional distribution of the volatility in dollar terms and as percentage of GDP.
Note: Includes all the countries where data is available.
Source: IMF, *International Financial Statistics*.

Table A2. Variability of net capital flows and current receipts* (1990–2002) (Shares)

	Variability	
	Current receipts + Net capital flows (US$ billions, share of total)	(Current receipts + Net capital flows)/GDP (in per cent, share of total)
Advanced economies	61.2	7.7
Major industrial	43.5	0.7
Of which US	20.9	0.1
Other industrial	17.6	7.0
Developing	31.1	72.4
Africa	3.7	32.0
Asia	12.6	12.3
Middle East	7.2	15.0
Western Hemisphere	7.5	13.0
Transition economies	7.8	19.9
	100.0	100.0

* Standard Deviation from centred 3-year trend. Shares represent the regional distribution of the volatility in dollar terms and as percentage of GDP.
Note: Includes all the countries where data is available.
Source: IMF, *International Financial Statistics*.

Notes

1 Presented at G-24 Technical Group Meeting, 2005, Manila, 17–18 March. I would like to thank Graciela Kaminsky for valuable comments and Ariel Buira for his guidance in the preparation of this paper. The views expressed herein are those of the author and not necessarily those of the G-24 Secretariat.
2 See the following sections for further details.
3 See Appendix I on quota formulas.
4 Like fiscal imbalances and monetary expansion leading to current account deterioration.
5 For a brief description of the different models of currency crises see Kaminsky, 2004. For a description of alternative approaches to financial crises see Calvo *et al.*, 2004; Calvo, 1996; Mendoza, 2001.
6 Procyclical capital inflows occur when capital inflows are positively correlated with domestic business cycle or real GDP cycle. For further analysis of procyclicality see Kaminsky, Reinhart and Végh, 2004.
7 Kaminsky, 2004.
8 Calvo and Reinhart, 2000 and 2002 document the impact of currency crises and sudden reversals in capital inflows on output. Also, see Kaminsky, 2003.
9 Calvo, Izquierdo and Fernando-Mejia, 2004. Although they cannot predict the causality, they explain that there is some evidence that capital flow reversals may precede high real devaluations as in their sample, 67 per cent of all devaluations in developing countries were preceded by a sudden stop in capital flows.

10 For a discussion on the Quota Formula see IMF, 2001; 2002a; 2002b; 2003; 2004.
11 In the five quota formula, two include the sum of current receipts and payments and the other three include current payments and openness ratio (current receipts divided by GDP). See IMF, 2002a; 2002b.
12 IMF, 2003, pp. 7, paragraph 11.
13 IMF, 2003; IMF, 2004.
14 op. cit.
15 We compute net flows in order to measure what would be the real adjustment required, that is, the net outflow that countries would have to finance.
16 This data excludes Fund credit and loans and exceptional financing, as also errors and omissions.
17 Appendix II presents the same results for all 184 countries where data was available.
18 See Footnote 11.
19 This Appendix is from IMF, 2004, pp. 9.

References

Aizenman, Joshua and Pinto, Brian, 2004, *Managing Volatility and Crises: A Practitioner's Guide Overview*, NBER Working Paper No. 10202, Cambridge: National Bureau of Economic Research.

Buira, Ariel, 1999, An Alternative Approach to Financial Crises, *Essays in International Finance*, Princeton: Princeton University, No. 212, February.

Buira, Ariel, 2002. *A New Voting Structure for the IMF*. Washington, DC: IMF.

Calvo, Guillermo and Reinhart, Carmen M, 2000, When Capital Inflows Suddenly Stop: Consequences and Policy Options, *Reforming the International Monetary and Financial System*, Kenen, Peter B and Swodoba, Alexander K (eds), Washington: International Monetary Funds, pp. 175–201.

Calvo, Guillermo and Reinhart, Carmen M, 2002, Fear of Floating, *Quarterly Journal of Economics*, May, 117, pp. 379–408.

Calvo, Guillermo, Izquierdo, Alejandro and Mejía, Luis-Fernando, 2004, *On the Empirics of Sudden Stops: The Relevance of Balance-Sheets Effects*, NBER Working Paper No. 10520.

Calvo, Guillermo, 1998, Varieties of Capital-Market Crises, *The Debt Burden and its Consequences for Monetary Policy*, The International Economic Association, London: Macmillan, 1 August.

Catao, Luis and Sutton, Bennett, 2002, *Sovereign Defaults: The Role of Volatility*, IMF Working Paper WP/02/149.

Gavin, Michael and Hausmann, Ricardo, 1996, *Sources of Macroeconomic Volatility in Developing Economies*, IADB Working Paper, Washington, DC: Inter American Development Bank.

IMF, 2001, *Alternative Quota Formulas-Considerations*. Washington, DC: Treasurer's and statistics Departments, September.

IMF, 2002a, *Alternative Quota Formulas-Further Considerations*, Washington, DC: Treasurer's and Statistics Departments, 3 May.

IMF, 2002b, *Twelfth General Review of Quotas—Preliminary Considerations and Next Steps*, Washington, DC: Treasurer's and Statistics Departments, January.

IMF, 2003, *Quota Distribution-Selected Issues*, Washington, DC: Finance Department, July.

IMF, 2004, *Quotas-Updated Calculations*, Washington, DC: Finance Department, August.

Kaminsky, Graciela, 2004, *Varieties of Currency Crises*, NBER Working Paper No. 10193.

Kaminsky, Graciela, Reinhart, Carmen and Végh, Carlos, 2004, *When it Rains, It Pours: Procyclical Capital Flows and Macroeconomic Policies*, NBER Working Paper No. 10780.

Kose, M. Ayhan, Prasad, Eswar and Terrones, Marco, 2003, *Financial Integration and Macroeconomic Volatility*, IMF Working Paper WP/03/50.

Masson, Paul, 2001, *Globalization: Facts and Figures*, IMF Policy Discussion Paper 01/4, October.

Mendoza, Enrique, 2001, *Credit, Prices, and Crashes: Business Cycles with a Sudden Stop*, NBER Working Paper 8338.

O'Donnell, Barry, 2001, *Financial Openness and Economic Performance*, (unpublished), Dublin: Department of Economics, Trinity College.

Lane, Philip R and Milesi-Ferreti, Gian Maria, 2003. *International Financial Integration*, IMF Working Paper WP/03/86.

Prasad, Eswar S, Rogoff, Kenneth, Shan-Jin Wei and Kose, M. Ayhan, 2003, *Effects of Financial Globalization on Developing Countries: Some Empirical Evidence*, IMF Occasional Paper No. 220.

World Economic Outlook, October 2001, Chapters III–V.

9

ENHANCING THE VOICE OF DEVELOPING COUNTRIES IN THE WORLD BANK: SELECTIVE DOUBLE MAJORITY VOTING AND A PILOT PHASE APPROACH[1]

Cord Jakobeit[2]

Abstract:

The paper looks into the pitfalls and promise of double majority voting as one element of a comprehensive reform package to enhance the voice of developing countries and countries in transition in the governance structure of the World Bank. It is argued that in order to effectively fulfil a mandate that is dramatically different from the one envisaged when the World Bank was created, the Bank must refashion its decision-making structure. Since there are, however, tremendous obstacles and reservations to the introduction of double majority voting, notably the legal requirement to amend the *Articles of Agreement* of the World Bank, I argue that a two-year pilot phase approach should be pursued. This would leave time to inform others about the promise of the idea and to gather support from key constituencies. Very much like the Global Environmental Facility (GEF) in its initial phase, a pilot phase approach would lower the resistance against 'definite' commitments, while also leaving a chance for agreed upon revisions in the light of lessons learned after a defined number of years.

Double majority voting is essentially a concept pioneered in the GEF over the last decade in the sense of a true North-South partnership. Ownership and 'voice' of all sides involved are an inbuilt feature of this innovative voting structure. Different stakeholders' claims are appropriately respected, including donors without whom the GEF could not function and recipient countries whose cooperation and participation is required to enable the institution to achieve its objectives. Contrary to common belief, double, special or qualified majority voting is not unique to the GEF. The regional development banks are successfully operating with a number of requirements for special majorities of regional member votes, without jeopardizing their financial solidity.

The arguments of financial solidity and the preservation of the World Bank's AAA rating are, however, not taken lightly. General policies, budget and strategic matters should continue to be based on consensus decision-making, whereas operational matters, such as project, program and personnel decisions (yet another PPP), would lend themselves as areas in which the two-year pilot phase with double majority voting should go ahead in the sense of a legally non-binding agreement. On more practical terms, the eight (out of 24) 'mixed' or multi-country constituencies on the Executive Board of the World Bank could be asked to cast two separate votes during the pilot phase, one reflecting the view of their members from the industrialized countries and a separate one for their members from the developing world and from countries in transition.

Introduction

The enhanced participation and voice of developing and transition countries in international economic and financial institutions has been on the international agenda for some time. The Millennium General Assembly of the United Nations in 2000 as well as the UN Conference on Financing for Development (Monterrey, March 2002) and the World Summit on Sustainable Development (Johannesburg, August 2002) listed this issue among their objectives. Within the World Bank, the issue of an enhanced 'voice and participation of the poor' has been discussed since the 2003 Spring Meeting and the Annual Meeting in Dubai in the fall of 2003. In Dubai, a consensus emerged that one was dealing with a multi-dimensional issue to be addressed in a wider context.

The World Bank has been under increased scrutiny for more than a decade with respect to the requirements of 'good governance' which are closely related to the 'voice' issue. Principles of transparency, accountability and participation must not only be applied to the borrowing governments but to the World Bank as well. However, some notable progress has been made on this front. Over recent years, significant steps have been taken to increase transparency and to make all sorts of data and information available to the public. With the creation of an independent inspection panel, the World Bank has made Bank policies open for public accountability. In addition, World

Bank operations and personnel have moved closer to the stakeholders in the developing world, thereby demonstrating a firm commitment to decentralize operations. The introduction of the Poverty Reduction Strategy (PRS) in low income and highly indebted countries has helped to lay the foundations for greater participation and ownership.

More closely related to the 'voice' issue, the Executive Boards of the World Bank and the IMF have started to address the lack of capacity, notably among the two sub-Saharan African Executive Directors who represent 22 and 24 countries each in the World Bank. Steps have been taken to help build capacity in national capitals and to promote the use of communication technologies to enhance dialogue between Washington and the capitals. An agreement to establish a new Analytical Trust Fund (ATF) was reached in December 2003. The ATF will provide additional policy advice and research support to the African chairs. In sum, the spring meeting of 2004 did not fail to notice that progress has been made on the 'voice' issue, but the tough problems still remain to be dealt with.

The complex problems of participation and representation need to be addressed within the 'voice' issue as well. Progress on this front has been incremental, if existing at all. In that sense, nothing but first and relatively 'easy' steps towards comprehensive reform have been taken so far. But the key Monterrey promises must go beyond capacity building. Some important alternatives and possible elements for a reform were already listed in a World Bank progress report dated September 2003.[3] But the Chairman of the Development Committee rightly pointed out in his letter dated 29 March 2004 that one is dealing with 'sensitive and complex political issues' with respect to voting rights and the operation of the Boards, whereby agreement 'is likely to be postponed for some time.'[4] The roadmap on process and procedures suggested by the Chairman of the Development Committee in March 2004 indicated the broad contours of a comprehensive reform package and made a suggestion on how to proceed from that year's Spring Meeting onwards. His roadmap listed a three-fold set of tasks for the next two years.[5] First, to ask the Boards of Directors to report on options for addressing the issue of basic votes over the next year; second, to ask the Boards of Directors to report within two years on options for addressing those situations where countries' quotas/capital shares are egregiously out of line with their economic strength; and third, to establish an independent 'Eminent Persons' Group' to evaluate the composition, structure and functioning of the Boards and to come up with recommendations over the next year. Therefore, provided that agreement was reached over reform on basic votes, quotas/capital shares and the composition and structure of the Boards, a comprehensive reform package could be on the table prior to the Annual Meeting in the fall of 2006.

It should be noted, however, that at this stage, most countries want to deal simultaneously with reform packages for the World Bank and the IMF. They favour a reform package including an increase in quotas at the IMF coupled with an increase in capital shares at the World Bank. Developing countries and countries in transition are equally keen to replace the measure of GDP at market exchange rates with purchasing power parities (PPPs) in the calculation of quota shares in order to better reflect their real weight in the world economy. During the spring meetings of 2005, the reform process on the 'voice' issue did not make significant progress not least due to the fact that the Bush administration has distanced itself from any substantial reform step in the IMF and World Bank that might weaken the position of the United States or threaten its status as a veto power. An additional question mark has been provided by the forthcoming change at the helm of the World Bank. Whether the designated new President of the World Bank, Paul Wolfowitz, will advocate a more compromising approach is open to debate. An incoming President must take some time to state his vision, priorities and position on all contested matters, thereby automatically postponing reform even further into the future. But all this should not be taken as a welcome excuse by other actors to delay any meaningful progress on reform until next year.

The official German view on the 'voice' issues is decisively in favour of a comprehensive and substantial reform package including a change in the present voting and capital structure of the World Bank.[6] This position was summarized in a position paper by the German Ministry for Cooperation and Development (BMZ) in the fall of last year.[7] It is based on three sets of recommendations. With respect to the PRS and the Poverty and Social Impact Analyses (PSIAs) initiated by the World Bank, Germany is arguing that efforts to strengthen ownership have often not gone far enough. Therefore, a further strengthening of the principle of ownership is advocated in order to ensure that developing countries participate more closely and effectively in the formulation and initiation of World Bank programs in their countries. Rather than supporting the impression that the 'final approval' of the PRS is granted in Washington, the World Bank should make better use of local knowledge by deliberately including and strengthening local institutions and capacities in the borrowing countries. It is argued that a sustainable and successful PRS should be anything but a blueprint since local conditions, institutions and capacities differ. To make substantial progress towards achieving the Millennium Development Goals (MDGs), there is no alternative to solutions that are genuinely 'country driven'.

With respect to voting and decision structures in the World Bank, the German priorities favour a substantial increase in basic votes of the 149 developing countries, bringing them back to their original level, thereby increasing their relative weight from the current 40 per cent to 43 per cent. It is also recommended to maintain the ratio of basic votes to total votes in the future, thus preventing the significant erosion in the proportion of basic votes to total votes that has happened over the last decades. With an increase in basic votes, the World Bank should be better able to achieve the commitment and cooperation of those members whose 'voice' must be heard when the Bank wants to fulfil its mandate. In addition, the position of the developing countries could be further strengthened by changing voting procedures in Board meetings. By introducing double majority voting, defined as a majority of shareholders and a majority of developing countries, as has been practiced in the Global Environment Facility (GEF) for the last decade, developing countries should be better positioned to make their views heard and reckoned with. However, in order not to jeopardize the World Bank's financial stability and AAA rating, the German plea for the introduction of double majority voting would be strictly limited to decisions taken at the operational level (e.g. projects, programs and personnel), while all financial and strategic matters would be dealt with according to the familiar decision-making procedures as laid out in the *Articles of Agreement*.

The purpose of this paper is to look deeper into the last recommendation—the introduction of a selective double majority voting in Board meetings and the likely consequences and implications thereof. What are the promises and pitfalls of selective double majority voting? To answer this question, Section 1 will explore the experience gained and the lessons learned with the double majority voting in the GEF over the last decade. What were the circumstances and underlying interest structures that brought the double majority voting inside the GEF into being? Are the developing countries in the drivers' seat in the GEF and what, if any, drawbacks of this voting system did occur? Section 2 will explore the legal and procedural consequences of the suggested introduction of the double majority voting in the World Bank. How, to what extent and where exactly can the double majority voting be applied to the Board meetings in the Bank? Are the intended effects likely to occur? And how likely is it that the introduction of selective double majority voting will lead to a different culture in voting behaviour by increasing the participation and ownership of developing countries? The paper concludes with a set of recommendations that can be fed into the negotiations following the roadmap over the next two years.

Reactions to the German idea have thus far oscillated between sheer ignorance and open resistance and it should also be noted that no other country, not even developing countries, have openly taken up this suggestion so far. Given this rather lukewarm, if not hostile reaction, a pilot phase approach could demonstrate the benefits over a limited number of years, thereby lowering the likely resistance against the necessary amendments of the

Articles of Agreement. Very much like the GEF in its initial phase, a pilot phase approach would lower the resistance against 'definite' commitments while also leaving a chance for agreed upon revisions after a defined number of years.

The Governance Structure of the GEF: Exception or Model?

The Formative Phase: Creation and Restructuring of the GEF

The different governance structures of the GEF in its pilot phase (from 1991 to 1994) and in its restructured phase (since 1994) are—as is the case with any other international institution—very much a product of the specific distribution of power, interests and ideas at the time of their creation. The World Bank and the IMF were largely products of the hegemonic role of the United States in 1944, thus mainly reflecting US interests, combined with lessons drawn from the failures of the 1930s and the imminent needs of post-war reconstruction. The GEF, on the other hand, started from the backdrop of a Franco-German financial commitment at the end of the 1980s at a time when, at the early preparatory stages of the United Nations Conference on Environment and Development (UNCED), Northern awareness and concern about global environmental problems started requiring international action. The developing countries, contrary to their non-existing role in 1944, were well aware at the end of the 1980s that steps to moderate global environmental threats emanating from or located in the South—notably the loss of biodiversity and issues related to climate change—could only be taken with their cooperation, consent and participation.[8] They were unwilling to consider transboundary and global environmental problems in their national politics and development plans 'unless additional funds from the industrial countries would be made available'.[9] The availability of these 'new and additional funds' from the North was seen as the prerequisite for cooperation of the South. Contrary to their relatively weak bargaining position in the debt crisis, the developing countries were confident that their cards were much better in international environmental negotiations.

The development of the GEF gained momentum when another international environmental governance structure began to move ahead. In the wake of the 'Montreal Protocol on Substances That Deplete the Ozone Layer' signed in 1987, formal agreement was reached three years later over a Multilateral Fund (MPMF) to finance the withdrawal of developing countries and countries in transition from the production and use of ozone depleting substances. Funds were made available from the developed countries to offset the incremental costs of projects defined as the extra costs incurred in the process of redesigning an activity to non-ozone-depleting technologies (ODT) *vis-à-vis* a baseline plan including ODTs. Although based mainly on consensus decision-making, in case of dispute, the MPMF operates with double majority voting, whereby decisions require a two-thirds majority vote that must represent a majority among the seven members of the Executive Council from the developed world in addition to a separate majority among the seven other members from the developing world.[10] The creation of the MPMF exclusively financed by the developed countries can be seen as a victory for developing countries, whereas a compromise prevailed with respect to the structure and decision-making. Both sides of the North-South divide must work together to effectively reduce and eliminate the production of ODTs. Neither the IMF/World Bank structure favoured by the developed countries (one dollar – one vote) nor the UN structure favoured by the developing countries (one country – one vote) prevailed. Interestingly enough, once the decision-making structures were operating, both sides discovered that the concerns they had voiced prior to the creation of the MPMF became largely irrelevant. Consensus decision-making has been the rule to the present day.

With respect to the nascent GEF, however, rapid action was perceived by the developed countries as one way to keep the drivers' seat. With the World Bank in the lead, it took only a year from the Franco-German financial proposal to finalize negotiations by the end of 1990. After additional pledges had been made to the Global Environmental Trust Fund (GET), the three-year GEF pilot phase was launched with the responsibility for the implementation of projects shared between UNDP, UNEP and the World Bank as implementing agencies. With hardly any formal or informal governance structure and the World Bank serving as administrator, taking care of the day to day control of the GEF activities, coordinating the projects and chairing the meetings of the GEF participants, the GEF got on its way as a 'loosely structured, action oriented entity'[11] heavily dominated by the World Bank.

From the very beginning, the critics of the GEF were up in arms. They scathed the dominant role of the World Bank and the OECD countries, deplored the limited role given to environmental NGOs, lamented about the limited transparency and participation on all levels and criticized the application of the policy of incremental costs as a new form of unwelcome conditionality. Deliberately designed as a pilot phase, it became obvious early on that the GEF would have to undergo major changes to win back the support of the developing countries and the NGOs. This urgent need for reform was reiterated by the conference of the parties of the Convention on Biodiversity (CBD) and of the Framework Convention on Climate Change (FCCC) signed at UNCED in 1992. The conferences of the parties of the two Conventions accepted the GEF as their financial mechanism on an interim basis, while also insisting that the GEF would have to follow the principles of good governance it was so obviously lacking in its pilot phase. A permanent relationship between the GEF and the CBD and FCCC was made contingent upon reforms within the GEF that would promote further transparency, accountability, democracy and universality of participation. The developed countries and the World Bank, on the other hand, argued in favour of the governance structure of the Bretton Woods system and held up high the notions of efficiency, cost effectiveness and strong management for the GEF.

The negotiations for the restructuring of the GEF began in the fall of 1992 and were finalized with the adoption of the 'Instrument for the Establishment of the Restructured Global Environment Facility' in the spring of 1994. The new charter explicitly pledges in its preamble 'to ensure a governance that is transparent and democratic in nature, to promote universality in its participation and to provide for full cooperation in its implementation among the UNDP, UNEP and the World Bank'.[12] With the focus on good governance and democracy, the restructured GEF was clearly reflecting the political climate and the dominating ideas of the early 1990s.

The Restructured GEF: Double Majority Voting in Practice

In many ways, the restructured GEF can be interpreted as a bridge or compromise between the UN system, dominated by the developing countries, and the World Bank, dominated by the industrialized countries. Neither side was able to get its way, thus turning the restructured GEF into a unique and pioneering institution[13] that was loosely based upon the experience gained with the MPMF.

The Assembly of the GEF members meets every three years and consists of representatives of all participant countries.[14] It reviews the GEF's general policies and the operations of the Facility. The Council is the main governing body of the restructured GEF. Meeting every six months, the Council comprises 32 members, representing 16 members from developing countries, 14 members from developed countries and 2 members from the countries of Central and Eastern Europe and the former Soviet Union. As long as the GEF serves as the financial mechanism for the CBD and the FCCC—that is, to the present day—the Council receives formal guidance from the conferences of the parties to the Conventions and is accountable to them. The GEF Secretariat services and reports to the Council and Assembly. It coordinates with the Secretariats of the Conventions and translates the decisions by the Assembly and Council into reality. As in the pilot phase, UNDP, UNEP and the World Bank serve as the implementing agencies for the GEF.

For the purpose of this paper, the most interesting part of the GEF is the double voting structure. Again, it can be read as a compromise between the

Bretton Woods and the UN model of decision making. Paragraph 25 (b) of the Instrument for the Establishment of the Restructured GEF states that 'decisions of the Assembly and the Council shall be taken by consensus'.[15] Where decisions cannot be reached by consensus,

> 'a formal vote by the Council shall be taken by a double weighted majority, that is, an affirmative vote representing both a 60 per cent majority of the total number of Participants and a 60 per cent majority of the total contributions'.[16]

Again, as with the MPMF, although slightly different, neither the developed nor the developing countries are able to prevail on their own. The consensus oriented decision-making and the double majority voting reflected the under-standing of the two major groups involved that successful policies to moderate global environmental degradation emanating from the South depended upon the cooperation and participation of every member, including the members from the developing countries. Hence, a deliberate attempt was made to build the GEF from the start into 'an exacting standard of good governance'.[17] To be effective in addressing the specified international environmental problems, the GEF had to be rebuilt in the sense of a true North-South partnership. The double majority voting brought the developing countries back on board and undoubtedly contributed to a strengthening of ownership, although contentious issues remained, such as limited financial resources made available by the developed countries in the replenishments and the incremental cost principle.

It should also be noted that the machinery for taking formal votes in the GEF is 'rather cumbersome'.[18] The 'Rules of Procedure for the GEF Council'[19] stipulate that votes require a written text of the motion that must be distributed to all members prior to the meeting during which the formal vote will take place, that members are allowed to make statements before the announcement of the start of voting or after the results of the vote have been announced, and so forth. Not surprisingly, votes have never been taken since 1994. Operations of the GEF assembly and council have proceeded without major confrontation. The two chairmen of the restructured GEF heralded the advice given by Keynes to the planned IMF in a written note to Viner in 1943: 'in actual working voting power is not likely to prove important. If the organization begins voting about everything, it will not be long before it breaks down.'[20]

It is no exaggeration to claim that the GEF is praised in the literature as a symbol for the needed cooperative spirit and vision to effectively fulfil its mandate. 'Innovative', 'unique' and 'role model' are common characterizations of the restructured GEF. The record of the GEF is equally impressive: 'During its first decade, GEF allocated $4.2 billion, supplemented by $11 billion in co-financing, for more than 1,000 projects in 160 developing countries and countries with transitional economies.'[21] The following quote sums up nicely the experience and lessons learned:

> 'Despite the differences in resources, ideology and interests among the Participants there is a common denominator accepted by all countries that cooperation is necessary to address global environmental issues. Altogether cooperation between North and South in the GEF is still better than in other forums. The increasing participation of developing countries over the years indicates a generally positive outlook of the GEF'.[22]

However, as the three independent evaluations of the GEF demonstrated,[23] not everything is coming up roses. The GEF project cycle is one of the most complex and cumbersome in the whole international system, the relationship between the conferences of the parties and the GEF leads to overly complex structures and processes, the sheer number of actors and institutions involved is sometimes resented as a weakness rather than a strength, the understanding of the GEF is very weak within many recipient countries and so forth. In sum, the GEF is anything but perfect. But as a learning organization built on a cooperative approach, these problems are openly addressed and dealt with. The independent evaluations are a strong sign of the culture of transparency, monitoring and accountability that have come to symbolize the GEF.

The Effects of Double Majority Voting Inside the GEF

A closer look at the GEF's governance structure reveals that, other than during the pilot phase, issues of governance have not hampered the development, effectiveness and performance of the institution. A double majority voting works towards consensus by restructuring the weight of arguments during a meeting. Although votes have never been taken within the GEF, the hypothetical vote on the basis of a double majority is able to ensure that all claims by different stakeholders are appropriately reflected in the consensual decisions. Woods (1998, pp. 93) described the behaviour of the actors as follows:

> consensual decisions will ... be arrived on the basis of informal tallies of "would be" votes based on opinions expressed around the table. In this sense, the double voting structure adds an important note of equal accountability—to contributors to the Fund and to recipient countries that host projects—while not detracting from the basic membership rights of all (otherwise equal) participants.

Ownership and 'voice' of all sides involved is an inbuilt feature of double majority voting. Different stakeholders' claims are appropriately respected, including donors without whom the GEF could not function and recipient countries whose cooperation and participation is required to enable the institution to achieve its objectives. The amount of financial contributions to the GEF, however, remained in firm control of the developed countries.

As personal communication with staff from the GEF secretariat and the World Bank showed, the exercise of strong ownership and full participation by Council members from the developing countries depends upon a high degree of technical expertise and pronounced concern about the environmental problems involved. Although often supported by representatives from the NGO community who are allowed to attend Council meetings—yet another innovative feature of the GEF—not all Council members from the developing world have the necessary knowledge base and strong interest to make the voice of the poor heard in decisions. The key to effective participation and influence in discussions is resources, intensive preparation and the calibre of support staff. The rotation of personnel and the amount of workload to be shouldered for competent participation in Council meetings is not always guaranteeing that the interests of the poor are really represented from the start. As we know from the analyses of policy cycles, key decisions are already taken at the defining stages of a problem and during the agenda setting phase, not necessarily when it comes to choosing among different options for decisions. Contrary to the Executive Directors at the World Bank who operate in 'continuous session ... and shall meet as often as the business of the Bank may require',[24] the GEF Council is only meeting twice a year. Whereas the Bank's directors might, at least in theory, be able to influence decisions already in their formative phase, members of the GEF council are bound by two constraints—the guidelines issued by the conference of the parties of the environmental conventions and by the fact that the GEF Council is meeting only twice a year. Therefore, the capacity problem should not be neglected in any advocacy of double majority voting. Every effort must be made to ensure that there is a level playing field for all members around the table.

The Governance Structure of the World Bank: The Need for Reform

The Pros and Cons of Consensus Decision-Making

Contrary to common belief, double, special or qualified majority voting is not unique to the GEF. Other than with the MPMF, qualified majority voting has been a central feature of the European Union since the middle of the 1980s leading up to the Common Market in 1992. The regional development banks have also a number of requirements for special majorities of regional member votes, apparently without jeopardizing their financial solidity. In the Inter-American Development Bank (IADB), special majorities of regional members are required for capital increases, quorum, Board seats, selection of President, suspension of membership and termination of operations and distribution of assets. The African Development Bank (AfDB) has similar provisions on the Board seats, election of the President and amendments of the Articles. Regional members' share of total voting power is fixed at 60 per cent. In the Asian Development (ADB), regional members' share of capital stock may not fall below 60 per cent. In the European Bank for Reconstruction and Development, the share of capital stock held by countries which are members of the European Community may not fall below a majority. Clearly, the Bretton Woods institutions are the exception, not the rule.

The decision-making procedures of the World Bank are dominated by Article V, Section 3 (b): 'all matters before the Bank shall be decided by a majority of the votes cast', whereby these votes are based on the 250 votes held by each member plus one additional vote for each share of stock held.[25] Since the amount of stocks depends upon relative economic and financial strength, the developed countries hold a clear majority within the World Bank. The current share of all 30 OECD countries amounts to 60 per cent. The share of the 35 industrialized countries or high income countries according to the World Bank classification amounts to 60 per cent. Nevertheless, on a number of matters, special majorities are required as well. Votes by the Board of Governors require a quorum of a majority of the Governors exercising at least two-thirds of the total voting power (Article V, Section 2 (d)) and votes by the Executive Directors require a quorum of a majority of the directors exercising at least one-half of the total voting power (Article V, Section 4 (f)). Several other specific actions by the Governors and Executive Directors require special majorities of total voting power, principally increases in capital (75 per cent majority), increases in the number of Executive Directors (80 per cent majority) and amendments to the Articles, which require approval by three-fifths of the members, having 85 per cent of the total voting power (Article II, Section 2 (b) and Article VIII (a)).[26] Other decisions requiring special majority votes relate to financial and administrative aspects of the Bank's structure. In practice, however, votes are rarely taken in Board meetings and consensus decision-making has developed as the standard procedure for most of the time.

While the basic structure of the World Bank is characterized by consensus decision-making against the back drop of the predominance of the developed countries, special majorities are essentially of interest to permit a smaller group of countries or just one country—given that the United States currently controls 16.40 per cent of the votes—to block or veto decisions by a larger group. This decision-making structure puts the developing countries in a clear minority position, thereby risking the alienation of the borrowers whose cooperation and participation is essential to enable the Bank to achieve its objectives. It is no wonder that the developing countries have attacked this governance structure since the end of the 1960s. Consensus decision-making has apparently not helped to reduce this grudge. How were and are the decision-making structures of the World Bank defended by their proponents? What are the merits of seriously considering the introduction of selective double majority voting?

The proponents of consensus decision-making have insisted that this procedure, while not obscuring the underlying structure of power, is opening up space for developing countries to make their views heard. Under these circumstances, a good and strong argument will not go unnoticed. The 'voice' of those who would not be able to win a vote will be listened to and they do have a forum to argue and even win their case on merit. The 'sense of the meeting', the consensus, must include the minority's point of view. In sum, the proponents of consensus decision-making cannot see anything wrong with current procedures.

In practice, however, to win a case on merit capacity is one key constraint. It takes time, preparation and highly trained staff to convince others of the quality of one's argument. Second, one should not neglect the effects of the underlying asymmetries in power. In the 'sense of the meeting', a good chairman will always make every effort to include some of the arguments voiced by the minority but ultimately the view of the majority will prevail. Voting power does always implicitly, if not explicitly, affect the outcome and all participants are always aware of it. At the same time, the standards of transparency and accountability held up high elsewhere in the operations of the Bank tend to be obscured by the voting structure and consensus-based procedures on the Board.

The price to pay for maintaining the current consensus decision-making structure is to risk further alienation of those whose consent, goodwill and participation is needed to meet the Bank's vision to succeed as the 'anti-poverty machine for the 21st century'.[27] The necessary ownership of borrowers will not be achieved by going on to pretend that they are equals on the Board when, in fact, they are not. Therefore, in order to effectively fulfil a mandate that is dramatically different from the one envisaged when the World Bank was created, a strong case can be made that the Bank must refashion its modes of operation.

On a more practical level, as has been noted in the past,[28] the Board has been hampered in its attempt to adequately hold Bank staff and management to account for several reasons. Many Executive Directors are in the job only for a short time, staff and management of the Bank tend to hide internal disagreements from the Board and many decisions are taken prior to Board meetings in the five committees (Personnel, Audit, Budget, COGAM and CODE) or in separate negotiations. Therefore, 'controversial cases and stand-off debates are rare',[29] although abstentions and objections have occurred in the past. In addition, the Executive Directors from many developing countries have not always helped, either because their prime interest is to get controversial projects through rather than having these projects opened up to peer pressure and possible redesign or reversal. The interpretation of what 'ownership' really means is notoriously open to contention and debate.

As we have seen, the requirement to amend the *Articles of Agreement* is the major stumbling block for the introduction of double majority voting as the new decision making structure in the Bank. Another is the historically developed structure with eight 'mixed' or 'multi-country constituencies'[30] out of 24, whereby developed, developing and countries in transition are grouped together and have to cast their votes on the Board of Directors 'as a unit' (Article V, Section 4 (g)), although fundamental differences on the issues at hand may prevail).

Whereas a selective capital increase would require the approval of the Board of Governors by a 75 per cent majority of total voting power (and the agreement of non-subscribing members not to exercise their pre-emptive rights), amending the *Articles of Agreements*, as illustrated above, depends on an 85 per cent majority of total voting power. Therefore, near unanimity seems to be a prerequisite for being able to carry the double majority voting forward in a formalized way. Every effort should be made to achieve unanimity when introducing such a major voting reform. If resistance to such a reform appears to be relatively strong at first, a more prudent approach should be taken.

Issue Areas for Double Majority Voting in the World Bank

Not even the proponents of double majority voting would insist on replacing the existing decision-making structure in full. As we have seen with the GEF, double majority voting is largely limited to operational matters, whereas strategic matters remain with the conferences of the parties of the environmental agreements, while the amount of financial contributions remains under full control of the developed countries. Control over their financial commitment is clearly a top priority for all developed countries. A Bank run exclusively by the borrowing countries is out of the question. The World Bank depends upon a good reputation on financial markets (AAA rating) to be able to raise funds at low interest rates. Therefore, not a single voice in the reform debate is willing to risk this financial solidity and life line of the World Bank. Anything related to strategic and general policies, profit distribution and so forth, should be kept under the current voting structure subject to further fundamental reform.

As we have seen, however, with the regional development banks, clearly spelled out and specific special majorities of regional members, that is developing countries, do not jeopardize a AAA rating. In addition, they provide the benefit of fostering the identification of the main borrowers with the objectives of the institution, while also better meeting the general requirements of accountability and participation. What specific areas would lend themselves to double majority voting at the World Bank?

The operations of an institution are carried out with the general objectives and strategic guidelines in mind. Whereas the latter should be formulated with as much consensus as possible, the former are based on specific and case by case interpretations where opinions might differ. If one wants to increase ownership of the borrowers in the day to day business, it is at this stage where double majority voting should come in. To exercise effective control of staff whose work is reaching the Board in the form of project and program proposals, the developing countries should really be more in the driver's seat without being able to manipulate projects to an exclusive advantage. The interests of donors and borrowers would be better reflected in projects and programs accepted by double majority voting rather than by consensus dominated by the majority.

Hardliners from the developing countries might argue that such a restricted and limited step would be hugely insufficient. To some extent, they are right. The approach is a compromise and obviously designed to provide a way out from the current impasse. Giving the idea a second and third thought, these critics might come around to value the merits of the approach. Consider the more controversial projects of the past, such as the Narmada dam or the Western China anti-poverty project and it would be clear that resistance generated largely by international and Northern dominated NGOs or by powerful shareholders could not as easily lead into a Bank withdrawal from these projects as had been the case in the past. A special double majority voting on the Board would certainly strengthen the position of the developing countries and reduce the influence of international NGOs whom some believe to have gained too much influence on the Bank, anyway.[31]

The *Articles of Agreement* of the World Bank list another item among the 'ordinary business of the Bank' carried out under the direction and subject to the general control of the Executive Directors:[32] 'organization, appointment and dismissal of the officers and staff.' Since programs and projects should be designed with a high level of participation by those affected by them, double majority voting for staffing decisions could be another way to increase borrowers' ownership with the Bank. This is not to say, of course, that every appointment or dismissal in the Bank should be subject to double majority voting on the Board. Identification with the Bank's objectives and procedures will increase on the side of the borrowers if the general requirements for recruiting, the guidelines for structure and background of staff and the broad organizational outlook of the Bank are made subject to double majority voting. The experience with the GEF would suggest that consensus will continue to be the rule. But this consensus will be shared more deeply by the developing countries.

How could the introduction of special double majority voting operate in more practical terms? As recommended, decisions on project loans and programs, such as a Country Assistance Strategy (CAS), county specific Poverty Reduction Strategies (PRS), and—probably most controversial—Country Policy and Institutional Assessments (CPIA) could be made subject to double majority voting. In addition, all matters on the agenda of the Personnel Committee of the Executive Board, such as compensation, benefits, diversity of staff etc., would also fall under double majority voting. This would translate into two rounds of decisions to be taken by the Board on these issues during the two-year pilot phase, one by the industrialized countries and one by the developing countries and the countries in transition. For a loan or program to pass, two different majorities would be required. In case of dissent, both sides will have to negotiate for a compromise.

But we would still be left with the problem of the 'mixed constituencies'. How are these eight multi-country constituencies on the Board to be dealt with? One way to handle this problem is to ask the eight 'mixed constituencies' to operate not as a unit during the pilot phase with respect to the decisions subject to special double majority voting but to cast two separate votes, one with the group of industrialized countries reflecting the view of the respective members and another with the group of developing countries and countries in transition. This way, there would be a separate majority among the 13 Executive Directors representing the industrialized countries (five plus eight) and another majority among the 19 Executive Directors representing the developing countries and countries in transition (eleven plus eight). Since this recommended procedure would leave the 'mixed constituencies' with an additional workload, they should be compensated by additional capacity enhancing measures financed by the reform group of industrialized countries willing to push the special double majority voting forward.

It should be noted that all recommendations above are based on **IBRD** majorities and that **IDA** issues have been left out. It is also clear from the above that the problem of the 'mixed constituencies' will most probably need to be addressed at the end of the pilot phase by a realignment of voting groups should member countries decide to permanently switch to special double majority voting in the future. Of course, for the pilot phase, one could extend special double majority voting fairly easily to the Board of Directors of the IMF as well.

Conclusions

It is certainly true that the GEF and the World Bank do not lend themselves easily to comparisons. While the former has started to operate in restructured form only a decade ago and is characterized by a limited mandate, scope and size of operations, the latter is clearly one of the most—if not the most— important player in the field of development with a significant size, scope and a broadbased mandate. Yet, the guidelines for good governance, participation and accountability should not only apply to the restructured GEF.

A special double majority voting, defined for practical purpose as a majority of shareholder votes, on the one hand, and a majority of developing country votes, on the other hand,[33] has been identified in this paper as an important step in the current attempt to increase the voice and participation of developing countries and transition countries in the World Bank. The time frame suggested by the Chairman of the Development Committee in the roadmap should be used to win broadbased support for this concept. However, since the voting structures in the Bank are clearly spelled out in the *Articles of Agreement*, there appears to be no alternative to a formal amendment if one wants to permanently introduce a new structure.

Again, the experience with the GEF can show a way out. The GEF started at the beginning of the 1990s with a pilot phase approach. Applied to our issue, such an approach falls short of a formal amendment while leaving time to gain experience with this new voting structure. If agreement can be reached among shareholders that for a limited number of years, a limited amount of matters and subject to proper evaluation, a special double majority voting should go ahead on the basis of a legally non-binding agreement, then there is no immediate need for an amendment of the *Articles of Agreement*. In case one of the shareholders wants to call a formal vote during the pilot phase, the current voting structures do apply. This argument should make it easier to get the green signal for the pilot phase approach from all shareholders, including the United States. After a defined number of years, I suggest a two-year pilot phase and depending upon the lessons learned based on a careful and independent evaluation of the experience, the approach might be formalized with an amendment of the *Articles of Agreement*. The pilot phase approach should be pursued to win over the opponents and to prove the merits of the idea. The extended time frame suggested by the Chairman of the Development Committee in the roadmap, an 'Eminent Persons' Group', reporting back on issues relating to composition, structure and functioning of the Board within a year, should be used to win broadbased support for the pilot phase approach on the voting issue. The introduction of double majority voting, albeit only on operational matters (projects, programs, personnel—PPP) and limited to a two-year pilot phase will be seen as a clear signal that the World Bank is willing to apply the requirements of accountability and participation to itself, thereby presenting the Bank as a learning organization. Moving forward on the 'voice' issue, nobody should settle for less.

Notes

1 This paper is also published by the German Ministry for Economic Cooperation and Development (BMZ) as a discussion paper (forthcoming).

2 The research for this paper was initially commissioned and financially supported by the German Ministry for Economic Cooperation and Development (BMZ) in the spring of 2004. The paper has undergone a number of revisions since then. For useful comments and suggestions, I am particularly indebted to Susanne Dorasil from the office of the German Executive Director at the World Bank in Washington, DC, Jürgen Zattler (BMZ, Berlin), Mirko Kreibich (formerly with BMZ, Berlin) and to the participants of the G-24 XX Technical Group Meeting, Manila, Philippines, 17–18 March 2005. I owe a special note of gratitude to Ariel Buira, Director of the G-24 Secretariat, for inviting me to the Manila Meeting and for a very constructive discussion on my conclusions. However, the usual caveat applies: the views expressed in this paper and the remaining errors are solely my own.

3 World Bank, 2003.

4 Manuel, 2004.

5 Manuel, 1994.

6 It should be noted, however, that there is not even intra-ministerial consensus on the reform issue at the Bretton Woods Institutions within the German government. While the German Executive Director at the World Bank reports to the BMZ, his German colleague at the IMF relates with the Ministry of Finance, where a much more sceptical view is taken on all reform issues.

7 BMZ, 2003.

8 On the creation, pilot phase and restructuring of the GEF, see Anderson, 1995; Bowles, 1996; Dernbach, 1993; Ehrman, 1997; Fairman, 1994 and 1996; Jordan, 1994 and 1995; Mott, 1993; Sharma, 1996; Sjöberg, 1994, 1996 and 1999; Streck, 2001; Wells, 1994; Wood, 1993; Young and Boehmer-Christiansen, 1997.

9 Streck 2001, pp. 72.

10 On the decision-making structure and the creation of the MPMF, see Biermann, 1997; de Sombre and Kauffman, 1996.

11 Streck 2001, pp. 73.

12 GEF, 1994a.
13 de Chazournes, 2003.
14 For the following section, see Streck, 2001 and GEF, 1994a.
15 GEF, 1994a.
16 op. cit., Paragraph 25 (c).
17 Woods, 1998, pp. 94.
18 op. cit., pp. 95.
19 GEF, 1994b, Paragraph 37–45.
20 Gianaris, 1991, pp. 920.
21 Christoffersen *et al.*, 2002.
22 Streck, 2001, pp. 85.
23 GEF, 1994c; Porter *et al.*, 1999; Christoffersen *et al.*, 2002.
24 World Bank, 1989, Article V, Section 3 (e).
25 World Bank, 1989, Article V, Section 3 (a).
26 Acceptance by all members is required for any amendment of the Articles which would modify the right of members to withdraw from the Bank (Article VI, Section 1) or to exercise pre-emptive rights in subscription to shares (Article II, Section 3 (c)) or would alter the limitation on liability on share to the unpaid portion of the issue price (Article II, Section 6).
27 Edwards, 1999, pp. 182.
28 World Bank, 1992; Woods, 2001.
29 Woods, 2001, pp. 87.
30 The Executive Director currently (summer 2004) sent by Austria (with countries in transition such as Kazakhstan and Belarus in this voting group), the Executive Director currently sent by Venezuela (with Spain as the largest share holder in this voting group), the Executive Director currently sent by the Netherlands (with countries in transition such as Ukraine and Romania), the Executive Director currently sent by Canada (with developing countries such as Jamaica and Guyana), the Executive Director currently sent by Italy (with Timor-Leste and Albania), the Executive Director currently sent by New Zealand (with Cambodia and Mongolia), the Executive Director sent by Iceland (with the three Baltic countries Estonia, Latvia, and Lithuania), and the Executive Director sent by Switzerland (with countries in transition such as Azerbaijan and Uzbekistan).
31 Mallaby, 2004.
32 World Bank, 1989, Article V, Section 5 (b).
33 Woods (2005) recently suggested a double majority not just of weighted votes but of all members. As the experience with the Montreal Protocol Fund and the regional development banks suggests, other forms of double majority voting are possible. Further detailed studies might be needed to determine the most appropriate and acceptable solution for the Bank and the Fund.

References

Anderson, Steven M, 1995, Reforming International Institutions to Improve Global Environmental Relations, Agreement, and Treaty Enforcement, *Hastings International and Comparative Law Review*, 18:4, pp. 771–821.
Biermann, Frank, 1997, Financing Environmental Policies in the South: Experiences from the Multilateral Ozone Fund, *International Environmental Affairs*, 9:3, pp. 179–218.

Boehmer-Chritiansen, Sonja, 1997, The International Research Enterprise and Global Environmental Change: Climate Change Policy as a Research Process, *The Environment and International Relations*, Vogler, John and Imber, Mark, F (eds), London: Routledge, pp. 171–95.

Boisson de Chazournes, Laurence, 2003, *The Global Environment Facility as a Pioneering Institution*, GEF Working Paper 19, Washington, DC: GEF. http://www.gefweb.org/Outreach/outreach-PUblications/2003-11WP19.pdf

Bowles, Ian A, 1996, The Global Environment Facility: New Progress on Development Bank Governance, *Environment*, 38:3, pp. 38–40.

BMZ, 2003, *For a Substantial Improvement of Participation of Developing and Transition Countries within the World Bank*, German Position Paper, Mimeo, Berlin: BMZ, September.

Christofferson, Leif *et al.*, 2002, *The First Decade of the GEF. Second Overall Performance Study*, Washington, DC: GEF.

DeSombre, Elizabeth R and Kauffman, Joanne, 1996, The Montreal Protocol Multilateral Fund: Partial Success Story, *Institutions for Environmental Aid: Pitfalls and Promise*, Keohane, Robert O and Levy, Marc A (eds), Cambridge: MIT Press, pp. 89–126.

Dernbach, John C, 1993, The Global Environmental Facility: Financing the Treaty Obligations of Developing Nations, *Environmental Law Reporter*, 23:3, pp. 10124–32.

Edwards, Michael, 1999, *Future Positive. International Organization in the 21ˢᵗ Century*, London: Earthscan.

Ehrmann, Markus, 1997, *Die Globale Umweltfazilität (GEF), in: Zeitschrift für ausländisches öffentliches Recht und Völkerrecht*, 57:2/3, pp. 565–614.

Fairman, David, 1994, Report of the Independent Evaluation of the Global Environment Facility Pilot Phase, *Environment*, 36:2, pp. 25–30.

Fairman, David, 1996, The Global Environment Facility: Haunted by the Shadow of the Future, *Institutions for Environmental Aid: Pitfalls and Promise*, Keohane, Robert O and Levy, Marc A (eds), Cambridge: MIT Press, pp. 55–87.

GEF, 1994a, *Instrument for the Establishment of the Restructured Global Environmental Facility*, Washington, DC: GEF. http://www.gefweb.org/Documents/Instrument/instrument.html

GEF, 1994b, *Rules of Procedure for the GEF Council*, Washington, DC: GEF. http://www.gefweb.org/participants/Council/Council_Rules/English_Council_Rules.pdf

GEF, 1994c, *Independent Evaluation of the Pilot Phase*, Washington, DC: GEF.

GEF, 2002, *Second Overall Performance Study*, Washington, DC: GEF. http://www.gefweb.org/1Full_Report-FINAL-2-26-02.pdf

Gianaris, WN, 1991, Weighted Voting in the International Monetary Fund and the World Bank, *Fordham International Law Journal*, 14, pp. 910–45.

Griffith-Jones, Stephany, 2002, Governance of the World Bank, http://www.gapresearch.org/finance/Governance%20of%20the%20World%20Bank.pdf

Jordan, Andrew, 1994, Paying the Incremental Costs of Global Environmental Protection: The Evolving Role of GEF, *Environment*, 36:2, pp. 12–36.

Jordan, Andrew, 1995, Designing New International Organizations: A Note on the Structure and Operation of the Global Environment Facility, *Public Administration*, 73:2, pp. 303–12.

Ladd, Paul, 2003, Options for democratising the World Bank and the IMF [Christian Aid], http://www.sarpn.org.za/documents/d0000527/Ladd_WB_IMF.pdf

Manuel, Trevor, 2004, Letter of the Chairman of the Development Committee, Joint Ministerial Committee of the Boards of Governors of the Bank and the Fund on the Transfer of Real Resources to Developing Countries (unpublished), 29 March.

Mott, Richard, 1993, The GEF and the Conventions on Climate Change and Biological Diversity, *International Environmental Affairs*, 5:4, pp. 299–312.

Porter, Gareth *et al.*, 1998, *Study of the GEF's Overall Performance*, Washington, DC: GEF.

Sharma, Shalendra D, 1996, Building Effective International Environmental Regimes: The Case of the Global Environment Facility, *Journal of Environment & Development*, 5:1, pp. 73–86.

Sjöberg, Helen, 1994, *From Idea to Reality. The Creation of the Global Environment Facility*, GEF Working Paper 10, Washington, DC: GEF.

Sjöberg, Helen, 1996, The Global Environment Facility, *Greening International Institutions*, Werksman, Jacob (ed.), London: Earthscan, pp. 148–162.

Sjöberg, Helen, 1999, *Restructuring the Global Environment Facility*, GEF Working Paper 13, Washington, DC: GEF. http://www.gefweb.org/Outreach/outreach-PUblications/WP13-Restructuring_the_GEF.pdf

Streck, Charlotte, 2001, The Global Environment Facility – a Role Model for International Governance?, *Global Environmental Politics*, 1:2, pp. 71–94. http://www.gppi.net/cms/public/aa069e41b3d818e5845522866af38321Streck%20GEP%202001.pdf

Wells, Michael P, 1994, The Global Environment Facility and Prospects for Biodiversity Conservation, *International Environmental Affairs*, 6:1, pp. 69–97.

Wood, Alexander, 1993, The Global Environment Facility Pilot Phase, *International Environmental Affairs*, 5:3, pp. 219–55.

Woods, Ngaire, 1998, Governance in International Organizations: The Case for Reform in the Bretton Woods Institutions, *International Monetary and Financial Issues for the 1990s*, Geneva: UNCTAD, 7 and 8, pp. 81–105.

Woods, Ngaire, 2001, Making the IMF and the World Bank more accountable, *International Affairs*, 77:1, pp. 83–100.

Woods, Ngaire, 2005, Does aid work?, *Prospect*, No. 110, 21 May.

World Bank, 1989, *Articles of Agreement* (as amended effective 16 February 1989), Washington, DC: World Bank.

World Bank, 1992, *Report of the ad hoc Committee on Board Procedures*, Washington, DC: World Bank, 26 May.

World Bank, 2003, *Enhancing Voice and Participation of Developing and Transition Countries: Progress Report by the World Bank* (unpublished) 11 September.

Young, Zoe and Boehmer-Christiansen, Sonja, 1997, The Global Environment Facility: An Institutional Innovation in Need of Guidance?, *Environmental Politics*, 6:1, pp. 193–202.

10

VOTING POWER IMPLICATIONS OF A DOUBLE MAJORITY VOTING PROCEDURE IN THE IMF'S EXECUTIVE BOARD

Jonathan R. Strand[1] and David P. Rapkin[2]

Abstract:

In this chapter, we simulate the effect that a double majority decision rule would have on the relative influence of members of the IMF's Executive Board. We first discuss the logic of double-majority decision methods and discuss several alternative ways to implement them. We then explain the importance of relative voting power and define two ways to estimate it. We then turn to simulations of how voting power would be redistributed were the IMF to adopt a double majority decision rule. The results, as expected, indicate that the voting power of developing countries would be increased if a double majority decision rule was implemented. We conclude that the chief virtue of double majority voting in the IMF would be to compel the developed countries to take into consideration more seriously the views and preferences of the developing countries which are, after all, most consequentially affected by the decisions and policies of the organization.

Introduction

One of the most fundamental governance issues facing international organizations concerns the methods by which members' preferences are aggregated for purposes of deciding upon and implementing collective action. From a slightly different perspective, what is at issue is how to reconcile the principle of sovereign equality with the reality of a hierarchical international system marked by large power disparities across member states. The strict Westphalian alternative—a one country – one vote rule, as practiced in the UN General Assembly—based as it is solely on the juridical equality of sovereign states, takes account of neither size, power, nor wealth (as reflected in financial contributions) and thus, assures that the larger, more powerful and wealthier members will not permit any matter of consequence to be decided by this decision method. At the other extreme, the great power veto system utilized by the UN Security Council provides a veto to the five permanent members, thereby creating problems of democratic representation as well as amounting to a recipe for inaction. The weighted voting systems employed in the Bretton Woods Institutions (BWI) represent an attempted compromise solution, in so far as each member country's number of votes is indexed primarily to its importance, or weight, in the world economy (as reflected in GDP, shares of world trade and international reserves). This decision method, however, has evolved in a way that privileges the developed donor countries at the expense of developing debtor countries, thereby engendering claims of unfairness and lack of representativeness and raising a chorus of calls for reforms to redistribute votes towards developing countries.

Among the many reforms that have been proposed to improve and make more fair the IMF and World Bank's decision methods and thus, also to better reconcile the sovereignty and power principles, we think any of three would produce sufficient structural change to serve as an effective centrepiece for a comprehensive overhaul of the IMF's regime of quotas, votes and representation—significantly increasing basic votes to a set percentage, a switch to a PPP-based version of GDP, or adoption of a double majority voting system. Our preferred alternative is a double majority voting scheme that O'Neill and Peleg (2000) call 'count and account', in which an initiative would need to be approved by a majority of the weighted votes *and* a majority of members in order to pass.

Another kind of problem that arises in weighted voting systems is that a member's *voting power*, defined as the ability to influence outcomes does not necessarily correspond to its *voting weight* (i.e. the simple percentage of total votes). Discrepancies arise because a country's voting power is a function not just of its percentage share of votes, but also of how votes are distributed across all members and of the majority required. Combined, these three types of information enable calculation of the combinatorial possibilities by which members can form winning coalitions. In short, a member's voting power may be greater (or lesser) than nominally indicated by its voting weight.

In this chapter, we first elaborate the logic of double majority decision methods and discuss several alternative ways to implement them. The next section discusses the importance of relative voting power and defines two ways to estimate it. We then turn to simulations of how voting power would be redistributed were the IMF to adopt a double majority decision rule. The results, as expected, indicate that the voting power of developing debtor countries would be enhanced *vis-à-vis* that of developed creditor countries. We conclude that the chief virtue of double majority voting in the IMF context would be to compel the US and other developed donor countries to take into consideration more seriously, the views and preferences of the developing countries that are, after all, most consequentially affected by the decisions and policies of the organization.

Double Majority Voting Systems

Count and account voting systems require an initiative to be supported by two majorities, one of members' weighted votes and a second of their unweighted votes.[3] The underlying logic of count and account approximates that of bicameral legislatures in which any piece of legislation must pass two legislative bodies, e.g. the US House of Representatives and US Senate. The majority of weighted vote requirement parallels the US House of Representatives, in which the number of representatives (votes) each state possesses is largely a function of its population; the majority of the unweighted vote requirement parallels the Senate, in which each state receives two votes regardless of its population.

In so far as developing countries far outnumber their developed country counterparts, adding the majority of the unweighted vote requirement (in effect, one country – one vote) would shift voting weights and we expect, also voting power, from the latter to the former. At the same time, however, the outnumbered developed country members would maintain a substantial majority of the weighted votes. In this fashion, double majority systems are expected to tend towards a rough kind of symmetry in which the interests and preferences of both developed and developing countries would have to be taken into account. Brauninger (2003, pp. 684), who develops the formal logic of bicameralism, argues that the most important condition necessary for bicameral decision-making to have these salutary effects is that 'societal actors are divided by one major conflict, but have several common interests', a condition that appears to be met by the relations between developed country creditors and developing country borrowers in the IMF. Furthermore, Brauninger (2003, pp. 701) contends that 'a bicameral or k-cameral voting rule will be more likely to produce outcomes that are stable and will be implemented'.

Although O'Neill and Peleg (2000, pp. 4) develop the idea using simple majorities, which they argue are more natural and easier to negotiate, they also point out that the count and account method is compatible with various qualified (or in IMF parlance, 'special') majorities. Not only does the method recognize straightforwardly both the principle of the sovereign equality of states (by requiring a majority of members) and the power hierarchy among them (by requiring a majority of weighted votes), it also manages, unlike the IMF's combination of basic and weighted votes, to reconcile these two considerations without compromising the logic or integrity of either. Adoption of some form of count and account would enable the determination of weighted votes to focus exclusively on mapping relative size/weight/importance in the world economy. For purposes of simplicity and without need to factor in juridical equality or need to access IMF resources, weighted votes could be determined only on the basis of GDP.[4] Basic votes could be discarded since one of the majority requirements already recognizes more directly members' juridical equality. Moreover, for the same reason, the IMF could rely exclusively on calculated quotas and dispense with the myriad ways in which actual quotas have been distorted by political influence, as well as by well-intentioned attempts to bend the system to accommodate the participation of developing countries. Count and account is also fully compatible with other needed reforms that have been proposed, e.g. leadership selection, personnel, Executive Board restructuring and separate algorithms for the distinct purposes of determining ability to contribute, vulnerability and need to access Fund resources.[5]

Another type of double majority voting system would require any initiative to be approved separately by a (simple or special) majority of the weighted votes of both developed and developing countries.[6] This version would be better suited to the World Bank, which has two categories of membership (donors and borrowers), than to the IMF, which in accordance with its 'uniformity' principle has only one category of membership. To adopt this version of double majority voting, the IMF would therefore have to establish two categories of membership—developed country creditors and developing country debtors. The uniformity principle has already been breached in practice since no developed country has used the IMF's loan facilities since the late 1970s, a fact that has created two *de facto* membership categories. We fear, however, that creating two formal types of IMF membership would leave unsolved and might even complicate further, the thicket of difficult issues surrounding the determination of quotas. Choice between these two types of double majority voting warrants further study, but we are inclined to think that the former provides a cleaner, more logical solution that better reconciles the Westphalian, one country – one vote and weighted voting principles.

A third (and simplest) type of double majority voting entails winning the separate majorities of *unweighted* votes of two (or more) categories of members. This type of decision rule is used in the Global Environment Facility (GEF), where, if members fail to reach a consensus decision, the decision rule defaults to a double majority requiring 60 per cent of the unweighted votes of recipient countries and 60 per cent of donating countries.[7] The International Seabed Authority likewise does not use weighted voting, but employs a quadrilateral voting system in which the approval of four groups of member states—consumers, investors, net exporters and developing countries, respectively—is required to pass an initiative.[8]

There are other instances of weighted voting in international organizations. In the European Union's Council of Ministers, a special majority of weighted votes and a two-thirds majority of countries are both required to pass certain resolutions. The EU's double majority method is favoured by small states because it ensures them a voice in decision-making. In fact, the IMF itself uses a double majority decision rule for amendment of its *Articles of Agreement*. Article XXVIII, Section A requires a 60 per cent majority of members and an 85 per cent majority of voting weight to change the *Articles*. A double majority is also required for certain other Fund decisions, such as the expulsion of a member or denying a member state benefits.[9] The possibility of a double majority decision rule is mentioned by the World Bank (2003, pp. 5) in the context of reforming the use of special majorities, but is dismissed because 'it does not seem that changes in this area are likely to engender broad support'. While support for implementing a double majority procedure may be limited at present, this may not always be so. Hence, in anticipation of a change in political climate in Washington and elsewhere, we simulate such a change later in this chapter in order to evaluate the prospective impact on voting power in the IMF's Executive Board.

The Logic of Voting Power

Analyses of weighted voting systems in international organizations have shown that voting weight, the percentage of votes held by each member, often deviates from the actual influence a member has over electoral outcomes.[10] This is due to the fact that voting weights fail to account for the overall number of members that can form winning coalitions and how voting weights are distributed across states. In other words, reference to voting weights alone does not fully describe the influence of actors. To illustrate this point, consider a committee comprised of three actors that uses weighted voting and makes decisions using a simple majority. Two of the three members of the committee have two votes each and the third has one vote. The first two members each have 40 per cent of all votes, while the third has 20 per cent, but it would be erroneous to infer from voting weights that the third actor has half as much influence or power than the other two. Since it takes three votes to pass a resolution, there are three possible minimum winning coalitions.[11] Each member of the committee is part of the same number of potential winning coalitions. Put differently, they each can contribute just as much to the passing or blocking of resolutions, so each has one-third of the influence in the committee. For an even more dramatic example, consider a committee in which one member has 99 votes, the second 98 votes and the third only two votes. A simple majority decision rule in this committee requires 100 votes to pass an initiative. Even though the third member has less than 1 per cent of the voting weight, it has an equal share of the influence (i.e., voting power) over electoral outcomes because of the manner in which minimum winning coalitions can form.

Several studies have examined voting power in the IMF Executive Board and Board of Governors.[12] Strand and Rapkin (2005), for example, calculate voting power in the Executive Board using three different measures of voting power in order to assess the potential of regionally defined voting blocs to diminish American power in the Executive Board. Leech (2002) calculates voting power in both the Executive Board and the Board of Governors. He finds that overall, the larger vote holders in the Fund have similar voting power in the Executive Board and the Board of Governors. Moreover, Leech's analysis underscores the importance of special majorities in determining the relative power of members.

The most commonly used measures of relative voting power are the Shapley-Shubik and Banzhaf indices.[13] Each power index has unique properties and no single index has emerged as the authoritative way to measure power.[14] Voting power indices assess voting power before any bargaining takes place and before any affinities based on preferences are considered. It is in this sense that power indices are described as *a priori*. The lack of a single, universally acceptable measure of voting power has fostered several criticisms of voting power indices, in part because results across these indices are not always consistent.[15] For the purposes of our simulation, however, voting power indices provide a useful way to assess systematically the potential effects of a double majority decision rule in the Executive Board.

The Shapley-Shubik and Banzhaf indices assess the relative influence of individual actors in a voting system.[16] To assess relative voting power we first define a voting game with n players as:

$$[q; w_1, w_2, \ldots, w_n]$$

In this definition, there are n players each with voting weight w_i, $(i = 1, \ldots, n)$. The total voting weight required for passage is q. Any non-empty subset of the players is a coalition $S \subseteq \{1, 2, \ldots, n\}$ and the voting weight of S is $w(S) = \Sigma_{i \in S} w_i$. A coalition is winning if and only if $w(S) \geq q$ and we assume $q > (1/2) \Sigma_{i=1}^{n} w_i$. Hence there cannot be disjoint winning coalitions.

A coalition, S, is a winning coalition such that, for player i in S, $w(S) - w_i < q \leq w(S)$. In this case, i is considered *critical* or *decisive* to S. For a vulnerable coalition S, $c(S)$ denotes the number of players critical to S. For any player i, let $V(i) = \{S: i$ is critical for $S\}$. We then define BP_i as the total number of times player i is a critical member to coalition S:

$$BP_i = \sum_{i=1} V(i)$$

To determine the relative power of players we normalize as:

$$BPI_i = \frac{BP_i}{\sum_{k=1}^{n} BP_k}$$

A player's Banzhaf voting power value is simply the number of times it is a critical actor divided by the total number of times all players are critical actors.[17]

The Shapley-Shubik index assesses players based on their abilities to serve as 'pivotal' members of winning coalitions. In short, a pivotal actor, by joining, turns a losing coalition into a winning coalition. Formally, the Shapley-Shubik index for player i is defined as:

$$SSI = \frac{(n - s!)(s - 1)}{n!} [v(S) - v(S - \{i\})]$$

$[v(S) - v(s - \{i\})]$ represents the votes (value) added to coalition S by player i, transforming the coalition from a losing to a winning coalition. This index divides the number of times (i.e. orderings) a player is pivotal, divided by the total number of possible orderings.

Results for the normalized Banzhaf index (BPI) and the Shapley-Shubik index (SSI) sum to 1 and can be expressed as percentages. In other words, the voting power of each member of a particular voting game is its *relative share* of voting power. Having discussed the usefulness of voting power analysis and defined two measures of voting power, we now report our results for the simulation of a count and account voting procedure in the Executive Board of the IMF.

Simulating Double Majority Voting in the IMF's Executive Board

This section presents the results of our data analysis. Figure 1 displays voting weights and voting power estimates of the current Executive Board under a simple majority decision rule.[18] Note that for the multi-member voting groups, the name of the country representing the group is listed. Both the Banzhaf index (19.7 per cent) and the Shapely-Shubik index (21.5 per cent) estimate that US voting power exceeds its voting weight (17 per cent), thus indicating that it has greater influence over outcomes than its hefty 17 per cent of all votes suggests. Japan, the second highest vote holder at 6.1 per cent, has slightly less voting power (5.8 per cent on BPI and 6.07 per cent on SSI) than voting weight. In fact, all other Executive Board members have less voting power than voting weight, although the difference is relatively minor. It is also worth noting that, as other studies have found, voting power results for BPI and SSI are generally similar for simple majorities.[19]

Figure 2 displays results for the Executive Board using the count and account method for decisions made with a simple majority decision rule. Quite strikingly, the United States has much less voting power than voting weight; it holds less than 10 per cent of the voting power according to both measures. Japan, Germany, France, UK and the voting groups headed by Belgium (shown as VG1 (Belgium) in Figures below), the Netherlands and Mexico also all have voting power values which are lower than their voting weights. While

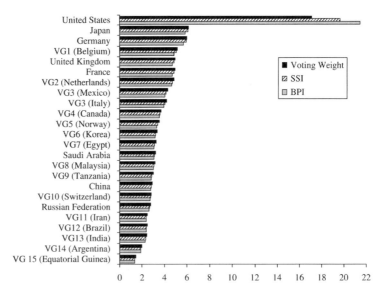

Figure 1. Current voting weight and power (simple majority).

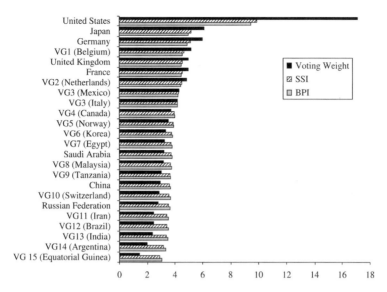

Figure 2. Voting weight and power with a double majority rule (simple majority).

these six Executive Directors would possess less influence over outcomes, the differences between their weights and power are smaller than the gap between US voting power and voting weight. Compared to the results in Figure 1, the United States would experience about a 50 per cent decrease in its voting power if a count and account system were to be adopted.

Several constituencies would have more voting power than voting weight. Consider for instance, the voting group currently represented by Argentina, which holds about 2 per cent of all votes in the Executive Board. This group's voting power, however, would be more than 50 per cent higher than its voting weight under the double majority rule. Similarly, China, Saudi Arabia, the Russian Federation and other constituencies would have more voting power than voting weight *and* more voting power than under current procedures.

As the Fund employs special majorities for a variety of decisions, we have also calculated the effect of the count and account decision rule on the distribution of voting power for the 70 and 85 per cent decision rules. Figure 3 presents voting power results for the Board under current procedures using a 70 per cent majority rule. The United States has 11.2 per cent of the voting power according to the Banzhaf index and 19.7 per cent according to the Shapley-Shubik index. The SSI appears to be almost entirely insensitive to changes in the level of majority required. The two were similar at the 50 per cent level, but diverge significantly as SSI estimates US voting power to be greater than its voting weight, while the US BPI value is lower than its voting weight.

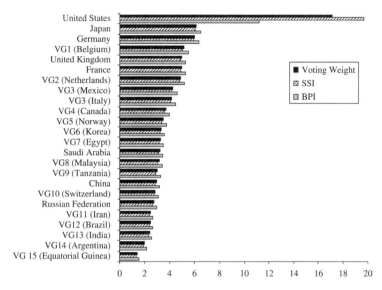

Figure 3. Current voting weight and power (70 per cent majority).

For all other members of the Board, their BPI values are higher than their voting weights and their SSI values are lower.

Adopting a double majority rule at the 70 per cent majority level would lower US voting power in the Board (see Figure 4). Voting power for the nine largest vote holders would decline. The other members of the Board would experience an increase in voting power. Consider the constituency represented by Equatorial Guinea, which has the lowest voting weight on the Board, 1.4 per cent. This group's voting power would increase by a factor of more than two if a count and account rule were implemented.

In Figure 5, we present results for the 85 per cent majority rule under current procedures. As in Figure 3, the results for BPI and SSI diverge as the decision rule is increased to 85 per cent—the BPI estimates US power as less than its voting weight while the SSI estimates it as higher. BPI values for Germany and Japan are also lower than their voting weights. For all other Board members, BPI values are higher than voting weights. SSI values for every member except the US and Japan are lower than their voting weights.

Figure 6 displays results for the 85 per cent special majority decision rule with the adoption of a count and account decision method. US voting power would decrease according to both measures, although its SSI value is four times as large as that of any other Board member. The voting power of the smaller vote holders increases greatly in percentage terms. The constituency represented by India, for example, has 2.4 per cent of all votes but under this scenario would have a BPI value of 4.1 per cent and a SSI value of 3.5 per cent.

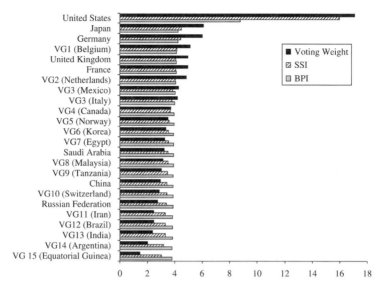

Figure 4. Voting weight and power with a double majority rule (70 per cent majority).

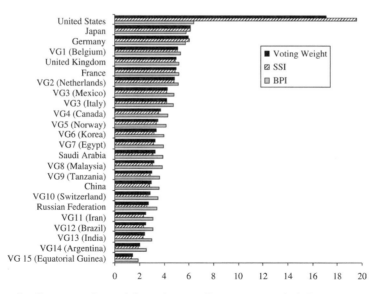

Figure 5. Current voting weight and power (85 per cent majority).

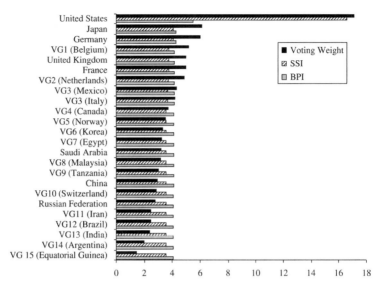

Figure 6. Voting weight and power with a double majority rule (85 per cent majority).

In sum, Figures 1, 3 and 5 report voting weights and two measures of voting power (SSI and BPI) for the IMF's current single majority, weighted voting system using, respectively, 50, 70 and 85 per cent decision rules. For all three of these special majorities, SSI estimates the voting power of the US Executive Director as significantly higher than its voting weight; all others' SSI voting power is very slightly lower than their voting weights. One finding that is important from a technical standpoint is that SSI estimates are virtually invariant across the three decision rules. The BPI estimates, in contrast, vary significantly as the decision rule increases from 50 to 70 to 85 per cent. Indeed, the BPI assesses US voting power as greater than its voting weight for a 50 per cent majority, but as less than its voting weight for a 70 per cent majority and as much less in the case of an 85 per cent majority requirement. In each case, of course, US losses of BPI voting power are matched by gains by smaller voting groups. This makes intuitive sense in that as the majority requirement increases, it becomes harder for the US to form winning coalitions and correspondingly easier for smaller vote holders to form blocking coalitions.

Given the purposes of this chapter, however, the more interesting findings are found in the comparisons of Figures 1 and 2, 3 and 4, and 5 and 6, which enable us to assess the impact of double majority decision making on voting power. At all three majority levels, a count and account system would result in a voting power distribution that reduces American voting power while concomitantly enhancing that of smaller vote holders. In practice, this would require the United States to consider more seriously other Board members' views as it would have to rely on others more for coalition building than it currently does.[20] Obviously, it would not eliminate the potential for an American veto for decisions requiring an 85 per cent majority of votes. Nevertheless, the United States and other large vote holders would have to be more sensitive to the preferences of smaller vote holders. A double majority procedure would still provide the United States and other large members the ability to express their interests through the use of weighted voting, but not without consideration of developing country voices.

Conclusion

This chapter has undertaken two related empirical tasks—estimating voting power in the IMF's Executive Board and examining how voting power would be affected by implementation of a double majority voting system. As explained earlier, a member's voting weight does not necessarily describe accurately its influence over outcomes because an exclusive focus on the percentage of votes does not take into consideration the various ways voters can form themselves into winning coalitions. A measure of relative voting power that incorporates this consideration is therefore needed.

We favour some form of a count and account decision rule, not only because it would provide greater voice for developing countries, but also because it does so in a way that simplifies or eliminates other arbitrary and problematic aspects of 1) the IMF's existing weighted voting regime and 2) other reform proposals. In addition to neatly reconciling two contradictory regime principles—the sovereign equality of states and the necessity of empowering capital contributors—a double majority system makes basic votes dispensable; can be compatible with consensual decision processes if used only in cases of dissensus and would be consistent with a rationalized schedule of special majorities. Most importantly, our simulation results (as reported in Figures 2, 4 and 6) suggest a double majority decision system would compel the largest donor countries to take into account the interests and preferences of the much larger number of developing countries that actually use IMF loan facilities. In other words, it would provide more influence to those countries that must live with the conditionality measures that the IMF requires of borrowers.

Change from the existing weighted voting regime to one based on a double majority decision rule would require amendment of the Fund's Articles of Agreement, no doubt a formidable political obstacle as it would require approval, ironically, by a double majority (a 60 per cent majority of members and an 85 per cent majority of weighted votes). This poses a daunting, indeed seemingly insurmountable, obstacle since it would be subject to veto by the United States—which has opposed almost every reform proposal. Perhaps the political infeasibility of a double majority system can be reduced by some of the steps described by Jakobeit (Chapter 9)—a phase-in, or trial, period to allow members to see how they fare under the new regime; restriction of double majority voting to operational and project decisions, while retaining the existing procedures for the more critical strategic and financing questions and; resort to actual double majority voting only in cases where a consensual decision cannot be attained. In any event, we think this or some other thorough going reform will be necessary to restore the legitimacy and effectiveness of this important institution.

Notes

1 Department of Political Science, University of Nevada, Las Vegas, NV 89154-5029, email: strand@unlv.nevada.edu

2 Department of Political Science, University of Nebraska, Lincoln, NE 68588-0328, email: drapkin@unlserve.unl.edu

3 For a more formal presentation of the advantages of a double majority system over a single majority 'account' system, see Peleg, 1992.

4 Note that adoption of a count and account voting system as described here presupposes solution of the assignment problem, i.e. creation of separate formulas for the distinct purposes of determining ability to contribute, vulnerability and need to access Fund resources and the allocation of voting weights.

5 Rapkin and Strand, 2005.

6 Bradlow, 2001, pp. 33; World Bank, 2003, pp. 5.

7 See Jakobeit's chapter in Woods, 1999, pp. 54–5.

8 Brauninger, 2003.

9 Gold, 1972.

10 Leech, 2002; Strand and Rapkin, 2005; Strand, 2003.

11 There is a fourth winning coalition, comprised of all three members, but it is not consequential for the calculation of voting power since it contains a superfluous member. In other words, the defection of one of the coalition members would not change the electoral outcome.

12 Among early studies see Dreyer and Schotter, 1980.

13 The clearest and most comprehensive study of power indices is the book by Felsenthal and Machover, 1998.

14 Some indices have been favored over others. Mercik (1997) suggests that since results obtained by the Shapley-Shubik index most closely resemble the actual voting weights of members of the EU, it should be adopted as the most reasonable index. Holler (1997) argues that choosing an index because it fits our intuition defeats the purpose of trying to analyze relative (voting) power. Others have suggested that all existing power indices lack 'reasonableness' because they often provide counterintuitive results (Felsenthal, et al., 1998). We believe that finding counterintuitive results is precisely the reason to employ power indices because it offers an opportunity to question our expectations and

understandings of a particular social system and assess the method (power index) we are employing. Voting power indices, like all models, are merely simplifications of complex relationships. For critiques and responses on the use of power indices, see Gelman, *et al.*, 2004; Garrett and Tsebelis, 1996, 1999a, 1999b; Holler and Widgren, 1999; Lane and Berg, 1999.

15 e.g. Felsenthal, *et al.*, 1998.

16 See Shapley and Shubik, 1954 and Banzhaf, 1965. As discussed at length by Felsenthal, *et al.* (1998), the Banzhaf and Shapley-Shubik indices measure different notions of voting power. The normalized Banzhaf index taps power over electoral outcomes (i.e. *I power*) while the Shapley-Shubik index measures power as a fixed prize (i.e. *P power*). See also Felsenthal and Machover, 2005.

17 Results for SSI and BPI were calculated using Bräuninger and König's (2001) program.

18 Our data for the Fund are from the IMF's web site, accessed 11 March 2005.

19 Dubey and Shapley (1979) have demonstrated that there is no unproblematic way to calculate one from the other, yet SSI and BPI often produce similar results. While this is generally true, as Straffin (1994) has demonstrated, there are instances where these two measures of power will diverge as they do in this chapter; namely when there is one large vote holder and many smaller vote holders with similar weights.

20 Note that adopting a count and account rule as simulated here would not address the issue of mixed constituencies. Several of the voting groups with both developed and developing country members are represented by a developed country. Under current rules, Directors from voting groups cannot split their weighted votes. Countries not elected as a group's representative 'can at best express a divergent opinion orally but cannot bring it to bear in the form of a vote' (Gerster, 1993, pp. 124).

References

Banzhaf, John F, III, 1965, Weighted Voting Doesn't Work: A Mathematical Analysis, *Rutgers Law Review*, 19, pp. 317–43.

Bradlow, DD, 2001, Stuffing New Wine into Old Bottles: The Troubling Case of the IMF, *Journal of International Banking Regulation*, 3:1, pp. 9–36.

Bräuninger, T, 2003, When Simple Voting Doesn't Work: Multicameral Systems for the Representation and Aggregation of Interests in International Organizations, *British Journal of Political Science*, 33, pp. 681–703.

Bräuninger, Thomas and König, Thomas, 2001, *Indices of Power*, IOP 2.0 (Release 2/01), Department of Politics and Management, Konstanz, Germany: University of Konstanz.

Dreyer, J and Schotter, A, 1980, Power Relationships in the International Monetary Fund: The Consequences of Quota Changes, *Review of Economics and Statistics*, 62:1, pp. 97–106.

Dubey, Pradeep and Shapley, Lloyd S, 1979, Mathematical Properties of the Banzhaf Power Index, *Mathematics of Operations Research*, 4, pp. 99–131.

Felsenthal, DS and Machover, M, 1998, *The Measurement of Voting Power: Theory and Practice, Problems and Paradoxes*, Cheltenham: Edward Elgar.

Felsenthal, DS and Machover, M, 2005, Voting Power Measurement: A Story of Misreinvention, *Social Choice and Welfare*, forthcoming.

Felsenthal, DS, Machover, M and Zwicker, W, 1998, The Bicameral Postulates and Indices of *A Priori* Voting Power, *Theory and Decision*, 44, pp. 83–116.

Garrett, Geoffrey and Tsebelis, George, 1996, An Institutional Critique of Intergovernmentalism, *International Organization* 50:2, pp. 269–99.

Garrett, Geoffrey and Tsebelis, George, 1999a, Why Resist the Temptation to Apply Power Indices to the European Union?, *Journal of Theoretical Politics*, 11:3, pp. 291–308.

Garrett, Geoffrey and Tsebelis, George, 1999b, More Reasons to Resist the Temptation of Power Indices in the European Union, *Journal of Theoretical Politics*, 11:3, pp. 331–8.

Gelman, A, Katz, JN and Bafumi, J, 2004, Standard Voting Power Indexes Do Not Work: An Empirical Analysis, *British Journal of Political Science*, 34, pp. 657–74.

Gerster, R, 1993, Proposals for Voting Reform within the International Monetary Fund, *Journal of World Trade*, 27, pp. 121–36.

Gold, J, 1972, *Voting and Decisions in the International Monetary Fund*, Washington, DC: IMF.

Holler, Manfred J, 1997, Power, Monotonicity and Expectations, *Control and Cybernetics*, 26:4, pp. 605–07.

Holler, MJ and Widgren, M, 1999, Why Power Indices for Assessing European Union Decision-making?, *Journal of Theoretical Politics*, 11: 3, pp. 321–30.

Lane, Jan-Erik and Berg, Sven, 1999, Relevance of Voting Power, *Journal of Theoretical Politics*, 11:3, pp. 309–20.

Leech, D, 2002, Voting Power in the Governance of the International Monetary Fund, *Annals of Operations Research*, 109, pp. 375–97.

Mercik, Jacek W, 1997, Power and Expectations, *Control and Cybernetics*, 26:4, pp. 617–21.

O'Neill, B and Peleg, B, 2000, Voting by Count and Account: Reconciling Power and Equality in International Organizations, manuscript, http://www.stanford.edu/~boneill/%26a.html

Peleg, B, 1992, Voting by Count and Account, *Rational Interactions: Essays in Honor of John C. Harsanyi*, Shelton, Reinhard (ed.), Berlin: Springer-Verlag.

Rapkin, David P and Strand, Jonathan R, 2005, Reforming the IMF's Weighted Voting System', paper presented at the Inter-Governmental Group of Twenty Four (G-24) XX Technical Group Meeting, Bangko Sentral ng Pilipinas, Mabini Manila, Philippines, March.

Shapley, LS and Shubik, Martin, 1954, A Method for Evaluation the Distribution of Power in a Committee System, *American Political Science Review*, 48, pp. 787–92.

Straffin, PD, 1994, Power and Stability in Politics, *Handbook of Game Theory, Volume 2*, Aumann, RJ and Hart, S (eds), Amsterdam: Elsevier Science, pp. 1127–51.

Strand, Jonathan R, 2003, Power Relations in an Embedded Institution: The European Bank for Reconstruction and Development, *Journal of European Integration*, 25:2, pp. 113–27.

Strand, Jonathan R and Rapkin, David P, 2005, Regionalizing Multilateralism: Estimating the Power of Potential Regional Voting Blocs in the IMF, *International Interactions*, 31:1, pp. 15–54.

Woods, Ngaire, 1999, Good Governance in International Organizations, *Global Governance*, 5:1, pp. 39–61.

World Bank, 2003, Issues Note: Enhancing the 'Voice' of Developing and Transition Countries at the World Bank, Washington, DC: World Bank, 2 June, Annex 1.

11

POWER VERSUS WEIGHT IN IMF GOVERNANCE: THE POSSIBLE BENEFICIAL IMPLICATIONS OF A UNITED EUROPEAN BLOC VOTE[1]

Dennis Leech and Robert Leech

Abstract:

We discuss the nature of bloc voting and show that there is a fundamental distinction between voting weight and voting power. We analyse voting power, assuming that the G-7 countries form a bloc and find that it would disenfranchise all other countries while greatly enhancing the power of the United States, already more powerful than supposed. We consider some of the implications of a proposed reform of the voting system of the IMF in which EU countries cease to be separately represented and are replaced by a single combined European representative. The voting weight of the EU bloc is reduced accordingly. We analyse two cases—the Eurozone of 12 countries and the European Union of 25. We show that the reform could be very beneficial for the governance of the IMF, enhancing the voting power of individual member countries as a consequence of two large countervailing voting blocs. Specifically, we analyse a range of EU voting weights and find the following for ordinary decisions requiring a simple majority: (1) All countries other than those of the EU and the United States unambiguously gain power (measured absolutely or relatively); (2) The sum of powers of the EU bloc and the United States is minimized when they have voting parity; (3) The power of every other non-EU member is maximized when the EU and the United States have parity; (4) Each EU member could gain power—despite losing its seat and the reduction in EU voting weight—depending on the EU voting system that is adopted; (5) The United States loses voting power (both absolutely and relatively) over ordinary decisions but (6) retains its veto over special majority (85per cent) decisions (and the EU bloc gains a veto).

Introduction

The governance of the IMF is based on a system of weighted voting in which the number of votes assigned to each member country is a reflection of its quota. The principle behind this is the idea that influence ought to be inextricably linked with financial contribution, rather as in voting capital of a joint stock company. Thus, for example, the 371,743 votes at the disposal of the United States are supposed to give it 17.09 per cent of the voting power, which is its percentage of the votes. On the other hand, Italy is supposed to have 3.25 per cent of the voting power based on its 70,805 votes. At the other end of the scale, the member with the smallest quota, the Pacific island of Palau, has 281 votes representing 0.01 per cent of the total weight.

In the language of the Bretton Woods Institutions, the number of votes each country has is universally referred to as its voting power. But this terminology is misleading because voting power, where power is defined as the extent of a country's influence as a member of a voting body, depends on its ability to affect the results of ballots or divisions and therefore decisions. A country has power if it can make a difference to the outcome by using its vote, that is, if it can be the 'swing' voter. The likelihood of its being able to do that is different from its fraction of the total votes and therefore its power and weight are not directly related. This is illustrated by the well known example of the voting system adopted by the original European Economic Community before its first enlargement in 1972. There were six members, varying greatly in size and weighted votes were allocated to each member such that Luxembourg had one quarter as many votes as West Germany, almost 6 per cent of the total, yet the voting rules ensured that its power was precisely zero.[2]

In this paper, we describe the voting power approach and show that it is a useful analytical tool for aiding in understanding the rules of decision making and the evaluation of their reforms. We show that in the current unipolar situation in the IMF, where there is a single large bloc, the weight of the United States being almost three times that of the next largest member, Japan, power and weight are a long way from an ideal of proportionality; the distribution of voting power among the members is far more unequal than claimed, the United States having an excess of power over weight at the expense of all other countries, which have lesser power than weight.

We investigate the power implications of two scenarios for change—a formal G-7 bloc and an EU bloc in which the individual countries belonging to the blocs give up their seats. We show that the G-7 bloc would be completely dominant and all other countries would be virtually powerless. The IMF would be completely controlled by the G-7 and the power of the United States, working indirectly through the G-7 bloc, would be greatly increased at the expense of other members. By contrast, in the other scenario, the formation of a European bloc with voting parity with the United States would mean a more equal power distribution in this bipolar voting body. All countries in the IMF would gain voting power with the single exception of the United States. Whether European members also gained or lost power would depend on the internal voting system in use.

We conclude that moving to a single European seat could improve the governance of the IMF by increasing both the absolute and relative voting power of all members except the United States—which currently enjoys more power than its voting weight. The EU member countries could also all benefit if an appropriate EU internal voting rule were adopted. These results are for ordinary decisions of the IMF, requiring only a simple majority. For decisions requiring an 85 per cent supermajority, the United States would retain its veto, but the EU would also have a veto.

In Section 1, we outline the voting power methodology and give some examples to illustrate the differences between power and voting weight. In Section 2, we describe the governance of the IMF. In Section 3, we consider the power implications of a formal G-7 bloc within the IMF and find that it would effectively disenfranchise all other countries and greatly enhance the power of the United States. In Section 4, we discuss European representation in the IMF and possible scenarios for a single European seat based on actual proposals that have been made. We examine the implications for both nonmembers and members of the European bloc. Our conclusion is that a single European voting bloc would be beneficial in increasing the voting power of all countries that were not members, except the United States, and that it is possible that the voting power of the members could also be increased depending on the voting rule that is adopted.

Voting Power Analysis and its Application to the IMF

Voting Power versus Voting Weight and Power Indices

The starting point of voting power analysis is the recognition that the power of any member of a weighted voting body—that is, one that uses a system of weighted majority voting, or qualified majority voting, to make decisions—is fundamentally different from its share of the voting weight. Its voting power is generally defined as its ability to influence the result of a ballot; the member has some power if it can change a vote that would fail to reach the threshold required for a decision without its support to one which does so with its support, that is, swing the decision; the more often it can do that, the greater power it has. A member is a swing voter for a particular ballot if the number of votes of the other members cast in favour of the decision falls just short of the required threshold by an amount less than the votes of the member. Then the member can add its votes to secure a majority decision. For example, the United States is a swing voter whenever the total number of votes cast by the other members falls below the majority threshold by less than 17.09 per cent. That is, the United States has voting power whenever the total number of votes of the other 183 members in favour of the decision is greater than 32.91 per cent and no greater than 50.00 per cent (assuming simple majority voting); in this case the decision will be taken only if the United States supports it.

Voting power is measured by the Penrose index, which is defined, for each member, as the proportion of all the voting outcomes that could occur (taking account of all the possible ways that members could vote on any issue) in which the member can swing the decision.[3] This is a very simple measure of the voting power of every member. The Banzhaf index[4] is the same measure *normalized*, that is, expressed in relative terms, with the power indices for all the members adding up to one. The Banzhaf index enables comparisons to be made between a member's voting power and voting weight, within the same voting body.

A member's voting power depends not only on its own weight, but also those of all other members, as well as the level of the majority threshold for a decision. We will illustrate this by considering a voting body in which the total number of votes equals 100 and the majority threshold for making a decision is 51 votes. A member with 20 votes might be very powerful, or not very powerful, depending on how the other 80 votes are distributed. Table 1 shows the power indices for two cases. In the first example, there are 80 other

Table 1. Power indices—two examples

Votes	No.	Power index (Penrose index)	Power share% (Banzhaf index)	Weight%
Example 1: One large voting weight				
20	1	0.9743	62.40	20.00
1	80	0.0073	0.47	1.00
Example 2: Two large voting weights				
20	2	0.5000	12.26	20.00
1	60	0.0512	1.26	1.00

Source: Authors' calculations using the program *ipgenf* on the website http://www.warwick.ac.uk/~ecrac, Leech and Leech (2003).

members with 1 vote each, and the 20-vote member has virtual control (its Penrose index is equal to 97 per cent) and its share of the voting power, measured by the Banzhaf index at 62 per cent, is much greater than its share of the votes. On the other hand, if there is another member that also possesses 20 votes and 60 members each with 1 vote, the 20-vote member's power is significantly lower (Penrose index 50 per cent) and its power share much less than its vote share (Banzhaf index 12 per cent).

Comparing the power indices for the 1-vote members shows an interesting phenomenon. In the first case (a single dominant 20 per cent voter), the Penrose index is 0.73 per cent (Banzhaf index 0.47 per cent) while in the second case (two voters with 20 per cent weight), the Penrose index increases to 5.12 per cent (Banzhaf 1.26 per cent). Thus, the small voters gain considerably in power where there are two large countervailing blocs, a bipolar situation, in comparison with a situation of a single dominant power; in this case, their power is greater than their weight.[5] In neither of these examples is power proportional to weight. We might assume this to be the usual case and the ideal of strict proportionality to be exceptional.[6]

The Importance of the Majority Threshold

The power of a member also depends on the level of the threshold needed for a majority decision. The above examples assumed a simple majority rule, where differences in weight led to great inequality of power. But if, to take an extreme case, unanimity were required to take any decision, then all members would have equal power regardless of the distribution of voting weights. Each member would have precisely one swing (that is, there is only one losing outcome that could become winning with the addition of its vote—when all other members are in favour of the proposal), so its Penrose index would be equal to $1/2^{n-1}$ and its Banzhaf index equal to $1/n$ (where n is the number of members), regardless of its weight and those of others. Each country has a veto under this voting rule.

If (to take another hypothetical example of relevance to the IMF), the majority threshold is set at 85 per cent, then the powers of the members may still not be very unequal, even though their weights may be. To continue Example 1 from the last section, the single member with a weight of 20 per cent in this case has not much more power than each of the 80 members having 1 per cent each. The 20 per cent member has a Penrose index of 0.0000007 per cent (or 7.057e–09), Banzhaf index 1.9 per cent, while a 1 per cent member has Penrose index equal to 0.00000045 per cent (4.46e–09), Banzhaf index of 1.2 per cent. Thus, power is relatively equal despite the extreme inequality in weight. This example illustrates the sensitivity of the results to the threshold. Essentially, a threshold set as high as 85 per cent means two things for voting power—that relative power (Banzhaf index) is much more equal than under a lower threshold and that the voting body is likely to be a very weak decisionmaker because very few of the possible voting outcomes lead to a majority decision, which substantially limits the measure of absolute voting power (Penrose index). In the terminology of Coleman (1971), the voting body has very little power to act. It is notable however that a voter with 20 per cent weight has a unilateral veto power.

The Powers of Bloc Members

One of the uses of voting power analysis is to analyse changes to the voting system consequent to the formation of blocs of countries, in which the members of the blocs give up their votes and work as members of the bloc, as in the examples of the G-7 and the European bloc. In this case, it is necessary to change the definition of voting power slightly and to define amended power indices. For countries that are not members of the bloc, the analysis proceeds as before, the only change being that the bloc replaces the individual countries which are its members before the power indices are computed.

For the countries that are bloc members, however, we need to redefine their power since they are now involved in two levels of decision-making. The bloc itself is a member of the changed voting body and each has greater or lesser power as a member of it. For example, we can find the power index for the European bloc within a reformed IMF. But in addition, each member has a degree of power within the bloc with respect to the bloc's internal voting rules. Each country's power within the European IMF bloc can be computed for the voting rules that apply internally to the bloc. In the case of the EU, this might be the system of qualified majority voting laid down in the Nice treaty. We then define the power of a bloc member as the indirect power it has by multiplying the two Penrose indices. This indirect power index measures absolute voting power, which is the basis of analysis of changes in voting structures and voting rules. The index for a European country, for example, can be used to evaluate the power implications of the assumed formation of the bloc by directly comparing it with the value obtained for the status quo.

Any member country may gain or lose power by becoming a member of a bloc. Whether joining a large, powerful bloc enhances a country's power depends on how much power it has over how the bloc votes. The theory of voting power under such two level voting systems is set out in Leech and Leech (2004b).

The Logic of Voting Power Analysis

It is important to be clear what voting power analysis is and is not. At the base of the approach is the assumption that all members of a voting body are sovereign, in the sense that they decide how to cast their votes on any issue independently of what others do and that they are just as likely to vote for as against. This is an idealization that is suitable for some purposes, most importantly when the focus is on the general properties of a system of voting rules—such as fairness and decisiveness—where voters' individual preferences are held to be completely irrelevant. This kind of voting power analysis has been called constitutional voting power in contrast to behavioural voting power, which takes account of voters' preferences or voting histories and therefore treats some voting outcomes as more likely than others. If we wish to model the actual disposition of power in a voting body in a positive sense, in order to make predictions, we should consider behavioural power. On the other hand, for normative analysis of voting rules in a designed constitution, voters' preferences are irrelevant and constitutional power measures are an appropriate analytical instrument.

The power indices used here do have an interpretation in behavioural terms. Instead of assuming each voter to be equally likely to vote for and against a motion, we can make the weaker assumption that each voter's probability of voting for a motion is chosen at random. Then, as long as the voters are independent, the Penrose and Banzhaf indices are suitable measures of behavioural power.[7] In the context of the IMF, this amounts to the assumption that the voting system is a means of deciding questions about the provision of global public goods in which the interests of different countries are likely to vary by issue. Voting power indices measure power in relation to an average issue and therefore preferences do not matter. If this model fits approximately, then the voting power indices will be a reasonable measure of behavioural power in this sense as well as being measures of constitutional power. On the other hand, power indices cannot give information about the likely results of voting on any particular issue, taking account of the preferences of particular voters. The model cannot be used to predict in this sense.

The voting power approach, involving rigorously calculated power indices, is a way of gaining insights into the properties of a voting body that cannot be obtained by verbal reasoning alone. Arguments about power in voting bodies are often put in verbal terms, but such qualitative analysis is often wrong. A good example is the case of the EEC with six members where commentators have erroneously claimed that the system of qualified majority voting favoured the small countries, particularly Luxembourg. Voting power analysis gives an insightful perspective and power indices provide a useful quantification that enable verbal arguments about voting power to be examined and also to be taken further.

The Governance of the IMF

The governing body of the IMF is its Board of Governors, corresponding to the shareholders of a corporation, which is made up of representatives of all the 184 member countries. Normally, governors are ministers of finance of the member countries and their alternates, their Central Bank Governors. As the body to which the Fund is ultimately accountable, the functions of the Board of Governors are largely formal and ceremonial, but it also makes decisions on essentially political questions. It controls, but does not manage, the IMF, analogously to the way that a company's shareholders as a group control their corporation.[8] The Board of Governors uses a system of weighted voting, in which the number of votes possessed by each member is determined by its quota. Unlike shares in a joint stock company, quotas cannot be traded, each member's quota being fixed by decisions of the Board of Governors itself. The most powerful member is the United States with over 17.09 per cent of the votes, followed by Japan with 6.13 and Germany with 5.99 per cent.

The main function of the Board of Governors is to receive reports and recommendations from the Executive Board which manages the organization as a board of directors does a corporation. The Executive is a much smaller body, comprising 24 directors who are either directly appointed by certain member countries or elected by groupings of members arranged in constituencies. Executive Directors are officials from member countries, not politicians, and the work of the Executive is technical rather than political. The Executive meets frequently, unlike the Board of Governors that meets biannually. However, unlike the board of a company, whenever it has to take an important vote, the IMF Executive uses a system of weighted voting based on that of the governors. This reflects the fact that its members have different lines of accountability, to their respective country or constituency, rather than the Board of Governors, whereas elected company directors are all accountable to the same shareholders meeting.

Eight directors are appointed by their governments and the other 16 are elected by constituencies. The eight appointed directors are those of the United States, Japan, Germany, France, UK, Saudi Arabia, Russia and China; each of the elected directors represents a constituency that is constructed on a more or less geographical basis. Thus, there are two African constituencies, three Latin American, one south Asian, one mainly south-east Asian and so on. One of the implications of the constituency system is that a director who is elected by a constituency casts all the votes of all its members. Moreover, they must cast them as a bloc regardless of any differences of view there may be among their constituents. A constituency may not split its vote although it can instruct is director to abstain. Procedures used internally by constituencies are, therefore, a very important part of the system of governance of the Fund. But they are not covered in the *Articles of Agreement* since constituencies are regarded as strictly informal groupings which can change from time to time and are not part of the constitution of the IMF. Constituencies are not well defined by the *Articles*, being formally just the group of members who voted for their director.

The Current EU Representation

The EU countries are currently over-represented in both the governing bodies of the IMF. Table 2 shows the current voting shares of the EU countries and the United States in comparison with shares of world GDP and population. The EU countries collectively are over-represented, both relative to their share of world GDP and compared with the United States—the EU countries (EU-25) command 31.9 per cent of the votes in the Board of Governors and have 31.1 per cent of world GDP. By contrast, the United States has 17.1 per cent of the voting weight with 29.3 per cent of GDP. The EU-25 has 86 per cent more voting weight than the United States with only a 6 per cent greater GDP. The Eurozone countries (Euro12) have 33 per cent more voting weight than the United States with a GDP that is 22 per cent smaller. Both the EU group and the United States are massively over-represented in comparison with their shares of world population.

In the Executive Board, out of a total of 24 directors, the EU countries supply between 6 and 8. Germany, France and UK appoint their own directors, while the remainder are elected or rotate to represent constituencies. Italy, Netherlands and Belgium provide their own directors as elected representatives of their constituencies. This is such a permanent arrangement that the constituencies are named after the country that represents it—the Italian

Table 2. Voting weight of European Union countries and the United States in the IMF Board of Governors (Share per cent)

	IMF vote	GDP	Population
EU-25	31.9	31.1	7.2
Euro-12	22.9	22.9	4.9
United States	17.1	29.3	4.6

Source: IMF and World Bank webpages.

constituency also includes Albania, Greece, Malta, Portugal, San Marino and Timor-Leste; the Netherlands constituency contains Armenia, Bosnia, Bulgaria, Croatia, Cyprus, Georgia, Israel, Macedonia, Moldova, Romania, Ukraine; and the Belgian constituency contains Austria, Belarus, Czech Republic, Hungary, Kazakhstan, Luxembourg, Slovak Republic, Slovenia and Turkey. All these three constituencies contain both EU members and non-members. The voting weight of the EU directors is enhanced by the fact that votes of all countries belonging to a constituency are aggregated. This effect is offset to some extent by the fact that two EU members are in other constituencies permanently represented by non-EU members: Ireland is in the constituency represented by Canada, while Poland is in the Swiss constituency. The two other constituencies with EU members have directors who are selected by rotation. The director of the constituency currently represented by Mexico rotates between it, Venezuela and Spain (the other members are the five Central American republics Guatemala, Honduras, El Salvador, Nicaragua and Costa Rica), while the Nordic/Baltic constituency, whose representation (currently Norway) rotates among its members, consists almost entirely of EU countries.[9]

Voting Power Implications of a Formal G-7 Bloc

Previous studies of the IMF using the voting power approach are Leech (2002) and Leech and Leech (2004a). There have been few previous voting power studies of the Bretton Woods institutions, although there is an extensive literature applying the approach to other weighted voting bodies especially the EU council of ministers and the US presidential electoral college.[10] We consider two possible scenarios—the formation of a formal voting bloc consisting of the G-7, the seven richest nations and the formation of a European bloc consisting either of the 12 countries that have adopted the euro or the union of 25 countries. We examine the first of these briefly in the next subsection and devote the next section to the second.

The G-7, consisting of the United States, Japan, Germany, France, UK, Italy and Canada, plays a powerful but informal role in global governance. Although it does not make formal decisions and has no agreed constitution for its meetings, and with Russia in the G-8, lead to a high degree of policy coordination that is extremely important for the international financial institutions. The suggestion is sometimes made that it should be formalized and constituted as part of the governance of the IMF. It is therefore of some interest to investigate what that would mean for voting power.

The weights of all the countries in the IMF are given in the first column of Appendix 1. The formation of a G-7 bloc would have the effect of reducing the number of independent voting members of the IMF from 184 to 178. The G-7 countries together have a combined weight of 45.30 per cent (Table 3), which is quite close to an absolute majority and therefore, we expect the power of the G-7 bloc to be very high indeed. Computation of the power indices for this voting body gives a Penrose index of precisely 1 for the G-7 and 0 for each of the other member countries.[11] Our conclusion is that the formation of a G-7 group within the IMF Governors would effectively disenfranchise every country that was not a member and all voting power over ordinary decisions requiring a 50 per cent majority would be with the G-7.

It is now of interest to examine how the formation of the G-7 bloc would affect the power of its members. For this, we need to make an assumption about the voting rule that it would use. Table 3 shows the results, assuming weighted majority voting with the IMF weights and a simple majority threshold. Since the bloc has all the power in the IMF, these power indices are also measures of power of the G-7 countries in the IMF.

The results show that the power of the United States would be dramatically enhanced by the formation of the G-7 bloc—with 17.09 per cent of the voting weight it has 55.01 per cent of the voting power. All G-7 countries have much more power than weight as measured by the Banzhaf index.

In order to ascertain how the formation of the G-7 bloc would affect the power of the G-7 countries, it is necessary to compare the indices in Table 3 with their powers in the status quo where there are no blocs. These are given in the first part of Appendix 1, from which it is apparent that the United States, Italy and Canada would increase their absolute voting power, while Japan, Germany, France and UK would lose power. The reason for this is the dominance of the United States in the assumed voting system in the G-7. However, in terms of relative voting power, all seven countries would gain.

Table 3. Power in the G-7 assuming weighted majority voting

	Votes	Weight%	Penrose index	Banzhaf index%
United States	371,743	17.09	0.84375	55.10
Japan	133,378	6.13	0.15625	10.20
Germany	130,332	5.99	0.15625	10.20
France	107,635	4.95	0.09375	6.12
UK	107,635	4.95	0.09375	6.12
Italy	70,805	3.25	0.09375	6.12
Canada	63,942	2.94	0.09375	6.12
Total	**985,470**	**45.3**	**1.53125**	**100.00**

Note: Majority threshold is 492,736 votes.

These results illustrate how power indices can reveal properties of weighted voting systems that are not apparent from the weights. The indices are the same for Japan and Germany although they have different weights. Thus it is not true that in this voting body Japan has more power than Germany. This is perhaps not too surprising since the weights of the two countries do not differ by very much. However, the other four countries also have identical power indices even though their weights are more variable. Canada with 2.94 per cent of the votes has the same voting power as France which has 4.95.

The results of this section show that the creation of a formal G-7 bloc would effectively reduce the voting power of developing countries (and all countries not members of the G-7) to nil and concentrate all power in the hands of seven countries, at the same time increasing the dominance of the United States. The analysis here is of constitutional power deriving from the formal voting rules. But the absence of a formal role for the G-7 does not mean that it is completely irrelevant and the results may be indicative of behavioural power to the extent that there is coordination among the group members. Greater real voting power for the developing countries and others requires that groups such as the G-7 do not collude behind the scenes but vote independently. We now consider a reform proposal that is being much more seriously debated: that there should be a single European seat at the IMF.

A Unified European Representation at the IMF

A key issue in the discussions surrounding the reform of the governance of the IMF is the representation of the European Union member countries. At present, each EU country is an IMF member with its own seat on the governing body but the suggestion has been made that greater economic and monetary cooperation among European countries, particularly following the introduction of a common currency, makes that unnecessary and that, moreover there would be advantages in a unified European representation. If all EU members decided to adopt a common policy on all matters concerning the IMF and agreed to vote together as a single EU bloc, they would become a very powerful force. In fact, it is obvious that if they retained their present voting weight they would become dominant with much greater voting power than the United States. However, as van Houtven (2004) has pointed out, the fact that the EU does not act as a bloc makes the United States more powerful.

The case for separate representation to be replaced by a single seat for the EU therefore has considerable force and has been made on two distinct arguments. On the one hand, the EU would be entitled to a much smaller share of the votes and that would increase the voting share of the other IMF members. The logical way to do this is by treating the EU bloc as a single country which would mean eliminating intra-EU trade from the formula which determines quotas and hence voting weights. On the other hand, European advocates of a single seat at the IMF see it as a logical corollary of greater cooperation over economic, monetary and foreign policy among EU member countries. A single seat would be very powerful because the voting weight of all the members would be combined. The result would be that the formal voting structure of the IMF would be transformed, from being dominated by the large weight of one country, to having two powerful voting blocs, the EU and United States.[12]

In this paper, we investigate the voting power implications of this change in structure, involving a simultaneous reduction in voting weight and a move to bloc voting, which are complex. First, a European bloc vote comparable in size to that of the United States will create a bipolar voting body in which the powers of the two rival blocs will be limited and those of the other members enhanced. Second, redistributing European voting weight will increase the relative voting weight of each of the other countries. This will affect their voting power in non-obvious ways. Third, we must also consider how the change affects the powers of the individual EU members, which would no longer be directly represented. They will not necessarily lose power since they will have indirect voting influence and may actually gain power if either the power of the bloc or their voting power within it (or both) is sufficient. It may be assumed that they would be unwilling to give up their separate seats otherwise.

Scenarios for a Proposed Single European Seat and Voting Power Analysis

A number of writers have discussed the possible adjustment of voting weights with a unified European representation in the IMF and various proposals for reform have been made.[13] van Houtven (2004) has proposed that the EU and United States be given equal representation and the number of Executive Directors reduced by the number of EU seats thereby lost. Buira (2002, 2003) argues that the introduction of the common European currency should lead to a recalculation of quotas of the countries of the euro area excluding their mutual trade. Such trade should be treated essentially as if it is domestic trade in the same way, for example, as between states of the United States. Kenen *et al.* (2004) suggest another model in which there are two European blocs— the Eurozone and the EU members outside the Eurozone. We have used these proposals as the basis of an investigation using the voting power approach to compute measures of voting power for all countries at different levels of the combined voting weight of the EU over a range of values.

An interesting feature of these proposed changes is that they do not appear to require extensive changes to the *Articles* and therefore, the formal agreement of the United States. The primary requirement is that the countries of the EU agree among themselves to coordinate their actions and reduce their quotas. We do not assume that there would be any consequent change to the quotas of countries outside the EU; however, it is obvious that there would be a redistribution of voting weight in relative terms.

It would clearly be desirable to consider other redistribution schemes based on changes to the quota formula but they would be much more radical and we do not consider them in the present paper. Nor do we consider in detail the implications of a single EU seat and the associated changes in voting weights for the structure of the Executive Board. Our analysis is confined solely to the Board of Governors where the scenarios can be simply defined.[14] In order to make a power analysis of the Executive, by contrast, the scenarios required would involve other assumptions about changes to the composition of constituencies as well as the size of the board and the analysis would be overly speculative.

Moreover, the voting power approach might not apply as well to the Executive, where the different constituencies have different decision rules. For example, some might reasonably be modelled on the assumption that they use majority voting, say, to elect directors, while others have a permanent representation, in the sense that their director is always from the same country, and still others have a rotating system of choosing directors from a different country in turn. Furthermore, many of them are mixed constituencies, comprising both industrial and developing or transition countries, and it is argued that in such a case, it would be wrong to assume that the elected director simply votes always on behalf of the majority within the constituency. The director has a responsibility to represent all constituency members and therefore, developing countries have a voice even if they have a minority of votes. This is a point however on which there are differences of opinion between industrialized and developing countries.[15]

Implications of a Single European Seat for Non-European Countries

In this section, we report the results of a voting power analysis assuming a single European bloc, all of whose member countries relinquish their individual seats. We investigate two cases:

- A bloc consisting of the 12 countries that have adopted the euro, which we designate Euro-12[16]
- A bloc consisting of the whole European Union of 25 countries, which we designate EU-25.[17] We assume that the bloc has voting parity with the United States.

As before, we assume a majority threshold of 50 per cent and therefore, our analysis applies only to ordinary decisions. Voting power analysis for decisions requiring a special majority of 85 per cent yields little of interest. In this case, the effect of unequal voting weights between countries becomes very small since the decision threshold is set so high that it is close to being a unanimity rule where all members have equal power whatever their weight, and the power of the governing body to act is very low.[18] The 85 per cent special majority rule is primarily important because it gives unilateral veto power to any member with more that 15 per cent of the votes, notably the United States, but also now the European bloc.

The detailed results for both Euro-12 and EU-25, assuming voting parity with the United States, are given in Appendix 1. The results, in general terms, are similar in both cases. There is a substantial quantitative effect. Before the introduction of a unified representation, voting is virtually dominated by the United States whose relative power at 24.49 per cent is well above its percentage of the votes of 17.09 and Penrose index of 0.7559. All other countries have a power share less than their vote share. The voting system can be said to redistribute power relative to weight to the United States. With a single European seat, however, all members except the United States gain voting power and a have a power share greater than their weight. So, to an extent, we can conclude that the reform would redistribute power to the smaller countries to some extent. The largest beneficiary would be Japan, whose power share would increase from 5.46 to 9.42 per cent with EU-25 (7.67 with Euro-12), but all countries would gain both in absolute and relative voting power. The voting power of both the European bloc and the United States would be much less than proportional to their weight. In the case of EU-25, they would each have 20.06 per cent of the votes and 16.71 per cent of the voting power and in the case of Euro-12, their weight would be 18.15 per cent and power, 16.06 per cent. These results therefore, show that the reform would be a significant improvement for all non-EU countries except the United States.

The results show that a Eurozone seat would increase the voting power of every other non-Eurozone member country, except the United States, over the entire range considered. Moving over to a structure with two large blocs of equal size would, therefore, have the effect of reducing US voting dominance even though the voting weight of the combined European countries would be substantially reduced on its current level. (It remains to be seen whether the Eurozone countries would also be more powerful and is discussed in the next section.)

Apart from the two blocs, each country's voting power reaches a maximum when the Euro-12 and the United States weights are equal, with 18.15 per cent of the votes. The ratios in Appendix 1 show that all countries, apart from the United States, would gain absolute voting power, as measured by the Penrose index, of at least 21 per cent compared to the status quo. The biggest gainers would be Japan and the UK, whose power indices would increase by 42 and 31 per cent respectively. The same pattern is shown for the changes in relative voting power.

The analysis of this section suggests that a unified representation for Europe, with reduced voting weight but parity with the United States, would enhance the voting power and therefore, influence in the decision-making of every member country outside Europe and the United States. However, the effects for developing countries with small voting weight would be small. To give them appreciably greater influence would also require changes to their voting weights, which are not considered in this paper.

Implications for the Voting Power of European Countries

Now, we investigate the effects of the single European bloc on the voting power of its members. Having found the power of the EU bloc in the last section, we can find the absolute power index of each EU member country as a compound of this with the member's power in internal European decision-making. This is the product of the two Penrose indices. The Banzhaf indices are not really meaningful in this case, since a change in the internal rules of the bloc can change the power indices of non-bloc members due to normalization.

Assumptions about the voting system within the European bloc

In order to make a voting power analysis for the EU bloc—considered as a voting body—requires us to make explicit our assumptions about the decision rule that it uses to determine its vote in the IMF Board of Governors. We consider a number of possible voting systems for each of the two cases as follows.

Euro-12

- IMF current weights: The Euro-12 works like an IMF constituency that uses weighted majority voting based on the actual current weights determined by the IMF quotas.
- GDP weights: a system of weighted voting based on the economic size of each country
- Population weights: a voting system based on population as an alternative measure of a country's size
- One Country – One Vote: all members have an equal vote; this is the basis on which the European Central Bank currently works

EU-25:

- IMF Current Weights
- Nice: the system of qualified majority voting established in the Nice treaty currently in use in the Council of Ministers
- Draft Constitution: the proposed alternative proposed by the European Convention to replace the Nice system
- GDP
- Population: both the Nice and the Draft Constitution voting systems are based on populations but they both require supermajorities for decisions, which means that these systems both give the EU-25 fairly low power to act (in the case of Nice, extremely low) and this will tend to limit the absolute voting power of members. In this system, we consider population weights with a simple majority decision rule
- Population Square Roots: proposals have been made that this would be a more equitable basis for EU voting weights[19]
- One Country – One Vote

In the case of the Euro-12, we assume a simple majority decision rule in all four schemes. In the case of EU-25, we assume a simple majority decision rule in all cases except the second and third, which are actual or proposed systems with a specified supermajority decision threshold.

Results

Appendix 2 gives the results for Euro-12. For each voting system, the table shows each country's voting power measured by its two-stage or indirect Penrose index and the ratio of that to its power under the status quo. This ratio gives a measure of whether its voting power has increased or decreased as a consequence of the introduction of unified European representation.[20]

The results from using current IMF weights are very favourable to a single EU seat, since all 12 countries would enjoy a substantial increase in voting power. On the other hand, all three alternative schemes give mixed results. The use of GDP weights is beneficial to 8 countries, but 4 lose power—the Benelux countries, especially Belgium and Finland. Population weights give broadly similar results, except that Austria replaces Finland as a loser of power; Spain and Portugal gain a lot of voting power. A system of unweighted voting gives a very different pattern of results. Now all countries gain voting power except France and Germany which lose power substantially; the smallest countries are all big gainers, especially Luxembourg which would have 28 times more voting power.

It is useful to compare power indices of different members under the status quo and a single Euro-12 bloc. Such comparisons can reveal changes in power rankings. For example, let us assume Euro-12 voting using current IMF weights. Germany becomes more powerful than Japan—Japan's power index increases from 0.169 to 0.239, while Germany's increases from 0.165 to 0.286. France and UK have the same power under the status quo, 0.138, but France becomes more powerful by being a member of a Euro bloc—its power index increases to 0.208, that of the UK increases to 0.18. There are many examples; another of which is Austria, which gains power relative to Argentina and Indonesia.

Appendix 3 reports the power analysis for the EU-25 countries for seven different weighted voting systems. As with Euro-12, the results for simple majority voting using the current IMF weights are unambiguous and show that all countries would gain voting power substantially. The biggest gainer would be Germany. Also, the population square root voting system would benefit virtually all members; only Belgium would lose very slightly.

The other voting systems considered would all produce mixed results and change the rankings of the power of individual countries in some cases. Under the Nice system, only the smaller countries would gain voting power and the large countries would lose substantially. This is largely a result of the fact that the Nice system requires large supermajorities of both weighted votes (74 per cent) and populations (60 per cent) and therefore, only a small proportion of possible votes lead to a decision. The EU council has very low power to act under this system. This is important for the analysis of power in a two-stage voting model. The same effect is apparent in the results for the Draft Constitution which also uses supermajorities—the countries that are currently most powerful in the IMF, all lose a lot of power. The use of GDP or population would enhance the power of the big countries, and the small countries would lose power, while under voting equality, only the big four countries would lose out and the small countries all gain considerably.

Our conclusion is that the voting system adopted by the single European bloc is crucial in determining whether the member countries gain or lose power. We have shown that it is possible that they could all gain absolute voting power under an appropriate European system of qualified majority voting.

Conclusions

We have argued in this paper that there is an important conceptual distinction between voting power and voting weight in systems of governance which are based on the use of bloc voting, such as the IMF. We have shown using examples that it can be quite substantial and have argued that it can be analysed using the power indices due to Penrose and Banzhaf. We made a power analysis of a possible formal G-7 bloc in the IMF.

We have considered the implications of voting power, of the introduction of a unified representation of the EU countries at the IMF with a reduced voting weight. We considered two versions of a European bloc—the Eurozone and the newly enlarged European Union. The IMF governing body would change from one with 184 members and a single dominant voter to one with slightly fewer members, two of which would be dominant rivals.

The effect of this (for ordinary decisions requiring a simple majority) would be to reduce the power of the United States and to enhance the power of all other members. However, the United States would retain its unilateral veto over decisions requiring a special majority of 85 per cent and the European bloc would gain the same veto.

Whether European countries gain or lose voting power depends on the internal voting arrangements within the European body that controls the votes of the European bloc. Some voting systems could be devised that would give members greater indirect voting power than they currently enjoy in the IMF, even if they give up their direct representation.

The reforms we have considered do not require any changes to the voting weights of countries outside the European bloc. Nor would they necessitate major amendment to the rules of the IMF.

Appendix 1

Voting power analysis of the IMF with a single European seat with voting parity with the United States

| | Status quo | | | | Euro-12/US parity | | | | | | EU-25/US parity | | | | | |
| | | | Power Indices | | | | Power Indices | | Ratios | | | | Power indices | | Ratios | |
	Votes	%	Abs	Rel	Votes	%	Abs	Rel	Abs	Rel	Votes	%	Abs	Rel	Abs	Rel
United States	371743	17.09	0.755917	24.49	371743	18.15	0.499745	16.06	0.66	0.66	371743	20.06	0.499991	16.71	0.66	0.68
Euro12					371743	18.15	0.499745	16.06								
EU-25											371743	20.06	0.499991	16.71		
Japan	133378	6.13	0.168548	5.46	133378	6.51	0.238587	7.67	1.42	1.40	133378	7.20	0.281973	9.42	1.67	1.73
Germany	130332	5.99	0.16513	5.35												
France	107635	4.95	0.138111	4.47												
United Kingdom	107635	4.95	0.138111	4.47	107635	5.25	0.18028	5.79	1.31	1.29						
Italy	70805	3.25	0.091691	2.97												
Saudi Arabia	70105	3.22	0.090793	2.94	70105	3.42	0.113549	3.65	1.25	1.24	70105	3.78	0.124767	4.17	1.37	1.42
China	63942	2.94	0.082879	2.69	63942	3.12	0.103089	3.31	1.24	1.23	63942	3.45	0.113424	3.79	1.37	1.41
Canada	63942	2.94	0.082879	2.69	63942	3.12	0.103089	3.31	1.24	1.23	63942	3.45	0.113424	3.79	1.37	1.41
Russian Federation	59704	2.74	0.077423	2.51	59704	2.91	0.09599	3.09	1.24	1.23	59704	3.22	0.105656	3.53	1.36	1.41
Netherlands	51874	2.38	0.067321	2.18												
Belgium	46302	2.13	0.060117	1.95												
India	41832	1.92	0.054331	1.76	41832	2.04	0.066669	2.14	1.23	1.22	41832	2.26	0.073370	2.45	1.35	1.39
Switzerland	34835	1.60	0.045262	1.47	34835	1.70	0.055381	1.78	1.22	1.21	34835	1.88	0.060935	2.04	1.35	1.39
Australia	32614	1.50	0.042381	1.37	32614	1.59	0.051811	1.67	1.22	1.21	32614	1.76	0.057008	1.91	1.35	1.39
Spain	30739	1.41	0.039949	1.29												
Brazil	30611	1.41	0.039782	1.29	30611	1.49	0.048602	1.56	1.22	1.21	30611	1.65	0.053473	1.79	1.34	1.39
Venezuela	26841	1.23	0.034888	1.13	26841	1.31	0.042577	1.37	1.22	1.21	26841	1.45	0.046837	1.57	1.34	1.33
Mexico	26108	1.20	0.033936	1.10	26108	1.27	0.041407	1.33	1.22	1.21	26108	1.41	0.045549	1.52	1.34	1.33
Sweden	24205	1.11	0.031465	1.02	24205	1.18	0.038373	1.23	1.22	1.21						
Argentina	21421	0.98	0.027848	0.90	21421	1.05	0.033941	1.09	1.22	1.21	21421	1.16	0.037331	1.25	1.34	1.33
Indonesia	21043	0.97	0.027357	0.89	21043	1.03	0.03334	1.07	1.22	1.21	21043	1.14	0.036669	1.23	1.34	1.38
Austria	18973	0.87	0.024667	0.80												
SouthAfrica	18935	0.87	0.024618	0.80	18935	0.92	0.029989	0.96	1.22	1.21	18935	1.02	0.032982	1.10	1.34	1.38
Nigeria	17782	0.82	0.02312	0.75	17782	0.87	0.028158	0.91	1.22	1.21	17782	0.96	0.030967	1.04	1.34	1.38

Norway	16967	0.78	0.022061	0.71	16967	0.83	0.026864	0.86	1.22	1.21	16967	0.92	0.029544	0.99	1.34	1.38
Denmark	16678	0.77	0.021685	0.70	16678	0.81	0.026405	0.85	1.22	1.21						
Korea	16586	0.76	0.021565	0.70	16586	0.81	0.026259	0.84	1.22	1.21	16586	0.89	0.028879	0.97	1.34	1.38
Iran	15222	0.70	0.019792	0.64	15222	0.74	0.024095	0.77	1.22	1.21	15222	0.82	0.026498	0.89	1.34	1.38
Malaysia	15116	0.69	0.019655	0.64	15116	0.74	0.023927	0.77	1.22	1.21	15116	0.82	0.026313	0.88	1.34	1.38
Kuwait	14061	0.65	0.018283	0.59	14061	0.69	0.022254	0.72	1.22	1.21	14061	0.76	0.024473	0.82	1.34	1.38
Ukraine	13970	0.64	0.018165	0.59	13970	0.68	0.02211	0.71	1.22	1.21	13970	0.75	0.024314	0.81	1.34	1.38
Poland	13940	0.64	0.018126	0.59	13940	0.68	0.022062	0.71	1.22	1.21						
Finland	12888	0.59	0.016758	0.54												
Algeria	12797	0.59	0.01664	0.54	12797	0.62	0.020251	0.65	1.22	1.21	12797	0.69	0.022269	0.74	1.34	1.38
Iraq	12134	0.56	0.015778	0.51	12134	0.59	0.0192	0.62	1.22	1.21	12134	0.65	0.021114	0.71	1.34	1.38
Libya	11487	0.53	0.014937	0.48	11487	0.56	0.018175	0.58	1.22	1.21	11487	0.62	0.019986	0.67	1.34	1.38
Thailand	11069	0.51	0.014394	0.47	11069	0.54	0.017513	0.56	1.22	1.21	11069	0.60	0.019258	0.64	1.34	1.38
Hungary	10634	0.49	0.013828	0.45	10634	0.52	0.016824	0.54	1.22	1.21						
Pakistan	10587	0.49	0.013767	0.45	10587	0.52	0.01675	0.54	1.22	1.21	10587	0.57	0.018419	0.62	1.34	1.38
Romania	10552	0.49	0.013721	0.44	10552	0.52	0.016694	0.54	1.22	1.21	10552	0.57	0.018358	0.61	1.34	1.38
Turkey	9890	0.45	0.012861	0.42	9890	0.48	0.015646	0.50	1.22	1.21	9890	0.53	0.017205	0.58	1.34	1.38
Egypt	9687	0.45	0.012597	0.41	9687	0.47	0.015325	0.49	1.22	1.21	9687	0.52	0.016851	0.56	1.34	1.38
Israel	9532	0.44	0.012395	0.40	9532	0.47	0.015079	0.48	1.22	1.21	9532	0.51	0.016582	0.55	1.34	1.38
New Zealand	9196	0.42	0.011958	0.39	9196	0.45	0.014547	0.47	1.22	1.21	9196	0.50	0.015997	0.53	1.34	1.38
Philippines	9049	0.42	0.011767	0.38	9049	0.44	0.014315	0.46	1.22	1.21	9049	0.49	0.015741	0.53	1.34	1.38
Portugal	8924	0.41	0.011605	0.38												
Singapore	8875	0.41	0.011541	0.37	8875	0.43	0.014039	0.45	1.22	1.21	8875	0.48	0.015438	0.52	1.34	1.38
Chile	8811	0.41	0.011458	0.37	8811	0.43	0.013938	0.45	1.22	1.21	8811	0.48	0.015326	0.51	1.34	1.38
Ireland	8634	0.40	0.011228	0.36					0.00	0.00					0.00	0.00
Greece	8480	0.39	0.011027	0.36					0.00	0.00					0.00	0.00
Czech Republic	8443	0.39	0.010979	0.36	8443	0.41	0.013355	0.43	1.22	1.21						
Colombia	7990	0.37	0.01039	0.34	7990	0.39	0.012638	0.41	1.22	1.21	7990	0.43	0.013897	0.46	1.34	1.38
Bulgaria	6652	0.31	0.00865	0.28	6652	0.32	0.010521	0.34	1.22	1.21	6652	0.36	0.011569	0.39	1.34	1.38
Peru	6634	0.30	0.008627	0.28	6634	0.32	0.010493	0.34	1.22	1.21	6634	0.36	0.011538	0.39	1.34	1.38
United Arab Emirates	6367	0.29	0.00828	0.27	6367	0.31	0.01007	0.32	1.22	1.21	6367	0.34	0.011073	0.37	1.34	1.38
Morocco	6132	0.28	0.007974	0.26	6132	0.30	0.009698	0.31	1.22	1.21	6132	0.33	0.010664	0.36	1.34	1.38
Bangladesh	5583	0.26	0.00726	0.24	5583	0.27	0.00883	0.28	1.22	1.21	5583	0.30	0.009709	0.32	1.34	1.38
Congo DR	5580	0.26	0.007256	0.24	5580	0.27	0.008825	0.28	1.22	1.21	5580	0.30	0.009704	0.32	1.34	1.38
Zambia	5141	0.24	0.006686	0.22	5141	0.25	0.008131	0.26	1.22	1.21	5141	0.28	0.00894	0.30	1.34	1.38
Serbia Montenegro	4927	0.23	0.006407	0.21	4927	0.24	0.007792	0.25	1.22	1.21	4927	0.27	0.008568	0.29	1.34	1.38

(continued)

	Status quo				Euro-12/US parity						EU-25/US parity					
	Votes	%	Power Indices Abs	Rel	Votes	%	Power Indices Abs	Rel	Ratios Abs	Rel	Votes	%	Power indices Abs	Rel	Ratios Abs	Rel
Sri Lanka	4384	0.20	0.005701	0.18	4384	0.21	0.006933	0.22	1.22	1.21	4384	0.24	0.007624	0.25	1.34	1.33
Belarus	4114	0.19	0.00535	0.17	4114	0.20	0.006506	0.21	1.22	1.21	4114	0.22	0.007154	0.24	1.34	1.33
Ghana	3940	0.18	0.005124	0.17	3940	0.19	0.006231	0.20	1.22	1.21	3940	0.21	0.006851	0.23	1.34	1.33
Kazakhstan	3907	0.18	0.005081	0.16	3907	0.19	0.006179	0.20	1.22	1.21	3907	0.21	0.006794	0.23	1.34	1.33
Croatia	3901	0.18	0.005073	0.16	3901	0.19	0.006169	0.20	1.22	1.21	3901	0.21	0.006784	0.23	1.34	1.38
Slovak Republic	3825	0.18	0.004974	0.16	3825	0.19	0.006049	0.19	1.22	1.21						
Trinidad Tobago	3606	0.17	0.004689	0.15	3606	0.18	0.005703	0.18	1.22	1.21	3606	0.19	0.006270	0.21	1.34	1.38
Vietnam	3541	0.16	0.004605	0.15	3541	0.17	0.0056	0.18	1.22	1.21	3541	0.19	0.006157	0.21	1.34	1.38
Côte d'Ivoire	3502	0.16	0.004554	0.15	3502	0.17	0.005538	0.18	1.22	1.21	3502	0.19	0.006090	0.20	1.34	1.38
Uruguay	3315	0.15	0.004311	0.14	3315	0.16	0.005242	0.17	1.22	1.21	3315	0.18	0.005764	0.19	1.34	1.38
Ecuador	3273	0.15	0.004256	0.14	3273	0.16	0.005176	0.17	1.22	1.21	3273	0.18	0.005691	0.19	1.34	1.38
Syrian Arab Republic	3186	0.15	0.004143	0.13	3186	0.16	0.005038	0.16	1.22	1.21	3186	0.17	0.005540	0.19	1.34	1.38
Tunisia	3115	0.14	0.004051	0.13	3115	0.15	0.004926	0.16	1.22	1.21	3115	0.17	0.005417	0.18	1.34	1.38
Angola	3113	0.14	0.004048	0.13	3113	0.15	0.004923	0.16	1.22	1.21	3113	0.17	0.005413	0.18	1.34	1.38
Luxembourg	3041	0.14	0.003955	0.13												
Uzbekistan	3006	0.14	0.003909	0.13	3006	0.15	0.004754	0.15	1.22	1.21	3006	0.16	0.005227	0.17	1.34	1.38
Jamaica	2985	0.14	0.003882	0.13	2985	0.15	0.004721	0.15	1.22	1.21	2985	0.16	0.005191	0.17	1.34	1.38
Kenya	2964	0.14	0.003855	0.12	2964	0.14	0.004687	0.15	1.22	1.21	2964	0.16	0.005154	0.17	1.34	1.38
Qatar	2888	0.13	0.003756	0.12	2888	0.14	0.004567	0.15	1.22	1.21	2888	0.16	0.005022	0.17	1.34	1.38
Myanmar	2834	0.13	0.003685	0.12	2834	0.14	0.004482	0.14	1.22	1.21	2834	0.15	0.004928	0.16	1.34	1.38
Yemen	2685	0.12	0.003492	0.11	2685	0.13	0.004246	0.14	1.22	1.21	2685	0.14	0.004669	0.16	1.34	1.38
Slovenia	2567	0.12	0.003338	0.11	2567	0.13	0.004059	0.13	1.22	1.21						
Dominican Republic	2439	0.11	0.003172	0.10	2439	0.12	0.003857	0.12	1.22	1.21	2439	0.13	0.004241	0.14	1.34	1.38
Brunei Darussalam	2402	0.11	0.003124	0.10	2402	0.12	0.003799	0.12	1.22	1.21	2402	0.13	0.004177	0.14	1.34	1.38
Guatemala	2352	0.11	0.003059	0.10	2352	0.11	0.003719	0.12	1.22	1.21	2352	0.13	0.004090	0.14	1.34	1.38
Panama	2316	0.11	0.003012	0.10	2316	0.11	0.003662	0.11	1.22	1.21	2316	0.12	0.004027	0.13	1.34	1.38
Lebanon	2280	0.10	0.002965	0.10	2280	0.11	0.003606	0.11	1.22	1.21	2280	0.12	0.003965	0.13	1.34	1.38
Tanzania	2239	0.10	0.002912	0.09	2239	0.11	0.003541	0.11	1.22	1.21	2239	0.12	0.003893	0.13	1.34	1.38
Oman	2190	0.10	0.002848	0.09	2190	0.11	0.003463	0.11	1.22	1.21	2190	0.12	0.003808	0.13	1.34	1.38

Cameroon	2107	0.10	0.00274	0.09	2107	0.003332	0.11	1.22	1.21	2107	0.11	0.003664	0.12	1.34	1.38
Uganda	2055	0.09	0.002672	0.09	2055	0.00325	0.10	1.22	1.21	2055	0.11	0.003573	0.12	1.34	1.38
Bolivia	1965	0.09	0.002555	0.08	1965	0.003107	0.10	1.22	1.21	1965	0.11	0.003417	0.11	1.34	1.38
ElSalvador	1963	0.09	0.002553	0.08	1963	0.003104	0.10	1.22	1.21	1963	0.11	0.003413	0.11	1.34	1.38
Jordan	1955	0.09	0.002542	0.08	1955	0.003092	0.10	1.22	1.21	1955	0.11	0.003399	0.11	1.34	1.38
Sudan	1947	0.09	0.002532	0.08	1947	0.003079	0.10	1.22	1.21	1947	0.11	0.003385	0.11	1.34	1.38
Bosnia	1941	0.09	0.002524	0.08	1941	0.003069	0.09	1.22	1.21	1941	0.10	0.003375	0.11	1.34	1.38
CostaRica	1891	0.09	0.002459	0.08	1891	0.00299	0.09	1.22	1.21	1891	0.10	0.003288	0.11	1.34	1.38
Afghanistan	1869	0.09	0.002431	0.08	1869	0.002956	0.09	1.22	1.21	1869	0.10	0.003250	0.11	1.34	1.38
Senegal	1868	0.09	0.002429	0.08	1868	0.002954	0.09	1.22	1.21	1868	0.10	0.003248	0.11	1.34	1.38
Azerbaijan	1859	0.09	0.002418	0.08	1859	0.00294	0.09	1.22	1.21	1859	0.10	0.003232	0.11	1.34	1.38
Gabon	1793	0.08	0.002332	0.08	1793	0.002835	0.09	1.22	1.21	1793	0.10	0.003118	0.10	1.34	1.38
Georgia	1753	0.08	0.00228	0.07	1753	0.002772	0.09	1.22	1.21	1753	0.09	0.003048	0.10	1.34	1.38
Lithuania	1692	0.08	0.0022	0.07	1692	0.002676	0.08	1.22	1.21						
Cyprus	1646	0.08	0.002141	0.07	1646	0.002603	0.08	1.22	1.21						
Namibia	1615	0.07	0.0021	0.07	1615	0.002554	0.08	1.22	1.21	1615	0.09	0.002808	0.09	1.34	1.38
Bahrain	1600	0.07	0.002081	0.07	1600	0.00253	0.08	1.22	1.21	1600	0.09	0.002782	0.09	1.34	1.38
Ethiopia	1587	0.07	0.002064	0.07	1587	0.00251	0.08	1.22	1.21	1587	0.09	0.002759	0.09	1.34	1.38
Papua New Guinea	1566	0.07	0.002037	0.07	1566	0.002476	0.08	1.22	1.21	1566	0.08	0.002723	0.09	1.34	1.38
Bahamas	1553	0.07	0.00202	0.07	1553	0.002456	0.08	1.22	1.21	1553	0.08	0.002700	0.09	1.34	1.38
Nicaragua	1550	0.07	0.002016	0.07	1550	0.002451	0.08	1.22	1.21	1550	0.08	0.002695	0.09	1.34	1.38
Honduras	1545	0.07	0.002009	0.07	1545	0.002443	0.08	1.22	1.21	1545	0.08	0.002686	0.09	1.34	1.38
Latvia	1518	0.07	0.001927	0.07	1518	0.002401	0.07	1.22	1.21	1518	0.08	0.002577	0.09	1.34	1.38
Moldova	1482	0.07	0.001914	0.06	1482	0.002344	0.07	1.22	1.21	1482	0.08	0.002560	0.09	1.34	1.38
Madagascar	1472	0.07	0.001854	0.06	1472	0.002328	0.07	1.22	1.21	1472	0.08	0.002480	0.08	1.34	1.38
Iceland	1426	0.07	0.001802	0.06	1426	0.002255	0.07	1.22	1.21	1426	0.07	0.002410	0.08	1.34	1.38
Mozambique	1386	0.06	0.001718	0.06	1386	0.002192	0.07	1.22	1.21	1386	0.07	0.002297	0.08	1.34	1.38
Guinea	1321	0.06	0.001674	0.06	1321	0.002089	0.06	1.22	1.21	1321	0.07	0.002238	0.07	1.34	1.38
Sierra Leone	1287	0.06	0.001652	0.05	1287	0.002035	0.06	1.22	1.21	1287	0.07	0.002201	0.07	1.34	1.38
Malta	1270	0.06	0.001646	0.05	1270	0.002008	0.06	1.22	1.21	1270	0.07	0.002172	0.07	1.34	1.38
Mauritius	1266	0.06	0.001624	0.05	1266	0.002002	0.06	1.22	1.21	1266	0.07	0.002057	0.07	1.34	1.38
Paraguay	1249	0.06	0.001538	0.05	1249	0.001975	0.06	1.22	1.21	1249	0.07	0.002036	0.07	1.34	1.38
Mali	1183	0.05	0.001523	0.05	1183	0.001871	0.06	1.22	1.21	1183	0.06	0.002034	0.07	1.34	1.38
Suriname	1171	0.05	0.001522	0.05	1171	0.001852	0.06	1.22	1.21	1171	0.06	0.002015	0.07	1.34	1.38
Armenia	1170	0.05	0.001507	0.05	1170	0.00185	0.06	1.22	1.21	1170	0.06	0.002010	0.07	1.34	1.38
Guyana	1159	0.05	0.001499	0.05	1159	0.001833	0.06	1.22	1.21	1159	0.06	0.002008	0.07	1.34	1.38

(continued)

Appendix 1. (continued)

	Status quo				Euro-12/US parity						EU-25/US parity					
	Votes	%	Power Indices		Votes	%	Power Indices		Ratios		Votes	%	Power indices		Ratios	
			Abs	Rel			Abs	Rel	Abs	Rel			Abs	Rel	Abs	Rel
Kyrgyz Republic	1138	0.05	0.00148	0.05	1138	0.06	0.0018	0.06	1.22	1.21	1138	0.06	0.001979	0.07	1.34	1.38
Cambodia	1125	0.05	0.001463	0.05	1125	0.05	0.001779	0.06	1.22	1.21	1125	0.06	0.001956	0.07	1.34	1.38
Tajikistan	1120	0.05	0.001457	0.05	1120	0.05	0.001771	0.06	1.22	1.21	1120	0.06	0.001947	0.07	1.34	1.38
Congo	1096	0.05	0.001425	0.05	1096	0.05	0.001733	0.06	1.22	1.21	1096	0.06	0.001906	0.06	1.34	1.38
Haiti	1069	0.05	0.00139	0.05	1069	0.05	0.00169	0.05	1.22	1.21	1069	0.06	0.001859	0.06	1.34	1.38
Rwanda	1051	0.05	0.001367	0.04	1051	0.05	0.001662	0.05	1.22	1.21	1051	0.06	0.001827	0.06	1.34	1.38
Burundi	1020	0.05	0.001326	0.04	1020	0.05	0.001613	0.05	1.22	1.21	1020	0.06	0.001774	0.06	1.34	1.38
Turkmenistan	1002	0.05	0.001303	0.04	1002	0.05	0.001585	0.05	1.22	1.21	1002	0.05	0.001742	0.06	1.34	1.38
Togo	984	0.05	0.00128	0.04	984	0.05	0.001556	0.05	1.22	1.21	984	0.05	0.001711	0.06	1.34	1.38
Nepal	963	0.04	0.001252	0.04	963	0.05	0.001523	0.05	1.22	1.21	963	0.05	0.001674	0.06	1.34	1.38
Fiji	953	0.04	0.001239	0.04	953	0.05	0.001507	0.05	1.22	1.21	953	0.05	0.001657	0.06	1.34	1.38
Malawi	944	0.04	0.001228	0.04	944	0.05	0.001493	0.05	1.22	1.21	944	0.05	0.001641	0.05	1.34	1.38
Macedonia	939	0.04	0.001221	0.04	939	0.05	0.001485	0.05	1.22	1.21	939	0.05	0.001633	0.05	1.34	1.38
Barbados	925	0.04	0.001203	0.04	925	0.05	0.001463	0.05	1.22	1.21	925	0.05	0.001608	0.05	1.34	1.38
Niger	908	0.04	0.001181	0.04	908	0.04	0.001436	0.05	1.22	1.21	908	0.05	0.001579	0.05	1.34	1.38
Estonia	902	0.04	0.001173	0.04	902	0.04	0.001426	0.05	1.22	1.21						
Mauritania	894	0.04	0.001163	0.04	894	0.04	0.001414	0.05	1.22	1.21	894	0.05	0.001554	0.05	1.34	1.38
Botswana	880	0.04	0.001144	0.04	880	0.04	0.001392	0.04	1.22	1.21	880	0.05	0.001530	0.05	1.34	1.38
Benin	869	0.04	0.00113	0.04	869	0.04	0.001374	0.04	1.22	1.21	869	0.05	0.001511	0.05	1.34	1.38
Burkina Faso	852	0.04	0.001108	0.04	852	0.04	0.001347	0.04	1.22	1.21	852	0.05	0.001481	0.05	1.34	1.38
Chad	810	0.04	0.001053	0.03	810	0.04	0.001281	0.04	1.22	1.21	810	0.04	0.001408	0.05	1.34	1.38
Central African Republic	807	0.04	0.001049	0.03	807	0.04	0.001276	0.04	1.22	1.21	807	0.04	0.001403	0.05	1.34	1.38
Lao People's Democratic	779	0.04	0.001013	0.03	779	0.04	0.001232	0.04	1.22	1.21	779	0.04	0.001355	0.05	1.34	1.38
Mongolia	761	0.03	0.00099	0.03	761	0.04	0.001203	0.04	1.22	1.21	761	0.04	0.001323	0.04	1.34	1.38
Swaziland	757	0.03	0.000984	0.03	757	0.04	0.001197	0.04	1.22	1.21	757	0.04	0.001316	0.04	1.34	1.38
Albania	737	0.03	0.000958	0.03	737	0.04	0.001165	0.04	1.22	1.21	737	0.04	0.001281	0.04	1.34	1.38
Lesotho	599	0.03	0.000779	0.03	599	0.03	0.000947	0.03	1.22	1.21	599	0.03	0.001042	0.03	1.34	1.38
Equatorial Guinea	576	0.03	0.000749	0.02	576	0.03	0.000911	0.03	1.22	1.21	576	0.03	0.001002	0.03	1.34	1.38
Gambia	561	0.03	0.00073	0.02	561	0.03	0.000887	0.03	1.22	1.21	561	0.03	0.000975	0.03	1.34	1.38

Belize	438	0.02	0.00057	0.02	438	0.02	0.000693	0.02	1.22	1.21	438	0.02	0.000762	0.03	1.34	1.38
Vanuatu	420	0.02	0.000546	0.02	420	0.02	0.000664	0.02	1.22	1.21	420	0.02	0.000730	0.02	1.34	1.38
SanMarino	420	0.02	0.000546	0.02	420	0.02	0.000664	0.02	1.22	1.21	420	0.02	0.000730	0.02	1.34	1.38
Djibouti	409	0.02	0.000532	0.02	409	0.02	0.000647	0.02	1.22	1.21	409	0.02	0.000711	0.02	1.34	1.38
Eritrea	409	0.02	0.000532	0.02	409	0.02	0.000647	0.02	1.22	1.21	409	0.02	0.000711	0.02	1.34	1.38
St. Lucia	403	0.02	0.000524	0.02	403	0.02	0.000637	0.02	1.22	1.21	403	0.02	0.000701	0.02	1.34	1.38
Guinea-Bissau	392	0.02	0.00051	0.02	392	0.02	0.00062	0.02	1.22	1.21	392	0.02	0.000682	0.02	1.34	1.38
Antigua Barbuda	385	0.02	0.000501	0.02	385	0.02	0.000609	0.02	1.22	1.21	385	0.02	0.000669	0.02	1.34	1.38
Grenada	367	0.02	0.000477	0.02	367	0.02	0.00058	0.02	1.22	1.21	367	0.02	0.000638	0.02	1.34	1.38
Samoa	366	0.02	0.000476	0.02	366	0.02	0.000579	0.02	1.22	1.21	366	0.02	0.000636	0.02	1.34	1.38
Solomon Islands	354	0.02	0.00046	0.01	354	0.02	0.00056	0.02	1.22	1.21	354	0.02	0.000616	0.02	1.34	1.38
Cape Verde	346	0.02	0.00045	0.01	346	0.02	0.000547	0.02	1.22	1.21	346	0.02	0.000602	0.02	1.34	1.38
Comoros	339	0.02	0.000441	0.01	339	0.02	0.000536	0.02	1.22	1.21	339	0.02	0.000589	0.02	1.34	1.38
St. Kitts Nevis	339	0.02	0.000441	0.01	339	0.02	0.000536	0.02	1.22	1.21	339	0.02	0.000589	0.02	1.34	1.38
Seychelles	338	0.02	0.00044	0.01	338	0.02	0.000534	0.02	1.21	1.20	338	0.02	0.000588	0.02	1.34	1.38
St. Vincent Grenadines	333	0.02	0.000433	0.01	333	0.02	0.000527	0.02	1.22	1.21	333	0.02	0.000579	0.02	1.34	1.38
Dominica	332	0.02	0.000432	0.01	332	0.02	0.000525	0.02	1.22	1.21	332	0.02	0.000577	0.02	1.34	1.38
Maldives	332	0.02	0.000432	0.01	332	0.02	0.000525	0.02	1.22	1.21	332	0.02	0.000577	0.02	1.34	1.38
Timor-Leste	332	0.02	0.000432	0.01	332	0.02	0.000525	0.02	1.22	1.21	332	0.02	0.000577	0.02	1.34	1.38
SãoTomé Príncipe	324	0.01	0.000421	0.01	324	0.02	0.000512	0.02	1.22	1.21	324	0.02	0.000563	0.02	1.34	1.38
Tonga	319	0.01	0.000415	0.01	319	0.02	0.000504	0.02	1.21	1.20	319	0.02	0.000555	0.02	1.34	1.38
Bhutan	313	0.01	0.000407	0.01	313	0.02	0.000495	0.02	1.22	1.21	313	0.02	0.000544	0.02	1.34	1.38
Kiribati	306	0.01	0.000398	0.01	306	0.01	0.000484	0.02	1.22	1.21	306	0.02	0.000532	0.02	1.34	1.38
Micronesia	301	0.01	0.000391	0.01	301	0.01	0.000476	0.02	1.22	1.21	301	0.02	0.000523	0.02	1.34	1.38
Marshall Islands	285	0.01	0.000371	0.01	285	0.01	0.000451	0.01	1.22	1.21	285	0.02	0.000496	0.02	1.34	1.38
Palau	281	0.01	0.000365	0.01	281	0.01	0.000444	0.01	1.22	1.21	281	0.02	0.000489	0.02	1.34	1.38
Totals	2175345	100	3.086340	100.00	2048461	100.00	3.111206	100.00			1853506	100	2.991795	100.00		

Both absolute and relative power indices are given (Penrose and Banzhaf indices). Ratios for both allow before and after comparisons. Calculations have been done using the program *ipmmle* in Leech and Leech, 2003.

Appendix 2

Voting Power Comparison for the Euro 12 Member Countries Assuming Euro12/USA Voting parity

	Status quo			Current IMF weights				GDP weights				Population Basis				Equality		
	Votes	%	Power	Weight%	Power	2-stage	Ratio	GDP	Power	2-stage	Ratio	Population	Power	2-stage	Ratio	Power	2-stage	Ratio
Germany	130332	5.99	0.1650	26.14	0.5723	0.2860	1.73	29.37	0.6201	0.3099	1.88	26.97	0.6162	0.3079	1.87	0.2256	0.1127	0.68
France	107635	4.95	0.1381	21.59	0.4160	0.2079	1.51	21.38	0.3799	0.1898	1.38	19.51	0.3565	0.1781	1.29	0.2256	0.1127	0.82
Italy	70805	3.25	0.0917	14.20	0.2949	0.1474	1.61	17.93	0.3604	0.1801	1.96	18.83	0.3486	0.1742	1.90	0.2256	0.1127	1.23
Netherlands	51874	2.38	0.0673	10.40	0.1904	0.0952	1.41	6.26	0.0889	0.0444	0.66	5.30	0.0986	0.0493	0.73	0.2256	0.1127	1.67
Belgium	46302	2.13	0.0601	9.29	0.1709	0.0854	1.42	3.70	0.0518	0.0259	0.43	2.38	0.0635	0.0317	0.53	0.2256	0.1127	1.88
Spain	30739	1.41	0.0399	6.16	0.1006	0.0503	1.26	10.23	0.1357	0.0678	1.70	12.43	0.1787	0.0893	2.24	0.2256	0.1127	2.82
Austria	18973	0.87	0.0247	3.81	0.0703	0.0351	1.42	3.08	0.0518	0.0259	1.05	2.63	0.0420	0.0210	0.85	0.2256	0.1127	4.57
Finland	12888	0.59	0.0168	2.58	0.0518	0.0259	1.54	1.98	0.0264	0.0132	0.79	1.70	0.0361	0.0181	1.08	0.2256	0.1127	6.73
Portugal	8924	0.41	0.0116	1.79	0.0332	0.0166	1.43	1.83	0.0264	0.0132	1.14	3.33	0.0596	0.0298	2.57	0.2256	0.1127	9.72
Ireland	8634	0.40	0.0112	1.73	0.0313	0.0156	1.39	1.82	0.0264	0.0132	1.17	1.29	0.0283	0.0142	1.26	0.2256	0.1127	10.04
Greece	8480	0.39	0.0110	1.70	0.0313	0.0156	1.42	2.12	0.0303	0.0151	1.37	3.49	0.0635	0.0317	2.88	0.2256	0.1127	10.23
Luxembourg	3041	0.14	0.0040	0.61	0.0117	0.0059	1.48	0.32	0.0029	0.0015	0.37	0.15	0.0029	0.0015	0.37	0.2256	0.1127	28.52
Total	498627	22.92		100.00				100.00				100.00						

Analysis assumes voting parity between the United States and Euro-12. The power index for Euro-12 is 0.499745. The power indices are the Penrose indices. Status quo refers to the present IMF. Two-stage is the two-stage Penrose index: the product of the power index in the Euro-12 with the power of the Euro-12 bloc in the IMF Governors (0.499745). The status quo is the current IMF Board of Governors. The ratio is the ratio of the power index to the status quo power index of the country. GDP and population figures are for 2003. Calculations of power indices for the members of Euro-12 have been done using the program *ipfdirect* in Leech and Leech, 2003.

Appendix 3

Voting power comparison for the EU-25 members assuming EU-25/United States parity

	Status quo			Current IMF weights				Nice system					Draft constitution system		
	Votes	%	Power	Weight%	Power	2-stage	Ratio	Weight	Pop%	Power	2-stage	Ratio	Power	2-stage	Ratio
Germany	130332	5.99	0.1651	18.79	0.4855	0.2428	1.47	29	18.21	0.0551	0.0275	0.17	0.158	0.0790	0.48
France	107635	4.95	0.1381	15.52	0.3803	0.1902	1.38	29	13.09	0.0551	0.0275	0.20	0.113	0.0565	0.41
United Kingdom	107635	4.95	0.1381	15.52	0.3803	0.1902	1.38	29	13.15	0.0551	0.0275	0.20	0.114	0.0570	0.41
Italy	70805	3.25	0.0917	10.21	0.2273	0.1136	1.24	29	12.79	0.0551	0.0275	0.30	0.111	0.0555	0.61
Netherlands	51874	2.38	0.0673	7.48	0.1750	0.0875	1.30	13	3.5	0.0272	0.0136	0.20	0.058	0.0290	0.43
Belgium	46302	2.13	0.0601	6.68	0.1537	0.0769	1.28	12	2.27	0.0251	0.0126	0.21	0.050	0.0250	0.42
Spain	30739	1.41	0.0399	4.43	0.1000	0.0500	1.25	27	8.75	0.0522	0.0261	0.65	0.098	0.0490	1.23
Sweden	24205	1.11	0.0315	3.49	0.0795	0.0398	1.26	10	1.97	0.0210	0.0105	0.33	0.048	0.0240	0.76
Austria	18973	0.87	0.0247	2.74	0.0622	0.0311	1.26	10	1.79	0.0210	0.0105	0.43	0.470	0.2350	9.53
Denmark	16678	0.77	0.0217	2.40	0.0546	0.0273	1.26	7	1.18	0.0148	0.0074	0.34	0.044	0.0220	1.01
Poland	13940	0.64	0.0181	2.01	0.0456	0.0228	1.26	27	8.58	0.0522	0.0261	1.44	0.083	0.0415	2.29
Finland	12888	0.59	0.0168	1.86	0.0422	0.0211	1.26	7	1.15	0.0148	0.0074	0.44	0.043	0.0215	1.28
Hungary	10634	0.49	0.0138	1.53	0.0348	0.0174	1.26	12	2.24	0.0251	0.0126	0.91	0.050	0.0250	1.81
Portugal	8924	0.41	0.0116	1.29	0.0292	0.0146	1.26	12	2.22	0.0251	0.0126	1.08	0.050	0.0250	2.15
Ireland	8634	0.40	0.0112	1.24	0.0282	0.0141	1.26	7	0.83	0.0148	0.0074	0.66	0.042	0.0210	1.87
Greece	8480	0.39	0.0110	1.22	0.0277	0.0139	1.26	12	2.34	0.0251	0.0126	1.14	0.051	0.0255	2.31
Czech Republic	8443	0.39	0.0110	1.22	0.0276	0.0138	1.26	12	2.28	0.0251	0.0126	1.14	0.050	0.0250	2.28
Slovak Republic	3825	0.18	0.0050	0.55	0.0125	0.0062	1.25	7	1.2	0.0148	0.0074	1.49	0.044	0.0220	4.42
Luxembourg	3041	0.14	0.0040	0.44	0.0099	0.0049	1.25	4	0.1	0.0085	0.0043	1.08	0.037	0.0185	4.68
Slovenia	2567	0.12	0.0033	0.37	0.0083	0.0042	1.25	4	0.44	0.0085	0.0043	1.27	0.039	0.0195	5.84
Lithuania	1692	0.08	0.0022	0.24	0.0055	0.0028	1.25	7	0.82	0.0148	0.0074	3.37	0.041	0.0205	9.32
Cyprus	1646	0.08	0.0021	0.24	0.0054	0.0027	1.25	4	0.17	0.0085	0.0043	1.99	0.038	0.0190	8.87
Latvia	1518	0.07	0.0020	0.22	0.0049	0.0025	1.25	4	0.54	0.0085	0.0043	2.16	0.040	0.0200	10.13
Malta	1270	0.06	0.0017	0.18	0.0041	0.0021	1.25	3	0.08	0.0064	0.0032	1.92	0.037	0.0185	11.20
Estonia	902	0.04	0.0012	0.13	0.0029	0.0015	1.25	4	0.32	0.0085	0.0043	3.63	0.038	0.0190	16.20
Total	693582	31.88		100.00					100.00						
IMF Total	2175345														

The analysis assumes voting parity between the United States and EU-25. Status quo refers to the present IMF. Two-stage is the two-stage Penrose index; the product of the power index in the EU-25 with the power of the Euro-12 bloc in the IMF Governors (0.499991). The status quo is the current IMF Board of Governors. The ratio of the power index to the status quo power index of the country. GDP and population figures are for 2003. Calculations of power indices for the members of EU-25 have been done using the program *ipdirect* in Leech and Leech, 2003.

Appendix 3. (continued)

	GDP weights				Population weights			Population square root weights				Equality		
	GDP %	Power	2-stage	Ratio	Power	2-stage	Ratio	Cpop	Power	2-stage	Ratio	Power	2-stage	Ratio
Germany	21.88	0.5332	0.2666	**1.61**	0.4962	0.2481	**1.50**	4.267	0.3544	0.1772	**1.07**	0.1612	0.0806	**0.49**
France	15.93	0.3432	0.1716	**1.24**	0.3203	0.1602	**1.16**	3.62	0.2938	0.1469	**1.06**	0.1612	0.0806	**0.58**
United Kingdom	16.36	0.3548	0.1774	**1.28**	0.3219	0.1610	**1.17**	3.63	0.2945	0.1473	**1.07**	0.1612	0.0806	**0.58**
Italy	13.36	0.2652	0.1326	**1.45**	0.3121	0.1561	**1.70**	3.58	0.2900	0.1450	**1.58**	0.1612	0.0806	**0.88**
Netherlands	4.66	0.1102	0.0551	**0.82**	0.0820	0.0410	**0.61**	1.87	0.1469	0.0734	**1.09**	0.1612	0.0806	**1.20**
Belgium	2.75	0.0621	0.0310	**0.52**	0.0534	0.0267	**0.44**	1.51	0.1178	0.0589	**0.98**	0.1612	0.0806	**1.34**
Spain	7.62	0.1908	0.0954	**2.39**	0.2063	0.1031	**2.58**	2.96	0.2363	0.1181	**2.96**	0.1612	0.0806	**2.02**
Sweden	2.74	0.0618	0.0309	**0.98**	0.0463	0.0232	**0.74**	1.40	0.1096	0.0548	**1.74**	0.1612	0.0806	**2.56**
Austria	2.29	0.0516	0.0258	**1.05**	0.0421	0.0210	**0.85**	1.34	0.1045	0.0522	**2.12**	0.1612	0.0806	**3.27**
Denmark	1.94	0.0436	0.0218	**1.01**	0.0278	0.0139	**0.64**	1.09	0.0847	0.0423	**1.95**	0.1612	0.0806	**3.72**
Poland	1.91	0.0430	0.0215	**1.19**	0.2008	0.1004	**5.54**	2.93	0.2338	0.1169	**6.45**	0.1612	0.0806	**4.45**
Finland	1.47	0.0331	0.0166	**0.99**	0.0271	0.0135	**0.81**	1.07	0.0836	0.0418	**2.49**	0.1612	0.0806	**4.81**
Hungary	0.75	0.0169	0.0085	**0.61**	0.0527	0.0263	**1.90**	1.50	0.1170	0.0585	**4.23**	0.1612	0.0806	**5.83**
Portugal	1.36	0.0307	0.0153	**1.32**	0.0522	0.0261	**2.25**	1.49	0.1165	0.0582	**5.02**	0.1612	0.0806	**6.94**
Ireland	1.35	0.0305	0.0152	**1.36**	0.0195	0.0098	**0.87**	0.91	0.0709	0.0355	**3.16**	0.1612	0.0806	**7.18**
Greece	1.58	0.0355	0.0177	**1.61**	0.0550	0.0275	**2.49**	1.53	0.1196	0.0598	**5.42**	0.1612	0.0806	**7.31**
Czech Republic	0.78	0.0175	0.0087	**0.80**	0.0536	0.0268	**2.44**	1.51	0.1181	0.0590	**5.38**	0.1612	0.0806	**7.34**
Slovak Republic	0.29	0.0065	0.0032	**0.65**	0.0282	0.0141	**2.84**	1.10	0.0854	0.0427	**8.58**	0.1612	0.0806	**16.20**
Luxembourg	0.24	0.0054	0.0027	**0.68**	0.0024	0.0012	**0.30**	0.32	0.0246	0.0123	**3.11**	0.1612	0.0806	**20.38**
Slovenia	0.24	0.0054	0.0027	**0.80**	0.0103	0.0052	**1.55**	0.66	0.0516	0.0258	**7.73**	0.1612	0.0806	**24.14**
Lithuania	0.17	0.0037	0.0019	**0.85**	0.0193	0.0096	**4.38**	0.91	0.0705	0.0353	**16.02**	0.1612	0.0806	**36.63**
Cyprus	0.10	0.0023	0.0012	**0.54**	0.0040	0.0020	**0.93**	0.41	0.0320	0.0160	**7.48**	0.1612	0.0806	**37.64**
Latvia	0.09	0.0020	0.0010	**0.50**	0.0126	0.0063	**3.19**	0.73	0.0571	0.0286	**14.47**	0.1612	0.0806	**40.82**
Malta	0.04	0.0008	0.0004	**0.24**	0.0019	0.0009	**0.58**	0.28	0.0220	0.0110	**6.65**	0.1612	0.0806	**48.78**
Estonia	0.08	0.0017	0.0009	**0.73**	0.0075	0.0037	**3.20**	0.57	0.0440	0.0220	**18.73**	0.1612	0.0806	**68.70**
		2.2511			2.455			20.58						

The analysis assumes voting parity between the United States and EU-25. The power index for the EU-25 is 0.499991. The power indices are the Penrose indices. Status quo refers to the present IMF. Two-stage is the two-stage Penrose index: the product of the power index in the EU-25 with the power of the Euro-12 bloc in the IMF Governors (0.499991). The status quo is the current IMF Board of Governors. The ratio is the ratio of the power index to the status quo power index of the country. GDP and population figures are for 2003. Calculations of power indices for the members of EU-25 have been done using the program *ipdirect* in Leech and Leech, 2003.

Notes

1 Paper commissioned by the G-24, presented at the G-24 Technical Group meeting, 2005, Manila, 17–19 March. We thank the Centre for the Study of Globalizaton and Regionalization at the University of Warwick for financial support. Contact Information: Dennis Leech, Department of Economics, University of Warwick, Coventry CV4 7AL, Tel:02476523047, d.leech@warwick.ac.uk, http://www.warwick.ac.uk/~ecrac

2 Leech and Leech, 2004a.

3 Penrose, 1946. The Penrose measure is more usually referred to as the Absolute Banzhaf index. The Normalized Banzhaf index is the same measure but normalized to make all members' indices sum to one. Most of the power indices in literature have tended to emphasize the latter. We consider that both are needed and have different roles in the analysis and therefore, it is useful to have a separate terminology for them. We prefer to use the term Penrose index for the non-normalized version, after its original inventor, and to use the Banzhaf index for its normalized version.

4 Banzhaf, 1965.

5 See Leech and Leech, 2004b, for the full mathematical details and numerical analysis.

6 See Holler, 1982, for a discussion of proportionality in weighted voting systems.

7 Straffin, 1977.

8 See van Houtven, 2002, for an authoritative account of the governance of the IMF.

9 A detailed account of representation of EU countries is given in Bini Smaghi, 2004.

10 See Felsenthal and Machover, 1998, for a literature survey. See Holler and Owen, 2001, for a collection of recent studies.

11 Logically, the power index for the G-7 must be strictly less than 1 and those for the other countries greater than zero, but our calculation to six decimal places could not detect this and the numbers were rounded. Therefore, we can say that the indices were greater than 0.9999995 and less than 0.0000005.

12 In this paper, we are taking the voting system laid down in the *Articles of Agreement* quite literally. It is often said that votes are rarely taken at the IMF and decisions are made by consensus. We take it as axiomatic that the voting structure matters in a fundamental way; that it is an exogenous factor conditioning the way decisions are taken. Many decisions are actually taken by voting.

13 Buira, 2002, 2003; Benassy-Quere and Bowles, 2002; Kenen *et al.*, 2004, Mahieu *et al.*, 2003; van Houtven, 2004.

14 Such limited voting power analysis of scenarios for changes to the Executive that we have done has given results which differ little from the Board of Governors.

15 Mahieu *et al.*, 2003, argue in favour of mixed constituencies like that led by Belgium. Belgium has 2.13 per cent of the voting weight but the Belgian director casts the total combined votes of all members of its constituency, some 5.15 percent. Buira, 2002, however, argues from experience that for developing countries, voice not backed by voting power is not enough: 'This writer recalls occasions when a major industrialized country would not be prepared to engage in the discussion they could lose on logical grounds. After listening to the arguments, the director would simply state they had not changed their position on the issue.'

16 Austria, Belgium, Finland, France, Germany, Greece, Ireland, Italy, Luxembourg, Netherlands, Portugal, Spain.

17 Euro-12 plus Cyprus, Czech Republic, Denmark, Estonia, Hungary, Latvia, Lithuania, Malta, Poland, Slovakia, Slovenia, Sweden, UK.

18 See Leech, 2002, for an analysis of this effect.
19 Based on the arguments of Penrose, 1946, hence the name, Penrose square root rule.
20 Normalized power indices are not meaningful here because they would depend on the internal voting rules of the Euro bloc. The power of a non-Euro-12 country is obviously independent of that. Comparisons can be made for countries using the Penrose indices, however.

References

Benassy-Quere, Agnes and Bowles, Carlos, 2002, A European Voice at the IMF, *La Lettre du CEPII*, No. 216.

Bini Smaghi, Lorenzo, 2004, A Single EU Seat in the IMF?, *Journal of Common Market Studies*, 42:2, pp. 229–48.

Buira, Ariel, 2002, *A New Voting Structure for the IMF*, Washington: G-24, www.g24.org/

Buira, Ariel, 2003, *Adjustment of European Quotas to Enhance the Voice and Participation of Developing and Transition Countries*, Note Prepared by the G-24 Secretariat, Washington: G-24, www.g24.org/

Coleman, James S, 1971, Control of Collectivities and the Power of a Collectivity to Act, *Social Choice*, Lieberman, B (ed.), New York: Gordon and Breach; reprinted in Coleman, JS, 1986, *Individual Interests and Collective Action*, Cambridge: Cambridge University Press.

Coleman, James S, 1973, Loss of Power, *American Sociological Review*, 38, pp. 1–17.

Felsenthal, Dan S and Machover, Moshe, 1998, *The Measurement of Voting Power*, Cheltenham: Edward Elgar.

Holler, Manfred, 1982, *Power, Voting and Voting Power*, Vienna: Physica-Verlag.

Holler, Manfred and Owen, Guillermo, 2001, *Power Indices and Coalition Formation*, London: Kluwer Academic Publishers.

IMF, 2004, *IMF Members' Quotas and Voting Power, and IMF Board of Governors*, http://www.imf.org/

Kelkar, Vijay L, Yaddav, Vikash, Chaudhry, Praveen K, 2004, Reforming the Governance of the International Monetary Fund, *The World Economy*, 27 May, pp. 727–43.

Leech, Dennis, 2002, Voting Power in the Governance of the IMF, *Annals of Operations Research*, 109, pp. 373–95.

Leech, Dennis, 2003, Computing Power Indices for Large Voting Games, *Management Science*, 49:6, pp. 831–8.

Leech, Dennis and Leech, Robert, 2003, Website: *Computer Algorithms for Voting Power Analysis*, www.warwick.ac.uk/~ecaae/

Leech, Dennis and Leech, Robert, 2004a, *Voting Power in the Bretton Woods Institutions*, Discussion Paper 154/04, Centre for the Study of Globalisation and Regionalisation, University of Warwick, forthcoming chapter in Paloni, Alberto and Zanardi, Maurizio (eds), *The IMF, World Bank and Policy Reform*, London: Routledge, in press.

Leech, Dennis and Leech, Robert, 2004b, *Voting Power and Voting Blocs*, Discussion Paper 153/04, Centre for the Study of Globalisation and Regionalisation, University of Warwick.

Mahieu, Géraldine, Ooms, Dirk and Rottier, Stéphane, 2003, The Governance of the International Monetary Fund with a Single EU Chair, *Financial Stability Review*, Brussels: *Banque National de Belgique*.

Penrose, Lionel, 1946, The Elementary Statistics of Majority Voting, *Journal of the Royal Statistical Society*, 109, pp. 53–7.

Straffin, Phillip D, 1977, Homogeneity, Independence, and Power Indices, *Public Choice* 30, pp. 107–118.

van Houtven, Leo, 2002, *Governance of the IMF: Decision Making, Institutional Oversight, Transparency and Accountability*, IMF Pamphlet Series no. 53, IMF: Washington.

van Houtven, Leo, 2004, Rethinking IMF Governance, *Finance and Development*, September.

12

CHANGING IMF QUOTAS: THE ROLE OF THE UNITED STATES CONGRESS[1]

J. Lawrence Broz[2]

Abstract:

Increasing IMF quotas (or changing their distribution) requires the approval of the United States, which maintains enough votes at the IMF to block such decisions. Any change in the US quota, in turn, must be approved by the US Congress—a feature of US law which gives Congress a central role in quota determination. In this paper, I analyse congressional votes on legislation to increase the US quota subscription to the IMF. I argue that legislators are more likely to support a quota increase (1) the more 'liberal' their ideology, (2) the larger the share of high-skilled 'pro-globalization' voters residing in their districts and (3) the larger the share of campaign contributions they get from banks that specialize in international lending. Statistical tests of congressional voting on requests for quota increases in 1983 and 1998 support these arguments.

Introduction

The United States is positioned at the International Monetary Fund (IMF or Fund) to unilaterally veto changes in the size or distribution of 'quotas'.[3] This is because altering quotas requires an 85 per cent majority in the IMF's Board of Governors, and the United States has never held less than 17 per cent of the votes. No matter how intensely other members feel about the need for increasing or redistributing quotas, opposition by the United States alone can block any quota adjustment. On quotas, the United States is predominant.

In this paper, I investigate the sources of US policy toward quotas. Rather than treating the United States as a single entity with a unified 'national interest' towards the Fund, I consider the preferences of the political actors within the United States who exert power over quotas. Specifically, I analyse how members of Congress vote on requests for quota increases. Although many actors within the United States battle to influence US policy toward the IMF—the President, the Treasury Secretary, US officials at the Fund, commercial banks, environmental lobbies, peak associations, think tanks, etc.—Congress is crucial because its members have the final authority to approve or deny any change in the US quota.[4]

Voting for a quota increase is a straightforward way to support the IMF. It increases the resources the Fund has for its lending activities. My goal is to explain why some members of Congress vote in favour of such increases while others vote against them. My arguments and evidence suggest that the votes of US representatives in Congress are responsive to personal ideology, district constituencies and interest groups. Of these three factors, I find that personal ideology has the largest impact on how members vote on quota increases. Members with conservative ideologies tend to view international organizations like the IMF as remote and opaque bureaucracies that engage in wasteful interventions in the marketplace. I use data on member ideology to estimate the effect of conservative ideology and find that a one standard deviation increase in conservatism decreases the likelihood that a member will vote for a quota increase by 30 percentage points, on average (27 points for Democrats; 33 points for Republicans). The implication is that a more conservative US Congress is likely to be a greater hurdle to changing quotas than a liberal one.

I also find that representatives are responsive to the preferences of voters in their districts. I argue that voters view the IMF as a force for global economic integration, which is good for high-skilled workers, but bad for low-skilled workers, who must compete with the low-skilled workers in developing countries. I reason that the proportion of high-skilled workers in a district should influence a member's vote on increasing the US quota to the IMF. Members of the House of Representatives, who represent more low-skilled workers, should vote against the IMF, as the IMF supports policies of increased global integration, while those representing high-skilled workers should support the IMF. This hypothesis is supported by the evidence that increasing the share of district population with high skills by one standard deviation increases the probability a member will support IMF funding by 7.5 percentage points, on average (10 points for Democrats; 5 points for Republicans).

As for interest groups, I focus on 'money centre' banks that specialize in international lending, such as Citigroup, J. P. Morgan Chase and Bank of America.[5] These banks have an interest in supporting quota increases because a strong IMF mitigates the risks of lending to developing countries. If the

IMF can help rescue countries when they face an economic crisis, there is a better chance that such countries will not default on loans they owe to these banks. Thus, US representatives who rely on campaign contributions from money centre banks should be more likely to support US quota increases than members who do not. This is precisely what I find. The greater the proportion of campaign contributions that come from money centre banks, the more likely a representative will be to vote in favour of increasing the US contribution to the IMF.

The effects of ideology, the skill levels of voters and campaign contributions from banks are surprisingly statistically significant, even when I control for factors such as political party (which is important because Republicans typically oppose contributions to the IMF, while Democrats have, by and large, supported them). The strength of these findings suggests that the United States does not act as a singular entity on quota changes. While there are members within Congress who are obstacles to quota increases, there are also members who are allies of the IMF—those who want to give the Fund more resources and more authority to stabilize world financial markets. I examine the battle that occurs at the congressional level because, depending upon who wins it, Congress can be just as much an ally as an obstacle to quota reform.

The paper is organized as follows. In the following Section 1, I provide a summary of the functions and organization of the IMF, emphasizing the role of quotas. Section 2 contains my arguments and evidentiary strategy, and Section 3 is the empirical analysis of congressional roll-call votes. The final section is the conclusion, which discusses implications.

Functions of the IMF and the Role of Quotas

The IMF's mandate is to support global trade and economic growth by providing assistance to countries facing balance of payments difficulties. IMF assistance is meant to enable countries to rebuild their reserves, stabilize their currencies and continue paying for imports, while they adjust policies and make reforms to correct their payments problems. There are two main components to Fund programs—financing and conditionality. Access to and disbursement of Fund finance is conditioned on the adoption of policy measures negotiated by the IMF with the recipient country. This 'conditionality' usually takes the form of performance criteria (e.g. inflation and spending targets) and policy benchmarks (e.g. tax reform and privatization). The aim is to alleviate the underlying economic difficulties that led to the balance of payments problem.

The IMF's financial resources come from members' subscriptions, which are known as 'quotas'. Each country's quota is calculated by a formula reflecting the relative size of its economy, using various measures of output and trade.

Total quotas in August 2004 were SDR 213 billion, or about $311 billion.[6] Quotas are also significant because they determine members' voting power in the organization. Each member has 250 'basic' votes, plus one additional vote for each part of its quota equal to SDR 100,000. As basic votes comprise only a small fraction of total votes, control of the IMF is heavily weighted toward its larger members. To illustrate, the United States, with its quota of SDR 37.1 billion (about $54.2 billion) has 371,743 votes (17.1 per cent of the total), while Palau has 281 votes (0.013 per cent of the total). Large members have even greater clout because important decisions are subject to special majorities. The United States, with over 17 per cent of the votes, has veto power over decisions that require 85 per cent approval, such as changing quotas.

Quotas can be changed in several ways—by increases for all members under a 'General Review of Quotas', by the addition of new members and by individual members requesting a selective increase due to a change in their position in the world economy. General Reviews are the most common source of increases and most increases have been equiproportional (equal percentage increase for all members). Table 1 provides summary information on these reviews.

Table 1. General reviews of quotas, 1950–2003

(1) Review of quotas	(2) Board of Governors' adoption of resolution	(3) Equiproportional increase in quotas (per cent)	(4) Overall increase in quotas (per cent)	(5) Entry into effect
First (1950)	No increase proposed	0	0	
Second (1955)	No increase proposed	0	0	
Third	2 February 1959	50	60.7	6 April 1959
Fourth	31 March 1965	25	30.7	23 February 1966
Fifth	9 February 1970	25	35.4	30 October 1970
Sixth	22 March 1976	Increases determined on the basis of different groups of countries	33.6	1 April 1978
Seventh	11 December 1978	50	50.9	29 November 1980
Eighth	31 March 1983	19	47.5	30 November 1983
Ninth	28 June 1990	30	50.0	11 November 1992
Tenth (1995)	No increase proposed	0	0	
Eleventh	30 January 1998	33.75	45.0	22 January 1999
Twelfth (2003)	No increase proposed	0	0	

Notes: The IMF conducts general quota reviews about every five years. Quota increases comprise an equiproportional percentage increase for all members and a selective increase, which adjusts certain members' quota shares in order to align them with their relative economic size. Column 4 is the sum of the equiproportional increase and the selective increases.
Source: Updated from Cooper et al., 2000.

While General Reviews are occasions to assess the adequacy of Fund resources, they also offer the only real opportunity for countries to try to raise their own *relative* quotas, with an eye towards increasing their voting power. This is because quotas can only go in one direction—with the exception of Honduras in 1948, no country has ever requested a reduction in its quota.[7] Thus, a country trying to increase its voting power will aim for a larger selective share of an overall quota increase during a General Review. As Boughton (2001, pp. 564) put it with respect to the Eighth General Review, 'Without a general increase, no redistribution was possible; the larger the increase, the more (in principle) could be accomplished on improving the distribution by allocating increases selectively.' Thus, to redistribute quotas, IMF members must also consent to increase quotas.

General Reviews are held about every five years and have produced eight major increases since 1946.[8] On each occasion—including those where the IMF's Board of Governors chose *not* to propose any increase—a major factor affecting outcomes was the difficulty in obtaining authorization from the US Congress for an increase in the US quota.

Although every member country must consent to its quota increase, the procedures for domestic ratification vary and certain countries, such as the United States, require legislative approval and appropriations. Since the United States is predominant at the IMF, Congress commands extraordinary leverage in the process of changing quotas. According to Pauly (1997, pp. 113), 'Quota increases, although strongly preferred by the Fund, sometimes entail legislative affirmation within member states. They certainly do in the United States, a reality which has complicated the life of the Fund since the beginning.' Indeed, Boughton (2001, pp. 858–72) cites several cases where quota negotiations at the Fund were influenced by Congress, as in the Seventh General Review, where the size of the quota increase was reduced to expedite congressional approval. Woods (2003) argues that Congress is 'recalcitrant' and 'feisty' with respect to funding the IMF and this may increase the influence of the United States at the Fund:

Each time an increase in IMF quotas…has been negotiated, the Congress has used the opportunity to threaten to reduce or withhold the funds, being yet more prepared than even the Executive agencies— Treasury and State Department—to set down special preconditions for US contributions. As a result, other shareholders and officials within the [IMF] have grown used to placating not just the powerful Departments of State and Treasury, but also the feisty US Congress. The overall result seems to have enhanced the capacity of the United States unilaterally to determine aspects of policy and structure within…the IMF.

No general increase in quotas has taken effect without Congress consenting to the US increase (Boughton, 2001, pp. 858). Furthermore, anticipation of congressional opposition has affected the size of increases proposed by the IMF. For example, during the Eighth General Review in 1982–83, technical analyses led most of the Fund's management and membership to favour a 100 per cent increase. However, US authorities refused to commit to any increase, due to anticipated congressional opposition. Bowing to the power of the United States, the IMF's Board of Governors ultimately voted to raise quotas by 47.5 per cent, which was, according to Boughton, 'as much as the US authorities were prepared to ask Congress to approve' (2001, pp. 868).

Congress, however, is not a single, unified entity. It is composed of 535 legislators with varied interests and beliefs on the value of funding the IMF. I examine the motivations of legislators because the factors that shape their votes are important in understanding the constraints and opportunities that the US Congress imposes on the process of changing quotas.

In summary, changes to IMF quotas require broad support within the IMF, since 85 per cent of the votes are required to approve quota changes. With over 17 per cent of the votes, the United States is the pivotal actor on quota changes. But US officials at the Fund cannot act independently of Congress. Congress formally approves changes in the US quota, which means that anyone seeking an increase—the President, the Treasury Secretary, the US Executive Director to the IMF, other member governments—must be sensitive to congressional sentiment.

Approach and Arguments

Which members of Congress will vote in favour of quota increases? Which will vote against? Legislator positions are influenced by many factors, including partisan identity and expectations about the future consequences of IMF rescues (such as the moral hazard problem). I make the standard assumption that legislator behaviour is self-interested and derives, at least in part, from the desire to remain in office. However, because IMF policy is not a 'high salience issue' (of concern to most voters, most of the time), legislator's should have some flexibility to vote on the basis of their personal convictions. Therefore, legislator 'ideology' should be very important to legislators' vote decisions. While factors that affect a member's re-election prospects should also matter— the preferences of voters and interest group pressures proxied by campaign contributions—personal ideology should matter more.

The average citizen is not likely to be aware of the content or existence of most IMF-related legislation. This lack of knowledge implies that, following the 'salience hypothesis,' legislators need not be perfect agents of constituent preferences. They will have some room to vote their personal beliefs.[9] What then shapes legislator beliefs about the IMF?

I argue that 'ideology' provides legislators with a simple schema for evaluating votes on funding the IMF. Indeed, almost all issues in Congress fall on a single liberal-conservative dimension epitomized by the role of government in the economy.[10] Funding the IMF is no different. Conservative politicians who believe in a small role for government regulation of the domestic economy should oppose financing the IMF because Fund programs distort economic incentives in the international economy. Conservatives see IMF programs as 'bailouts' that insulate investors and borrowers from the risks of their actions and thereby promote greater instability in international finance. Conservatives also oppose the expansion of the government sector and see international organizations like the IMF as particularly prone to waste and inefficiency.[11] Conversely, liberals focus on market failures at both the domestic and the international levels and see a positive role for IMF 'rescues' in mitigating the economic and social costs of financial crises. They also tend to be more optimistic about the operations of international organizations and the motivations of the officials that inhabit them.[12] In short, ideology should provide the foundation upon which legislators evaluate the IMF.

Although personal ideology matters, legislators are not completely unrestrained either by constituent or interest groups pressures. To a limited degree, they must also consider how IMF quota increases will affect them electorally. This means they have to be responsive to the preferences of voters and special interest groups. To derive these preferences, I ask, who benefits and who loses from IMF policies? I look to the economics literature on economic globalization and financial rescues to derive such distributional effects.

With respect to voter preferences, I expect members representing districts with greater proportions of net 'winners' from economic globalization to be more likely to favour increasing the IMF's resources. This is because the IMF, by pursuing its mandate to protect the world economy from financial shocks, encourages globalization and its attendant distributional consequences. Stolper and Samuelson (1941) and Mundell (1957) identified the winners and losers from economic globalization in terms of factors of production, such as high-skilled and low-skilled labour, from which factor owners derive their incomes. Owners of locally abundant factors tend to gain more than average from globalization, while owners of scarce factors tend to lose. In the United States, the relatively scarce factor is low-skilled labour and thus, the group most likely to lose from globalization is low-skilled labour.[13] As trade has increased with nations where low-skilled labour is relatively abundant (and hence cheap), organized labour in the United States has mobilized against globalization and received protection in less-skilled intensive industries in return.[14] By contrast, highly skilled labour is abundant in the United States relative to the rest of the world and thereby benefits from globalization. Indeed, individual level data from public opinion surveys provide support for the argument—workers with college degrees or high skills support further liberalization of international trade, while those with less education and fewer skills resist such initiatives.[15]

My extension of trade theory to IMF funding recognizes that the IMF's mandate to protect the world economy from financial disorder is a benefit to voters who gain from global economic integration. I thus expect voters with high (low) skills to support (oppose) the IMF. Although these interests are diffuse and unorganized, I expect to see them represented in the electoral calculations of legislators.

Among organized interest groups, money centre banks comprise a key constituency for the IMF and lobby on its behalf. IMF financial rescues provide *de facto* insurance to these banks, allowing them to retain the gains from international lending while distributing losses, when they occur, to the public sector. Thus, I expect campaign contributions from money centre banks to have a positive impact on the propensity of a member of Congress to vote in favour of increasing the US quota.

I am not the first to identify money centre banks as an important constituency for the IMF. A radical '*dependencista*' version dates to the 1960s and a more orthodox variant is currently circulating.[16] Bhagwati (2002, pp. 8–9) speaks of a 'Wall Street Treasury complex', in which bankers rotate in and out of government, influencing IMF programs to the benefit of Wall Street. But I am less concerned with the reasons why large international banks have influence on the details of IMF programs than with the reasons why such banks might endorse granting more resources to the Fund, via a quota increase. A quota increase gives the IMF greater resources to support the international payments system. It does not dictate how these resources are used or to whom they are allocated. Hence, I emphasize a broader reason why banks endorse quota increases—they benefit directly from the moral hazard created by Fund financial rescues.

Even if intended to stabilize the international financial system, IMF rescues are a form of insurance for private creditors and thus, a source of 'moral hazard'.[17] Moral hazard is an action that encourages the very behaviour that the action seeks to prevent. With respect to the Fund, moral hazard arises when its crisis assistance encourages banks to take on risks that they might otherwise shun, in an attempt to reap greater financial returns. Creditors may over-lend to emerging economies because of the expectation, based on previous experience, that the IMF will provide the foreign exchange liquidity that will allow them to exit the country in times of crisis, without bearing their full losses. Bird (1996, pp. 489) finds that the financial assistance the Fund provides to debtor countries is often used to repay loans to commercial banks. In fact, in some instances, debt service is an explicit component of IMF programs. Gould (2002, pp. 22) cites the case of a Stand-By arrangement with Ghana in 1983, which required the new IMF loan to be held in the Bank of England and used to service Ghana's debt to a British commercial bank.

Some evidence suggests financial market participants are aware of the risk transfer to the public sector. Demirguc-Kunt and Huizinga (1993) found that unanticipated increases in US financial commitments to the IMF caused the stock market capitalization of the exposed banks to increase.

While there is ongoing debate on the extent of the moral hazard problem, everyone agrees that it exists.[18] IMF Deputy Managing Director Krueger sees it as a major concern: 'Private institutions may be encouraged to lend and invest recklessly by the belief that the Fund will ensure that their creditors can repay them.'[19] So did the International Financial Institutions Advisory Commission (the 'Meltzer Commission'), which Congress chartered to evaluate and recommend US policy toward the IMF after the Asian crisis.[20] Rogoff (1999) has perhaps the most pragmatic view, arguing that some moral hazard is an inevitable consequence of stabilizing the international payments system, a view reflected in policy circles as well. Thomas Dawson, Executive Director for the United States at the IMF from 1989 to 1993, stated in congressional hearings that 'The problem of moral hazard is [that] nobody has figured how you save the system without bailing out at least some investors'.[21] My argument is simply that banks with assets in developing countries are among the most direct beneficiaries of IMF-created moral hazard. I expect these banks to lobby Congress to expand the resources of the IMF.

Data and Analysis: Congressional Votes on IMF Quota Increases

The IMF conducts a general review of the adequacy of quota resources at least once every five years. If it determines that a quota increase is needed, the US Congress must first ratify the US increase. Historically, these ratifications have been occasions for rigorous congressional examinations of the IMF. Roll-call votes that occur during such debates provide an opportunity to test my arguments.

I analyse congressional votes in 1983 and 1998 on quota increases. These are the only quota increases for which 'clean' roll-call votes were taken. Usually, when Congress considers a quota increase, it does so by including

IMF funding in a big omnibus spending bill, which makes it impossible to isolate legislator positions' on the IMF issue. However, I identified three amendments to a 1983 spending bill and one motion in 1998 that dealt exclusively with IMF quotas. These are clean votes, in the sense that a vote for or against captures a member's position on increasing US contributions to the IMF, and nothing else.

Table 2 provides summary information on these roll-call votes. Three of the votes (V286, V287 and V313) occurred in 1983 following the IMF's Eighth General Review. The context was the Latin American debt crisis, which provoked worries among some conservatives that a quota increase would fund a bailout of commercial banks.[22] These members were reluctant to provide more resources to the IMF without also tightening regulatory control over commercial banks. This they did with the International Lending Supervision Act of 1983, which required banks to maintain minimum levels of capital.[23] This Act was conjoined in a single bill (H.R. 2957) that, in addition to funding the IMF, also extended the authority of the Export Import Bank, encouraged worldwide economic growth and provided for continued US participation in the multilateral development banks. Just before this omnibus bill passed the House by a close vote of 217–211, several members proposed amendments that would strip the bill of the IMF quota increase. I analyse votes on these three amendments.

The fourth vote (V109, 105th Congress) came in 1998 during the Asian financial crisis and involved a motion to an emergency supplemental spending bill (H.R. 3579). What prompted the motion was that the House and the Senate were considering two different versions of the same bill. The Senate version included funding for the US peacekeeping missions in Bosnia and the Middle East, disaster relief for storm victims in the United States, as well as $18 billion for an IMF quota increase and to fund the establishment of the IMF's New Arrangements to Borrow (NAB). However, the House broke these funding requests into two separate bills—H.R. 3579 included funding for Bosnia, the Middle East and disaster relief, while H.R. 3580 funded $18 billon for the IMF/NAB and provided $500 million to pay down US arrears to the United Nations.

With the House bill diverging from the Senate's, IMF funding was under threat. Procedure requires that for a bill to reach the President for signature, it must pass both Houses of Congress in identical form. In an attempt to reconcile the legislation, Obey (D-WI), ranking member of the House Appropriations Committee, offered a motion to instruct conference committee members to put the IMF money back in the emergency bill. This would allow the House and Senate to pass identical bills, providing the IMF with $18 billion in new commitments. On 23 April 1998, Congress defeated Obey's

Table 2. IMF quota votes in the US Congress

Roll-call Number	V286 H.AMDT. 306 (HR 2957)	V287 H.AMDT. 307 (HR 2957)	V313 H.AMDT.341 (HR 2957)	V109 Motion to instruct conferees (HR 3579)
Congress	98th	98th	98th	105th
Date	29 July 1983	29 July 1983	3 August 1983	23 April 1998
Sponsor	McCollum (R-FL)	Patman (D-TX)	Corcoran (R-IL)	Obey (D-WI)
Summary	To amend H.R. 2957 to strike the language authorizing the Governor of the IMF to consent to an increase in the quota of the United States. [A 'No' vote supports the IMF quota increase.]	To amend H.R. 2957 to eliminate provisions in the bill requiring continued US participation in the IMF. [A 'No' vote supports the IMF quota increase.]	To amend H.R. 2957 to strike the language that increases US participation in the IMF General Arrangements to Borrow from $2 billion to $4.25 billion and authorizes the Secretary to consent to an increase of the US quota in the IMF. [A 'No' vote supports the IMF quota increase.]	To allow the House and Senate to pass identical spending bills, providing the IMF with $18 billion for a quota increase and to establish the New Arrangements to Borrow (NAB). [A 'Yes' vote supports the IMF quota increase and the NAB.]
Result	Y = 182, N = 227	Y = 178, N = 226	Y = 174, N = 249	Y = 186, N = 222
Partisan split	Dem:Y = 90,N = 158 Rep:Y = 92,N = 69	Dem:Y = 89,N = 155 Rep:Y = 89,N = 71	Dem:Y = 82,N = 177 Rep:Y = 92,N = 72	Dem:Y = 164,N = 28 Rep:Y = 22,N = 193

motion by a vote of 186 to 222, stalling the appropriation of funds for the IMF and the NAB for another six months. The spread of the crisis to Russia and Brazil, along with President Clinton's admonishment of congressional foot-dragging as 'irresponsible', finally helped convince opponents that they would be blamed if a global recession took place.[24]

I have three hypotheses. First, I expect legislators with conservative ideologies to oppose new funding requests for the IMF. Conservative members should oppose increasing the quota because they see the IMF as a remote bureaucracy whose interventions create moral hazard. Second, I anticipate that the higher the skill level of constituents in a congressional district, the more likely a member will be to support a quota increase. This captures my argument that members see the IMF as an organization that promotes global economic integration and take positions that reflect the impact of globalization on the real incomes of constituents. Third, I expect the probability a member will vote in favour of funding the IMF to increase with a member's affinity to money centre banks. This affinity is proxied by the amount of campaign contributions each member receives from these banks.

My proxy for legislator ideology is the first dimension of the DW-NOMI-NATE score.[25] The scores ranges from −1 to +1, from most liberal to most conservative and is based on the member's voting behaviour on issues related to government expansion.[26] I measure constituent skill levels in two ways—by educational attainment and by occupational classification. COLLEGE is the share of district population with four years or more of college. SKILLS is the percentage of district workers in executive, administrative, managerial, professional and professional specialty occupations. To identify money centre banks, I use the regulatory classification in the Federal Financial Institutions Examination Council's (FFIEC) 'Country Exposure Lending Survey'. Since the FFIEC identifies the specific banks that comprise the money centre group, I was able to obtain a list on which to base the collection of campaign contribution data.[27] For campaign contributions, I use the Federal Election Commission's data on contributions from Political Action Committees (PACs). My constructed variable is BANK_PAC—the sum total of money centre bank contributions to each House member, as a percentage of that member's total receipts in the previous electoral cycle.[28] See Appendix 1 and 2 for variable descriptions, sources and summary statistics.

Table 3 presents results of Probit analyses of the three 1983 votes. Models 1–3 contain my three variables of interest, all of which are correctly signed and highly statistically significant even when controlling for a members' political party affiliation. Model 4 includes controls for INCOME (median district household income) and MEXICAN ORIGINS (share of district population

Table 3. Probit analyses of IMF quota votes in the 98th Congress

	(1) V286	(2) V287	(3) V313	(4) V313
DW-Nominate	−4.267***	−4.437***	−3.352***	−3.454***
	(0.489)	(0.510)	(0.440)	(0.461)
College	12.464***	13.456***	11.644***	15.870***
	(3.664)	(3.727)	(3.467)	(4.227)
Bank_PAC	59.276***	74.695***	37.765**	37.738**
	(15.432)	(20.241)	(16.464)	(16.833)
Party	1.918***	2.085***	1.294***	1.374***
	(0.320)	(0.327)	(0.294)	(0.305)
Income				−0.432*
				(0.026)
Mexican origins				−0.725
				(0.759)
Constant	−1.590***	−1.725***	−1.127***	−0.638*
	(0.264)	(0.262)	(0.230)	(0.364)
Observations	405	400	419	419
Prob > chi^2	0.0000	0.0000	0.0000	0.0000
Log likelihood	−194.464	−189.393	−216.896	−215.100
Pseudo R^2	0.301	0.310	0.240	0.242

Notes: Robust standard errors in parentheses, *$p < 0.10$, ** $p < 0.05$, *** $p < 0.01$.
Dependent variable: 0 = Yes, 1 = No (a 'No' vote *supports* funding the IMF)
DW-Nominate: First dimension; higher values denote a more conservative ideology.
College: Share of district population with four years of college.
Bank_PAC: Campaign contributions to candidates from money centre bank PACs in the previous electoral cycle, divided by the total receipts per candidate from the previous cycle.
Party: 0 = Democrat; 1 = Republican.
Income: Median household income in a district.
Mexican Origins: Share of district population of Mexican ancestry.

of Mexican ancestry). The latter control is intended to capture any effect that proximity to Mexico—the first victim of the debt crisis—might have on member voting. My core results are not affected by the inclusion of these controls.

Table 4 contains results after substituting SKILLS (share of population working in high-skills industries) for college attainment. The findings are robust to this alternative specification.

Table 4. Probit analyses of IMF quota votes in the 98th Congress

	(1) V286	(2) V287	(3) V313	(4) V313
DW-Nominate	−4.196***	−4.344***	−3.278***	−3.305***
	(0.485)	(0.508)	(0.452)	(0.462)
Skills	2.376***	1.868**	2.214***	2.287***
	(0.847)	(0.913)	(0.804)	(0.879)
Bank_PAC	59.864***	75.425***	38.955**	39.141**
	(15.874)	(21.050)	(16.288)	(16.598)
Party	1.906***	2.079***	1.278***	1.291***
	(0.320)	(0.329)	(0.296)	(0.305)
Income				−0.009
				(0.023)
Mexican origins				0.916
				(0.733)
Constant	−1.713***	−1.621***	−1.224***	−1.085***
	(0.318)	(0.333)	(0.292)	(0.384)
Observations	405	400	419	419
Prob > chi^2	0.0000	0.0000	0.0000	0.0000
Log likelihood	−196.799	−193.586	−219.222	−218.436
Pseudo R^2	0.293	0.294	0.227	0.230

Notes: Robust standard errors in parentheses, $*p < 0.10$, $** p < 0.05$, $*** p < 0.01$.
Dependent variable: 0 = Yes, 1 = No (a 'No' vote *supports* funding the IMF).
Skills: Share of district population aged 16 years and over employed in executive, administrative, managerial and professional specialty occupations.

The vote on Obey's 1998 motion (V109) should be difficult for my arguments since members voted very strongly along party lines. Nevertheless my main variables are signed correctly and significant in several alternative models, as shown in Table 5. Model 1 includes my three variables of interest. Model 2 substitutes SKILLS for COLLEGE, and Model 3 controls for other potentially relevant district characteristics. MEXICAN+KOREAN+THAI is the share of district population of ethnic groups originally from three countries that suffered major currency crisis in the 1990s. My estimates do not support a relationship. NET IMPORTS and NET EXPORTS capture the effect of district industrial characteristics. Since the IMF pursues an essentially pro-trade mandate, members representing districts that face strong import competition might be expected to oppose funding the IMF. Members with export oriented industries in their districts, on the other hand, might support IMF funding.[29] These results are only suggestive, at best. The coefficients are correctly signed but insignificant.

In Table 6, I provide a substantive interpretation of the results. Using models from Tables 3 and 5, I simulated the predicted probability of observing a vote in

Table 5. Probit analyses of IMF quota vote in the 105th Congress

	(1) V109	(2) V109	(3) V109
DW-Nominate	−1.098***	−1.082***	−1.022***
	(0.405)	(0.402)	(0.397)
College	3.508***		3.121**
	(1.163)		(1.242)
Skills		3.507***	
		(1.387)	
Bank_PAC	24.965***	25.087***	24.505***
	(8.144)	(8.130)	(8.194)
Party	−1.675***	−1.650***	−1.726***
	(0.360)	(0.361)	(0.352)
Net imports			−1.472
			(1.128)
Net exports			1.194
			(2.029)
Mexican+Korean+Thai			0.326
			(0.739)
Constant	−0.089**	−0.307	0.125
	(0.279)	(0.386)	(0.374)
Observations	403	403	403
Prob > chi^2	0.0000	0.0000	0.0000
Log likelihood	−133.839	−135.636	−132.873
Pseudo R^2	0.518	0.511	0.521

Robust standard errors in parentheses, *$p < 0.10$, ** $p < 0.05$, *** $p < 0.01$.
Dependent variable: 0 = No, 1 = Yes, (a 'Yes' vote supports funding the IMF).
Net Imports: Per cent district population employed in net import industries.
Net Exports: Per cent district population employed in net export industries.
Mexican+Korean+Thai: Share of district population of Mexican, Korean and Thai ancestry.

favour of an IMF quota increase for both Democrats and Republicans and then examined how these probabilities change as each explanatory variable is increased by one standard deviation above its mean.[30] The effects are substantively large. For example, a one standard deviation increase in DW-NOMINATE reduces the likelihood of a Republican supporting the IMF by as much as 48 percentage points (V286). The effect of conservatism is also large for Democrats—the average effect across all votes of moving a Democrat one standard deviation toward conservatism is to reduce their chance of voting for IMF funding by 27 percentage points. Note that conservatism has a smaller (but always significant) impact on members of both parties during the 105th Congress, due to strong party line voting on V109.

I also obtain large substantive effects for COLLEGE and BANK_PAC. Increasing the share of district population with a college diploma by one

Table 6. Substantive effects of campaign contributions from international banks, district skill levels and member 'ideology'

	DEMOCRATS			REPUBLICANS		
	Bank_PAC	*College*	*DW-Nominate*	*Bank_PAC*	*College*	*DW-Nominate*
V286 (98th Cong) Table 3, Model 1	0.158***	0.104***	–0.287***	0.047***	0.035***	–0.481***
V287 (98th Cong) Table 3, Model 2	0.197***	0.111***	–0.279***	0.044***	0.030***	–0.471***
V313 (98th Cong) Table 3, Model 3	0.102***	0.104***	–0.342***	0.0482***	0.050***	–0.413***
V313 (98th Cong) Table 3, Model 4	0.101***	0.141***	–0.342***	0.0485***	0.058***	–0.417***
V109 (105th Cong) Table 5, Model 1	0.074***	0.078***	–0.186***	0.073***	0.079***	–0.103***
V109 (105th Cong) Table 5, Model 3	0.071***	0.068***	–0.164***	0.072***	0.067***	–0.093***
Average effect:	*0.117***	*0.101***	*–0.267***	*0.055***	*0.053***	*–0.330***

Notes: Values represent the change in the predicted probability of voting in favour of an IMF quota increase, as each variable of interest is increased by one standard deviation over its mean, holding other variables at their means. For Democrats, 'Party' is held to zero; for Republicans 'Party' is held to 1. $*p < 0.10$, $** p < 0.05$, $*** p < 0.01$.

standard deviation increases the probability a member will support IMF funding by as much as 14 percentage points (V313). Although the effect is evident for members of both parties, Democrats are about twice as sensitive to these factors than Republicans. Increasing the share of workers with college degrees yields a 10 percentage point increase in the probability a Democratic member will vote to fund the IMF but just a 5 percentage point increase for a Republican, on average. Similarly, increasing campaign contributions from international banks by one standard deviation hikes the probability that a Democrat will support the IMF by 12 percentage points on average, but the same change in contributions to a Republican yields but a 6 percentage point increase in the likelihood of voting in favour of funding the IMF. These partisan differences in the responsiveness to district skill-levels and campaign contributions from money centre banks probably reflects the fact that Democrats have had historical ties to anti-globalization unions and a populist distrust of big finance. This would suggest that increases in pro-globalization workers and campaign money banks would have a larger impact on Democrats than on Republicans.

Conclusions

Few aspects of the IMF are as contentious in the United States as requests for new resources and, due to a feature of US law that requires any change to the US quota to be approved by Congress, few are as directly observable. I have analysed these roll-calls and found that three political factors influence the votes of legislators: (1) legislator 'ideology' with respect to the role of government in the economy, (2) the impact of globalization on worker incomes within a congressional district, and (3) the share of campaign contributions legislators receive from banks that specialize in international lending. Each factor has implications for increasing (and perhaps redistributing) IMF quotas.

According to my estimates, economic conservatism is an important source of anti-IMF sentiment in the US Congress. Conservatives view the IMF as a profligate bureaucracy that distorts incentives in international financial markets. To quote Gingrich, the 1998 quota increase was 'typical liberal foreign policy...we're not turning over $18 billion to a French Socialist to throw it away'.[31] Although extreme, Gingrich's position is not uncommon in Congress and conservatism does appear to have a negative impact on the willingness to support the IMF independent of political party affiliation.

Does a more conservative Congress actually make it more difficult for the IMF to increase quotas? Do officials at the Fund consider congressional conservatism when they determine the size of the quota increase they will support at the Board of Governors? These are complicated questions because many factors—economic and political—shape Fund requests for quota increases. But historical evidence from Boughton (2001, Chapter 17) suggests that there may be a relationship between the timing and size of IMF quota increases and the average level of conservatism in Congress. Table 7 plots the percentage increase in quotas (left axis) from all IMF General Reviews since 1950 against the average ideological position of the US House of Representatives (right axis).[32]

The proxy for ideology is DW-Nominate, averaged for all members and ranges from -1 (very liberal) to $+1$ (very conservative). Four General Reviews produced 'no increase' in quotas—the First (1950), Second (1955), Tenth (1995) and Twelfth (2003). Note that these reviews occurred during periods when Congress was markedly conservative. Conversely, all of the large quota increases between the Third and Ninth General Reviews (1960–1990) came during liberal Congresses. The only exception is the Eleventh Review (1998), in which a 45 per cent increase occurred during a conservative Congress. Arguably, the new resources needed to cope with the Asian financial crisis swamped the effect of conservatism in this instance—if conservatives in

Table 7. Average 'Ideology' of the US House of Representative and IMF quota increases, 1950–2004

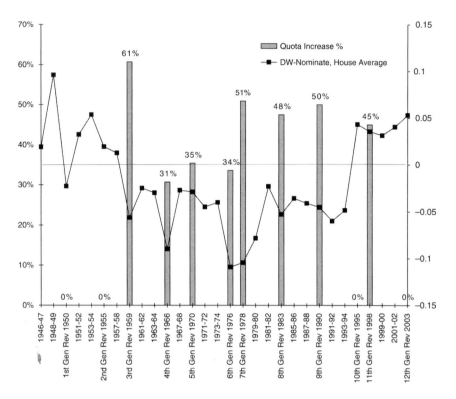

Notes: DW-Nominate (right scale) is the average ideological score of the US House of Representatives on the broad issue of government intervention in the economy. Higher values denote a more conservative ideology. IMF quota increases (left scale) are quota increases approved by the IMF's Board of Governors during a General Review of Quotas.

Congress had rejected the increase and the Asian crisis had taken a turn for the worse, liberals might have blamed them in the next election. Further research might explore the extent to which conservatism in the US Congress (and other parliaments) set limits on the timing and level of support the IMF can muster within powerful member countries.

My second finding, relating to the Stolper–Samuelson theorem, is also relevant to the process of changing IMF quotas. Convincing Congress to increase support for the IMF is a difficult political challenge, especially in light of the current 'backlash' against globalization in the United States. Indeed, my estimates suggest that political divisions on the IMF mirror divisions on globalization more generally. Members representing districts with large numbers of high (low) skilled workers are more likely to vote in favour (against) funding the IMF. My inference is that legislator positions on the IMF are shaped by the relative wage effects of globalization, which the IMF promotes. In future research, I intend to explore the inference directly by analysing survey data; if it is valid, I should find a correlation between individual attitudes toward trade and the IMF.

An alternative possibility is that my inference is flawed and that my skill-level estimates have a different interpretation. It might be that more educated/skilled constituents are more 'cosmopolitan' intellectually and have better knowledge about the need for the IMF. But while a college education or a high-skill occupation could give rise to an internationalist outlook, there is no compelling reason why these attributes imply support specifically for the IMF. Academic economists are highly divided on whether the IMF does more harm than good, with several taking public stances against the IMF on moral hazard grounds.[33] While more education might make people more likely to support trade liberalization, where the overwhelming majority of academic opinion favours free trade, it should not make people more apt to support the IMF, because no such unanimity exists. Therefore, it is difficult to attribute my results to constituents' intellectual capacity.

My third finding, on the impact of money centre bank contributions, should resonate with scholars and policymakers that suppose banks are active in the politics of the IMF.[34] To my knowledge, however, this is the first analysis showing that representatives in Congress who are supported by banks are more likely to approve increased funding for the IMF. This finding extends the established research on the role of private financiers by showing that banks are active politically at multiple levels—on the specifics of IMF programs, they communicate directly with IMF officials and staff.[35] But on matters of funding the IMF, they work though Congress, which controls the purse strings.

The banking industry has long been one of the largest contributors to congressional campaigns and commercial banks rank in the top ten in terms of total giving (PAC, individual, soft money) to Congress among over 80 industries.[36] In addition, money centre banks appear to carefully target members with particular influence over banking and financial policy. Table 8 shows that all but two of the top twenty recipients of bank contributions in my 1983 sample were members of the Committee on Banking, Finance and Urban Affairs. Eighteen of 20 also voted in favour of the IMF quota increase. This targeting may derive from the decentralized nature of congressional decision making—bankers may understand that money allocated to the banking committee is more efficiently spent.[37] It may also reflect an understanding of the committee assignment process since banks are more likely to find a sympathetic audience in this committee.[38]

This analysis also speaks on the question of how international public goods are financed. While the IMF's capacity to stabilize financial markets—a global public good—depends on contributions from member countries, the incentives that drive large members to bear a disproportionate share of the financial burden have not been clearly identified. It has long been suspected that the United States uses its voting power at the IMF to advance its own interests, which might explain why the US Executive has a stake in funding it. But Congress controls the purse, not the Executive and members of Congress tend be motivated by local, as opposed to national or diplomatic, concerns. To specify the motivations of the political actors that formally decide levels of US funding, I identified two constituencies—money centre banks and high-skilled citizens—that benefit from a well-funded IMF and tested to see if connections between these pro-IMF groups and Congress shaped member voting. My strong, positive results suggest that the United States funds the

Table 8. Top 20 recipients of campaign contributions from money centre bank PACs

Name	State	District	Party	Committee	Bank_PAC	Vote on IMF V286	V287	V313
Lafalce, J	NY	32	Dem	Bank & Fin	0.0642	No	No	No
Barnard, D	GA	10	Dem	Bank & Fin	0.0474	No	No	No
Lundine, S	NY	34	Dem	Bank & Fin	0.0463	No	No	No
St Germain	RI	1	Dem	Bank & Fin (chair)	0.0451	No	No	No
Green, S	NY	15	Rep		0.0333	No	No	No
Hubbard, C	KY	1	Dem	Bank & Fin	0.0328	No	No	No
Annunzio, F	IL	11	Dem	Bank & Fin	0.0324	-	-	Yes
Wortley, G	NY	27	Rep	Bank & Fin	0.0313	No	No	No
Towns, E	NY	11	Dem		0.0306	No	No	No
Ridge, T	PA	21	Rep	Bank & Fin	0.0305	No	No	No
Neal, S	NC	5	Dem	Bank & Fin	0.0297	No	No	No
Wylie, C	OH	15	Rep	Bank & Fin (ranking)	0.0264	No	No	No
Fish, H	NY	21	Rep		0.0255	No	No	No
Carper, T	DE	1	Dem	Bank & Fin	0.0199	No	No	No
Erdreich, B	AL	6	Dem	Bank & Fin	0.0191	Yes	Yes	Yes
Mckinney	CT	4	Rep	Bank & Fin	0.0175	No	No	No
Levin, S	MI	17	Dem	Bank & Fin	0.0174	No	No	No
Lehman, R	CA	18	Dem	Bank & Fin	0.0144	No	No	No
Roukema	NJ	5	Rep	Bank & Fin	0.0142	No	No	No
Bereuter	NE	1	Rep	Bank & Fin	0.0140	No	No	No

Notes: A 'No' vote *favours* funding the IMF (see Table 2). **Bank_PAC** is the sum of campaign contributions from money centre bank PACs in 1981 and 1982, as a percentage of total receipts for the 1981–1982 electoral cycle. **Bank & Fin** denotes a position on the House Committee on Banking, Finance and Urban Affairs.

IMF at least partly because private actors have individual stakes in seeing the IMF funded.

Appendix 1

Data and Sources

Party: 0 = Democrat; 1 = Republican.

DW-Nominate: The first dimension of the DW-Nominate score, capturing a member's ideological position on government intervention in the economy. DW-Nominate estimates the position of each legislator, using roll-call voting and scaling techniques. Scores range from -1 to $+1$, with higher values denoting a more conservative ideology.[39]

Bank PAC: Campaign contributions from money centre bank political action committees to candidates in the previous electoral cycle, divided by the total receipts per candidate from the previous electoral cycle. Money centre banks are identified by the Federal Financial Institutions Examination Council, *Country Exposure Lending Survey* (various years). In 1983, the FFIEC list included Bank of America, Bankers Trust, Chase Manhattan Bank, Chemical Bank, Citibank, Continental Illinois, First National Bank of Chicago, Manufacturers Hanover and Morgan Guaranty. By 1998, consolidations and takeovers had reduced the list of money centre banks to JP Morgan, Chase Manhattan, Bank of America, Citicorp, First Chicago and Bankers Trust. Bank_PAC in Table 5 was calculated from the contributions of these six banks. PAC contributions are from the Federal Election Commission (http://www.tray.com).

College: Share of district population with four years of college (*Congressional Districts of the United States*, US, Bureau of the Census).

Skills: Share of district population aged 16 years and over employed in executive, administrative, managerial and professional specialty occupations (*Congressional Districts of the United States*).

Income: Median household income (*Congressional Districts of the United States*).

Mexican Origins: Share of district population of Mexican ancestry (*Congressional Districts of the United States*).

Mexican+Korean+Thai: Share of district population of Mexican, Korean and Thai ancestry (*Congressional Districts of the United States*).

Net Imports: Per cent district population aged 16 years and over, employed in net import industries. Net import industries are two-digit SIC manufacturing sectors where the ratio of imports to consumption is greater than the ratio of revenues from exports to total industry revenue (Textiles 22, Apparel 23, Lumber 24, Furniture 25, Paper 26, Petroleum 29, Rubber 30, Leather 31,

Stone, Clay and Glass 32, Primary metals 33, Fabricated metals 34, Industrial machinery 35, Electronic goods 36, Transportation equipment 37, Other manufactures 39). *County Business Patterns 1997* CD-ROM, Bureau of the Census. County-level employment data was aggregated up to the congressional district level using the following procedure. If a county contains more than one congressional district within its borders, the number of workers from an industry who are in each district is estimated by using the fraction of the county's population residing in each district. For example, if 10 per cent of a county's population lives in a district, that district receives 10 per cent of the county's workers in each industry. I obtained the geographic information from the MABLE '98/Geocorr v3.0 Geographic Correspondence Engine [http://plue. sedac.ciesin.org/plue/geocorr].

Net Exports: Per cent district population aged 16 years and over, employed in net export industries. Net export industries are two-digit SIC manufacturing sectors where the ratio of revenues from exports to total industry revenue is greater than the ratio of imports to consumption (Food 20, Tobacco 21, Printing 27, Chemicals 28, Instruments 38). See Net Imports and the text for the concordance procedure.

Appendix 2

Summary Statistics

	V286, V287, V313 (98th Cong)			
	Mean	*Std Dev*	*Min*	*Max*
DW-Nominate	−0.0529	0.3707	−.7780	0.9870
Party	0.3839	0.4869	0	1
Bank_PAC	0.0026	0.0070	0	0.0642
College	0.0569	0.0226	0.0100	0.2075
Skills	0.3534	0.0902	0.1450	0.8540
Income ($1000s)	16.915	3.560	7.154	28.181
Mexican Origins	0.0393	0.0891	0.0007	0.7156

	V109 (105th Cong)			
	Mean	*Std Dev*	*Min*	*Max*
DW-Nominate	0.0645	0.4637	−0.7600	1.150
Party	0.4747	0.4999	0	1
Bank_PAC	0.0044	0.0098	0	0.0967
College	0.2007	0.0799	0.0530	0.5138
Skills	0.2584	0.0634	0.0918	0.5282
Mexican+Korean+Thai	0.0581	0.1154	0.0013	0.7057
Net Imports	0.1353	0.0801	0.0085	0.4263
Net Exports	0.0536	0.0452	0.0002	0.4606

Notes

1 Prepared for the *International Economic Cooperation for a Balanced World Economy* conference, 2005, 12–13 March, Chyonking. Sponsored by the World Economic Forum, the Reinventing Bretton Woods Committee (RBWC), the Ministry of Finance of China, and the People's Bank of China. Also presented at the Political Science Seminar, Brigham Young University, 17 March 2005. I thank Scott Cooper and other members of the BYU seminar for comments and Mark Farrales for excellent research assistance.

2 Contact information: J.Lawrence Broz, Associate Professor, Department of Political Science, University of California, San Diego, jlbroz@ucsd.edu

3 Quotas are the capital subscriptions that member governments make to the IMF. Quotas serve as the main resource for IMF lending activities and determine members' voting power at the Fund.

4 The Bretton Woods Agreement Act of 1944 states that 'Unless Congress by law authorizes such action, neither the President nor any person or agency shall on behalf of the United States request or consent to any change in the quota of the United States under the *Articles of Agreement* of the Fund' (USC. Title 22, Section 286c).

5 Money centre banks are located in financial centres like New York, Chicago and San Francisco. Their clients include governments, corporations and other banks.

6 Special Drawing Rights (SDRs) serve as the unit of account of the IMF. Its value is based on a basket of key international currencies

7 Horsefield, 1969, pp. 196.

8 Article III, Section 2(a) of the IMF's Articles of Agreement provides that 'the Board of Governors shall at intervals of not more than five years conduct a general review, and if it deems it appropriate propose an adjustment, of quotas of members'.

9 Miller and Stokes, 1963.The 'salience hypothesis' holds that voters are more likely to become informed and monitor legislator behaviour as salience increases. Legislators respond to constituents' preferences on salient issues because the probability of retribution at the ballot box is high relative to less salient issues.

10 Poole and Rosenthal, 1997.

11 See, for example, Armey (Rep TX), 1998.

12 See, for example, LaFalce (Dem NY), 1998.

13 Wood, 1994.

14 Haskel and Slaughter, 2000; Baldwin and Magee, 2000.

15 Scheve and Slaughter 2001; O'Rourke 2003; Mayda and Rodrik. 2005.

16 Stiglitz, 2002; Barro, 1998; Soros 1998.

17 Bulow and Rogoff, 1990; Rogoff, 1999.

18 See e.g. Dell'Ariccia, Schnabel, and Zettelmeyer, 2002; Jeanne and Zettelmeyer, 2001; Dreher and Vaubel, 2004.

19 Address by Anne Krueger, given at the National Economists' Club Annual Members' Dinner American Enterprise Institute, Washington DC, 26 November 2001.

20 Report of the International Financial Institutions Advisory Commission, March 2000.

21 Dawson, 1998, pp. 105.

22 Bordo and James, 2000, pp. 32.

23 The Act was also a precursor to the bank capital standards of the Basel Accord in 1988.

24 Frankel and Roubini, 2001, pp. 36.

25 Poole and Rosenthal, 1997.

26 Similar results obtained using interest group ratings of legislators.

27 See the Data Appendix for the banks that make up this group.
28 Alternate specifications of the variable—the amount of money-centre bank contributions to each member, or the share of members' total receipts that come from the financial industry in general—provide nearly identical results.
29 See the Appendix for the construction of these variables.
30 The simulations were performed with 'Clarify' (Tomz *et al.*, 1998; King *et al.*, 2000).
31 The 'French Socialist' is Camdessus, Managing Director of the IMF from 1987 to 2000. Speech before the Christian Coalition, 18 September 1998, Washington, DC. Quoted in Shapiro, 1998.
32 I thank Mark Farrales for suggesting this graph.
33 Barro, 1998; Calomiris, 1998; Meltzer, 1998; Schwartz, 1998.
34 Stiglitz, 2002; Bhagwati, 2002.
35 Gould, 2003; Oatley, 2002; Oatley and Yackee, 2004.
36 Makinson, 2003; Kroszner and Stratmann, 1998.
37 Grier and Munger, 1991.
38 Shepsle, 1978.
39 McCarty, Poole and Rosenthal, 1997.

References

Armey, Dick (Rep, TX), 1998, The Moral Hazard of IMF Expansion, Remarks as prepared for delivery on the House Floor, 2 October.

Baldwin, Robert E and Magee, Christopher S, 2000, *Congressional Trade Votes: From NAFTA Approval to Fast-Track Defeat*. Washington DC: Institute for International Economics.

Barro, Robert, 1998, The IMF Doesn't Put Out Fires, it Starts Them, *Business Week*, 7 December, pp. 18.

Bhagwati, Jagdish N, 2002, *The Wind of the Hundred Days: How Washington Mismanaged Globalization*, Massachusetts: MIT Press.

Bird, Graham, 1996, The International Monetary Fund and Developing Countries: A Review of the Evidence and Policy Options, *International Organization*, 50 (Summer), pp. 477–511.

Bordo, Michael D and James, Harold, 2000, *The International Monetary Fund: Its Present Role in Historical Perspective*, NBER Working Paper 7724, Cambridge: National Bureau of Economic Research, June, pp. 1–57.

Boughton, James M, 2001, *Silent Revolution: The International Monetary Fund, 1979–1989*, Washington, DC: IMF.

Bulow, Jeremy and Rogoff, Kenneth, 1990, Cleaning Up Third-World Debt Without Getting Taken To the Cleaners, *Journal of Economic Perspectives*, 4 (Winter), pp. 31–42.

Calomiris, Charles W, 1998, The IMF's Imprudent Role as Lender of Last Resort, *Cato Journal* 17:3 (Winter), pp. 275–94.

Cooper, Richard N, *et al.*, 2000, *Report to the IMF Executive Board of the Quota Formula Review Group*, Washington, DC: IMF, September.

Dawson, Thomas C, 1998, Statement to the Subcommittee on General Oversight and Investigations, Committee on Banking and Financial Services, US House of Representatives, Review of the Operations of the International Monetary Fund, 21 April, pp. 105.

Dell'Ariccia, Giovanni, Schnabel, Isabel and Zettelmeyer, Jeromin, 2002, *Moral Hazard and International Crisis Lending: A Test*, IMF Working Paper No. 181, Washington, DC: IMF, October, pp. 1–53.

Demirguc-Kunt, Asli and Huizinga, Harry, 1993, Official Credits to Developing Countries: Implicit Transfers to the Banks, *Journal of Money, Credit and Banking* 25:3, pp. 430–44.

Dreher, Axel and Vaubel, Roland, 2004, Does the IMF Cause Moral Hazard and Political Business Cycles? Evidence from Panel Data, *Open Economies Review*, 15:1, pp. 5–22.

Frankel, Jeffrey and Roubini, Nouriel, 2001, *The Role of Industrial Country Policies in Emerging Market Crises*, NBER Working Paper No. 8634, Cambridge: National Bureau of Economic Research, December.

Gould, Erica R, 2003, Money Talks: Supplementary Financiers and International Monetary Fund Conditionality, *International Organization* 57:3, pp. 551–86.

Grier, Kevin B and Munger, Michael C, 1991, Committee Assignments, Constituent Preferences, and Campaign Contributions, *Economic Inquiry* 29, pp. 24–43.

Haskel, Jonathan E and Slaughter, Matthew J, 2000, *Have Falling Tariffs and Transportation Costs Raised US Wage Inequality?*, NBER Working Paper 7539, Cambridge: National Bureau of Economic Research.

Horsefield, J Keith, 1969, *The International Monetary Fund, 1945–1965: Twenty Years of International Monetary Cooperation*, Chronicle. Washington, DC: IMF, Vol. 1.

Jeanne, Olivier, and Zettelmeyer, Jeromin, 2001, International Bailouts, Moral Hazard, and Conditionality, *Economic Policy*, October, 33, pp. 409–32.

King, Gary, Tomz, Michael and Wittenberg, Jason, 2000, Making the Most of Statistical Analyses: Improving Interpretation and Presentation, *American Journal of Political Science*, March, 44:2, pp. 341–55.

Kroszner, Randall S and Stratmann, Thomas, 1998, Interest-Group Competition and the Organization of Congress: Theory and Evidence from Financial Services' Political Action Committees, *American Economic Review*, 88:5, pp. 1163–87.

Krueger, Anne, 2001, International Financial Architecture for 2002: A New Approach to Sovereign Debt Restructuring, Speech given at the American Enterprise Institute, Washington, DC, 26 November.

LaFalce, John J (Dem, NY), 1998, The Role of the United States and the IMF in the Asian Financial Crisis, Address before the Institute for International Economics, Washington, DC, 27 January.

Locke, Mary, 2000, Funding the IMF: The Debate in the US Congress, *Finance and Development*, September, 37, pp. 3.

Makinson, Larry, 2003, *Open Secrets: The Encyclopaedia of Congressional Money and Politics*, http://www.opensecrets.org/

Mayda, Anna Maria and Rodrik, Dani, 2005, Why Are Some Individuals (and Countries) More Protectionist than Others?, *European Economic Review* (forthcoming).

Meltzer, Allan H, 1998, Asian Problems and The IMF, *Cato Journal*, 17:3(Winter), pp. 267–74.

Miller, Warren and Stokes, Donald, 1963, Constituency Influence in Congress, *American Political Science Review*, 57, pp. 45–56.

Mundell, Robert A, 1957, International Trade and Factor Mobility, *American Economic Review*, June, 47, pp. 321–35.

Oatley, Thomas, 2002, *Commercial Banks and the International Monetary Fund: An Empirical Analysis*, University of North Carolina at Chapel Hill: Mimeo.

Oatley, Thomas and Yackee, Jason, 2004, American Interests and IMF Lending, *International Politics*, 41:3, pp. 415–29.

O'Rourke, Kevin, 2003, *Heckscher-Ohlin Theory and Individual Attitudes Towards Globalization*, NBER Working Paper No. 9872, Cambridge: National Bureau of Economic Research.

Pauly, Louis W, 1997, *Who Elected the Bankers? Surveillance and Control in the World Economy*, Ithaca: Cornell University Press.

Poole, Keith T and Rosenthal, Howard, 1997, *Congress: A Political-Economic History of Roll Call Voting*, New York: Oxford University Press.

Rogoff, Kenneth, 1999, International Institutions for Reducing Global Financial Instability, *Journal of Economic Perspectives*, 13:4 (Fall), pp. 21–42.

Scheve, Kenneth F and Slaughter, Matthew J, 2001, What Determines Individual Trade-Policy Preferences?, *Journal of International Economics*, August, 54, pp. 267–92.

Schwartz, Anna J, 1998, *Time to Terminate the ESF and IMF*, Cato Foreign Policy Briefing No. 48, Washington DC: The Cato Institute, 26 August.

Shapiro, Walter, 1998, Newt the Plagiarist, *Slate*. Friday, 18 September, http://slate.msn.com/id/1000171/

Shepsle, Kenneth A, 1978, *The Giant Jigsaw Puzzle: Democratic Committee Assignments in the Modern House*, Chicago: University of Chicago Press.

Soros, George, 1998, *The Crisis of Global Capitalism: Open Society Endangered*, New York: Public Affairs.

Stiglitz, Joseph E, 2002, *Globalization and Its Discontents*, New York: W.W. Norton.

Stolper, Wolfgang and Samuelson, Paul A, 1941, Protection and Real Wages, *Review of Economic Studies*, 9, pp. 58–73.

Thacker, Strom, 1999, The High Politics of IMF Lending, *World Politics*, October, 52:1, pp. 38–75.

Tomz, Michael, Wittenberg, Jason and King Gary, 1998, CLARIFY: Software for Interpreting and Presenting Statistical Results. Version 1.2, Cambridge MA: Harvard University.

Wood, Adrian, 1994, *North-South Trade, Employment, and Inequality: Changing Fortunes in a Skill-Driven World*, Oxford: Clarendon Press.

Woods, Ngaire, 2003, The United States and the International Financial Institutions: Power and Influence within the World Bank and the IMF, *US Hegemony and International Organizations*, Foot, Rosemary, MacFarlane, S Neil and Mastanduno, Michael (eds). London: Oxford University Press.